The Portable Writer's Conference

Your Guide to Getting Published

Edited by Stephen Blake Mettee

Quill
Driver
Books
Q

Sanger, California

Quill Driver Books\Word Dancer Press, Inc.
1254 Commerce Ave,
Sanger, CA 93657

Printed in the United States of America

Quill Driver Books\Word Dancer Press books may be purchased
at special prices for educational, fund-raising, business
or promotional use. Please contact:

Special Markets
Quill Driver Books\Word Dancer Press, Inc.
1254 Commerce Ave,
Sanger, CA 93657
1-800-497-4909

To order a copy of this book
call 1-800-497-4909

ISBN 1-884956-57-2   **13-digit: 978-1884956-57-7**

Quill Driver Books/Word Dancer Press Project Cadre:
Doris Hall, Linda Kay Hardie, Stephen Blake Mettee, Carlos Olivas

The portable writer's conference : your guide to getting
    published / edited by Stephen Blake Mettee.
      p.   cm.
    Includes bibliographical references.
    ISBN 1-884956-57-2. -- (pbk.)
      1. Authorship--Marketing.   2. Authors and publishers.
    3. Publishers and publishing.   I. Mettee, Stephen Blake,
1947 -
    PN155.P67   1996
    808' .02--dc21

                                                96-45131
                                                CIP

To Josh,
Annette,
Christopher,
Hannah Marie,
and Grace Lynn

Contents

KEYNOTE

——— Writers' Resources ———

Foreword

EVERY WEEK IN THE UNITED STATES SOMEONE, somewhere, is holding a writer's conference, and anywhere from a couple of dozen to several hundred writers or would-be writers are putting down their money to attend. For some, it is a chance to meet professional book people—the all-important editors and agents on whom one day they will have to depend. For others, experienced, long-published authors, it is a matter of networking, keeping in touch, polishing a sense of the marketplace.

But not everyone who wants to go can get to such conferences. Perhaps there isn't time, the nearest one is too far away, they cost too much; perhaps a would-be writer is even embarrassed at being perceived as such, sharing his hopes and fears with dozens of fellow hopefuls he has never seen before. What then?

The Portable Writer's Conference is here to solve just that: to bring together a list of qualified and experienced contributors who can deliver on the page the same kind of no-nonsense advice they would offer from the podium during lunch or dinner, or in the workshops that take up much of the time at writer's conferences. Here between book covers, without the hassle of travel and reservations and sitting through presentations that aren't really very helpful, just because you've paid to be there, is the best of all possible worlds for the would-be writer: An anthology of advice that is very specific to the needs of many different kinds of writers, that can be referred to at will, where you don't have to take notes or buy tapes or struggle to stay awake.

I've been to many writer's conferences in my time to speak my piece about how authors can best relate to book publishers including ones in locations as glamorous as Maui and Lake Tahoe. This book may not transport you to such idyllic spots, but I can safely say that none of these conferences has offered so wide a range of speakers and subjects as this book does. You can learn in the following pages about dozens of subjects, from improving your grammar to researching online, from writing for kids to writing for romance readers, from putting down authentic sounding dialogue to conducting interviews that sell, and lots of excellent information on tough subjects like copyrights and contracts. The contributors are the kinds of people who are often invited to conferences: publishers, editors, literary agents, authors with a proven track record in a dozen different genres.

There'll always be a need for "live" writer's conferences, for many writers like to get together, to network and get a chance to show their work to people who just may want to publish it—or at least to hear why they won't or can't. But for a lot of the nuts-and-bolts information such conferences offer, *The Portable Writer's Conference* is an excellent one-stop shopping choice.

—*John F. Baker,*
Former Editorial Director,
Publishers Weekly

Introduction

Dare to Wet Your Line

" **Y**ou can't catch any fish if you're not willing to get your line wet," Kenny advised as he fixed his fiberglass pole into a contraption he'd made by sticking two twigs into the dusty river bank.

Kenny was the dad who occasionally let me tag along with him and his sons on weekend fishing trips. Heaven only knows why he felt driven to expound such. Maybe I had been dragging my feet getting my line in the water. But, as these things sometimes are to twelve-year-olds, the comment provided something of an epiphany to me. I understood him to be speaking universally: Without the chance of failure, there is no chance of success.

I thought of Kenny the other day when I arrived to do a book signing at a Barnes & Noble. Two young clerks were excited—at least they acted excited—to meet a book publisher. Both said they were dedicated writers. The young man wrote science fiction stories, the woman, poetry and essays on life as a female college student. Both were intelligent and articulate and from this I imagined both were decent writers. I asked where they had been published and they both said they weren't published yet. But they hoped to be someday.

I knew the answer to my next question, but I asked it anyway: "Have you ever submitted anything to a publisher?" Neither had.

They offered me a bottle of Evian and we sat down to talk for a minute. I asked them why, if they were so excited about writing, they hadn't tried to get published. There was a bit of hemming and hawing, then they both admitted, albeit sheepishly, that they feared getting rejected.

Rejection to them would be proof that their writing was bad and if their writing was bad their dream of someday getting published would be dashed. Rejection would be embarrassing; their family and friends knew they wrote and hoped to be published. Rejection would damage their self respect. And, while they truly wanted to see their work in print, to garner the validation this would provide, they hadn't summoned the courage required to submit their work to publishers. They weren't willing to get their lines wet.

How about you? Have you wet your line recently? Or have you written great stuff only to let it grow moldy in your desk drawer? Does fear of failure stop you from sending your short stories to magazines or your book proposals to book publishers? If so, Teddy Roosevelt has some advice for you.

In a rousing speech Roosevelt gave before Chicago's Hamilton Club in 1890, he said, "Far better it is to dare mighty things, to win glorious triumphs, even though checkered by failure, than to take rank with those poor spirits who neither enjoy much nor suffer much, because they live in the gray twilight that knows not victory nor defeat."

If you find yourself shoulder to shoulder with Roosevelt's "poor spirits," face down your fears, step out of the gray twilight into the warm sunshine of the bold and the published. Dare to wet your line. Submit your work to an agent or an editor.

And be persistent. Don't stop at the first "No" you get, or the second or the forty-sixth. You've probably heard the stories about such 'n' such book, rejected by umpteen editors, finally picked up, goes on to sell millions of copies, securing for its author a place in literary history and a lifetime of ease.

Well, it happens. Book and periodical editors have many reasons for rejecting manuscripts that have nothing to do with the inherent worth of the work. Getting published, like selling insurance, is a numbers game. The more you pitch the more you hit. Any writer worth her salt can paper her office wall with rejection slips. Don't be afraid. You haven't failed until you stop trying.

Now dig into this book and I'll watch for your byline.

Workshops

The Mother of all Attitudes

What fiction writers can learn from football players

By James N. Frey

RANDY, A KID IN MY NEIGHBORHOOD, was recently cut from his college football team, the "Soaring Eagles," in his senior year because, the coach said, he had "failed to develop an attitude."

Randy mows my grass from time to time, waters my lawn when my wife and I are away, keeps the storm drain clear. I've known him all his life. He's a sweet kid, brainy, likable, easy-going. He asked me if I'd call the coach and find out what he meant by "developing an attitude." I wanted to know, too, so I went over to the college to ask, thinking maybe I could help the kid get back on the team.

On the way over, I was thinking how much football is like fiction writing. Football is mythic, a clash of titans, protagonist pitted against antagonist in a winner-take-all struggle with the outcome uncertain. Football, like fiction writing, has a game plan, rises to a climax, and is performed with art and grace. Works of fiction are about the struggles of living. Football is a metaphor for the same thing. Often, the excitement mounts as the clock runs down, just as in fiction the climax often comes at the end of a race against time. Football teams are characters of a sort: The fans identify with them the way readers identify with fictional characters. The Forty-Niners are slightly effete, the team of finesse, timing, precision; the Chicago Bears are a Popeye-type team, they play smash-mouth, in-your-face hardball; the Raiders are outlaws. In both fiction writing and football what's being created is a contest of wills, a drama, played out for the pleasure of an audience. Tension is built and released. There's suspense, and character is being tested. Things are at stake.

I found the Soaring Eagles coach at the practice field. Coach Davis turned out to be a big bruiser of a man with the wide face of a panda bear and hands that could go halfway around a prize watermelon. He said he didn't mind me asking for the kid. Putting his foot up on the bench and looking out over his players bashing each other under the hot August sun, he said what he meant was that the kids who didn't have an attitude didn't want to hit hard, whined too much when they got banged up, and didn't seem to mind losing. As an example, he said, take Randy, the kid who cuts my grass. There was nothing wrong with his talent: He had a fair amount of skill, good hands, and was plenty quick, but he'd never developed an attitude, so he couldn't be a Soaring Eagle.

I still didn't get it, I said.

He explained that having an attitude means that you don't want to just beat your opponents, you want to humiliate them. When you hit, you want the man you hit to think he was hit by a freight train. When you carry the ball, you don't want to make just a first down: You want to score. You're hungry. Running with the ball, you don't go down with the first hit, even the second, and in a pile-up, you keep your legs pumping. Losing makes your shorts crawl up. You'd rather drink drain cleaner than lose. Linebacker Hacksaw Reynolds once sawed his Volkswagen in half to relieve his frustrations after a loss. That's what having an attitude means. Guys with an attitude come to practice early and leave late. They're ready to listen to anyone who can help them better their technique. Winning, Davis said, is a matter of doing a million small things well, and the guy with an attitude wants to master them all.

> "It's a matter of having an attitude, hating rejection, doing a million little things well."

And that, I thought, exactly describes fiction writing. It's a matter of having an attitude, hating rejection, doing a million little things well.

Davis went on. In a game, he said, guys with an attitude might be down by three touchdowns with two minutes to go and they'll still be trying to score. Guys with an attitude never lose a game, they just run out of time.

To be a Soaring Eagle, he said, you must have an attitude or we don't want you—no matter how much innate ability you have.

I got to thinking about the Soaring Eagles when I drove south to conduct a workshop for a writers group called the Santa Cruz Forum which meets twice monthly to schmooze, read each other's work, and munch cheese and crackers. They're nice people, open, friendly, easy to get along with. They're well educated, well read, and most have talent. Their writing is generally crisp, their metaphors both apt and colorful, their humor hip, their grammar impeccable. Most have interesting stories to tell. Some tug a tear occasionally— even from a hard-hearted old writing coach like me. They choose nice fonts, like Times Roman and Palatino, when they print drafts on their laser printers. They know correct manuscript form. But none of them has an *attitude*.

The first time I'd had a workshop with them, they each had hammered out a good outline for a novel and had a good running start at it. They'd all left knowing where they were heading, and the plan was that each would have a first draft when I came back six months later.

In between my visits, these nine people had produced almost nothing except great excuses. Only one had a first draft, and that was so sketchy it read more like a synopsis. Another had been on a European vacation, she said, and another had to move her business. A talented romance writer said she had a husband who bought a sailboat and so she had to go sailing with him every weekend during her writing time. A short story writer, one who'd published a few things over the years, said he was busy looking for work. Another had computer problems. Blah, blah, blah. They all swore blood oaths that they were *now* ready to really get rolling. Really. When I came back again next year, they'd all have at least a first draft. Some even promised to be ready to submit their novel to a publisher.

But they won't. Not a one of them. None of them has an attitude. Like Randy with football, they have the skills, some even have talent, but they aren't prepared to do what it takes. As writers, just like football players, we're in a game with brutal competition. We can't humiliate an opponent on the field, but if we're going to write with an attitude, we need to write not just to sell a story, but to create a masterpiece. Not to be "good enough to publish," but to write something that will knock an editor on his or her keister with the very first page.

Football players have to play with pain, the way fiction writers have to write with pain. We're selling emotion, and putting emotion on paper means we first have to feel it in our hearts. And that's painful. More painful that getting hit by a 240-pound fullback. Losing—in the writer's case rejection—hurts, but it's a hurt we have to endure with alacrity. To increase your success rate, it's been said, you simply have to increase your failure rate. We may have to suffer humiliation at the hands of an inconsiderate editor or fellow member of a workshop. But if we're going to get to play in the Super Bowl, we're going to have to stand up to a lot of hurt and humiliation.

On the way back from Santa Cruz, I was thinking a creative writing workshop leader is more like a football coach than he or she is like a teacher. A teacher instructs, that is, shows the students how to approach a math problem, or how to look for symbols in *The Red Badge of Courage*. In creative writing, the trick is to teach people how to read with a critical eye. How to think in terms of rewrite to bring about certain effects. A workshop leader, like a football coach, looks at performance and makes suggestions on how to improve that performance.

Football players must show up for practice, and they must be ready to learn. As a writing coach, I've found, there are innumerable would-be writers who show up for writing workshops who are not ready to learn. They have come to be praised, have their heads patted and their backs slapped, to be flattered, coddled, and encouraged. As football players they would not last five minutes.

To become a writer, one must be open to learn techniques, such as controlling point of view, creating believable characters, learning how they develop, putting them in conflict and so on, just as a football player has to learn to block high on the pads to stop a bull rush, to cut below the knees to take a blocker down on a kickoff return, to throw his body into a hole in the line to stop an onrushing fullback twice his size. A football player with an attitude is ready to sacrifice his body if he has to. Anything to win.

And football players must play with pain. It hurts to be hit. Players often have their "bells rung," which means they suffer a mild concussion. Writers, too, must learn to write with pain. Sometimes it just does not go well. How many times do we hear our writing colleagues whine that they have to do a rewrite and it's just too painful to throw out what they've written, or that they got a few rejections and aren't sending out that story anymore.

Mame garnered something like fifty-two rejections before it sold. The number of books that became hits after being rejected is enormous. The reason is, really good work is *different*, and different means risk to an editor. Having an attitude as a writer means you have to take risks, which means you'll scare the hell out of some editors and you'll have to suffer rejection as a result. Jean Auel took a risk. Everyone told her that if she wrote about prehistoric people no editor would buy it, too risky. But she had an attitude. Her books have now sold in the millions.

Football is an intensely competitive game, but it doesn't begin to compare with writing. The odds of making it to the Super Bowl for a high school football player are probably 10,000 to one. For a writer starting out, the odds of making it to the *New York Times* best-seller list are probably as great, if not greater. There are fewer than 300 best-sellers a year, and over a half million people start writing a novel every year—luckily only about 20 percent ever finish, and fewer yet are ever submitted.

Making it to the Super Bowl, coaches say, is a matter of "staying focused." The same applies to writing. Staying focused means for a football player that no matter what happens—if they're way ahead or way behind in a game, if they're ahead in the league standings, if their star quarterback just got carried from the field—no matter what, they will stay focused on their job and perform up to their maximum capacity.

As a writing coach, I can testify that most writers fail for this very reason: They can't stay focused. In the Santa Cruz Forum, the lack of focus spreads like a case of the flu. Instead of encouraging each other to write, they commiserate about each other's troubles and cry on each other's shoulders about why they can't write. Boo-hoo, I had to entertain my relative, I had to have my kitchen remodeled, I had to clean out my closets.

> "We're selling emotion, and putting emotion on paper means we first have to feel it in our hearts."

They're using up all their creativity in making excuses. If they were on Coach Davis' Soaring Eagles, they'd be carrying water buckets.

Living in the San Francisco Bay Area, and being a creative writing teacher, I'm invited to a lot of parties, often attended by writers and would-be writers. Over the past ten years or so, I've bumped into a would-be writer—let's call her Sarah Sommersby—who was working as a waitress in San Francisco by day and working on her novel at night. She attended workshops, spent thousands of hours in the library doing research, and rewrote and rewrote and rewrote. The manuscript was 2,000 pages long.

A couple of years ago, as the novel was in its "semifinal" draft, she had an accident and severely injured her back. She could not stand without great difficulty. Because the prescription pain pills affected her writing, she refused them. Over-the-counter pain medication helped, but she was still in agony. Bedridden, she continued to work using a contraption to hold her keyboard. She stayed focused; she had an attitude. She wrote six hours a day, seven days a week. Like a football player playing with pain, she was writing with pain.

I saw her at a party the other night. Her health is much improved. Her book has just come out. She got enough from the American advance and the German rights that she will never have to work again at her day job, and she was ecstatic.

Marv Levy's Buffalo Bills had lost three successive Super Bowls and were about to play their fourth. When asked by a reporter if this was a "must win," he said, "World War II was a 'must win'; this is a football game." Marv Levy does not have an attitude.

Vince Lombardi, coach of the Green Bay Packers, was asked once if football was the most important thing. He said no, "it is the only thing." He'd made the Packers, the perennial doormats of the league, into the dominant team in football and won two consecutive Super Bowls. The Super Bowl trophy is now called the Lombardi Trophy in his honor. He had an attitude.

I asked Coach Davis the all-important question about attitude. Are you born with it, or do you develop it? He considered the question for a long time as he looked out on his scrimmaging players. Finally he spit between his teeth and said that some are born with it and some develop it. I then asked the most important question of all: If you're not born with it, how do you develop it?

Fear, he said.

Fear? I didn't get it.

Fear of losing, fear of not measuring up, he explained. That's how it starts. Fear is the mother of an attitude. First you've got to hate the feeling of losing, of feeling worthless, feeling that you let your fans down. The first sign of getting an attitude is when they start gritting their teeth when they hit the practice dummy. Then they start coming to practice early and taking notes on new plays. You can see the fire in their eyes growing brighter.

And then he walked off to yell at a player for running with the ball held away from his body, in what the coach called the Fumble Zone. One of the million little things.

When I think of the writers who have developed an attitude over the years, who became, by God, possessed, maniacally determined to make it as a writer, it seems to me what happened to them is that success did not come easy as they'd first thought it would. It was then they became afraid. Afraid they would fail. And it's this fear that did lead them to develop an attitude.

So anyway, Randy was over yesterday and told me he no longer cared about football, that he'd found something much better—he was taking a creative writing class. Three units, he said, and he only had to write two short stories. An easy "A," he said, and maybe he'd get something published. His teacher said he had a lot of talent.

But what's that without an attitude? I asked.

You're talking football, not writing, he said. In writing you don't have to have an attitude.

Which left me chuckling.

James N. Frey is the author of nine novels, including Winter of the Wolves and The Long Way to Die, *nominated for an Edgar by the Mystery Writers of America. He is also the author of* How to Write a Damn Good Novel; How to Write a Damn Good Novel II: Advanced Techniques; The Key: How to Write Damn Good Fiction Using the Power of Myth; *and* How to Write a Damn Good Mystery *by St. Martin's Press. Frey teaches novel writing at private workshops.*

Telling Tales

A short story workshop

By Shelly Lowenkopf

> With a tale forsooth he cometh unto you,
> with a tale which holdeth children from play,
> and old men from the chimney corner.
> —Sir Philip Sidney

A SHORT STORY IS LIKE A GENIE IN A BOTTLE. Once the cork is pulled, out gushes a force that may grant you wishes or hound you with malicious intent.

Even if you are able to get the genie back in the bottle or the effects of the story out of your mind, some residue will forever affect your response to bottles and fiction.

If this makes the short story seem volatile, daunting, and difficult to control, I've been successful in alerting you to the dangers of taking on one of your own. On the other hand, if your goal as a writer is to grant wishes to your readers, disturb them, or transport them, you've come to the right place. Short stories, especially good ones, seem easier to execute than they are. But if launched with proper momentum, they illustrate the human condition in ways that enlighten and entertain.

The first thing to look at in planning your short story is scope. Novels often set forth to capture life with a wide-angle lens, portraying time, movement, differing perspectives, and change. The short story is an event, a moment in time, captured as if by accident. Seemingly informal or without design, the story is like a snapshot in a photo album, revealing something quite unintentional and remarkable—after the fact of the event.

If the novel is a landscape, the short story is a close-up. Alice Munro, Margaret Atwood, William Maxwell, and William Trevor are able to cram longer passages of time into their short form narratives but even they are sparing about doing so, focusing more often on time frames associated with a single event: a meal, a family gathering, a concert, a wedding, a funeral.

Novels have multifarious characters; short stories are limited. Too many front-rank characters in too brief a time produce the same effect you get when attending a party where nearly all the guests are strangers. Remarkable and different as they may seem, their names and faces become a jumble until you get to know them at some length.

Edgar Allen Poe, Nathaniel Hawthorne, and Somerset Maugham, authors who gave the short story its unique shape, emphasize the importance of striving for one effect, achieved by selecting events, incidents, and complications that build to one combustive response. The best way for you to put your fingerprints on your own short story is to decide on the payoff, the single effect you wish to leave with the reader at the end.

Choose the time frame, setting, and events for your story as you would the ingredients, condiments, and spices in a recipe. Just as you want fresh ingredients and condiments that do not cancel one another, you want incidents, individuals, and recognizable conflicts in your story that promise—and deliver—some notable personality and an agreeable aftertaste.

> "The short story doesn't have the luxury of depicting change; the closest it can come is awareness."

Novels provide a sense of change, growth, solution to problems. The short story doesn't have the luxury of depicting change; the closest it can come is awareness. Thus the final effect of a story—the aftertaste—is based on opportunity for understanding being offered. This opportunity is most often presented to the protagonist, the principal person in the narrative; it may be accepted, ignored, or misinterpreted, depending on the effect you want to leave with the reader.

The propellant

There are two basic types of fiction, plot-driven and character-driven. Stories propelled by plot tend to have a broader audience appeal, appear in mass-market publications, earn their authors respectable sums of money. Such stories often come from authors whose grasp of plot allows them to see or contrive a dramatic, related series of events with little effort and indeed, these authors seem to be able to produce an unending stream of stories in which the narrative is reminiscent of the famed English garden mazes, with twists, frustrations, dead-ends, surprises, and last-minute discoveries.

A notable example of a plot-driven writer is O. Henry, whose story "The Gift of the Magi" is a classic model for study. Two appealing people want to commemorate their love for one another with a gift at Christmas. But alas, they're both quite broke and so he sells his most prized possession, the pocket watch of his late father, in order to buy her splendid tortoiseshell combs for her long, luxuriant hair. And she? Ah, she has sold her locks to a wig maker in order to buy him a watch chain. Result: unselfish love, sacrifice, surprise, for a payoff of some depth and warmth. Based on the scores of stories he wrote with such surprise endings, O. Henry (William Sidney Porter) had the knack of plotting his famous reversals and payoffs, if not from the very beginning then soon into the writing process. Many of his plots are remembered—but few of his characters.

Character-driven stories are set in motion by the agendas, behavior, and interaction of the participants. Writers of this kind of story tend to begin with a concept or an incident between two or more individuals they know quite well, rather than from a plot that has been worked out in advance.

Character-driven stories usually appear in journals or so-called "little" magazines and reviews, where payment is in free copies or subscriptions. I have been paid five dollars for such stories by one magazine, a ballpoint pen from another, and a T-shirt featuring the logo of the magazine from yet another (the publisher offered me an extra large T-shirt for any subsequent acceptances). Some character-driven stories end up in prestigious publications such as *The Georgia Review*, where payment is ten dollars a printed page; others still appear in *The New Yorker*, where payment starts at about fifty cents a word.

Stories of this nature are usually undertaken in the same spirit of the pure scientist (if *that* is not a contradiction of terms) pursuing a line of enquiry for the passion of curiosity, or of a musician chasing after an improvisation for the thrill of discovery. This is by most accounts the art-for-art's-sake story. Such wildly diverse practitioners of it are Bobbie Ann Mason, Alice Adams, Bob Shaccochis, and Michael Chabon.

One of the earliest practitioners of this kind of story—if not the "inventor" of it—is worth your study nearly a hundred years after the fact. Any of the stories in James Joyce's volume *Dubliners* would fit without notice were they to appear in a current issue of *the* New Yorker under some other byline. The payoff or aftertaste in each story is a resounding emotional awareness. (Character-driven stories pay off in a feeling or with a mood; plot-driven stories can have an emotional payoff but usually deliver on some physical action associated with a mistaken perception. Notable example: Ambrose Bierce's "Occurrence at Owl Creek Bridge," which does both.)

Single character point-of-view

As the writer you are setting up an intriguing landscape with a compelling cast of characters who are responding to some kind of pressure. The reader wants a guide. Perhaps you could have been that guide fifty or sixty years ago, easing us into short fiction the way Somerset Maugham and F. Scott Fitzgerald so artfully set their narratives into motion. That was then—this is now.

Pick the character best suited to be the guide for the reader, then hand over the controls to this first-person or third-person narrator. You must stay out of the narrative unless it becomes absolutely necessary in order to avoid some long, unwieldy passage.

Modern short stories, even plot-driven ones, are most often told by one character, speaking as an I (Louise Erdrich comes to mind with her stunning "Love Medicine") or by a third-person narrator who "tells" your story by experiencing its events before our very eyes. In recent years some writers have been telling short stories through the point of view of more than one character. Tempting as it is to try this, you should know you may be limiting your chances with editors, who seem to favor a one-person approach.

Authors such as William Trevor can get away with an omniscient point of view without sounding antiquated or appearing to have a jerky style. You probably shouldn't try omniscient until you've written forty or fifty stories.

Such venerable publishers of short stories as *Saturday Evening Post* and *Collier's* had a simple guideline for characters—no stories about people their readers would not invite to their homes as guests. This left the door open for some agreeable eccentrics and marginal misfits, but some of the more memorable persons in modern literature would have had to grab a bite at Burger King instead. Imagine the author of *Silence of the Lambs* being offered condensation rights only if Dr. Hannibal Lecter were rewritten as a vegetarian.

Contemporary characters need not be likable or even redeemable, but they must be interesting. Some sure ways to enlist reader sympathy and interest:

- Make your characters vulnerable.

- Give them some flaw, defect, or adversity to overcome.

- Show them struggling to keep their lives from careening out of control.

Quick start

Literary agents and editors, as examples of professional readers, and bookstore browsers, as examples of readers for pleasure, will give a novelist three or four pages to get things going, establish rapport, and effect traction. Otherwise the manuscript goes back to the author or the book goes back to the shelf.

> "Contemporary characters need not be likable or even redeemable, but they must be interesting."

Short story writers have even less leeway; if nothing happens by the end of the first page of manuscript, the editor is a sure bet to bail out. If nothing happens by the end of the first printed page, the reader will begin skipping ahead in search of a more hospitable climate.

Accordingly, we come to out next plateau.

Start with some provocative and relevant action. This adjuration applies to both types of short story. Even though the action does not have to be physical in the violent or combative sense, it must be physical in the sense of not being cerebral. If a character is thinking things over as your story begins, as in "How had her life gotten so befuddled, she wondered," you have already lost the necessary momentum associated with beginnings and are well on your way to putting your reader beyond your reach.

Time is of the essence. Begin with two or more people present, having just reached some kind of boiling point. Make your opening sentence as provocative as possible. One of my favorite approaches for getting novice writers off to a jump start is to ask them to imagine having just left home and settling into the living situation of their fondest dreams only to have a parent—you know the one I mean—arrive at the front door, take one look, then say, "How can you let yourself live this way?"

One character left alone for too long, especially at the onset, is likely to go cerebral on us—a fatal mistake. Unless the one character alone is doing something covert or illegal, say exhuming a body, going through a loved one's purse or wallet, eavesdropping, hiding something, or waiting in ambush, get another character on stage fast. Play on the fear of discovery. Exploit the reader's suspicions of the unthinkable come to pass. Stay away from interior monologue, background, and setup until the story is well in progress.

But how, you ask, will I interest the reader without being able to give relevant backstory and description?

• Let your characters define themselves and their goals through what they do.

• Withhold vital information for as long as possible (which, come to think of it, is a pretty good definition of suspense).

Scenes as bursts of energy

Just as a point of view is a window into the attitudes and agendas of a character, scenes are windows into the personality of the story. Each scene must in some material way advance the story, must show the characters as they try to keep their heads above water while swimming against an ever-increasing current.

Throwing complications at your characters is not enough. You must also provide tension, variety, and yes, even surprise. It is not a scene if you bring two or three characters into a locale merely to argue about their backgrounds and explain their motives; you must supply as well some opposition, and you must be sure to evoke some kind of mood such as despair, vulnerability, fear, nostalgia, regret.

> "Start with some provocative and relevant action."

Scenes require the energy of reversals, opposition, and suspense to keep them moving. Even if the time has come for description and backstory, don't assume the reader will sit still for large doses without frequent pit stops for refueling.

Think of a scene as a small tub in which you are going to attempt to wash a large, unwilling dog.

Succinct = success

Because short stories are briefer than novels, they are less forgiving of excess. This makes detail a vital element. Too much detail robs the story of its movement. One ill-chosen word, one resounding cliché, one unintentional repetition can bring disaster. One line of dialogue too much (or too cute) can make a *Titanic* of the most original narrative yet contrived.

The best way to approach this critical area is through the reader, as in Don't tell the reader what he already knows. Most readers know what it's like to be hungry, to have insomnia, to experience grief. Most readers know what cheap hotel rooms look like, how lawyers' offices are furnished, how difficult it is to cut a cheap steak.

Spare the reader descriptions of things the reader is already bored with—sunrises, sunsets, views of Los Angeles from on high, handsome men, and attractive women come to mind—and concentrate on two matters of more immediacy:

• Look for the essential character trait of a person or place, then try to express it as a throwaway phrase.

• Describe familiar objects and places only when there is something unexpected and surprising about them that relates to the story.

Define with dialogue

Dialogue is the way people talk *in fiction*; it is meant to advance story, reveal—repeat, reveal—character. Dialogue that gets chatty and begins to sound like transcripts of courtroom proceedings grows old fast, the more so in short fiction. Use dialogue to poke, prod, enhance, and define; use it to make the other characters nervous or edgy. Two characters who agree with each other represent a loss of dramatic tension. If your characters seem to be in agreement, your readers should suspect this is because each is agreeing to something different.

Story, drama, and narrative are about blunted expectations and frustrations. Dialogue should mirror these feelings, demonstrating the differences between your characters. One character at rest becomes another character's resentment. One character's praise or approval becomes another character's occasion for suspicion.

Check every exchange of dialogue with a relentless eye for such throw-away lines as "Oh." "Oh, really?" "Well, I guess so." "OK." "It's all right with me." They and all other similar equivocations pull the switch on tension and bring the story to a stop.

Anticlimax

If you've done well with your choice of characters, your beginning, pacing, and skillfully led up to the moment of combustion in which things not only get out of hand but become unthinkable—if you've let the characters tell your story and have resisted the temptation to be a control freak by bombarding the reader with endless detail, there is a final check point where you need to show your writerly credentials.

One of the most important words to be understood in fiction—short fiction in particular—is anticlimax.

In a literal sense, anticlimax means against the ending, which is close to the way I ask you to consider it in the context of the short story. A story ends at some significant emotional point where as much of the dramatic energy as possible has been dissipated. Cycles have come to as much of a return as possible; settlements have been negotiated and some bit of wisdom or understanding is presented for the characters and the reader.

Try not to tell the reader more than the reader wants to know. The more you withhold and the longer you withhold it, the more you engage the reader's imagination, supplying the very elements the reader wants and the very elements genies offer in the form of wishes: transportation, riches, and enlightenment.

Beginning writers have a tendency to want to explain the ending in minute detail and, by doing so, defeat the very effect they have labored to achieve. A good way to illustrate this point is found in an anecdote concerning two of the most towering forces in jazz during the past fifty years. John Coltrane, a major harmonic innovator on the tenor and soprano saxophone, was known for his long solos and extended improvisations. Although his solos were not only tolerated but admired by many other musicians because they were so fresh and powerful, many of his peers teased him about his tendency to go on at such length. One day Coltrane confessed to his admired friend and often employer Miles Davis that he played at such length because he was not always sure how to end his solos. "Just take the instrument out of your mouth," Davis said.

A story is over when relevant action is done; it need not be repeated in the manner of a nervous stand-up comic, trying to milk a joke. It need not be spelled out to make sure the reader has understood the point. It needs no gradual fade-out, no transition—nothing but a final period at the end of the sentence.

The modern short story, whether plot- or character-driven, has an elliptical quality, shading toward the opaque as the medium moves from mass-market to the more literary. A defining event brings some but not all the dramatic elements to rest, allowing a few speculative moments in the reader's mind to linger and resonate.

Shelly Lowenkopf has held major editorial positions with general trade, scholarly, literary, and mass market publishers. He has been an adjunct professor at the University of Southern California Masters in Professional Writing Program since 1974 and has led the late night fiction workshop at the Santa Barbara Writers Conference since 1980. His book reviews have appeared in metropolitan and national periodicals as well as his present weekly column in the Montecito (CA) Journal. *Since the early nineties, his fiction interests have focused on short stories, which appear in the literary press. His most recent book will be* The Fiction Writers' Handbook. *He continues to serve as a freelance editor and consultant to literary agents, publishers, and authors.*

How to Write a Dynamite Love Scene

Sizzle sells more than just steaks:
Learn how to add steam to your novel or short story

By Suzanne Forster

FLASHES OF HIS COLD FACE AND HOT EYES came back to her unbidden. She could feel the dominating power of his hands, the muscled strength of his arms. The cologne permeated her senses as she remembered the heat and the sweat and the scathing kiss. It was his scent, she was sure of it. She felt as if she'd been marked, as if the irrefutable evidence of his manhandling were all over her body.

So begins the tortuous dance of love for Jessie, the heroine of my 1994 novel *Shameless*. The passage quoted above occurs on the very first evening, immediately after Jessie has her first encounter with the dark, dangerous Luc. You see, love scenes don't start after the characters take off their clothes. They start from the very first moment your characters meet. Sometimes they even start before that. Readers can begin to anticipate a love scene, or a romantic moment, as soon as a character is described on your pages.

For example:

As she unbuttoned her black cashmere cardigan, she was aware of the fullness of her breasts against the inside of her wrists. For so long she had not thought of her body as anything but an efficient machine, that the contact surprised her. Her flesh was oddly responsive tonight...

That scene is also from *Shameless*, page two to be exact.

As you've probably guessed by now, I'm going to be exploding the process for creating dynamite love scenes. (Pardon the pun but I just couldn't pass that up!) One of the most important things we, as writers, must remember is that what makes for love scene dynamite is not so much the sex itself, but all the great stuff that *builds* to it. So how do we create anticipation? Read on.

If you're writing a romance novel, virtually everything you do in your story is going to contribute to the anticipation. If you're writing in another genre, but you have a romantic subplot, the same standard applies. All or most of the elements of that subplot will contribute. When I say they *will*, what I mean is they *should*. You, the writer, should set it up that way. Be calculating.

Even if your characters meet and hate each other on sight, that charged moment is an impetus toward the love scene. Everything you write—the scene setting, your characters' thoughts, fantasies, their dialogue, even the subliminal stuff, the subtext and the body language—all of that adds to the build. It's a cumulative effect, like feeder streams flowing into a river that's heading for the rapids. Oh, I should warn you, I do have a tendency to launch into water metaphors when I'm talking about sex. I'll try to control myself.

Love scenes are built through a very, very mysterious process called *sexual tension*. There are a lot of interchangeable terms for sexual tension. You can call it *romantic chemistry* or *mood setting*. But it's really all about the balance you create between the two characters who are attracted to each other.

Definition: Sexual tension is the balance between the conflict and the attraction your characters feel.

Now let's talk about how to create sexual tension

Let's look at it from a couple of different angles. First I want to talk about the character factors involved in writing sexual tension, then the story factors.

Sexual tension does not exist in a vacuum. It is built from details—the wonderful, evocative details you choose to include in your story, the imagery, the scene setting. And it is also built from the personality traits and characteristics that you choose to include in your characters. Sexual tension has to be motivated. And we have to believe the motivation.

Characters' factors that promote sexual tension

Emotions. I've divided emotions up into two categories. The first category is emotional intimacy. These are the underlying emotions, or the character's deepest needs. The longing for completion. The yearning to connect with another human being. The search for a soulmate.

Your characters may not be in touch with these needs. They may even have cut themselves off from such needs, because of the pain of not having them met in the past. But the longing is there, and it is driving the character. Emotional intimacy with others is a basic human need that drives us all.

Another basic need is to be loved unconditionally, to be acknowledged and accepted for who we are. These needs will probably come into play later in your story as your characters realize they're falling in love.

The second category of emotions are the visceral responses, the feelings we associate with physical or sexual attraction: pounding heart, rapid breathing, flushed skin, dilated eyes. They have a direct effect on the sexual tension in your story.

Love beats

Psychology Today did a study in which they discovered that anything that makes the heart beat faster (including jogging) will make the opposite sex seem more attractive. A second study showed that the emotions that make the heart beat harder will make the opposite sex more attractive to you—and make you more responsive to the opposite sex under the right conditions.

The two emotions they tested were fear and anger. The condition is that the emotions experienced have to be fairly mild. They're not talking about a high level of emotion like terror or rage that will trigger the survival instincts. They mean a moderate level of arousal, a little jolt of fear, a little jolt of anger. Anything that stirs the pulse and heats the blood. A spirited argument can be great foreplay. We've all seen the classic movie scenes where the hero and heroine are arguing one minute and kissing the next.

Fear works well, too. But again, it has to be the right degree. Just a touch of it. What they call a "thrill of fear." I particularly like to use elements of mystery and danger in my hero. There's a built-in arousal factor. The heroine's adrenaline is flowing.

One of our most basic fears is loss of control

Whenever you feel your control slipping away, in any situation, the tension rises. In a sexual/romantic situation, the tension skyrockets because there is so much at stake. There is an instinctive fear of someone else taking control over your will. Or of surrendering your will to someone.

Deprivation

I've already discussed the unfulfilled emotional needs: the needs for closeness and intimacy, the longing to connect with another human being.

Now I want to talk about unfulfilled physical needs. This could be a character who's been deprived of physical gratification, either by choice or by circumstance. Or they're disappointed or disillusioned by that aspect of their life.

Basically, I think we all know what we're talking about here. This is a person who's been doing without for a long time. At first blush, deprivation doesn't sound like a very sexy situation for a book, but it can be an incredibly powerful motivator, because so much has been unfulfilled. The longing, both sexual and emotional. The needs, the hunger.

In *To Love a Man* by Karen Robards, the heroine was married to a gay man for seven years with no physical gratification. She meets the book's hero under unusual circumstances. She's caught in the cross-fire of a third-world coup, is knocked out and wakes up in his arms. She hasn't been held or touched by a man in years, but he misinterprets her responsiveness. He doesn't think of her as needy, he thinks of her as "easy," which sets up the conflict for the early part of book.

Senses

Seeing, hearing, touching, tasting, smelling. The five senses are so important in creating sexual tension that I could spend this entire workshop on them alone. Obviously I don't have space to do that, so I'm going to refer you to a wonderful book on the subject: *A Natural History of the Senses* by Diane Ackerman.

To give you an idea how powerful the senses are, here's a paragraph about the sense of smell from her book: "Smells spur memories. They also rouse our senses, pamper and indulge us, help define our self-image, stir the cauldron of our seductiveness, warn us of danger, lead us into temptation, fan our religious fervor, accompany us to heaven, wed us to fashion, and steep us in luxury." The author discusses all of that, at length, in her book. And that's just one sense. I suggest you get a copy and use what you learn in your writing.

She also said something I thought was fascinating. She said that mothers of school-age children can pick out T-shirts worn by their own child. Men cannot do this. Fathers don't recognize the smell of their infants, but men can tell if a T-shirt has been worn by a male or a female, just by smelling it.

Be sure to use the senses in your scenes. They will enrich your story and give it texture. And they will personalize your story when shown through your character's point of view.

Imagination

The brain is the sexiest organ in the body. You can do so much with the characters' thoughts and fantasies. You can even suggest things that might push the envelope a bit, because they're not actually doing anything. They're just thinking about doing it. Jimmy Carter, lusting in his heart.

Also, in reality our repressed erotic impulses do break through in our dreams. So dreams are great material.

In my novel *Shameless*, the heroine, Jessie Flood, tries to kill the hero in the first chapter. She shoots him, is what she does. She doesn't actually kill him, but when he gets a look at where she's got that gun aimed, he figures he might as well be dead.

It's a love/hate thing between the characters (as if you couldn't figure that out). But there was a time when Jessie adored Luc Warnecke. They grew up together, and he was the object of all her adolescent fantasies. And that's what finally allows her to let down her guard and to be close to him.

She fantasizes about her fantasies. She had dreams about going to the prom with him, dancing close, winding up in the back seat of his car. There's a sweetness to the daydream that cuts through the hostility between them for a brief time.

Dialogue

Dialogue is another powerhouse technique for creating sexual tension. Especially when it's challenging, provocative dialogue. Characters who keep each other slightly off-balance.

From my novel *Shameless*:

> "Giddy?" She nodded, her heart pounding wildly. "Maybe we both had too much to drink," she suggested.
>
> "I'm high all right, but it isn't the wine. It isn't even the music or this place, Jessie. It's this rush of feeling. It's incredible." He shook his head, laughing huskily as if he didn't quite know what to make of the situation.
>
> "Luc, don't laugh like that," she implored, velvet-voiced and breathy.
>
> "I beg your pardon?"
>
> "I just wish you wouldn't laugh like that, and maybe you shouldn't look at me that way either—"
>
> "Not look at you? Jessie, I—"
>
> "You *promised*," she reminded him quickly, extricating herself from his arms.

"I promised not to look at you?"

"No, but you promised it would be one dance. Nothing more."

"True, but who knew this was going to happen, who knew we were going to feel like this." He drew in a deep breath as if he were about to declare himself in some way. "There's something I've been wanting to tell you," he said. "Something besides the fact that you look irresistible tonight. Jessie, I—"

"No!"

Sexual signals

Body language. Nonverbal communication. Seventy-five percent of our communication with other people is nonverbal, so the signals we send each other are crucial in what they convey.

I came across a super book called *Sex Signals, the Biology of Love* by Dr. Timothy Perper, and a couple of journal articles on the same subject. I found that the signals people send to each other are loaded with sexual tension.

I want to give you the seven most common signals that women give to men. These signals say "It's OK to approach me," or "I'm available." They are:

- smiling at a man

- glancing around the room

- solitary dancing

- laughing

- darting glances

- flipping her hair

- leaning toward the man

According to the author, these signals are much more important than the opening line of conversation in terms of what they communicate. The nonverbal communication is much more powerful than the verbal communication in the initial stages of attraction.

The author points out that in reality—not necessarily in fantasy or in our romance novels—but in reality, men are not the sexual aggressors in a courtship situation. Women initiate the first interaction by their signals. Someone has to physically get up and walk over to the other person. The man is the one who almost always does this, so it *looks like* he's making the first move.

But most men will approach a woman only if they've had signals that it's safe to approach. According to the author, this is the hardest part of all for men. The men he interviewed reported that they feel absolutely raw, sheer terror. (Note: If you're single and want him to approach, use the above seven signals.)

More sexual signals: (women)

Adjusting the collar of a blouse or toying with the top button whispers a fantasy that the blouse may be removed. Twirling a bracelet around the wrists or adjusting the belt often is a signal of female aggressiveness, as is the posture of hands on hips, feet apart. Wetting the lips with the tongue, rocking of a crossed leg both signal invitations.

If a woman is interested in a man as a potential partner, she may gradually expose the smooth soft skin of her wrists to him. If she's fondling a cylindrical object, she's a sure thing. (Only kidding.)

Then there's something called the shoe fondle and this one is supposed to drive men wild. The woman dangles her shoe, preferably a high heel, from her toes, slipping the shoe on and off occasionally. She's not supposed to use her hands for this one—just her foot. Anyway, the effect of all this, according to one article, is supposed to be "stimulating" (actually, the word used was phallic) because the woman's foot is "thrusting in and out of the shoe."

> "Then there's something called the shoe fondle..."

Sexual signals: (men)

Men use preening gestures. The man may reach for his throat and straighten his tie, smooth his collar, brush imaginary dust from his shoulders or rearrange his clothing. An unbuttoned shirt collar, loosened tie and rolled-up sleeves are symbolic of strength.

The most aggressive sexual signal a man can give a woman is to hook his thumbs in his belt, which highlights his pelvic area. The man may also turn his body toward the woman and point his foot at her. He may stand with his hands on his hips to accentuate his physical size or sit with his legs spread.

One last male signal, and then we'll move on. Apparently, some of the best signals are given off by the eyes. They say when a man's excited, his eyes will dilate up to four times their normal size. The woman, even though she may not be consciously aware that his eyes are dilating, is picking up the signal. And she responds. Her eyes start to dilate, too.

The author didn't elaborate on what happens after this, but I found myself hoping that these people weren't going to be driving anywhere.

Description of characters

Details, details, details! Details are crucial if you're trying to create sexual tension. Imagery is great, too. Also, be sure to get inside your character's head. See things through the character's eyes. What does the heroine see when she looks at the hero?

> "Step into the light," she ordered.
>
> He moved into the room, throwing off the shadows. The lamplight climbed his body, revealing lean, aggressive hips, a clenched gut and wide shoulders, heavy with muscle. A sensual shadow of a mustache snaked from the curve of his upper lip into the hollows of his cheekbones, then flared with the blunt angles of his jaw. His hair was sable black, a tumult of waves and flames that swept back from a widow's peak on his forehead and spilled onto his shoulders. Taken all at once, the dark sensuality of his unshaven features was breathtaking.
>
> Full recognition didn't come instantly. Jessie's senses were too stunned by the sight of him. But within seconds, she had begun to shake so violently she could hardly hold the gun steady. Nerves sparked painfully along the raised tendons of her hand.
>
> "Luc," she breathed. "You bastard."

Vice versa.

> He glanced up and saw her coiled in a wingback chair by the room's marble fireplace. She wore a black satin nightshirt, and with her legs drawn up and her heavy copper hair tumbling around her shoulders, she was the picture of privileged womanhood at ease. But the hush in her voice and the lethal weapon pointed in his direction spoke volumes about her state of mind.

Conflict

Here you need to think about the difference between internal and external conflict. Internal conflict is what's going on inside the characters, their personal fears and concerns. External conflict is what's going on outside the characters, the events that impinge upon them from outside and interfere with their relationship.

With regard to conflict as it relates to sexual tension, ask yourself two questions:

• Why are the characters attracted to each other? (Whether or not they'll admit their attraction).

• Why can't or won't they act on the attraction? What stops them? That's the key to the conflict.

In *Shameless*, Jessie was in love with Luc at one time. Very intense adolescent love. She also literally saved his life when they were kids. So they were bonded. And then that bond was shattered. That's the internal conflict.

The way the bond was shattered sets up the external conflict for the story. *Shameless* is about two families—one white trash and one wealthy—on a collision course. It's also about a woman who is determined to keep the past buried, and a man who is equally determined to dig it up.

The catalyst for all this happens on one night ten years before my story starts. On that one night, everything explodes—a man is murdered, a child is conceived, bonds are broken, friendships are betrayed. As a result Jessie implicates Luc in a murder. He is then disinherited and banished by his father.

In the ensuing years, Jessie ends up married to his father, and she inherits the entire empire when the father dies. So that's the backstory. My story actually starts when the hero returns, and he wants some answers.

The internal conflict is how Jessie and Luc feel about each other—love/hate stuff because of their past. The mysteries to be solved are the external conflict.

Plot

What I've just described in *Shameless* are the elements of a romantic suspense plot. The only thing I would add is when you're plotting your book, be sure to plan for those sizzling moments. Think them through strategically. Be calculating. Don't leave them to chance.

Setting

When you're trying to pick the "right" setting for your love scene, consider not just the romantic aspects, but the symbolic aspects. For example, a cave or grotto for a love scene. Of course, the cave itself has sexual symbolism, lots of plants at the mouth and perhaps a bubbling natural hot spring—water, the timeless symbol of sexuality—all symbolic of fertility.

You can also turn things around. Sometimes the "wrong" setting is exactly perfect for a love scene. I did a book a couple of years ago called *Private Dancer*, and one of the love scenes takes place on a kitchen counter top. The very fact that they're in the kitchen where you're not supposed to be doing such things gives the scene a forbidden aspect and increases the tension.

Let's talk about love scenes. Love scenes are a wonderful way to explore the building relationship between your characters—their thoughts and feelings—everything from tenderness to lust. They're also the perfect opportunity to explore character. They can provide insights into your characters and reveal psychological facets that might not be done nearly as effectively in any other way.

There's a tendency to overlook the fact that our characters aren't just physically unclothed or naked in love scenes, they're emotionally naked as well, and vulnerable. This presents you, as a writer, with an opportunity to reveal the strengths and weaknesses in your characters.

Love scenes can also provide the pivotal moments in your plot.

There's more than one love scene in *Shameless*, but the crucial scene looks as if it's going to be the BIG reconciliation between the characters. It actually turns out to be the story's dark moment. And it drives a wedge between them that seems insurmountable. (It even seemed insurmountable to me when I was writing it. I was thinking, how am I ever going to get these people back together after this!)

Six quick tips for writing dynamite love scenes

1. Several of the factors I recommended for building sexual tension are also important for writing the actual love scene: The emotions, the senses, the imagination, dialogue, and description.

2. Read love scenes. I'm giving you the perfect excuse to thumb through books to the "good parts." Read and study other authors' techniques. Study their style, the scene's situation, the dialogue, the tone, the texture, the dramatic build, the pauses—everything that makes the scene work. My rationale is that if I can figure out how this author has done it, maybe I can do it.

3. Tune in to your own feelings. This might be the most important tip I can give you. It's easy for us to get caught up in details and positions and

genre buzzwords, but when we do that we forget to allow ourselves to enjoy the scene and to become excited by what we're creating.

It starts with us—the writers. And in that context, one of the most important things we can do to create exciting scenes is to be open to the things that stimulate and turn us on. *Don't write what you think will turn the reader on. Write what turns you on.*

4. Pleasure and pain. I'm not talking about S&M or B&D, but there are varying degrees of sensory experience, and I am suggesting that you explore the entire range. There's a very thin line between the sensations of pleasure and pain, and you can blur that line a little.

For example, fingernails on bare skin is an interesting sensory experience. Or the sensual use of one's teeth. A kiss that starts or ends with a nip. Something sweet with a little sting in it. Even nature understands that concept. Every rose has thorns. Pleasure can be enhanced by the contrast of a little pain. It alerts the nerves and the brain. It heightens everything.

Keep in mind that there's infinite variety out there, an entire spectrum of sensation. Don't be afraid to try something different. Blur distinctions occasionally. Bring in contrasts that will really intensify the scene.

5. Point of view. One of the first rules of writing I learned was to stay in one viewpoint throughout a scene. I break that rule regularly now. I believe any time a scene is enhanced or made more powerful by switching viewpoints, then that's what you should do.

For love scenes, I have found it works best if you stay in one while the excitement's building, then when it naturally plateaus a little, you can move into the other. You can double the impact of a scene that way. We get to experience all of the excitement of the female's arousal, and we get to experience the male's excitement as well.

6. One last tip. Once you've written the scene, you should let someone you trust take a look at it. When they're done, watch closely for signals. If they expose their wrists, point their foot at you or hook their thumbs in their belt, you know you've written a pretty darn good love scene.

*In case you had any doubts, **Suzanne Forster** writes romantic fiction. Her awards include* Romantic Times' *Career Achievement Award for Sensuality and multiple Reviewer's Choice Awards. Her mainstream novel,* Shameless, *won the National Readers' Choice Award for Best Single Title Contemporary.*

Suzanne teaches and lectures frequently and served as an advisory board member in the development of a creative writing curriculum at California State University, Fullerton. She jointly taught seminars on women's contemporary fiction at UCLA and UC Riverside. She is also an award-winning screenwriter.

Selling Your Novel to An Agent

Develop a High Concept Pitch to Hear an Agent say Yes!

by Adam Marsh

Even with the decade-long upsurge in numbers of independent book publishers, the publishing of novels (as opposed to nonfiction books) is mostly the realm of the large, New York-based publishers. These publishers usually require an author pitch his or her novel to them through a literary agent.

However, the world is changing and I predict, as independent publishers of novels gain in numbers, they will follow the path of independent nonfiction book publishing houses and not require that an author be represented by an agent. (Not to say you won't want to employ an agent. Good agents do much more than find a publisher for your book.)

In this piece I refer only to agents, but, whether you are pitching a novel to an agent or directly to an editor at a publishing house, the pitch remains the same.

In my six years as a literary agent, I read thousands of queries and synopses, and I came to find that I could easily place just about every plotline into a particular, familiar category.

It's not plot alone

The most important, fundamental thing a novel can do, I believe, is to simply entertain. Yet plot alone rarely ever hooked me into wanting to read a manuscript. For me, the attention-getter almost always had to do with a fresh combination of some unexpected aspect of a character's dilemma within a well-structured plotline. The juxtaposition of the objective thread of the story involving the practical dilemmas faced by the main character to the subjective, psychological thread of the main character's journey—usually involving an interesting moral or existential dilemma—is what made me sit up and take notice.

A story can be about the *activity* of building a bridge, but the shadow-drama of what that bridge represents to the protagonist, what demons its creation will exorcize, how the hero will grow and change, is the second storyline and perhaps the most interesting one.

When a book can effectively entertain readers with a compelling plot and at the same time travel on at least one additional level by offering subjective insights into the main character, the readers are rewarded with a sense of self-discovery seeing aspects of themselves in the hero. Long after the thrill of the drama has dissipated, readers have these ideas to hold onto.

I call this type of book a "high concept narrative." These are the books that snare agents, publishers, *and readers*.

The high concept pitch

The most effective way to convey the multidimensional nature of your book to an agent is by way of the "high concept pitch." The high concept pitch expresses the book's premise in one or two compelling sentences. It's a hook that makes the agent want to read more. Be sure your hook conveys the multilevel nature of your storyline.

Here is an example from the film "ET":

"A meek and alienated little boy finds a stranded extraterrestrial and has to find the courage to defy authorities to help the alien return to its home planet."

In this example we are told of *both* storylines, the objective (the discovery of the alien) and the subjective (the meek child's search for strength).

Devising a high concept pitch is not always easy. It forces writers to look for aspects of their plotlines and characters in ways they might not have considered previously. But the high concept pitch is a writer's best friend when pitching to agents and editors. It makes a great lead, or beginning, to a query letter. Memorize it in case you find yourself pitching an agent face-to-face.

When considering your work's high concept premise, a few things should be considered:

• Give heroes flaws that keep them from achieving their worthwhile goals.
• Introduce a life-changing event, usually instigated by an opponent.

• In the process of responding to the life-changing event, and with the help of an ally, force heroes to overcome their flaws before they do battle with their opponents.

• Incorporate irony, as in the above example, where the meek alienated boy must find strength in order to assist an alien.

Be it genre fiction (horror, suspense, romance, mystery, thriller, etc.) or literary fiction, a high concept narrative achieves its compelling effect by way of anticipation mingled with uncertainty. Readers become seduced by the narrative's fictive spell desiring to know how the story will resolve itself and how its characters will fare, and *this* is exactly what agents and publishers are looking for.

As for the anxiety producing quality of high concept narratives, I like the word "lacuna," as it suggests a gap containing a vacuum, and that vacuum, as I see it, is the reader's desire to fill that gap, to restore order and balance by having the questions generated by the narrative answered. The wish to fill those gaps of knowledge is the very ingredient that propels the audience into the storyline and into the lives of the characters.

> "Give heroes flaws that keep them from achieving their worthwhile goals"

This leads us to the high concept narrative proposal. Literary agencies have different submission guidelines, but in general they accept a single-page query letter, a one- to two-page synopsis, and anywhere from the first page to the first three chapters of the manuscript.

The query letter

So let's get to some of the basics of the query letter itself. It should be a single page, single-spaced. Always address the letter to a specific agent. Never begin a query with a salutation such as, "Dear Agent," or, "To Whom it May Concern," or "Dear Sirs." It's important to let the agent know that you are aware of his or her particular agency, and have done some research as to the types of literature this agency handles. Queries sent out "shotgun" style are rarely worth an agent's time, and they do not receive the same attention that a polite, professional, well-targeted query does.

Also, never convey arrogance or negativity about previous rejections or the publishing business, and always go for a clear conveyance of your work instead of cleverness. Keep in mind that readers at agencies want to find quality works, but often they become a bit bleary-eyed from going through the slush pile. Clear and concise expression is always appreciated, and will give your query the best chance of gaining an agent's attention.

After the high concept hook, provide the agent with the technical aspects of your novel, such as the title, genre and word count. State why you think your novel is a good fit for this particular agency. Mention it if you have met the agent, or heard him or her speak at a conference.

Then get to the story. In one paragraph describe the novel by introducing your main character and some of the main conflicts that drive the narrative. Reveal what the main character wants to ultimately accomplish. Remember, you will not have an opportunity here to include all your great plot points, so focus on only the major obstacles and how the main character deals with them, both physically and psychologically.

As we've discussed, the high concept narrative works on at least two levels so don't focus solely on the practical, concrete obstacles the hero must contend with. Give the agent a clear knowledge of what drives the hero toward his or her ultimate desire, and indicate the ways in which the hero changes inside. You will have more ample opportunities to describe the plotline and characterization in the synopsis.

After the one paragraph narrative description, include a paragraph about yourself: previous publications, literary awards, your inspiration for writing the book, what qualifications you have for writing this particular book, and writing groups you belong to. If you do not have previous publications, there is no need to mention it.

To finish off your query letter, be sure to thank the agent for his or her time and consideration. Be sure to mention that you have included a self-addressed, stamped envelope for the agent's convenience.

The synopsis

The synopsis should be one to two single-spaced pages. The synopsis is used as a tool for the reader to not only gain insight into the characteristics of the narrative, but it also provides a structural context to help better judge the effectiveness of the beginning pages or chapters. The synopsis conveys the nuts and bolts of the story by illustrating the major plot points, and relates to the agent how the main characters react or don't react to the internal and external obstacles they face.

Since we are addressing the high concept narrative proposal, remember not to focus exclusively on the concrete, practical aspects of the plot. Convey the subjective narrative threads of the main characters, so the agent will have a clear understanding that the narrative operates on more than one level. It is worth repeating: The best high concept narratives tend to have combinations of objective practical dilemmas and internal existential (the search for meaning, or of one's place in the world) and moral (deciding between right and wrong) dilemmas.

Keep it short

I've seen many experienced, professional authors stymied by the notion of composing a synopsis; the idea that they would have to condense an entire book into a page or two. Keep in mind the synopsis does not have to contain all the wonderful stuff of the narrative. Focus on only the major plot points, and the characters' main motivations and reactions. Besides the plotline the agent will want to know what drives the characters. As I stated earlier, for me, plot alone rarely made a story stand out. It is the combination of the objective and subjective threads that usually hooks agents into wanting to read more. And that in itself is the objective of the query letter and synopsis.

Along with the query letter and synopsis, most agencies request sample pages of text, usually anywhere from the first page to the first three chapters. Unfortunately, no matter how much text the agent requests, it is common that he or she only reviews a page or two before bailing out to move on to the next project.

I have received many calls from authors wanting to know how much an agent can tell about a work and an author's ability by reading only a page or two. The answer: plenty. Here are some thoughts about first pages.

In a page or two, I cannot not tell if a novel is good, but I can tell at what stage of development the text and the writer are. There are telltale signs of an early draft and of authors who are not quite ready to write a blockbuster, such as the overuse of passive verbs, word repetitions, pat phrases, and a pedestrian narrative eye.

For me, the acuity of the narrative eye has always been a vital issue when judging the initial pages. Exceptional writing conveys a fictive world in sharp, interesting detail. Avoid words that serve as narrative shortcuts (for example: handsome/beautiful, fantastic/ordinary, simple/difficult) and instead focus on specific imagery to carry meaning.

An acute narrative eye is one that utilizes, in cinematic terms, wide-angle perspectives, medium shots, and close-ups at optimum times. Thus, the narrative eye is akin to the directorial eye in cinema.

A common mistake is to enter scenes by way of medium shots and close-ups, and to maintain these close perspectives—common in dialogue—while negating wider points of view that reveal the stages upon which the scenes play out. Many writers take setting for granted, and reading such narrative is like watching a theatrical production with inadequate stage lighting, where only the faces of the characters and a few choice props are illuminated. It's drama in a vacuum. Show the fictive world clearly and with interesting detail. I'm not suggesting an overabundance of detail, but carefully chosen, interesting detail that conveys meaning. Imagery trumps words every time. So, when sending your initial pages to agents, make sure that you employ a clear vision of the fictive world in order to induce a fictive spell upon them.

A final few words of advice: Don't get antsy. Wait until your novel is in its final stage of development before sending out your queries. The best writing will be successful.

I look forward to seeing your novel on the bookstore shelves.

Adam Marsh is a graduate of the M.F.A. Creative Writing Program at San Francisco State. Upon graduation he was hired as in-house editor at Reece Halsey North Literary Agency, and eventually became an agent with that firm, where he represented clients for six years. In October of 2006, he left Reece Halsey North to start Adam Marsh Editorial Services. (marshadam@msn.com)

Literary Agents
Getting and working with the right one

By Natasha Kern

CONTRACTING WITH A LITERARY AGENT can be compared to hiring a lawyer to defend you in court or a doctor to operate on your child. It is of crucial importance for you as a writer to have the right one to preserve artistic freedom and have your creations of the mind and spirit well cared for in the arcane and difficult world of publishing. You want someone to tell you what is going to happen and to be on your side when there are problems—and there are *always* problems.

Before beginning this search, a writer must decide whether an agent is even needed. Many books, including scholarly books, professional books and textbooks, do not require agency representation. And, if you plan to write an occasional category romance, a poetry book or a narrow niche book to be published by a small publisher, it may not be necessary to engage an agent.

Conversely, because these types of books often earn only modest royalties and since agents are paid with a percentage of these royalties (usually 15 percent), it may not be worth an agent's time to represent you.

There are other reasons not to use an agent. If you are the type of person who prefers to do everything for yourself, or are uncomfortable without a sense of complete control, you may want to go it alone.

However, if you hate to argue about money, decipher fine print in legal contracts, market yourself and/or your work to editors, or have no idea what a long-term career plan looks like, then you probably will feel more comfortable having an agent assist you.

There are several stages of your writing career ("Writing *career?*" you ask. Well, this may come as a surprise to some of you, but agents are much more interested in clients who plan to write more than a single book) when you should consider getting an agent. The first, and most obvious, is when you want to sell your first book. Yet this is probably the most difficult time to get one, in part because agents are flooded with queries and submissions from people who have not prepared to write a book.

It will never cease to astonish me how many people who would never dream of trying to get a booking in the most modest of music halls without taking music lessons, or running a marathon without getting into shape, have no compunction about trying to get published without investing even a few months in learning the craft and art of writing. As a result, agents, who are always thrilled to find a beautifully written work that deserves a "yes," reject hundreds of poorly written and thought out submissions at the query stage because there's no time to look through stacks of second- or third-rate manuscripts in hopes of finding that one jewel.

A second common reason for looking for an agent is when you are unhappy with the agent you already have. Perhaps you feel neglected or are unhappy with your contracts or your career.

Another is when you are in trouble in one of the hundreds of ways a publishing career can go wrong. You signed a multi-book contract and can't meet your deadlines. You are writing for several houses and don't know which one should get your next book. You have written ten books and are still getting four-figure advances. Your publisher has pushed publication of your book to three years after completion. Your publisher will not accept your option book. You've just discovered your publisher is holding 90 percent of your royalties as a reserve against returns. Or, as happened to one unhappy author who called me, you have just received your first royalty statement and, on a book that is selling very well, you owe the publisher $6,000 and have already contracted for your next book with the same house.

Agents prefer to take new clients who are not having serious problems, but it is often when problems arise that writers realize how much they need one.

You may also decide to get an agent when you get an offer from a publisher. Let me offer a caveat: Do not say yes to any offer until you have thought about it at least overnight. If you do accept an offer, and then decide to use an agent, the agent most likely will be unable to change basics such as the advance or royalties paid or anything else you have already agreed to. If you prefer to be agented, thank the editor politely (or enthusiastically) for her interest in your work and tell her you plan to have an agent negotiate the deal. Don't be afraid this will hurt the deal; many editors, especially those at the larger houses, prefer working with an agent. These editors feel they will spend less time explaining the basics to an agent and that there is less chance of a significant misunderstanding.

Last, and perhaps most important: You should get an agent when you are ready to think of yourself as a professional writer and not someone who is just writing as a hobby.

There is no doubt that the challenges facing a writer are formidable and that agents can help. There is also no doubt that you must take responsibility for yourself and for choosing an agent who will work for you and support you through problems as they arise.

Why use an agent?

Although agents are essentially commissioned sales representatives, agents do a lot of things for their clients besides making the sale. If it were an agent's function simply to find a publisher, writers like John Grisham or Danielle Steel would not have one. These writers have publishers clamoring for their work. A good agent helps you to get not just a deal, but the best possible deal for you. She will help you to understand publishing as a business and guide you in building your career.

What do agents do?

In order to know whether an agent is right for you, you must first understand what agents do. Agents are negotiators, strategists and managers. They must have an entrepreneurial temperament and a knowledge of the publishing business. Their advice is often crucial for authors deciding which book to write, how to revise a manuscript or develop a proposal for a nonfiction book, and how to successfully sell their work to publishers. Beyond being a negotiator of contracts, an agent literally represents the author's wishes to the editor, publisher, art department, marketing team and everyone associated with the book.

Good agents know which editors are interested in a particular type of book, understand the importance of a book's place on a publisher's list and know whether a book-signing tour or other time-consuming promotion is a good idea. A good agent is competent to conduct an auction (two or more publishers bidding on a book—usually conducted over the phone), alter boilerplate clauses in contracts and track down missing royalty or subsidiary rights payments.

Agenting requires understanding sales and marketing (nope, they are not the same thing), literary law, editing, publishing business practices; industry standards, requirements and protocols, publicity and promotion (also not the same), counseling and career development; international, film and audio rights markets, arbitration and a myriad of other things, including the rapidly burgeoning opportunities in high-tech publishing.

Because there is such a broad range of expertise required, no one starts out thinking: I'll be a literary agent when I grow up. We come to this job with different backgrounds. Most agents were formerly editors, attorneys, subrights managers or sales reps. Keeping this in mind will help you to make a match. What specialized talents in an agent will complement your own?

Agents who are lacking in one or more areas of expertise usually work with independent editors, lawyers or subagents.

"Good agents know which editors are interested in a particular type of book..."

All agents, to stay in business, must at least know what properties to represent, having applied solid standards of literary merit and marketability to make her choices.

Obviously, every agent must start somewhere. A new agent may not have a long list of clients or properties, but she may have strong contacts in the industry and be well respected, and she may be more open to acquiring new clients. However, you should be very cautious about committing your work and your career to an agent who is not listed in *Literary Market Place* (available at most libraries), has no professional references or a list of recent sales or has no background in publishing. Anyone can call herself an agent and even though it seems that having a poor agent is better than no agent, this is not the case.

There are many disaster stories about writers who were badly represented and got stuck with contracts or decisions that negatively impacted their careers for years. At first it is tempting to be grateful to anyone who will take you as a client, but do exercise caution. Think of your book as your child who is about to undergo surgery and you need to select a doctor. You may know nothing about medicine, but you are going to do your very best to pick someone who is competent!

Selecting an agent

This leads to the number-one concern in selecting an agent: Is he or she competent to represent you? What is her work history and her relationships with other clients, colleagues, editors and subagents? Does the agent know your genre? Has she sold similar books before?

Do you feel you would like the personal attention of a small agency or the perception of glamour of being a client at a large agency? Keep in mind the wide disparity between agencies in terms of their size, how many writers they handle, the number of publishers they deal with, what kinds of books they represent, and how they work, not to mention the personality and tastes of the agent who would work with you.

A very important concern is: Does the agent like your work? If you sent a partial, did the agent seem excited about seeing the whole manuscript? Has she really read and understood your work and your strengths and weaknesses as a writer?

A sense of championship for your work is the second most important thing to look for, after competence. It is this enthusiasm that helps the agent to feel positive about your work and be able to continue to sell it when difficulties arise, such as when nothing has sold in a year or two. Keep in mind that more writing careers develop slowly like Rosamund Pilcher's than overnight like Amy Tan's. You don't want an agent who will drop you at the first hint of trouble or one who works hard for other writers on her list but not for you. You want the concern and support that can only come from someone who believes in you and what you are trying to achieve.

If the agent expresses interest in you and your work and offers a contract, ask to see a client list and to talk with a few of her clients. Ask to see a list of recent sales. (If the agent is unwilling to supply this information, be wary.)

Check to see if the agent is a member of the Association of Authors Representatives. While some good agents are not members, membership is a check in the "pro" column because she will have had to meet some standards of performance to become a member. Is she recommended by a writer's organization like Romance Writers of America or Mystery Writers of America? If you already have an editor, ask your editor about the agent you plan to select. I know of more than one case in which the writer was told the editor would not work with a certain agent, and, as a result, the writer lost a contract that had already been offered.

The Association of Author's Representatives has a checklist (see writer's resources section at the back of this book) for authors that includes asking a potential agent important questions about how long she has been in business, how clients are informed about the agent's activities on their behalf and how commissions or charges for expenses are collected.

Here are some basic financial questions you should ask:

• How much does the agency charge?

• Will you be billed for expenses? Which ones? Will they be deducted from your income on the sale, billed direct, or credited against an initial deposit?

• Is there a marketing fee?

• Does the agency maintain a client trust account?

• How soon are funds forwarded to clients?

Ask every question you can think of regarding the disbursement of your money, how legal or public relations problems will be handled and even what provisions are made in the event of the death or retirement of the agent while she is representing your work.

A compatible work style matters a great deal. Some agents are in frequent contact with clients, make payments promptly, and consult closely about submission strategies. An agent you hear from rarely may be working just as hard for you. But, before signing with an agent, make sure you will receive copies of all correspondence and be informed about progress.

Consider specific problems you would like your agent to resolve: Can she help you make a jump from category to mainstream? Has she done it before with another author? Can she advise you about if, when and how you should quit your job and write full time? Can she help you to decide whether to write for only one house or several, use a pseudonym or not, switch genres, get more money, handle publicity more effectively, get your synopsis in better shape? If you write for a broad market, can the agency represent all of your work?

She should be able to help you when your editor moves to another house, your publisher is sold or changes its list and no longer wants your book. You should feel confident that your agent has handled a variety of contracts and can find all the problems in the one you are offered.

She should be able to explain to you the vagaries of joint accounting, reserves against returns, pass-through clauses and every other aspect of the deal. Since it is your signature that goes on a book contract and you who must fulfill its terms, you should not have a feeling of being left in the dark.

Probably the last thing to consider is location. Does it matter where your agent is located? Since my agency is located in Portland, Oregon, I am frequently asked whether this poses difficulties for me. I usually respond, "I'm never sure whether revealing my eight years of working and living in New York is an asset or a liability."

The best answer I've heard came from a senior editor when we were on a panel together at a writers' conference. She said there were agents in New York who had offices less than two blocks from hers whom she had never met and agents from out of town whom she saw several times a year. Furthermore, she said that what mattered to her was getting good books and good deals. She didn't care where the agent was located or where the writers lived. In these days of overnight mail service, e-mail, fax machines and cellular phones, an agent can be successful anywhere.

The important thing to conclude from all of this is that it is the responsibility of each writer to assess what you want from an agent and to learn as much as you can about the agents you are considering. Or you can use the criterion of last resort which one fiction writer expressed by saying, "I want a local agent so I have a throat I can easily get my hands around when things go wrong."

Where to look

Now that you have determined the qualities you want in an agent, how do you go about finding this paragon of excellence? Look in the front matter of books you like or authors you admire to see if the agent is acknowledged. If not, call the publisher and ask who the agent is. Ask all the professional writers you know about agents and check with professional writing groups, both local and national. Look in *Literary Market Place* and the other publications in your library that list agents and explain what each agent represents and their submission requirements. Make agent appointments at writer's conferences. Check with publishers; many will provide a list of agents they like to work with.

The more clearly you understand what you need and want, the easier it will be to assess whether the agent you choose can meet your needs. Develop a written list of these needs. Then start listing agents who seem to be appropriate, i.e., they represent the genre you write, they have a good track record and are well respected, etc. When you query, request whatever information the agency has available. One enterprising writer asked about my agency on an electronic bulletin board and got a surprising number of responses.

Submitting your work

Be sure to find out each agent's requirements for submission and follow them carefully. Some agents prefer a simple query letter; others, a formal nonfiction book proposal. Regard this as a test. If you can't follow simple instructions and, say, send a full manuscript when only three chapters have been requested, ask yourself if the agent will feel confident about communicating and working with you.

Some agents do not accept multiple submissions, so in that case, you must decide whether or not to risk weeks or months on the chance the agent will accept you. I accept multiple submissions because I want a client to choose to work with me because she decides I am the best agent for her, not because I am the only one who expressed interest. If I take too long and lose a possible client, that is a risk I think it is fair I take.

Contracts

I think it is important to have a written agreement with your agent so that rights and responsibilities are spelled out clearly and you know how to terminate the agreement if you want to. Is the agency contract acceptable to you? Is there an escape clause? Avoid commitment for a long period of time. If you have a disagreement with the agent and the contract period isn't up, what will you do? Stop writing?

Make sure you will be working with the agent you like and will not be passed on to someone else in the agency now or in the future. This happens frequently, sometimes with alarming results. Two of my present clients had to leave their former agency because they were reassigned to someone who did not like their work or with whom they were incompatible.

If the contract is terminated, is it spelled out what happens to works that are sold or are under submission? Does the contract state clearly what will be included or excluded if you write a column or articles or other genres?

Talk and listen

You should communicate your hopes, dreams, and career aspirations to your new agent and she should talk frankly with you about the possibilities for fulfilling them. Talk about problems you have encountered in the past or are concerned about, and see what kinds of solutions she proposes. Find out what kind of marketing plan she has in mind for your work—submitting single or multiple copies; changing houses or writing a better book for your current publisher as a means of advancement; doing your own publicity to increase readership or getting more support from the house. She may not have everything nailed down at this early stage, but she should have a view of you and your career.

Always keep in mind that communication is a two-way street. Your agent cannot help you if she doesn't know what is on your mind. Many times writers have called me with concerns about their agents. Most of the time, a simple conversation with their agent resolved the problem and a change of agents was not needed.

Be realistic

Agents are troubleshooters and have to deal daily with dozens of disasters from dreadful covers to poor distribution to missed deadlines resulting from writers' personal problems. One former agent told me he had quit agenting because it was his job to take care of the thousand things that could go wrong, and even if he saved the day with 995 of them, he would get blamed for the other five. There is a real germ of truth in his comment. Agents aren't gods, nor are they magicians, but most are honest and hard working. The important thing is that you feel comfortable and that your expectations are realistic.

Trust

A sense of mutual trust is extremely important. Writers must trust the agent to handle their financial affairs and their careers properly. Agents must trust clients to comply with contract terms, to let us know if they cannot make their deadlines and to tell us about problems. Once this trust is lost, it is time to consider a frank talk with your agent and if issues are not resolved, time to change agents.

Getting the right agent is an important step in becoming a professional. Writing books is difficult and trying to earn a living at it daunting. You want an agent you can rely on to help you with all aspects of your career.

Natasha Kern has personally sold more than 750 books and launched the careers of dozens of new writers. Natasha has a strong commitment to acquiring and developing new talent even though she represents best-selling writers like Connie Mason, Leigh Greenwood, Nina Bangs, Eliot Pattison and Robin Lee Hatcher. She represents a wide range of commercial fiction as well as non-fiction. The agency has sold books to every major publisher and to many medium-sized presses. Information about the agency is available on the Internet at www.natashakern.com.

Writing Every Magazine & Newspaper's Staple

How to craft the feature article

By Donna Elizabeth Boetig

DASHING OUT OF THE OPERATING ROOM of Pittsburgh Children's Hospital, Dr. Thomas Starzl, a world-renowned transplant surgeon, confronted the two worried mothers. Penny Thomas and Nancy Point could see the urgency in his expression. "Which child is it?" they each wondered.

Candi Thomas, a six-year-old with a halo of finger curls, lay anesthetized on the operating table, waiting for Dr. Starzl to perform her second liver transplant. Scar tissue had clogged her liver ducts, and digestive fluids were spilling into her blood. By sheer coincidence, her best friend, Jason Point, another towhead, also six, had been rushed to the same hospital, delirious with pain. Doctors had just completed his exploratory surgery.

The surgeon spoke quietly. "This is the situation," he began. "Candi needs a new liver, but we can stabilize her for now. Jason's liver is gangrenous; he's going to die tonight unless he gets a new one."

Besides everything else they had in common, the two children had the same blood and tissue type, making them eligible for the same organ. Dr. Starzl knew that technically Candi had a right to the one available liver because she was at the top of the donor list. But he believed the human side of the dilemma had to be considered, too. It would only be fair to give those who would be most affected by the choice a part in making it—even if it meant asking Candi's mother to make the toughest decision of her life.

Turning to Penny, he said: "What should we do?"

This was the crux of the feature article "Leap of Faith," published in *Family Circle* (December 1990), and in *Reader's Digest* (March 1992).

Every feature article I write teaches me more than it teaches the reader. Writing feature articles is like rearing children: Each one presents a unique challenge, but with a lot of work, and a little luck, the experience leaves you wiser.

Today, more than ever, feature articles written with flair are in demand by editors. In this workshop I'll share with you the insights I've learned from nurturing editors, talented writers, my hard-working students, and my own mistakes, made while writing hundreds of feature articles for newspapers and national magazines. These techniques will make you a more successful writer— even better, they'll make you a happier writer—I promise.

"Leap of Faith" taught me a few surprising lessons. Just because a story has already appeared in print doesn't mean it can't be written again—if you spot a gap in the original piece. Two national newspapers reported the facts in "Leap of Faith," but failed to explore the story's universal theme: the toughest decision any parent will ever make, or to exploit its incredible drama.

Mirror, mirror on the wall: leads that reflect

When I proposed the story to my editor at *Family Circle*, she was intrigued but cautioned me not to begin the drama the way I presented it to you now. She believed few parents could identify with such a dilemma and the pathos should be saved for later, when the reader is entrenched in the piece. She instructed me to begin by seducing the reader with a lead that mirrors the reader herself—the way a savvy salesman subtly mimics the speaking style and mannerisms of a prospective customer. We began the story this way:

> Penny Thomas glanced at the kitchen clock in her rural Accokeek, Maryland, home. She wondered why six-year-old Candi, the youngest of her four children, wasn't up yet. [What parent can't relate to a child dawdling on a school morning?] Candi loved first grade. She enjoyed choosing what to wear and having her mother sculpt her long, golden hair into finger curls.
>
> Penny found her daughter still asleep in her room, surrounded by her favorite stuffed animals. Candi's cheeks were almost as scarlet as the leaves outside her window that crisp October morning. [Again, nearly every parent has found her child flushed with fever at least once. But now, very quickly, something has to happen to keep the reader's interest.] Penny was alarmed. A fever could signal a serious infection in a child like Candi.

With the reader joined at our hip, we were off: to the hospital, to a decision no mother should ever face, to pages of milking the nail-biting tension.

This new thinking on writing leads that mirror the reader runs contrary to the traditional ploy of shocking the reader with the most startling image or information. Perhaps it's a sign of the times that we question what it is we could write that would surprise anyone anymore. While we still launch our story with a captivating scene, or intriguing fact, sensationalism takes a back seat.

Besides offering reader identification, our lead also suggests a good story. Leads might also promise information, even inspiration. Finally, the lead presents an element of mystery. While stating that a fever in a child who has had a liver transplant can signal a serious infection, it poses a question in the reader's mind: "What's going to happen to Candi?" Suddenly the reader is no longer a bystander, but a participant in the drama.

In a nut shell

After writing your lead, consider inserting a powerful device known as a nut graph, an old journalistic term for "in a nut shell." The paragraph that began "Every feature article I write teaches me more than it teaches the reader" is the nut graph of this feature. In a few sentences the nut graph gives the reader the direction of the piece, makes a sales pitch for reading it, and exploits any news peg associated with the story. Besides helping the reader understand the significance of the piece, the nut graph is the writer's best friend, too. It forces her to step back from the details to see the big picture, the real value of the story to the reader. The nut graph answers the reader's subconscious question of why she should read this story now.

To write a nut graph you need the time to let the information settle in so the story's significance can come out. Your story doesn't exist in a time vacuum; it has a past and it has a future. Its full extent stretches beyond the boundaries of your strong focus in your feature article, but thanks to the nut graph you're able to present its full ramifications neatly wrapped up in a few sentences.

The nut graph in "Leap of Faith" was disguised in Penny's thoughts: "Now as Penny looked at Nancy she wondered how she could weigh her own child's life against another's. She had felt so fortunate that this time there was a liver ready for Candi. How could she gamble that another one would become available in time?"

The take: seeing it through your eyes

Most important, your nut graph spotlights your take or slant on the story.

Unlike a news story that has more to do with the facts than the writer's view of them, crafting a feature article means establishing your perspective on the information by putting it through your life's lens with all your experience, insight and perceptions.

It takes time to consider an idea, and patience for you to move around in your thoughts to get the right angle. You have to consider what's in it for the reader, and determine what one message you want to convey. By far this is the most crucial aspect of any feature article. This is the way you—and maybe you alone—view the facts.

While you must be true to what your subject says, how she feels, and of course, the facts, how you view these things is your prerogative as long as you write with integrity and fairness.

Forcing yourself to think about your story before you write it increases the chances you'll hit the bigger point. Only you can develop this big picture. Your subjects aren't likely to spout it out in a interview. And even if they did, it would be *their* perspective on the piece, not necessarily yours.

You can begin developing this big picture as soon as you begin researching the article. In fact, a strong focus guides your research and helps shape your story. Occasionally, you'll learn your first hunch was off the mark and you may need to adjust your take a bit. Rarely will your intuition be so skewed that you have to scrap your first take completely.

This creative process shapes a good story into a great one. But it can be a temptation to skip it. There's something falsely satisfying about seeing words on paper. The trouble is that too often we marry them. I still have to pinch myself not to jump right in and start writing. I've seen how much better a story can be when I've explored it in my head, brainstormed angles on scrap paper, and talked it through to myself or others. The more time spent thinking before putting fingers to computer keyboard, the less time wasted later trying to pump up an anemic piece, or band-aiding one full of holes. In the end, a half-baked feature never quite lives up to the full-bodied work that slowly and thoughtfully matured.

After pitching an idea to a *Family Circle* editor, I'll never forget her reply. "Sounds interesting. Let me massage it a bit." That's the key. Writers, too, need to massage ideas—before we propose them to editors.

This mental posturing doesn't stop when you determine the angle of your story: It's only the beginning. As you research, write, and rewrite your feature, stay alert to how you can fine-tune your take to make the piece more powerful. For instance, when I wrote the story of Grace Corrigan's spiritual journey ten years after the death of her daughter, teacher-in-space Christa McAuliffe, for *McCall's*, the take evolved three times before the piece was published.

When I proposed the piece, I knew that Christa's influence on education was worldwide. My tentative take on Grace's story was to explore this gold mine. But after getting the assignment and spending two days of heartfelt talks with this engaging woman at her home outside Boston, I came away with a slightly different slant. Not only had Christa influenced teachers worldwide, she influenced her mother, too. Grace, a former homemaker, had become an international lecturer since her daughter's death, speaking on a topic close to Christa's heart: the importance of teachers to the future of our country. When I submitted "The Whole World Loved My Daughter," my editor at *McCall's* very astutely observed that by tweaking the as-told-to piece, it could be far more poignant. Based on my quotes from Grace, he saw that Christa's influence on Grace was not past tense. Instead Christa, like an angel, continues to lovingly guide her mother's life. Here are a few of the passages, in Grace's words, substantiating that take:

> "In a way, Christa has taken over my life these past ten years. She's guided me—a housewife and substitute teacher—through challenges I never dreamed I could surmount...I feel her presence whenever I visit the Christa Corrigan McAuliffe Center...She inspired me to write *A Journal for Christa*...Sometimes I question whether Christa is happy about what I'm doing...I am now 71. There are occasions when I don't want to travel. But then I hear Christa's voice, 'Come on, Mom. You can do it,' and I'm off again."

Proving your point

You've promised the reader the world in your lead, showed her its relevance in your nut graph, now it's time to prove your premise in a few well chosen points.

The first point—the one that buttresses the nut graph—is the most important since it's most closely related to this big picture. You can make your point by either stating it in a topic sentence, then using facts, statistics, quotations, or anecdotes to support your statement, or you can allow your reader to discover it for herself by presenting the facts first, then declaring the point they make.

Research until you begin to hear the same things twice. You should always know more than you write because no amount of effort spent learning about your story is wasted. While researching "Lost in the Desert"—a *Reader's Digest* drama in real life about a two-year-old found by a young woman volunteer and her German Shepherd after being lost in the Arizona desert for four days—I spent a week in the desert and on the mountain tops of Utah, living with the Rocky Mountain rescue dogs and their trainers. If you gather material for ten anecdotes but write only three, those three will be the crème de la crème, written with the authority and conviction that a writer who researched only to word count could never produce.

With your reader clearly in mind, digest, simplify, and put the facts in perspective for her. Quote experts with credentials your readers will respect. While letters after a name impress readers, "experts" with real life experience, whom readers identify with, score high, too, so include both.

Visualize your reader as you interweave your anecdotes, quotations, statistics, and facts. What questions is she asking? Are you answering them? Did you satisfy her query: "So what?" Is she yawning? If so, pitch that paragraph, paraphrase it, or put the boring but important information in a sidebar, a chart, or a graph.

If you're writing a narrative feature article such as "Leap of Faith," your points may be scenes, or moments, as my *Family Circle* editor liked to call them. She encouraged me to listen for the occasions that tug at the reader's heart when interviewing, then fully flesh them out with details using all the senses. These moments, which may be a complete anecdote or simply a scene, are linked with narrative, or telling, to create the drama.

Give a little of yourself

Though readers want the facts, they want to know you, too, through the way you present your story. The job of a feature writer is to create an experience for a reader, whether it's the experience of how to wallpaper a room or a heart-stopping drama. Most of the time, the subjects or the facts speak for themselves. But occasionally, if the people involved are not able to articulate their lust for whatever it is you're writing about, then it's your job to step gingerly into the story. As your reader's advocate, you experience that situation, and translate that passion to the reader. Often it takes no more than a sentence or two from you, now and then throughout the piece, to make the experience happen for the reader.

Don't fret about violating your objectivity. Every time you write a lead, choose whom and how much to quote, and what examples to use, you reveal your viewpoint on the story—like it or not. And that's the way it should be, as long as you're fair.

Strong voice

The invisible force that reaches out and gently but firmly leads your reader through your story is your strong voice. It should be able to transform a mundane subject into a memorable piece. It's the voice you'd speak in while conversing with a good friend. It's opinionated. It's outspoken. It's saying stuff timid writers would never put on paper, but would share with a confidante. A writer with a strong voice takes risks because she knows it's the only way to distinguish herself from the pack. But mostly she takes risks because readers like it.

You've got a strong voice—think of the way you spoke as a child. But that free, confident, and uninhibited voice may have been muffled by an overzealous English teacher, or a heavy-handed editor. Now's the time to unearth it. The surefire way to regain your strong voice is to become a quick study on your subject. Other strategies include reading writers with strong voices to stimulate the flow; writing your draft in the first person, even if you have to switch the final version to third person point of view; and going back after you've "finished" a piece and inserting something a bit judgmental. At first, you may feel as awkward as trying on a bathing suit in Loehmann's community dressing room. But do it anyway—for your reader.

You don't say, or quotable quotes

As writers we take to heart our role as guardians of our subject's words—often to a fault. Surely, we want to preserve the tone and intent of their statements, but our job is to write what our subject would say—not necessarily what she did say. How often do you speak off-the-cuff in perfect printable prose? Our reader is our god. Our god is not the people we interview, nor the information we gather. And we should keep this in mind when making all the decisions involved in feature writing. Right now, post this above your computer: "My reader is my god." The truth is that once we commit ourselves to our reader, we will simultaneously serve our subject, and the material as well. When we present the subject's words and information in the most intriguing fashion, she and her message are more compelling to the reader.

> "Our reader is our god."

There are three techniques to creating quotable quotes: First, set up your quotes by providing the reader with a framework, a few sentences of background or perspective, to help her interpret the subject's words. Second, join related thoughts that were not expressed together. And finally, after you've polished your quotes, consider cutting them by 30 to 40 percent. A quote is like a magnificent brooch. If it's the sole piece of jewelry a woman wears, it

shines. If it competes with necklaces, jangle bracelets, and rings on every finger, its brilliance is lost. So it is with quotes: Less is more. If you've quoted
someone for five sentences, pare it down to two. If the deleted sentences provided background necessary to interpret the quote, paraphrase them. The
sentence or two that remain will sparkle.

Transitional treasures

Transitions, or bridges between blocks of similar text, are often under-
valued as parts of a feature article. Besides seamlessly joining sections of your
piece, transitions are the opportunities for the writer to insert her voice. It's
here, at the end of one paragraph, or the beginning of the next, that the writer
adds her thoughts in a phrase, or a few sentences to help the reader understand the significance of what is ahead.

"A Friend in Need," *Family Circle* (July 1995), told of a young woman
who was rescued as a child from a life of abuse and poverty by a volunteer
from Big Sisters of America. After a lead that puts the reader in ten-year-old
Mary's world, filled with drugs, rock music and theft, I introduce her savior,
Big Sister Janet. I transitioned from Mary's hellish existence to one of caring
and tranquility this way:

> The year was 1983, and little Mary Ta had already suffered a
> lifetime of tragedy. When she was six years old, her family had fled
> Vietnam after being accused of treason for harboring American sol-
> diers during the war. In a rickety boat, they escaped to Hong Kong.
> Months later, they embarked on a rough voyage to America.
> But life on these shores proved treacherous as well...

Notice, please, that the opening sentences of both paragraphs are a bit
judgmental. Neither Mary not Janet had made those statements directly. Instead, as a writer I drew those conclusions, then later supported them with
facts. Both sentences prepare the reader for what is to come.

Eternal endings

The ending of a feature article should almost catch the reader by surprise, leaving her breathless but satisfied. It's like watching a great movie
and when the credits scroll down the screen you're disappointed; you wish it
could last longer, but you know it should end.

There are as many types of endings as there are leads, and next to the
lead this is the most important part of your piece. Endings can circle back to
the beginning of the article, completing an anecdote begun in the lead; or they

can look to the future; or wrap it up with a quotation that says exactly the sentiment you want to leave with the reader. What's important is that the ending nails down your story's message.

The ending in "Leap of Faith" does just that:

> Says Penny, "I gave Candi's liver to Jason knowing that somehow God would provide for Candi. I thank him every day for answering my prayers."

***Donna Elizabeth Boetig** is a freelance writer, a former newspaper reporter, and a former corporate publication editor whose articles appear in national magazines such as* Reader's Digest, McCall's, Family Circle, Woman's Day *and dozens of others.*

A popular speaker at writer's conferences, Donna conducts seminars and workshops throughout the country. She is based in Crownsville, Maryland.

Unforgettable

Seven secrets to creating memorable characters

By Sara Ann Freed

F ACE THE FACTS. NO ONE—NO READER, bookseller, or librarian—ever recommends a book because he or she admires the sentence structure, loves the setting, or adores the publisher. People read, reread, and recommend novels because of *people*—characters they can identify with. (Sometimes the emotional attachment is so strong that readers get angry with authors who dare to take liberties with their own creations!) The characters that readers love are etched forever in human memory.

Could I ever forget my first introduction to Atticus Finch in *To Kill a Mockingbird*? Or Anna Karenina? Or one of my favorite mystery characters, that great Victorian archaeologist Amelia Peabody, created by Elizabeth Peters. Larger than life, full of herself, tenderhearted, romantic, Amelia is utterly unique. She's a wonderfully independent woman in a time when conformity was almost a duty, a scholar when "unseemly" knowledge was swept under the carpet, a mother who refuses to go by her society's rulebook. It would be foolhardy for any other writer to try to breathe life into her. Downright stupid. Amelia is so real to me I refuse to recognize the fact that she is a fictional character. It's impossible.

How can a writer dream up such an unforgettable character? Margaret Maron, who created the Edgar award-winning series featuring Judge Deborah Knott, helped me come up with these suggestions:

Physical characteristics

As you are creating your character—I'm sure you already know a great deal about him or her— try to put yourself under this character's skin. What does she like about herself? Is she proud of her baby blond hair, a color so pure that no hairdresser has come close to matching it? That she is fifty years old without a wrinkle to mar her forehead? Does she hate her stocky upper arms? Is a male character proud of his flat stomach when he sees his beer-guzzling compatriots at the twenty-fifth reunion? Does he bite his nails or chew his mustache?

Use all five senses

Throughout the novel, you need to address the character's senses. Too many writers concentrate only on what their character sees. You should be thinking about other senses as well. What does she hear at night when she can't fall asleep? What does she taste when she orders in her favorite Chinese food? What does she smell when she's out jogging at dawn? What does the new puppy's skin feel like when she touches him?

Genes and early childhood

What did his family history contribute? Obviously, a writer knows from the very beginning if his character will be Chinese-American or a Connecticut WASP. That's how he or she popped out of the womb. But what about the other things that shaped his personality? What about his birth order? Is he an only child, responsible oldest, peace-making middle child, indulged youngest? Did he set a good example or a bad example in the neighborhood? Was he blamed or praised for everything? Bright in school? Dyslexic? Anorexic? Overweight? Underweight? The ninety-pound weakling? Cheerleader? Quarterback? Glasses or contacts?

Was there a "Leave It to Beaver" family life? Or did his parents divorce when he was seven and his father move across the country to L.A.? Is his mother an alcoholic? Does he live in the poor part of town? Did he dream his way through school or was he the "perfect student"?

Did this contribute to his being a take charge person or a reluctant hero? A Harrison Ford or a Tom Hanks?

Friends and associates

Are most of the character's friends of the same or the opposite sex? Why? What kind of adventures do they get into—Huck Finn or otherwise? Is he a giver or taker in these relationships? Does he cherish his family and friends? Remember their birthdays or anniversaries? And what do his associates think of him? Is he overvalued or under-praised?

Addictions and habits

Is she a clotheshorse? A shop-till-she-drops type? A fashion victim or a preppy dresser? Does she get up at dawn to jog? Does he watch "Nick at Night" after he gets back from the danceteria? Does her thought turn to food, is her favorite magazine *Gourmet,* her secret wish to eat herself through a three-month tour of France? Or does he wish all his nutritional needs would be taken care of by vitamin pills and his meals five-minute microwave reheats?

Does he or she smoke cigars? Hide candy bars (any kind) in her desk drawer? Is her desk sloppy or neat? Does she cuss like a drunken sailor? Think pot should be a legal substance? That there should still be a prohibition against alcohol?

Goals and outlook

Now that you've thought about your character, you should decide what you want him to achieve before the novel ends. If this is a mystery novel, of course you want him to solve a crime. But what are the roadblocks to that achievement? What kinds of things are environmental or otherwise beyond his control?

> "When something climactic happens, how would your character react?"

How would individual events that take place in the course of the novel impinge upon this character? When something climactic happens, how would she or he react: happy, sad, scared, bewildered, angry? Honest or devious? Fair-minded or prejudiced?

Your character is born: Who cares?

What is it about this character that made you want to write about him? If he's a funny guy, will other people think he's amusing, too? (Or is his humor self-serving and juvenile?) Does he have a noble side, given to idealistic outbursts? (Or is he just a whiny prig?) Is she outrageous and over-the-top? (Or just a loudmouth?)

As you ponder these questions, fill a notebook with your answers. Return to this notebook from time to time as you write, fleshing out—pun intended—your character and checking to be sure your character "stays in character."

Unforgettable

Do all of this and you'll have created a character who will live as long as there are bookstores, libraries, audiobooks, the Internet—and memory. This character will be loved or hated by your readers in a fairly literal way. Readers will often confuse you and the character, will love you when your character pleases them, despise you when he or she doesn't. You will have succeeded in creating an unforgettable character. Readers will want more of your character—and so will your publisher.

Sara Ann Freed joined Mysterious Press, an imprint of Warner Books, in 1985 as a freelance editor working with Marcia Muller, Aaron Elkins and Charlotte MacLeod among others, getting paid to read what she enjoyed most: crime detection. She served as executive editor of Mysterious Press and senior editor for Warner Books.

Humor Impaired?

The hows and "wise" of humor for writers

By Roger Bates

I DON'T LIKE TO GENERALIZE...at least generally speaking. But as a humor consultant, I have found that most writers who have trouble incorporating humor into their work simply need to develop their "humor eye." Blind to humor, or to the benefits of humor, these writers usually fall into one of three categories:

- writers who believe humor is unimportant and unnecessary

- writers who would like very much to be funny but are convinced they have no sense of humor

- writers who use humor that is inappropriate or ineffective.

If you sometimes feel humorously impaired, here's how and why to change.

The benefits of humor

Do you often see humor as being frivolous, trite, insignificant, or worthless? If you do, you may have a "serious problem." Life without humor is no laughing matter. Although life would be better without lame jokes (like these), humor truly is essential to your happiness, mental health and overall well-being.

Without humor you would lose your healthy perspective and be unable to cope well with adversity. Life would become a serious and grim trek, offering little relief or reward. The future would loom ahead—dark, gloomy and dismal. You'd complain all the time in a high, whiny voice about every tiny, insignificant, unimportant thing anybody said or did. In short, you'd be just like my Aunt Mae when she's off her Prozac.

Just as humor adds a sense of perspective, balance, joy and relief to your life, it can lend these same qualities to your writing. Through humor you add color, attitude, depth, warmth and emotion, and much more. If you want your written words to have a life of their own, to be interesting, realistic, emotional and convincing, humor can help.

> "Even a hint of humor or small quip can provide important relief..."

People enjoy laughing. Look how many best-sellers are written by comedians. Whether reading a book, magazine article, letter from a friend, or watching a movie or television commercial, humor gives us a feeling of warmth. It opens us up and relaxes us. People like material that has a humorous side because it makes them feel good.

Even a hint of humor or small quip can provide important relief, especially if your writing is of a serious nature. In fact, the darker and more serious the writing, the more comic relief is appreciated and the bigger the impact a touch of humor will have.

By activating your sense of humor, you reduce stress and stay calm and clearheaded, which is important if you are writing under a deadline. You even sharpen your creative ability through humor because the thought process for being creative and being funny are the same!

You have a great sense of humor

A sense of humor is just that, a "sense." Although some people's sense of humor is better developed than others, everybody has one. If you have laughed just once in your life, you have a sense of humor. Though not a good one. But don't despair. Like a muscle, you can build and develop your funny bone, just by using it!

Since everybody's sense of humor is unique and different, nothing is funny to everyone. You can't please all the people all the time. I think it was

Abe Lincoln who first said that...or maybe I said it on my honeymoon. But the point is, expressing your sense of humor often requires "letting go" and taking a chance. The more chances you take with humor, the better your odds of making someone laugh.

It's important to realize we each have a wonderful sense of humor...no matter what our friends may tell us. Funny people usually *believe* they are funny and *see* themselves as being funny.

How and where to find humor

Unlike road construction, where you just lean on your shovel all day, in joke construction you build jokes with two basic parts, the *setup* and the *punch line*. Together they provide the foundation for all humor.

The punch line always comes after the setup. If a punch line is delivered before the setup, the joke is completely gone. *"Please...take my wife"* does not work. No one will laugh, and you may suddenly find yourself living alone.

If you ask any humorist what the single most important element of comedy is, the answer might surprise you. That's the answer... "surprise." In order to maximize surprise and catch you off guard, a good punch line is usually different from what is expected.

This is why a humor trick called the "reverse" is so effective. The reverse sets the reader up by heading them off in one direction and then revealing a different, and hidden, direction with the punch line.

My son keeps a hamster in his bedroom. At first the smell was terrible ...but then the hamster got used to it. At first the reader attributes the smell to the hamster. With the punch line, the reader suddenly realizes the smell belongs to the son, and that is a surprise...unless of course the reader also has a young son.

Notice how the hidden meaning—that the son is causing the smell rather than the hamster—is not revealed until the last few words of the punch line. A good punch line always comes at the end and is often just one or two words. By placing the punchword at the very end of the last sentence of the joke, you keep the listener in suspense. This increases the surprise for your listener and creates a bigger laugh.

Bob says, *"I left work because of illness and fatigue. My boss got sick and tired of me."*

Erma Bombeck says, *"When you look like your passport photo, it's time to go home."*

Erma's setup is straight ahead, giving you no clue of what's to come. Not until the last word can you realize what angle she's taking, and you still must deduce that she is saying passport pictures are terrible. If she had given you more information, *"When you look terrible like your passport photo,"* she would have given away the direction she was taking and lessened the surprise. This example of humor is resolved indirectly. Indirect resolution makes for a bigger surprise and therefore a bigger laugh.

Here's another example of an indirect resolution. David Brenner describes how fast and reckless New York cabbies drive:

"They go around corners on two wheels, 90 miles an hour. I always feel like I should be hanging out the window shooting at the car behind us."

Rather than *say, "I feel like I'm in a car chase,"* he *implies* it. He paints a nice picture but leaves something for the reader to figure out. The reader has to make the connection.

The best way to gain confidence in your sense of humor is to use it. Probably the least risky way to be humorous is through self-deprecation. Self-deprecation is inoffensive since you are the target of the humor.

For example, a divorcee might tell a friend, *"My ex-husband and I had a communication problem. He wouldn't even tell me who he was dating."* A Richard Lewis-type character might say something like, *"I suffer from such low self-esteem when we make love, I fantasize I'm someone else."* An old character might say, *"It's tough getting old. I get out of breath playing cards. I order a three-minute egg, and they want the money up front."*

You can give a character (or yourself) likability, warmth, strength and humility by giving him or her a self-deprecating line.

Puns and other wordplay

Writers often have a predilection for humor based on wordplay. Caution is advised, especially when using puns. They can reek of corniness, and they don't always work on paper.

A young woman announced at work that she was getting married and that everyone from the company was invited to the wedding. One of her co-workers asked incredulously, *"We're all invited?"* The bride-to-be replied, *"Absolutely. We want your presence."*

Written out, we realize what type of presence she was referring to. When spoken, however, we don't know if she means presents or presence. We laugh at the double meaning.

The more relevant humor is to the situation at hand, the funnier it is. Wordplay is stronger and less corny when it is not a joke, but a punch line to something someone actually says. Take the example of the colorful, quick-witted elevator operator. When asked by a smart aleck if she minded all the ups and downs she responded, *"Not at all. It's the jerks that bother me."*

Wordplay humor is often inadvertent. Back in high school there was much discussion about the Vietnam war. When a friend asked what I thought of euthanasia I replied very earnestly, *"I'm against sending our boys to Asia or anywhere else to fight."*

Malapropisms, the misuse of words, are usually unintentional and can be used to paint a character as a nonintellectual or earthy type. Sam Goldwyn is credited for coming up with beauties like, *"In two words, the answer is 'n-o.' Include me out."* Casey Stengel said, *"If people don't want to come to the ballpark, no one can stop them."* Foreign characters are naturals for malapropisms. A Middle Eastern friend of mine once said after telling someone off, *"I really gave him a piece of my ear."* He'll say, *"I have a funny joke to tell you. Stop me if I have heard this before."* I always stop him.

Figures of speech become colorful and interesting with humor, as long as they are original. Many humorous figures of speech are based on exaggerations, such as: *hungry as a bear, big as a house, fat as a pig, stubborn as a mule, etc.* These clichés are not funny because we've heard them so many times the surprise is gone. But the first time someone said, *"I'm so hungry I could eat a horse,"* people were probably rolling on the ground with laughter. *"Ha, ha, ha. Grog say he so hungry he eat horse. Me hungry too. Me want another dinosaur toe."*

Hyperbole

You can make characters come alive by putting energy into what they say. A great way to achieve this is through exaggeration. Instead of saying, *"This town is too small,"* try, *"This town is so small they have the yellow page. It's so small you've got to leave town to unfold a map. It's so small, the 7-11 closes at 5."*

To show how conceited someone is, her acquaintance might say, *"She thinks highly of herself. She'd walk through a garden so the flowers could smell her."*

Discussing a bad movie, a character might remark, *"That movie was so bad, Siskel and Ebert cut their thumbs off."*

Performing stand-up comedy, I sometimes mention the dive I stayed in where *".....the walls were so thin, when I got up during the night to go to the bathroom, the guy in the next room asked me to bring him a glass of water."*

In comedy, a good verbal exaggeration is similar to a good caricature or impression. The funniest characteristics are greatly distorted, and yet, the subject can still be recognized. The more unique and clever the exaggeration, the funnier it tends to be. The bigger the exaggeration, the bigger the laugh, up to a point. The laughter falls off quickly if the caricature or impression loses its semblance to the original subject.

The callback

Another great humor trick is the callback. With a callback you take a bit of humor used earlier and repeat it in a different context. In other words, you are making reference to the same punch line, only with a different setup. Callbacks provide an easy and safe laugh. As long as the readers found it funny the first time, they will laugh again just at the reminder. (Kurt Vonnegut, Jr. is a master of this technique.)

As an example, take the following scene: Telling a group of friends about her new flame, Denise describes him as *"a licensed psychologist."* The group finds the word "licensed" very funny. Someone kids her by asking if she would still date him even if he were not licensed. When another woman mentions that her boyfriend is a good cook, someone asks, *"Yes, but is he a* licensed *cook?"* References are made to "licensed lovers."

This scene provides the writer with an inside joke that can be called back throughout the book—sparingly, so it wears well—any time friends from this group are together. The callback helps tie these people together and provides an easy means for the writer to create warmth and humor at will.

Use common sense to choose appropriate and effective humor

Writers often ask me what rules or guidelines they can follow when using humor. The first rule of comedy is there are no rules. (But here are some anyway.)

Humor is funniest when it is believable, when it fits within the context of the story, or fits the personality of the humorist delivering it—whether it is you or one of your characters. In other words, make humor relevant to a character or to a point you are trying to convey. Just as a pun becomes funnier when it is delivered in response to a remark someone makes, rather than in joke form, any humor is stronger when it is spontaneous (or appears to be spontaneous) and relates to the experience of the moment.

Comedian Rodney Dangerfield says, *"I don't get no respect. I told my dentist my teeth were getting yellow. He told me to wear a brown tie."* We laugh because this bit fits his loser image so well. If a brash, arrogant comic were to use the same bit we probably wouldn't find it nearly as funny. We wouldn't "buy it." Likewise, you don't want a cool, hip character telling a corny pun or a cerebral character coming off like Curly of "The Three Stooges." (Moe or Larry either, for that matter.)

When I help a writer add humor to a text, I look for anything and everything from which to build punch lines. Then we go through and pick the humor that is most fitting for the story or for the writer's objectives.

A setup can be something someone says or *does*. Take a simple scene where Jack is fumbling to put on his tie while his wife Jill, patiently waits. Jill might say (or think to herself), *"Jack, you're so slow. This reminds me of the first time you tried to take my bra off."* (For a total reverse she might add, *"You never did explain why you had it on."*)

Jill could also use exaggeration and say, *"Come on, Jack. By the time you get that tie on, it's going to be out of style."*

To paint a humble character, Jack could use the same line targeting himself. *"Sorry I'm taking so long. This reminds me of the first time I tried to take your bra off."*

Jill might add, *"The first time? It's like every time you try to take my bra off. You've been slow at everything, Jack, since you fell down and broke your crown."*

Jack could retort, *"Well, you had to come tumbling after...and whack me in the head with the bucket."*

The preceding exchange would be great if you were writing slapstick but hardly appropriate for more somber and serious writing, such as a business manual.

One paradox of truly funny individuals is that although they don't mind taking chances with their humor, they (usually) know what needs to be edited for a particular audience. Through experience they have developed an intuitive feel for how people respond. To survive in the business, stand-up comedians must quickly develop a sixth sense as to what to use and what to edit. We quickly learn that a joke one audience finds hilarious may draw groans, or even completely turn off another group. If you keep your readers in mind and use common sense, your humor will be appropriate and effective—most of the time.

Humor, like life, is magical and mystical. If viewed with wide-eyed wonder, we catch more, appreciate more and feel more alive. By keeping your eyes open, you train yourself to see life's folly. In the words of that wise yogi, Yogi Berra (not to be confused with Yogi Bear), *"You can observe a lot by just watching."*

Roger Bates is a stand-up comedian, speaker and humor consultant. He is the author of several books. In his latest book— How to Be Funnier (Happier, Healthier & More Successful Too!)— *he shows the reader how to see, feel and share more humor by using the tips, tricks and secrets of the top comedians and humor writers. To contact Roger Bates call (919) 380-8169.*

So, You Want to Be a Columnist?

*Learn what periodical publishers
look for and how to supply it*

By Frances Halpern

IN MY EXPERIENCE, IF A WRITER WERE granted his or her career wish, it would almost always be to create a best-selling literary novel, author a widely-acclaimed poetry anthology or publish a book of inspirational advice which captures the world's attention; then, after accomplishing any or all of the above, *write a syndicated column.*

At one time or other, we all fantasize about authoring a column which showcases our humor, knowledge, philosophy, and keen insights. Of course the column would appear in hundreds of newspapers—or at least a major magazine. And we would be handsomely rewarded.

The reality is a little less grand. Columnists usually settle for careers with hometown newspapers or magazines. But they often become local celebrities, and the ambitious, talented and lucky graduate to major markets and eventually syndication.

At this juncture, you might be thinking, "Hey, I just want to get a regular column published somewhere." Assuming this is the case let me share a little anecdotal material about how many of us began.

I'm sitting in what is labeled the begging chair, positioned opposite the buyer of words. I have glibbed my way into this meeting with the editor of a small community newspaper. My purpose—to convince him to publish a weekly column I plan to write. He hears the pitch and responds wearily, "You housewives/retired engineers/teachers/etc. always think you want to write a column.

I need serious people who will maintain quality and meet deadlines. Nice try, lady," he says not unkindly, "but no thanks."

Would you slink away discouraged and depressed? My response was to send the editor three columns focusing on very local happenings. My cover letter assured him I would let nothing interfere with deadlines. He relented. How determined are you?

Aside from having a rich uncle who owns a chain of newspapers, there are two ways to get published as a columnist:

• Find a subject not covered and fill an editor's need to have it covered.

• Convince an editor that your expertise, writing ability and fresh approach will attract readers.

Either way, you'll need to prove to the editor that you can write regularly and better than anyone else about your specialty as a psychologist, plumber, economist, gardener, car mechanic or bargain hunter.

Where to start

Sit down with your favorite newspapers and magazines. Study them page by page. Don't skim. Notice the fillers, the features, the columns, news coverage, editorials and the ads. Pretend you're going to be tested on their contents. Become aware of regular features. Is there a gap? What isn't being covered? Does the newspaper or magazine include regional sections? Spot bits and pieces scattered throughout the newspaper or magazine which could be gathered under one banner.

For example: The column I have written for the past fifteen years (consecutively for three major newspapers) is a result of my observation that items about literary events were used as fillers or buried in a calendar list. There was no real focus on the writing world on a weekly basis. So, I queried an overworked—all editors are overworked, at least in their minds—editor about gathering that information into a regular column. And because writing and publishing is a business, I suggested in my query that giving booksellers, publishers and writers a regular forum could result in a tool for the sales department to sell advertising space.

Many now-syndicated columnists started by responding to this "fill the gap" concept. For example: Your newspaper may wish to print a neighborhood column about the activities of local residents. Not the most glamorous assignment—to write about little Herman Berman's birthday bash, or who attended the latest symphony board fund raising dinner and (ugh) what they wore. But, if that's what the newspaper needs, bring a fresh eye to that little neighborhood column (for which you will be paid in pennies), learn the craft and build a reputation.

While you're paying your dues, keep a sharp eye peeled for other opportunities. Newspapers are the obvious and easiest target for the beginning columnist. However, don't overlook the thousands of small, trade, general and specialty magazines which might be receptive to a column.

Check out the trade journals representing every interest group where you have, or conceivably could develop, a level of expertise: sports, travel, health, music, military, home decorating, computers, animals (note how many individual magazines focus on dogs, cats, horses, birds, etc.).

If you're getting to that stage where the cashier behind the counter at the pharmacy offers you a discount (or even if you're not), ask yourself what the subscribers to your local senior citizen journal might enjoy reading? Can you regale them with a column about travel, economic issues, sports, pursuing hobbies, health, writing, the arts?

While many retired folk hang it all up to smell the flowers, travel, visit the grandkids, pursue whatever their work schedules formerly precluded, your retirement might include taking up the pen to become a columnist. None of the following now-established columnists, who happen to be mature citizens, had serious literary credits before crashing the party.

Muriel Kauffmann, a divorced mother, bookkeeper by profession, and lover of theater and the arts, wrote the weekly "View From Over the Hill" for a Canadian newspaper chain. She says, "Research, persistence and knowledge made it happen." Her advice is: "Determine how a publication can benefit from your services and tell them so. Magazines and newspapers are businesses. I'm not above suggesting to editors that ads can be sold around my column, or that demographically, the readers have specific needs and interests that I can address." She continues, "Once you make the contact, even after a rejection, keep in touch. The editor of a California chain of senior publications took a full year to hire me as a first-time columnist. She later admitted that she signed me on because I never gave up calling her."

This successful columnist also reminds us to stick to subjects with which we possess a knowledge and enthusiasm level sufficient to impress an editor. Following her move to Canada, she sought new column assignments, and during a telephone conversation with an editor, who called simply to turn her down, her passion for her subject so impressed him, he agreed to take her "on trial." The resulting "View From Over the Hill" column first appeared every two weeks. It segued into a weekly feature.

Two of the perks of this columnist's persistence are invitations to attend all kinds of performances and the respect accorded to the chronicler of events.

Another success story (wildly so) illustrates the rites of passage of a woman widowed at fifty-five. She determines to plunge into the world, attends classes and writers' conferences, and uses her incredible sense of humor and experienced view of life to create sparkling columns which reflect her take on everything from crotchety conversations in the supermarket to traveling as a single woman. Her columns begin to appear in a small town paper in the Midwest. People buy the Sunday paper just to read "Midlife Musings." She decides to compile the columns and self-publish a book. More self-published books based on her hilarious and poignant columns follow, including *The Girls With the Grandmother Faces*. She becomes a sought-after speaker. The books fly out the door wherever she appears. A literary agent reads and loves *The Girls With the Grandmother Faces* and presents the book to a major publisher who offers a huge advance. (Yes, publishers actually seek self-published books with a track record to reissue to a broad audience.)

Another maturing citizen decided to go the nostalgia route. As a retired Hollywood producer, a million stories rolled around in his head. Leonard "Buzz" Blair began to write gossipy columns about old movies and legendary actors. A weekly newspaper took on the column, and film buffs who like to read about movies made during the heyday of the studios make the column popular. This producer-turned-columnist saw a niche and filled it.

How to start

To convince an editor of your commitment and expertise, write at least three columns. This is your query, your calling card. Make certain the writing is your best and your ideas fresh.

Editors always worry whether an untried writer can sustain an ongoing column. The first question asked is "will you have enough material to fill the column?" Your job is to show that you do and will continue to.

A surprising success story involves a young woman, newly divorced, with a doctorate in religion, and no job. She was casting about for something positive to do which would also give her a way to make a living. She attended a writer's conference where a panelist inspired her with a message about taking risks.

In response to a series of articles in her local newspaper about the controversy over school prayer, she took a mental deep breath and submitted her thoughts and comments. They were published in the paper's guest column section. This emboldened her to query about writing a religion column which would combine general analysis and her personal philosophy. As careful editors often do, they responded with "We'll give you a trial run."

Diana Butler's "Faith in Our Time" was picked up by the New York Times

Syndicate and approximately seventy newspapers are using the columns as one-shots, a term which means they are buying individual columns instead of a weekly series—but who knows where it will end? Diana Butler has gone on to author a number of books on religion and the role of the church in America.

On rejection

Editors are bombarded with column submissions and, unfortunately, reject over 95 percent, often in a very cursory manner. Why? Believe it or not, they report that people who haven't a clue muck it up for the talented writers by submitting ungrammatical, banal, plagiarized, and/or undecipherable work—or the columns are so painfully and privately autobiographical they would be of no interest to readers.

They admit a smaller group of submissions might have an element of interest, but other flaws make them unacceptable: a cleverly written political column with no original ideas, information or insights or the financial expert who submits a column brimming with fresh ideas but couched in incomprehensible economic jargon.

The editor has more important things to do than spend hours sifting through mountains of unacceptable material so she gives most proposals very little attention.

What else falls into the rejection pile?

• Clones of columns already published

• A concept too narrow: the care and feeding of bonsai trees

• Or too broad: a travel column full of generalizations about why the globe trotter/journalist loved or hated wherever.

The inevitable Erma Bombeck/Dave Barry humor column clones will be rejected by syndicators for an obvious reason: The niche is filled. However, heads up, here is an opportunity to hit your local newspaper or magazine with your version of those popular columns. Writers who submit clever, humorous or poignant observations of incidents and events with a local spin make names for themselves, are asked to speak at luncheons and dinners and are honored and quoted as community treasures.

What are the subjects inspired columnists write about? Anything. Everything. I remember reading a series of columns based on family names in the local phone book. Everything from color names (Brown, Green, White, etc.) to folks with names like Magazine, Doctor, Swindle, Godsick. There are hundreds of events which the creative columnist can observe and then write about. Ride with the police one day. Sit in with the local radio talk show host.

I spent a Christmas Eve doing just that and uncovered a world of lonely people who call talk shows on holidays. Great column material. Of course, the events in your own life, special anniversaries, a disaster in the house, animal antics involving birds, cats, horses, dogs, are all fodder—if you can spin a yarn in language which is both fresh and familiar.

Anything you write must appeal to the reader's need to know, touch emotions, make us care, or make us think. All good writing elicits that nod of recognition (yeah, that's how it is) or is a wake up call (glad you told me that). Every column you create should deliver either or both to readers.

Recycle ideas into new slants on subjects. Find an angle. Do you collect political items? How about a column dealing with the funny and/or crazy history of political campaigns and campaign ephemera in your community? An editor might love a lighthearted look at the loony bumper stickers, weird hats and campaign slogans your local politicos dream up.

Ecology and the environment are big topics. How does someone concerned with these issues beat the odds in getting an environmental column published? Focus on a segment of the population. One clever writer aimed his column at children (and of course their parents). Readers learn about environmentally safe toys, chemical–free cotton blankets, how to create gifts from recycled materials, etc.

> "Anything you write must appeal to the reader's need to know, touch emotions, make us care, or make us think."

A retired brigadier general who had thought long and hard about his 25-year military career decided to write a column based on his experiences which included 11 years with NATO dealing with geopolitical and military affairs. His passion was to suggest solutions to international problems. He developed a prospectus for a weekly opinion column which clearly delineated his objectives. He described his own qualifications, education and experience. His proposal included succinct paragraphs indicating the column's character, scope and orientation. He suggested an 800-word column and rates he expected to be paid based on circulation. All of this information, including his photo, was presented on one page. The prospectus included a self-addressed stamped card which editors filled out if they wished to use the column. With this simple, but organized method, the general, Henry Huglin, self-syndicated "Affairs of Nations" to eighteen papers.

You've learned a little about how so-called average citizens achieve column bylines. They are innovative, gutsy, clever storytellers. And generally outgoing personalities, with almost childlike curiosity about everything and everyone. Most columnists I know are passionate about many things. They are angered by events they perceive to be unjust and they also see humor in life, even in personal disasters. All of this becomes grist for their storytelling mills. In addition, successful columnists use the following information to guide them on a difficult, competitive journey.

Lauren Roberts absolutely loves books. Mostly nonfiction titles about words, books publishing and art. When a new weekly newspaper opened its doors in her community, she sent a query about doing a column called "Review & Reflections." She received an immediate responce from an editor who said he was impressed by the query letter. He signed her on, told her she could review any book that appealed to her, and requested only that she also focus on some local publishing events.

Unfortunately the newspaper shut down two years later. However, Lauren moved "Reviews & Reflections" to her Internet site bibliobuffet.com which provides an outlet for writers interested in literary subjects, and is open to submission of books for reviews. Contact the site at www.bibliobuffet.com.

Lesson learned here. The Internet is an enormous market for potential columnists and essayist who want to practice the craft and who can meet deadlines.

The business end

Here's where you make choices. You can write a column for one publication (local, regional or national) and be content to remain at your post forever. There are happy, successful columnists all over the nation who are doing just that.

Or self-syndicate. After studying the market, submit simultaneously to as many non-competing publications as possible. Use the names of the periodicals that pick you up initially to open doors with the more reluctant ones. Continue to do this until you're happy with the exposure you have and the money you're making.

The third option is to be represented by a syndicator who does all the work (except the writing) and takes anywhere from 50 to 60 percent of your income. Most national columns are syndicated.

Tools of the columnist's trade

The Internet is a terrific source as is the library to find information about the following magazines and newsletters. Join organizations which will help you make the contacts needed to launch a column.

• *Editor & Publisher*, 770 Broadway, New York, NY 10003-9595. A weekly magazine which covers the newspaper and syndicate world. Also publishes a detailed syndicate directory every summer.

• *Association of Alternative Newsweeklies*, 1250 Eye Street N.W. suite 804, Washington DC 20005. E-Mail: Web@aan.org. An annotated and illustrated description of North America's metro newsweeklies. Call (202) 289-8484.

• *National Directory of Newspaper Op-Ed*, Communication Creativity, P.O. Box 909, Buena Vista, Colorado 81211-0909. Lists needs of newspapers published in North America. Although not complete, this state-by-state compilation will help familiarize you with what's out there.

• *Society of Professional Journalists*, Eugene S. Pulliam National Journalism Center, 3909 N. Meridian Street, Indianapolis, Indiana 46208. Hosts national and regional conferences and dinner meetings. Many active local chapters meet regularly. Members receive *The Quill Magazine*. (317) 927-8000.

• *National Society of Newspaper Columnists*, P.O. Box 156885, San Francisco, California 94115-6885. Hosts an annual conference and publishes a very helpful networking newsletter. (866) 440-6762.

• Gini Graham Scott has created a newspaper and syndicate database. Find her online at ginis@aol.com or at the website www.ginigrahamscott.com.

• *News Jobs Cafe*, Joe Grimm's online information source for writers online at jobspage.typepad.com/jobspage.

(See Magazines and Newsletters of Interest to Writers, page 368, and Associations for Writers, page 374, for more listings.)

Browse either the library or online through *Gale's Directory, Editor & Publisher Yearbook,* and *Working Press of the Nation.*

Most important of all, write well and be persistent.

Frances Halpern *is a broadcast and print journalist with expertise in politics and publishing. She delivered weekly columns covering literary events and the publishing business to three major daily newspapers for fifteen years including the "Words & Images" column which appears in the* Los Angeles Times *for six years. She is currently host of Beyond Words, a weekly literary talk show on KCLU, a National Public Radio affiliate. Beyond Words can be heard in Santa Barbara and Ventura counties and on the Internet at kclu.org.*

Frances authored "The Writer's Guide to Publishing in the West," contributed to "Chicken Soup for the Writer's Soul" and has been published in regional and national magazines and newspapers including the Los Angeles Times, Seventeen, Grit, Westways *and* Inflight Magazine. *She is a member of the American Society of Journalists & Authors and The Authors Guild. She's a regular on the lecture circuit and has moderated a number of panels at the annual Los Angeles Times Festival of Books.*

Watch Your Language!

*Taking the groan out of grammar and
the yuck out of usage*

By *Sierra Adare*

L ET'S FACE IT. WRITERS BEND, OR EVEN BREAK, the rules of grammar and usage on a daily basis. But nothing will get you a rejection slip more quickly than ignoring guidelines that have been carved in literary granite. For good reason, too. They keep your writing from sliding into that dark abyss of vagueness, confusion, wordiness and lifelessness.

When compiling my latest book, *What Editors Look For*, I surveyed editors in every facet of publishing—from regional presses to national magazines to the "biggies" in New York. Regardless of whether they handle fiction or nonfiction books, short stories or articles, editors stress the need for a "command of the language" and "knowing how to use it."

So, what exactly do editors mean by this?

The answer—grammar and usage—usually brings forth groans and an "oooh yuck" or two. These two ingredients, however, play a huge role in what makes for successful writing. For example, Ed Stackler, senior editor at NAL/ Dutton, sees hundreds of queries and synopses every single week. He finds the "quality of writing" the most common element missing in these submissions. "It invariably makes an editor doubt the quality of the work in question," Stackler confides.

Unfortunately, due to today's increasingly heavy workloads, editors are forced to make snap judgments. In other words, poor writing in a query letter results in a form rejection letter.

Overcome this stumbling block to getting published by learning the nuances that make the language work for you rather than against you. *The Elements of Style* by Strunk and White, a thin, little book (a total of seventy-eight pages), offers a concise cram course on basic grammar for good writing. Buy it. Study it. Keep it by your computer and refer to it often.

In addition to the guidelines you find there, be consistent with your grammar. If you begin using a comma before the "and" in a series (e.g. Nancy, Dave, and Paul), stick with it throughout the manuscript even though a series without a comma in front of the "and" is equally acceptable. By the same token, if you spell the word "skeptic" early on, don't switch to the equally correct "sceptic" later. Once you've mastered the fundamentals of grammar, it frees you to work on the more important facets of usage.

Content—the words you choose and how you string them together—can turn bland, everyday language into compelling writing, provided you follow a few simple rules.

Avoid passive verbs

Nothing kills your writing faster than the "to be" verb in all its forms. The following sentence offers a typical example of what editors see all too often in query letters.

> "Nothing kills your writing faster than the 'to be' verb in all its forms."

"Killer Thief" *is* a story about a thief who *is* framed for the murder of a politician.

What exactly does this sentence tell an editor? Content-wise, it says very little. Structure-wise, it screams, "Composed by a beginner." Furthermore, the above example "shows" nothing. Compare it to this.

In my mystery *Killer Thief*, attorney William Cartwright *devises* a way to knock off his opponent, Senator Bob Brown. Cartwright *hires* the notorious cat burglar, Rogue Allen, to *steal* Brown's coin collection, then *frames* the thief for the murder.

Not only do the action verbs (italicized here for easy recognition) add pizzazz, they also help characterize the characters. Cartwright must be devious. He *devises* and *frames*.

Stating the obvious wastes words

Look at the first example of *Killer Thief* again. In theory, the author did some market research to obtain the editor's name and address and knows the type of book this editor acquires for the publisher. Fiction editors assume every submission "is a story." What they want to know is what kind of story. This example could propose a murder mystery, a men's adventure or a thriller. Hence the phrase in the second example "in my mystery."

Paul Zimmer, the director of the University of Iowa Press, puts it this way: "They should not begin, 'I am writing to you...' Of *course* they are!"

Avoid vague words

You might as well print one of those pointing-finger dingbats next to such words as *sometimes, may, plenty, little, few* and *most.* They convey an immediate message to the editor: You skimped on your research. Which means you either haven't bothered to dig into your subject or you don't know how. Therefore, can the editor trust your data in the article or book? Hardly. Instead, the manuscript comes back with a nice rejection letter that's as vague as you were.

Rather than writing:

> Several million visitors drive through the gates of Yellowstone National Park each year.

try:

> A record 2,912,193 people drove through the gates of Yellowstone National Park in 1993. Of this figure, 795,471 arrived through the south entrance and 474,033 used the east entrance.

Watch out for extra, uncalled-for information

Be as specific as possible without throwing in extraneous information you have no intention of expounding on.

For example: Unless you plan to list and discuss each of the negatives, avoid starting a paragraph with something like:

> I find hiking alone has two advantages and five disadvantages.

It is better to focus on what you plan to actually elaborate on in the paragraph:

Although I've hiked in a group and alone, I prefer the latter. I find the solitude invigorates my spirit and reduces my stress levels.

Keep the tone straightforward

Just as you employ black ink, white paper and a readable font to promote an image of proficiency, the contents of your submission must promote your writing skills. Michael Seidman, an editor at Walker and Company, calls it "calm professionalism." He says, "Get to the point; tell me what I need to know, and finish."

Instead of

> If you like taking the family dog for long walks, you're going to just love my fun-filled article on packing with goats.

how about this?

> Goats display the same characteristics of loyalty, friendliness and companionship as dogs, which lends packing with goats the air of a family outing—only the goats carry the gear.

In the first example, the editor reaches the end of the sentence without learning the connection between dogs and goats. Sure, it might be intriguing enough for the editor to read on, but why create extra work? Recall that stack of up to 100 queries and manuscripts awaiting the editor's bloodshot eyes? Why risk it?

Avoid long paragraphs

Visually speaking, these look daunting to the eye. Pick up a copy of the short story "The Beast in the Jungle" by Henry James if you need proof. His "stream of consciousness" style consists of internal monologue that runs on for pages. At times, a single paragraph hogs an entire page. No quotation marks or unusual punctuation offer a bit of visual relief on such pages. I think college professors relish assigning a paper about this none-too-short story just to see which students can wade through seemingly endless prose. But you can bet your computer, the only wading editors do involves fly fishing.

Vary sentence lengths and structures

Reading one long, clause-ridden, compound sentence after another tends to make your eyes burn, cross, or wander to something more interesting—like the dumb saying on your coffee mug that you already know by heart.

Think of a paragraph as a roller coaster ride. The lengthy sentence piles on the information until the editor perches on an apex of data. Now, toss in a short one. Fill it with action, and watch the way the editor's eyes zoom through it and into the next.

On another front, consider sentence structure. Starting every single sentence with a noun followed by a verb should appear in the dictionary as a definition for monotony. Turn this:

> The hikers lose their maps in a wind storm. They find a game trail. They follow it. It leads them in the wrong direction. They become lost. They run out of food. They panic.

into this:

> When the wind storm blows away their maps, the hikers look for a game trail to follow. Unfortunately, the one they find leads them in the wrong direction. They become lost. Nevertheless, they don't panic until the food runs out.

The first example also exhibits another structure problem—beginning almost every sentence in the paragraph with the same word. Note how one sentence begins to sound like the next and the next.

Be positive

You can write just about any sentence in either a positive or a negative way. Watch for the negative connotation of words such as *not, can't, no* and *don't*. For example:

> This is not the only book about mountain climbing in Montana, but mine deals with walk-ups that require no specialized gear.

Remove negatives by restructuring the phrase or sentence:

> While six other books stress mountain climbing in Montana, only mine features walk-ups that require no specialized gear.

Note: The phrase "no specialized gear" indicates a positive aspect of the book. Learn to spot the difference.

Are you saying what you think you are?

From time to time, our wonderful English, which draws words and components from many languages, confounds our best efforts to command it. The following example comes straight from the desk of a New York publisher.

Dear Editor,
I have just completed a truly horrifying novel.

Obviously, the author of this cover letter hoped this sentence would convey the emotional level of terror the story line would generate for the reader rather than announcing how poorly written the novel is. You can easily avoid this by handing your letter or manuscript to a friend or family member to read. A second set of eyes sees the words we, as the author, miss.

Read *everything* you write out loud

Fiction pros tell beginning writers this is one of the standards to live by. But "read it out loud" also applies to query and cover letters, synopses and book proposals. Had the author of the above example read that sentence out loud, the little editor who lives inside every individual's ear would surely have caught the double meaning.

Trust your ear to help you fine-tune everything you submit to an editor. When, as you read out loud, you stumble over a word, phrase or an entire sentence, put yourself on red alert. Something doesn't work. After you've checked for a mismatched noun and verb combination, look for phrases that dangle by spider threads.

Adherence to the above rules, combined with solid, uniform grammar, adds clarity to your prose and assists you in creating a winning writing style. This will very often mean the difference between an contract and a rejection letter. And when you do decide to bend those rules of grammar and usage, you'll do so for the right impact, putting language to work for you in producing a dynamic piece editors can't put down, instead of one they can't wade through!

> ***Sierra Adare*** *teaches and lectures on writing and marketing techniques, and writes marketing and submissions columns for* Roundup Magazine *and several newsletters. Her book* What Editors Look For: How to Write Compelling Queries, Cover Letters, Synopses & Book Proposals *developed out of work sheets, questions and discussions generated during her classes. Adare has written five other books. For more than fifteen years, Adare's how-to, marketing, travel and cooking articles have appeared in both regional and national publications. She has also published essays, book reviews, poems and a newspaper column.*

Meet a Jerk,
Get to Work

Find your fiction characters and settings in everyday life

By Jaqueline Girdner

FIRST OFF, LET ME CONFESS. I kill people for a living. Fiction-
ally, of course. In other words, I'm a mystery writer, one of those
lucky few who spend their day thinking about murder and committing it. Am
I punished for these sinister deeds? No, I'm paid for them, criminally little,
but paid nonetheless.

How did I get so lucky? you might ask. Then the question gets a little
stickier. You might even ask me about character, plot, and setting. Then you'd
really see me panic. Because I know I should think up something profoundly
academic in answer to such questions, but in fact I don't really think a lot
about character, plot, and setting when I'm starting a new book. I think about
people. I observe.

Okay, okay, what I really do is meet people. Actually, I meet "Jerks." And
I meet their "Victims."

"So what is a Jerk?" you might ask. Or maybe you already have your
own ideas. A Jerk is someone who is supremely insensitive to the hurt that
arises from their actions, or sometimes, someone who realizes the hurt all too
well…and relishes it.

I talk to people a lot, but I listen too. I can't help it. I believe the curse of
the fiction writer is that very inability to turn off observation even while interacting. And when I meet Jerks and their Victims, somehow it always turns
into a murder motive for me.

Let me tell you about some of the Jerks and their Victims that I've met. The Jerks (also known as the "murderees") include people who hurt their children, writers who would do anything for a story, people who spread false rumors and threaten blackmail, and people who do evil work without thinking of the ultimate consequences of their work. Not to mention people who think that their own righteousness (in this life and even in *former* lives) is the primary determining factor in the quality of their lifestyle, so they damn well deserve better than the next guy.

Their Victims? (Also known as the "murderers.") Victims might be people protecting their children, people protecting their lives, and people protecting their livelihoods. Victims might be people who have been abused themselves and are angry about it, angry with the system…and angry with the Jerks.

You've met them. I've met them. An example, perhaps?

I was visiting a friend one day, and when I asked her how she was, she began to cry. And I mean real crying, long gulping sobs that seemed endless. I put my arms around her and asked her what was so terrible that it could cause her so much distress. "It's a man," she told me. And I said, "Oh," a little disappointed. My friend had seemed too sensible to let romantic entanglements cause her this much grief. "No, not that kind of man," she said. "Not a lover." Then her voice lowered. "This man is a hater." And she told me her story.

A man (read "Jerk") at her place of work had become jealous of her popularity and was afraid of losing position because of it. So he decided to set her up, blackmailing someone in a weak position into accusing her of sexual harassment. A completely off-the-wall idea if you knew my friend, but still. Luckily, the would-be blackmail victim came to my friend first and warned her, but told her he wouldn't repeat the truth if asked. The Jerk had too much power. My friend had seen the Jerk at work before, had even seen a suicide result from his actions. But he was very powerful, in a much higher position than she was. We talked over the situation into the late hours of the night and she finally decided she had no recourse but to document her allegations to her union and then seek work elsewhere.

It was then that I found myself saying, "Really, the best way out would be to kill him." She shook her head and replied, "I wouldn't do that." "Nor would I," I told her. Then I smiled. "Except on paper." And she smiled back. "Would you do that for me?" she asked. So I did. Her situation, greatly disguised became the plot for…well, let's just say one of my mystery novels. You'll have to read them all to find out which. My friend was unjustly forced to find work elsewhere, but she felt some sense of revenge when her Jerk became my Jerk and died horribly on paper. And I had a book.

Another one of my plots came from a complete stranger who waited until almost everyone had left after one of my book signings and told me a story about a Jerk that would curl your hair. (Or straighten it if it's already curly.) And there wasn't a thing she could do about him legally. When she finally left she said, "Maybe I'll just have to kill the s.o.b." She said it with a smile, but it was a smile that made me shiver. And a smile that gave me my next book. And no, I won't tell you which one that became either.

And if she did kill her Jerk in real life, would I blame her? I'm not sure. I just hope I never hear about it.

Become the murderer

You may have noticed by now that I have some sympathy for my murderers. In fact, in some cases, I have a *lot* of sympathy for my murderers.

However, given the motive for the Victims to kill the Jerks, I, personally, still wouldn't beat someone over the head with a hammer. Nor would the woman who attended my signing. Probably. But who would? This is where it gets interesting. The Victim has the motive, but how does this Victim become a murderer? What person do they have to be to translate what we all feel at one time or another into murder? At this point in my thought process, I become that person. What would my childhood have had to be like? What would be important enough to trigger that murder? I pace the house in the Victim's shoes and become more and more murderous. Until I really feel the urge, viscerally. It has to make real sense to me, both intellectually and emotionally, or I don't write it.

> "It has to make real sense to me, both intellectually and emotionally, or I don't write it."

And then my mind is flooded with the experiences of that Victim/murderer, not to mention clues, red herrings, interactions, and other people who are angry. It gets deeper and murkier. And suddenly, I have the beginnings of, well, a character.

Living in Marin County, California, I meet a special kind of Jerk and a special kind of Victim. The Jerk/murderee is often the New Age, spiritually conscious Jerk. Have you ever heard that special phrase, "You create your own reality"? It's a comment which exemplifies the dark side of the New Age for me, using positive-speak to blame the Victim, whether victimized by sickness, poverty, or just plain bad luck. Well, I'd heard the phrase, about 500 times too many, when I decided to kill the messenger. It sprouted and twined and twisted and turned in my head until my third book, *Murder Most Mellow*, was born.

And the Victim/murderer? Well...gulp...they're often a lot like me. Sometimes, even vegetarians. They're human beings pushed to their limits, living out their human potential, so to speak, but often abruptly ending that of others—with weapons particular to Marin County's spirit: a Salad Shooter in *Fat-Free and Fatal* and organic herbal tea in *Tea-Totally Dead*.

Write what you know

I've always heard you should write what you know. I just take it a little further; I kill what I know. Every experience I've ever had is possible fodder for murder. And I've had a lot of experience: as a divorce lawyer, as a psychiatric aide in a mental hospital, and as a small-business owner. And of course, as a writer.

Wanna talk about Jerk/murderees? Have you ever been in a writers' critique group? Well, Slade Skinner was. And he was a mite bit insensitive in his verbal critiques as he methodically pumped a dumbbell up and down. I don't even have to tell you. I'll bet you can figure out the final use of that dumbbell in *A Stiff Critique*.

Character begets plot

So now I have my characters. My Jerks and their Victims. My murderees and murderers. But how about plot? Strangely enough, I have a hard time untangling character and plot. They weave together like warp and woof. Because once I'm in my Victim/murderer's shoes, I begin thinking how I will kill my Jerk/murderee. And then I know the problems I'll run into. And then I start thinking, and feeling, the anger that others may have towards this Jerk. And I realize all the interactions that might be sparked by this essential clash between Victim and Jerk. The plot begins to make itself, faster than I can keep up with it. Plot and subplots build as characters come alive. I keep pads of paper in every room of the house to write down each twist and turn as it comes off the skein. And believe me, my stories come alive. My Jerks and Victims, and now the whole cast of characters, follow me everywhere. They even come into my dreams to tell me what they will and will not do.

The plot and characters dance a sinister tango, entangling and weaving themselves into a story. And then the details come raining down.

I look around me and what do I see? Murder weapons. Everywhere I go. At the chiropractor's. Look at that metal bar. At the hairdresser's. All those chemicals. And those women sticking their heads into electric helmets. At the nursery, communing with all those poisonous plants. On the road with all those other people in their automotive death machines. Even my home becomes a Madame Tussaud's of murder. Knives, electrical appliances, even pinball machines appear as instruments of death. My book, *Most Likely to Die*, features the unlikely murder of a man by "Hot Flash." Not the usual change of life discomfort, mind you, but a pinball machine named "Hot Flash" that the Jerk rigs to make menopause jokes. What he doesn't know is that the Victim has rigged it to do another trick. When the Jerk steps up to play he is electrocuted, writhing in the agonies of his own "Hot Flash."

Use familiar, real-life settings

As for the setting, well, I do live in Marin County, California. I don't have to look any further for a bizarre and mysterious backdrop. To get to my house from San Francisco, you drive over the Golden Gate Bridge and keep going until you pass through the rainbow tunnel. The rainbow tunnel is a clue. You have just entered the land where the New Age is still new, where spirit guides outnumber the walking, breathing residents, and where "consciousness" is measured spiritually instead of medically. A land of moneyed, well-tanned, true enlightenment. Citizens with bad teeth or bad karma need not apply. How can a writer resist?

All I have to do is take a walk in my hometown of Mill Valley and my sense of place creates itself. One day, while I was standing at a corner waiting for the light to change, two women jogged up next to me. One woman said to the other, "I'm advising my clients against the futures market these days." Her friend said, "Oh, really. Why?" And the woman replied, "Because my channeler told me futures were just too dangerous considering my past lives." No, I'm not making this up! In fact, the incident was so strange I never did get to use it in a book. My real problem is toning down the reality of my real-life settings.

When I sent my first manuscript to my editor, she immediately called me on the phone. She couldn't believe they had tofu burgers at the local 7-Eleven in Mill Valley. But they do. Even my backdrops seem to pounce on me.

My husband says that every time I leave the house I come home with a new place for a murder. It's true. They follow me home like homeless kittens. Homeless kittens with teeth. I go to my chiropractor's and *bam*, someone gets their neck broken in *Adjusted to Death*. We go to a run-down health spa with gruesome brown, orange, and black paisley wallpaper and *The Last Resort* is born. And believe me, it's the last resort anyone would want to visit when I'm finished with it.

A comfy, warm soak in the hot tub leads to *Murder Most Mellow*. Of course, I started wondering how you could electrocute someone in a hot tub. I'm a mystery writer. I can't help it. Vegetarian cooking ends up *Fat-Free and Fatal*. A friendly family get-together blossoms into *Tea-Totally Dead* at the family reunion from hell. My mild-mannered mystery writers' critique group inspires *A Stiff Critique*. And attending my high school reunion...well, you remember the Jerk who was elected *Most Likely to Die*. The deserving Jerk.

Observe

So how do *you* find your own Jerks? Your own Victims? Don't worry, they'll find you. All you have to do is observe. When a drunk comes up to you at a party to regale you with tales of cruel revenge, listen. When a couple stands in front of you, arguing in hushed whispers, watch. When complete strangers yell at each other on the street, stand a little closer. You can probably smell their anger. If you work in a corporate office...'nuff said. There are fictional murders waiting to happen all around you.

> "When a couple stands in front of you, arguing in hushed whispers, watch."

It's amazing just how many potential homicides are in the air. Ask your friends if they've ever thought of murdering someone. You'd be surprised how many people have...in gruesome detail. I've had people tell me repeatedly that they've had friends who have literally gotten away with murder, and then those same people have described the gory circumstances to me. I try not to think that the "friend" might be the very person telling me the story. In fact, that might make an interesting plot right there. Now, let's think about it. What if the "friend"... Never mind. You see how it works. You can't run, you can't hide. The stories are just waiting to get you.

Experience

You can't write about something until you've experienced it. And you can't experience writing fiction until you've looked around you. And listened. And felt the emotional truth that lurks behind tears and false smiles. As writers, you can't help it. You're the ones who will go into a four-star restaurant and upon leaving neglect to discuss the great food but instead talk about the interactions you heard going on around you. "Did you see that couple? They'll be divorced in a year." "What do you think the relationship was between the white-haired lady and the young man with freckles? Lovers, mother and son, friends?" Victim and Jerk?

So, how do I plot and characterize? I meet people. But I never meet Jerks anymore. I only meet...*material*.

Jaqueline Girdner is the author of twelve Kate Jasper mysteries under her own name, and four Cally Lazar mysteries under the pseudonym of Claire Daniels. Jaqueline was also the Chair of the Mystery Writers of America Edgars Committee to choose the Best Mystery Novel of 2005. She lives, writes, and does tai chi with her husband, Greg, in Marin County, California.

Once You've Climbed Over the Transom

A book's progress from proposal to finished book

By Georgia Hughes

SO NOW YOU'VE HAD THE EXCITING CALL from your agent or an acquisitions editor with an offer from a publisher to publish your book. You thought this was the hard part, getting the agent to notice your work, finding the right editor at the right publishing house, waiting while the book proposal made its way through a labyrinth of meetings and readings, and finally, an offer!

Don't relax yet, the work is just beginning. Now the proposal must go on to become a manuscript suitable for a book, it must be set into type, a cover needs to be designed and printed, and, and, and...Enough! Let's back up and take this step by step.

You may be wondering about the meaning of this workshop's title. In publishing parlance, "over the transom" refers to manuscripts that come into a publishing house without being requested. Legend has it that when publishing houses were mostly small endeavors and when doors commonly had transoms over them which opened, writers would toss manuscripts through the open transoms to get them into editors' hands. Although manuscripts now arrive (often unrequested) via Federal Express, e-mail, and the postal service, the phrase has stuck.

And, while I'm going to assume you are writing a nonfiction book for the purposes of this workshop, most of what we will talk about applies to novels and other works of fiction. The big difference is that with a work of fiction—unless you are a well established author—you will be submitting a finished manuscript instead of a book proposal.

Publishing agreement (*the contract*)

This document grants the publisher the right to publish your book. It delineates the terms required of the author, what is expected of the publisher, and the payments due the author. This agreement also provides indemnity clauses for both the author and publisher. In other words, if the publisher decides against publishing the book, what happens? Or if the author collects the money but never delivers the book, what happens?

Most publishing agreements are based on an advance against future royalties. Simply stated, this means that the publisher is estimating the success of the book and offering you a bit of "up-front" money—the advance—in a gamble that the book will make that much in royalties for the author very soon. The royalties you will be paid as an author are stated as a percentage of the retail price of the book or as a percentage of the amount the publisher receives for each book.

The advance against future royalties is normally paid out to an author in stages, part on signing an agreement, part on acceptance of final manuscript for the book, and part on the publication of the book. Once a book is published, the royalties due are usually paid twice a year to the author, based on the continued sales of the book, and are accompanied by a royalty statement.

In addition to the royalties and the advance due, other agreement clauses that deserve special mention include: the grant of rights (what rights you are giving the publisher in addition to publishing the work in book form, which may include electronic rights, film rights, first and second serialization rights, and audio rights); territory in which the rights are granted (most publishers like to buy world rights); option clause (most publishers like to keep good authors; they want to have an option, usually with a time limit and usually in effect only after the time your first book is published, that grants them the right to decide whether they will publish your next book prior to your showing that book to other publishers); and the noncompetition clause (protecting the publisher from an author selling the same book to more than one house).

At the contract stage, the acquisitions editor will ask you when a final manuscript will be ready for publication. This is the "manuscript due date" that becomes part of the contractual agreement. As an author, you should be very careful when you provide this date to your editor. Publishing schedules hinge on these dates and your book can acquire the reputation of a "problem" book if it misses this important date.

Be realistic. Ask yourself, "When can the manuscript be ready?" Discuss this date with your editor. Find out if you deliver two months earlier if it can make an earlier season or if the marketing and editorial departments think your book might work better in one publishing season or another.

Cataloging

Most publishing houses work on either a two-season year or a three-season year, publishing a catalog featuring their new titles, called the front list, and listing their other titles, the back list, for each season. For a publisher using two seasons, the seasons are Spring (January through May) and Fall (June through December). Three seasons usually break down to Winter/Spring (January through April); Spring/Summer (May through August); and Fall (September through December). Traditionally, fall is the best time for gift books or high-priced books. The summer list is the list for good summer reading and lighter publishing. The season beginning in January is considered the best season for self-improvement books such as financial books, weight loss, healthy cooking books, and anything else having to do with New Year's resolutions. Your editor and publisher will have the best sense of where your book fits into the season, and they may have other concerns about the book's relation to other books on the list. Keep in mind that not all books are time sensitive.

The manuscript due date will be the peg from which your book's publication schedule hangs. If circumstances develop that make that date unrealistic, call your editor as soon as you are aware of the problem and discuss the date. As you read further in this workshop, you will see why dates become more and more unchangeable as the publication date approaches.

Now the agreement is signed, your advance is earning interest in your bank account, and the computer screen stares back at you each day when you sit down to write. While you ponder that blank screen, your acquisitions editor and publisher are busy deciding how to best present your book to the bookstores, wholesalers, and others they happily refer to as "the Trade."

Once a contract and due date are final, the editor assigns a publication date, a date on which the book will be in bookstores. That date then sets into motion all sorts of planning and activity. The book must have a cover; it must be assigned to editors who will line-edit; it must be put into the seasonal catalog; it must be presented to the sales representatives who then present it to bookstore buyers; it must be scheduled with the production department.

The usual production time for a text-heavy book (in other words, a book with mostly words that will be distributed through bookstores; textbooks and other technical books follow different schedules and require different approaches) is somewhere between nine months and one year. (Yes, the comparison to having a baby has been made before!)

Preparing your final manuscript

Be sure to ask your editor for manuscript preparation guidelines if these are not provided automatically. Most publishers now require manuscripts to be delivered on disk as well as in manuscript or hard copy form. Most also have preferences for the type of software you use. If you have an outdated program or what seems to be the wrong software, talk to your editor before racing out to buy new equipment or software. Typesetting service bureaus can translate disks from one format to another for minimal cost.

Keep any text formatting, such as bold or italic type and other type elements to a minimum. Type styles and special characters do not translate well from one computer format to another and a copy editor will be marking these things anyway. *Keep your text as clean and simple as possible!* If you want special layout or design elements, tell your editor, but don't try to lay out the book yourself. Double space the entire manuscript, including bibliography and note sections and any quoted material. Ask your editor if he prefers separate files for each chapter or part and if there are any specific ways to name the files.

Many manuscripts remain only in electronic form for many months into the production process. Editors review and request revisions using word processing programs that clearly show the editing and editor's comments. These files are emailed back and forth to the author and even to outside editors. Ask your editor if a printed copy is even necessary.

Book cover

Once a catalog season has been determined, the marketing, production, art, and acquisitions departments begin working with designers to design the best possible cover for the book. If you have always had a picture in your mind of what the cover should look like, by all means let your editor know. No promises will be made, but cover ideas must come from somewhere and publishers need fresh ideas.

The goal of a good cover is to convey the contents of the book in an inviting way, to appeal to the most likely audience of the book, and to clearly distinguish the book from others in the same category without looking like another category. You can see the challenge. While working on these issues, the designer and publisher will also need to adhere to a reasonable budget.

Catalog copy

Along with the progress of the cover design, someone—sometimes an in-house copywriter, sometimes an acquisitions editor, sometimes a marketing person, and sometimes a freelance writer—will be writing catalog copy. By the time a book is cataloged, the publisher has determined the price, estimated page count, format (either paperback or hardcover), trim size, and shelving category of a book. Since the catalog is the selling tool that is presented to the middleman—the buyer at independent bookstores and chain stores—the catalog copy should sell the book to bookstores and not to individual book buyers. Put simply, buyers are more concerned at this time with the appeal of this book to a wide audience than to the specific editorial content.

> "The usual production time for a book is somewhere between nine months and one year."

In addition to pricing, title, and cover, your book will be assigned an ISBN, which stands for International Standard Book Numbering, by the publisher. This number is unique to each book. The first number tells where the book was published and in what language (0 or 1 for the United States). The next series of numbers is the publisher number. This series can be as few as two or as many as six digits, depending on the size of the publisher and how many ISBNs they will need. The publisher also will obtain Library of Congress Cataloguing in Publication, or CIP, data. CIP data goes on the copyright page of the book and provides information used by librarians.

Production

Once your manuscript has been reviewed by an acquisitions editor, it is passed along to the production department. Usually, at this stage, the project editor takes over the project. This new editor will evaluate the manuscript for production purposes and schedule the manuscript's steps to become a book. Along the way, many more people will become involved in the book's progress, but your contact will remain the acquiring editor, who acts as ringmaster, keeping all of the performances going smoothly and juggling the schedule to make sure the book is published and in the stores at the appointed time.

Copyediting

Once the project editor has reviewed the manuscript, it will go to a copy–editor. Although every (or at least the best!) authors are extremely careful about checking spelling and grammar, everyone makes mistakes. The type of writing which works well for magazines or for other venues does not always measure up to a book length form. A copy editor, sometimes referred to as a line editor, goes through the manuscript word by word, correcting typing errors and other lapses and generally cleaning up the manuscript.

Copy editors also check for consistency in spellings of names or places, organization and repeated material, structure of the book, missing material, and all the other details necessary for a finished, final product. They may query authors about missing or unclear material or ask for citations for quoted material.

One other crucial aspect of their task is coding the manuscript for the typesetter. These codes are used by the typesetter or layout person to make sense of the various elements constituting a book design.

The copyedit on a book takes at least one month and may take much longer for longer or more complex books. If a book is technical in nature, it may need to be reviewed by a technical editor at the same time or prior to copyediting.

Once the edited manuscript is back, the production editor will go over the copyeditor's work and then send it along to the author. An author usually has two weeks to review the manuscript and answer any queries made. At this time, too, an author has the opportunity to question any changes a copy editor has made. Most production editors choose a copy editor carefully, mindful of what type of edit the book needs. Acquisitions editors suggest the level of edit: if the writing is weak and needs much work, the book may need to go through a developmental stage, with major revisions; if the ideas are well presented but the sentence structure is weak, the manuscript will need a heavy edit; if the manuscript is in very good shape, with just a few typos here and there, it will only need a light edit.

When you receive the edited manuscript, you may not understand the editorial marks used. (See Proofreader's Marks, page 362.) Many of the marks will be codes for the production aspect of the book. Authors should be most concerned about the contents and any changes to sentences.

Copy editors are chosen for their track records with similar books and their abilities to deal with different levels of editing. If you feel strong about your writing and don't want it changed, you should discuss this with your editor when you turn in the manuscript. Copy editors (and all editors) are working to make your book the best it can be, but it is your book. Be sure to question anything along the way that troubles you. All authors should know about the magic letters, STET, which stand, cryptically, for "let it stand." This notation, made in the margin of your manuscript, should override questionable changes the copy editor has made. Once you see the edited manuscript, you should talk to your editor if you think the editing is not right for your book.

Many houses are now doing the majority of their editing electronically. This system speeds up the process considerably and should help to avoid errors. Authors may receive a "clean" printout of the edited manuscript rather than a marked version. Changes made to a manuscript appear in different colors and whatever is then changed by the author appears in a third color.

Design

At the same time the manuscript is being copyedited it is being designed. Prior to working in a publishing house, I never thought about the interior of a book being designed. But it is.

The book designer makes the decisions about the size of type, the typeface to be used, the way the chapters open, how wide the margins are, and how the other parts of the book are put together. Often the interior design follows the cover design, incorporating whatever features are appropriate.

Layout

Once the design is approved, it is sent along with the manuscript to a layout person, sometimes called a compositor. The compositor takes the electronic version of the edited manuscript, creates a template using the design specifications, and flows the text into the design. A more difficult task than it may sound like, this takes approximately two weeks, depending on the complexity of the book. At this stage, the edited manuscript becomes page proofs, referred to as galleys. These used to be long sheets of preliminary printed pages, but with today's technology, these long galley sheets have become laser printed page proofs.

Flap and panel copy

While the manuscript is being prepared for book form in the editorial and production departments and the manufacturing department is ordering the paper and scheduling press time for the printing, the acquisitions department is working in conjunction with the sales and marketing department to produce copy that adequately describes the book to potential buyers—retailers, librarians, etc.—and consumers. This copy is often called the "flap and panel" copy, describing the places where the copy will appear—on the flaps of a book's dust jacket if it is hardcover or on the back panel of the cover if it is paperback.

To increase the book's appeal to the consumer market, the editor may solicit prepublication endorsements to be used as cover "blurbs." The editor will have a good idea of whether these are important for your book and how best to go about requesting them. However, editors depend on authors' expertise and personal connections in their fields to come up with experts from whom to solicit these endorsements.

The copy writer will put together the flap and panel copy, using the editor's guidelines and the final manuscript. Authors are consulted to make sure that the book is being represented correctly, and then the copy will be typeset and worked into the design of the jacket or cover of the book. If you have reviews of previous books or suggestions of marketing copy that should go on the book, be sure to pass these on to the editor.

Back in the production department, the page proofs are reviewed by the editor and by the author. At this stage, the pages are often proofread by a professional proofreader. However, proofreading is now often left up to the author and editor, mostly because of new technology. When books were actually typeset rather than electronically generated, typesetters could introduce errors. Now, in theory, the disk delivers the exact manuscript to layout and no errors can be introduced.

At the page proof stage, if the editors have decided one is appropriate, an index will be prepared. Most publishers prefer to have a professional indexer prepare an index—another task that is not as easy as it may sound.

On the home stretch

During this phase in a book's progress, the editor is assembling the final version of the book and making sure that any changes made along the way are being incorporated into the "good" version of the page proofs. This is a hectic time as the editor works to make the date scheduled for the book to be at the printer and the art department works to get the final cover art ready to be printed.

Finally, it is shipped to the printer and everyone waits, or more likely goes on to the next project, until the books come off the press.

The actual printing of the sheets, called signatures, which will become the book's pages, gathering and trimming these signatures, binding them, and putting on the cover, can take several weeks. The books are then shipped from the bindery to the warehouse, and review copies are sent to the publishing house. In a few more weeks, the books have worked their way from the warehouse into the bookstores that pre-ordered them, and it's time to begin publicizing the book.

Publicity

Actually, the publicity for a book begins months earlier, with advance copies of page proofs or bound galleys sent to advance reviewers such as *Publishers Weekly* and *Library Journal*. The majority of review copies are actual books sent to print media for review along with a press release. With book reviewers bombarded with new books, publicists sometimes group similar books, hoping for a review or feature article on the newest trend in cooking, for example, or another appropriate topic.

Publicists may set up radio tours, satellite tours, or live author tours. Many of the interviews broadcast on radio are not conducted face-to-face but via telephone. Publicists will also try to promote authors for television talk shows, especially in their hometown or where they have strong contacts.

> "Authors need to be as active as possible promoting their books."

Authors can assist publicists by keeping abreast of the events related to the publication of their books. If there has been attention to topics related to your book recently, be sure to let your publicist know.

Unfortunately, most publicity departments are understaffed and publicists will work on the books that they think have the highest sales potential and may not have time to do much for your book. Authors need to be as active as possible promoting their books. Even if your publicist is working hard to promote the book, keep in mind that each publicist works on many books each year and you've got only one book. Your promotions can be a determining factor in the book's sales. John Kremer's *1001 Ways to Market Your Books* is a valuable guide for authors and publishers and should be available at your bookstore or library.

Set up talks with groups you know will be interested in your topic. Call your local radio and television stations to see if they would be interested in interviewing you. If you have experience writing for magazines, try to put together articles related to your book to be published around the time of the book's publication. Are there any holidays or anniversaries of historic events related to your topic? If so, suggest the publicist focus on these. If your book is particularly appropriate for mothers, Mothers' Day may offer a good promotion opportunity, for example.

Contact any professional organizations or other groups who might have newsletters as possible reviewers of your book. A mention in an alumni magazine or a professional journal will reach many more people who might be interested than you might expect. Talk to bookstores in your area to set up a talk or storytelling with a book-signing. Although a book-signing may not sell many books, you may be able to attract media attention and be featured in the local paper.

Okay, so now the book has risen to the top of the best-seller list and all the people along the way who didn't see your book's potential are looking for other jobs in publishing. Sit back, relax, and think of the next book idea!

Georgia Hughes is editorial director at New World Library, where she acquires and edits nonfiction books in the areas of spirituality, personal growth, sustainable business, nature and animals, and women's issues. Before joining New World Library, Georgia worked in bookstores and at Harper San Francisco and Prima Publishing. According to Georgia, the acquisitions editor's job does not stop once the contract is signed. An editor should be the author's advocate and the book's champion throughout the publication process, shepherding the manuscript through the sometimes treacherous process of becoming a published book.

Writing the Compelling Novel

How to produce a page-turner

By Larry Martin

S O YOU WANT TO WRITE A NOVEL.
I'm constantly approached by folks who say, "I'm writing a novel and wonder where I should sell it," or "...would you take a look at it for me?" And I normally answer, "Have you written before?" and if the reply is "No," I ask, "Have you attended any writer's conferences?"

It's amazing to me how many "no's" I get to both questions. Why is it amazing?

If you were going to perform a heart transplant, wouldn't you expect to do a little research on blood vessels and muscle tissue? Especially if you wanted the recipient to live?

How about building a house? Wouldn't you set out to learn the secrets of the contractor's trade? Or at least learn to identify a claw hammer from a jigsaw?

If you set out on a complicated process like writing a novel—one you mean to sell—wouldn't you try to learn the basics? Not a lot of folks. I guess most of us—and I admit I was one of them—think that reading makes us an expert at writing.

It's not true. I found out the hard way, which is the reason I've compiled this workshop. And I'm pleased you're reading it, because I know you're already to the spot to which it took me years to get—because you've cracked the cover of *The Portable Writer's Conference*. Which means you're studying and trying to *learn* your craft. Believe me, you've made a great decision, and taken one major step toward getting published.

Take me. I'm a guy who loves to hunt and fish. I'll get outdoors for any excuse. I love the West and its history and think I'd have done just fine had I lived 150 years ago. As the song says, a country boy will survive. But to publish a novel in any genre—I write westerns—you need more than a love of your subject. Like all endeavors—be it driving an eighteen-wheeler, driving a nail or doing nails—there are tricks that make writing a novel easier. There are also pitfalls, but, like land mines, most of them are easily avoided if you know what they are and where they are.

Yet, even today, after selling twenty novels, I fight obvious errors and poor grammar, clumsy sentence structure and worse, *much worse*, boring text. I can't even begin to teach you all there is to know about writing novels or even all there is to know about writing a good letter to your mother. But if I can make your trail a little easier, then I've accomplished my purpose in writing this workshop.

So, what do you as a new novelist shoot for? The finest compliment I get as a novelist is, "I read your book in one sitting." Even if the reader hated it, it was compelling! A page-turner. OK, let me qualify that compliment by reminding you that generally, the westerns I write are short—other than an insomniac speed-reader, no one could read *War and Peace* in one sitting. Still, that your book is *compelling*—a page-turner—is, in my opinion, the greatest compliment a writer can get.

I've only been given space for the most basic look at the craft, so now that we know what we're shooting for, let's ride on.

A novel is a fictional story with a beginning, middle and end. It has characters, plot, time and place. The trick is to bring those four elements together in a *compelling* read.

Theme

But before we get to all that, let me toss is a quick word or two about theme. Your novel should have one. Editors and readers want your novel to have a theme—and so do you. Good triumphs over evil is probably the most common. You can't keep a good man down. A good woman is hard to find. As ye sow, so shall ye reap. Cheat me once, you're a fool; cheat me twice, I'm a fool. Themes. It helps you plot your novel if you have a theme. It helps drive you as you write your novel; it's the road map that gets you where you're going, to The End. Stay with it throughout the story, and prove it with what you write.

Plotting and conflict

Lonesome Dove, by Larry McMurtry, is the story of a cattle drive. It begins in Texas and ends in Montana and takes months. Simple. Straightforward. No complicated flashbacks to deal with. A Pulitzer Prize winner.

Your novel can be a simple journey—from here to there. Or it can be a quest—the sheriff goes after the killer or vice versa, the heroine wants the hero, the detective wants to solve the crime.

Seven Minutes takes place in seven minutes. Other novels are set over generations or eons in James Michener's case.

There are as many ways to approach the plot as there are motes of dust on the Chisholm Trail. Yet all plotting styles must be filled with drama. Drama in every scene. And conflict in every scene, for drama is conflict, and a scene is not a scene without conflict of some sort. I'm going to repeat that, because it's a critical part of writing *compelling* novels. Write no scene without conflict.

Every scene must have conflict of some kind or it shouldn't be in your story. (Got it yet?) If there's no conflict, then it's only a transition, getting your story from one place to another or from one time to another, and a transition deserves no more than a paragraph, usually at the beginning or ending of a scene. We'll get to more about scenes in a minute.

The conflict can be man against man, man against the elements, man against animal, man against woman, or man against himself. (Switch the genders in the previous sentence and it works just as well.) Your story is about your hero overcoming one or all of them. No one wants to read about a pleasant cattle drive across grass-filled plains dotted with water holes in wonderful weather where everyone gets along famously. Or to be more succinct, *where nothing happens*! Boring!

So, what's a plot?

Plot is defined by my trusty *Random House Dictionary* as:

> ..also called story line, the plan, scheme, or main story of a literary or dramatic work, as a play, novel, or short story.

There's that word drama again. So what exactly is drama? Drama is defined by *Random House* as:

> A composition in prose or verse presenting in dialogue or pantomime a story involving conflict or contrast of character...any situation or series of events having vivid, emotional, conflicting, or striking interest or results.

Notice: The definition of drama includes the words character and conflict.

A good novel, like any good drama format, is about trial and tribulation, success and failure, and, hopefully, riveting head-to-head conflict that makes it a compelling read.

So your plot, whether it be journey or quest, must have characters experiencing some sort of conflict. Your job is to fill 300 or so pages of 250 words each with compelling characters engaged in hard-hitting conflict.

I have taken you in a circle, plot, drama, conflict, plot, to say just this:

Conflict and its resolution make compelling reading.

Now, for those of you who are as hardheaded as I am, and who still don't get this conflict thing, go back to where I wrote "So you want to write a novel," and begin rereading this workshop. The rest of us, I think, can mosey on.

Where to start

I'm a character–driven writer. I like to create interesting characters and let them run with the story. Kat, my wife, who writes best-selling romance novels, is plot driven. She knows exactly where her story is going when she sits down and types "Chapter One." Neither approach is right or wrong. Well...her way is probably more right, and softens the dreaded, but always necessary rewrite, but it doesn't work for me. I have to hammer out my novels the hard way. Whichever way works for you is right, but either way, it helps to have your basic story in mind. Think it through first, at least the main plot points.

Point-of-View

I've got a point of view about most subjects, so do you, so does your mother-in-law, but that's not the kind of point of view we're talking about.

Point–of–view, as it applies to the craft of writing, is through whose eyes the action is seen. Before you plot your novel, you must determine in which point of view it is to be written.

Probably more otherwise good novels are trashed by editors because of inconsistent point of view than for any other technical reason.

Basically, you have two choices: First person point of view or third person point of view.

You can't wander away from the direct line-of-sight view of the storyteller if you write your novel in the first person. This is the "I" point of view.

> I made sure my Walker rode free and easy in the holster as the cackler rose from his ladder-back chair.

That's first person.

> Ethan hoisted his Walker, making sure it rode free and easy, as the cackler rose from the ladder-back chair.

That's third person.

If the point of view then shifts to the cackler, then to the barmaid across the room, it's third person omniscient. The all-seeing eye. It's the third person omniscient point of view that I chose to use in my book with Ethan as a character.

Since I chose omniscient, I could have gone on to begin the next paragraph or the next chapter:

> Meanwhile, back at the ranch...

You can't do that in first person. You can't go to the ranch in your writing unless you take your first person observer to the ranch. Simple? No, it's not simple for me. I still fight proper point of view every time I write, but at least now when an editor or another writer ask me, "What's your point of view?" I don't launch into a political observation or my opinion about the latest news story on the tube.

A first person point of view cannot have flashbacks unless the protagonist—99 percent of all first person novels are written from the hero's point of view—is the one thinking about the flashback. A first person point of view cannot see or hear something that's happening in the next room, next building, or next town. First person limits your plot...or at least your approach to your plot. For that reason, most novels and certainly most westerns and historicals are written in third person omniscient.

I keep a sign over my desk that says "Filter all description through point of view." Why? Because by not doing so, you're engaging in author intrusion; by doing so, it gives your reader a great insight into the character of your characters. Let me show you what I mean.

> Miss Mary Jane Petersen crossed the boardwalk and paused in front of the batwing doors. Taking a tentative breath, then a deep one, she smoothed her linen skirt. Finally, boldly, back stiff and chin held high, she entered.
>
> The room, filled with bawdy men, reeking of tobacco smoke and sweat, stopped her short. The clamor silenced as all eyes turned to her—but she was careful not to meet them. She strode on, moving to the plank bar and finding the gaze of the curious barkeep.
>
> "Your proprietor. Mr. Oscar Tidwell, please," she said, carefully keeping her voice from cracking.

Or:

> Miss Mary Jane Petersen crossed the boardwalk and paused

in front of the batwing doors. Tucking her loose-fitting blouse in tightly—purposefully straining it against her ample bosom, which she had long known was her best feature—she pushed boldly into the saloon. The smell of working men always made her pocketbook itch, and now was no different.

Bawdy men paused and surveyed her as she strode across the room to the plank bar, then went back to their faro and poker and whiskey.

The barkeep shined a mug as she approached. He, too, let his eyes drift to the straining fabric. It was all she could do not to openly smile. Men were so easily manipulated.

"The boss, please...Mr. Tidwell."

Do you get two different opinions about Miss Mary Jane? Even though the bar scene is basically the same?

Now that you've decided to write in a given point of view, you can proceed with your novel.

Pace and brevity

I can't think of a faster way to get me to lay a novel down than to layer in too much extraneous description. Many writers, and many editors too, love a novel dripping—no, gushing—with description. Many writers are great at this "purple prose," but give me a lean one every time.

Take, for example, *The Bridges of Madison County* by Robert James Waller. A small hardback which had a modest first printing—but a book that got legs, as they say in the trade, and became one of the best-selling novels of all time. The reason is that it says a great deal in its 171 pages. Waller does this with a simple turn of a number of great similes and metaphors. With brevity, when you're writing about unrequited love, and your character is aging with "dust on his heart," as is Mr. Waller's protagonist, you don't have to say a lot more.

If you want to keep your pacing fast, you do it with brevity. Read *The Bridges of Madison County* and find brevity at its best.

But here's a caveat about pacing. Readers want conflict. Give them conflict! A story with high emotion. But no one wants a single-emotion read. By that I mean your plot has to be well-paced. If your hero wakes up facing a band of hostile warriors, escapes them to run into a grizzly, escapes it to be chased by wolves—it's a single-emotion read and will be no more compelling than the cattle drive where nothing happened.

You want to build emotion throughout the novel to the climax. A series of conflicts is fine, in fact necessary, but intersperse a few relaxed, reflective moments at the campfire. He's in trouble, he's out, he's in deeper, he's out, he's in deeper yet, until the conclusion when he's home free—or however you end it. A great method to create compelling reading is to constantly throw your hero into deeper and deeper trouble, but only when paced with reflective scenes in between the action.

A Percy by any other name...

Just a quick note about character names. I don't know about you, but most people have a preconceived notion of names and the characters they're attached to. I wouldn't name my hero Percy. Not that Percy's not a nice name. But it connotes an English butler to me—unless my hero's an English butler, then Percy is fine.

Another hint about names that's important: It's tough enough to follow a novel, particularly one you pick up and put down, without having an author name a couple of primary characters Eloise and Elliott. There are twenty-six letters in the alphabet. Don't set out to confuse your readers. Make it as easy on them as you can by naming characters with easily identifiable handles. Name them Able, Bart, Charles, Darwin, Elliott, Ferdinand...not necessarily in that order, but you get the picture.

If you're writing historicals, use names from the time. Jed and Isaac, for instance, were common names in the mid 1800s and connote a feeling of time and place to the reader.

Scene

OK, let's get back to scenes. What's a scene? Now that you're off and away writing, and you know what's an acceptable novel length, who your primary characters are and something about your plot, write in scenes. A scene is an action sequence. By action, I mean where something happens that moves the plot forward or shows characterization. It doesn't have to be a fist fight or a car chase; it can be the hero having a conversation about going to the box social with the heroine and it can be in her point of view or in his, or you can change point of view in the middle of the scene—I don't recommend it, but you can. But remember, except for scenes that dramatically reveal characterization, there's a rule: The scene's primary ingredient is conflict. If it doesn't have conflict, it's not a scene and should be trashed.

Your heroine tells your hero she would prefer he didn't bid on her basket; he says it's a free world. Besides, she makes the best apple pie in town. That's conflict. Not the most exciting conflict, but it will make a scene. If they talk about going to the box social and there's no conflict, make it one sentence of another scene or a short paragraph of transition.

How long is a scene? How long does it take? You can have one scene to a chapter or several scenes. You can break chapters in the middle of a scene—a Louis L'Amour trick. It makes for compelling reading because many readers put a novel down only when they've finished a chapter. It's hard to do in the middle of some kind of conflict, even if the chapter has ended.

Louis L'Amour was a master of chapter endings and beginnings. He often ended his chapters with a question, a question the reader wanted answered, so the reader read on. When the reader finished, he told his friends he couldn't put Louie's novel down.

One of the best writing tips I can give you, the one that will help make your writing more compelling, is to enter a scene late and leave a scene early. No one gives a damn if your characters greet each other! "Hello, how are you?" generally adds nothing to a scene. Neither does "goodbye." Enter the scene just before the conflict, or during the conflict, and leave the scene during or just after the conflict.

Now that you know about plotting and conflict and theme and point of view and scenes, charge forward.

That's my advice: Put on your spurs and your chaps, climb into the saddle and charge forward. Writing the novel will present you with hard-to-anticipate questions we may or may not have discussed. You can't find the answers until you know the questions. But believe you me, plenty of sly questions will raise their fuzzy little heads as you write, and then you'll find the answers. And then you'll have a published novel.

Happy trails.

***Larry Martin** is the best-selling author of nineteen westerns, historicals, and thrillers and one western romance co-written with his internationally best-selling wife, Kat Martin, who has forty novels to her credit published in a dozen languages.*

Write for the Trades

Mine this 6,000-plus
magazine market for clips and cash

By Mary E. Maurer

MOST BEGINNING WRITERS DREAM of seeing their byline in one of the high-profile consumer magazines read by their friends and family. While that is a worthy ambition, the consumer magazine field is extremely competitive. Many writers get discouraged and give up. Others occasionally sell to the big names, but not often enough to pay the rent or even the light bill. Yet, you can supplement your income and your ego by writing for a somewhat hidden market: trade publications.

There are thousands of opportunities for writers in trade, technical, and professional journals. I stumbled upon the trade field quite by accident, as many writers do, when I agreed to write a profile about the business of a friend. Now half of my income is derived from trade magazines. These publications serve a readership united by occupation or industry, avocation or education. There are also many "trades" serving members of associations or unions. Here are some examples:

• *Corrections Today*—This is the official publication of the American Correctional Association. Typical topics? Here are a few titles from recent issues: "How to Improve Employee Motivation, Commitment, Productivity, Well Being, and Safety," "Jail Time Is Learning Time," "Girls in Gangs: On the Rise in America." Go to their website at aca.org and click on "publishing and periodicals" for article archives, editorial calendar, and submissions guidelines.

• *CIO*—This magazine serves the needs of information executives. Subjects of interest here are information technology, secrets of success, data management, etc. Visit their website at cip.com, scroll all the way to the bottom of the home page and click on "about us" for editorial information.

• *Fire Chief*—This publication caters to fire chiefs and emergency response managers. Recent concerns: evacuations, staffing, increased demand for services. Visit firechief.com and view their editorial guidelines at "about us."

• *Wildlife Society Bulletin*—The focus of this magazine is on wildlife conservation and appeals not only to those working in the field, but those contributing to the effort. Two of their recent titles: "White-Tailed Deer Management Practices on Private Lands in Arkansas," and "A Technique to Estimate the Approximate Size of Photographed Bats." For more information, go to wildlifejournals.com.

• *The Rotarian*—This monthly is aimed at Rotarian businessmen and their families. From their guidelines: "The best way to get acquainted with *The Rotarian* and for us to get acquainted with you, is to break in with a short itme in our monthly Field Reports section. Items in this section usually run 200 to 600 words and focus on the work of Rotarians in the field, highlighting successful, innovative Rotary programs and projects." Got to rotary.org and visit their "newsroom."

As you can see from this small sampling, trades have a lot to offer their readers. They carry business-related news of new products and trends, features on successful businesses and their owners or managers, and service pieces on solving employee and/or customer problems. Within major occupations and industries there are often magazines for specific aspects such as marketing, buying, selling, design, production, training, etc. Some publications carry more technical information than others. Association magazines tend to have the most general information, but others also cover general topics such as health, safety, and travel in regular departments.

Why write for the trades? Trades cater to the needs of their readers, but they also have a lot to offer writers. Writing for the trades is an excellent way for you to hone your craft and be published regularly. You'll gain confidence and build up that all-important clip file.

Once you become an expert in a particular field and have the clips from trade magazines to prove it, you'll have more clout with editors of consumer magazines. Consistent sales give your work more credibility. However, keep in mind that writing for the trades isn't just a stepping stone to "bigger and better." Editors of trade magazines deserve, and demand, your best effort. You may also find writing for them so satisfying that it becomes the mainstay of your career.

Writing for the trades enables you to build a relationship with an editor, since many work with small staffs and are eager to find hard-working, serious writers. You may find trade editors more willing to talk to you on the phone, more willing to make assignments, and more willing to listen to new ideas.

Writing for the trades can provide you with a steady income, even if you do get that byline in *The New Yorker.* Pay for trade articles averages $50 to $200 for 1,200 to 1,800 words.

Do you have what it takes? That depends on two things:

• Are you serious about writing? Articles written for the trades are informative, instructional, technical. They are rarely just entertaining. That means your writing must be clear and focused for a specific purpose and audience. Does your current writing contain a lot of profiles or how-to articles? Do you have a knack for explaining technical material?

• Are you willing to become an "industry expert"? Writers wishing to break into the trade market need to have or develop a strong understanding of the occupation or industry. You *must* know your subject thoroughly. Do you like to learn about other occupations? Do you like to talk to people about what they do and how they do it? Are you interested in advertising, new products, or business trends?

> "Trade magazine editors want new ideas; they don't require Pulitzer Prize winners."

Not intimidated yet? Good, because most skillful writers of nonfiction can write for the trades. According to Steven Austin Stovall, customer service expert and experienced trade writer, "Trade magazine editors want new ideas; they don't require Pulitzer Prize winners."

To become a trade expert, begin by examining your own profession, your "day job." What do you know? What skills do you possess? What is your educational background? What intrigues you?

Next, think about your hobbies. There are trade and business aspects of every hobby, from quilting to oil painting. If you like to sew you can interview the owner of your favorite fabric store. Or find out how fabric and thread are made and what new innovations are ahead. Wood carver? Write about logging, milling, carving tools. Artist? Write about appraisers, art galleries, arts management, architects. The possibilities are everywhere.

Whom do you know? Investigate the careers of friends or family members. Does anyone have an occupation you find fascinating? I wrote three articles, for separate publications, about a friend who developed a unique way of painting T-shirts and started a successful business. Look at your community. Is there a businessman who is particularly successful? One of my favorite articles was a profile for *Miniatures Dealer*. I wrote about two brothers who used their talents to open one of their city's best hobby shops. You may want to interview similarly successful people in your area.

Look at the larger area around your community. Is it rural or urban? Are you surrounded by farmers? Is your town or area of the country famous for a particular product? Do you live near a tourist attraction? How is it managed? Who would be interested in the technical or business aspects of it? Are you near a major highway with lots of truck traffic? Airport or rail station nearby?

> "Very often your general interests can be focused and developed so you can write for a trade publication..."

Now look at your current writing interests. Very often your general interests can be focused and developed so you can write for a trade publication in the same field. I took my interests in children and education and became an expert in preschool education. I have written for *Texas Childcare*, *Mailbox*, *Christian Education Counselor*, *Christian Home and School*, and others. Interested in gardening? Become an expert in commercial gardening and write for *Growertalks*, a publication catering to commercial greenhouse growers. Do you like to read about health topics? Increase your knowledge of physical fitness and write for *Fitness Management*, the magazine for commercial, corporate, and community fitness centers. Here are some other general topics and their trade counterparts:

- Religion—Church administration, education, counseling, childcare, education, school administration, religious education, teaching (by type, such as public school, private school, dance, theater, etc. and by grade)

- Sports—sports retailing, fitness, campground management, sports medicine

- Travel—transportation, manufacturing (autos, airplanes, recreational vehicles), travel industry

To consider yourself an expert in a given field you need to see beyond the basics of "who, what, when, and where," to "how" and "why" and "what's next." If you want to write for *Farm Journal*, you can't just back up your writing with those wonderful memories of grandpa's farm in Iowa. You need to understand the history of agriculture in our nation and its future in the global market. You need to understand the controversy between huge corporate operations and small farmers. You need to know the different challenges facing farmers raising crops and those raising animals. You need to know about new trends in agriculture, regulations regarding pesticide use, the growing interest in exotic animals, etc. You need to give farmers accurate, practical information about farm management in today's economy. And more specifically, for *Farm Journal*, you need to write about corn, wheat, milo, soybeans, cotton, dairy cows, beef cattle, or hogs. By contrast, for *Western Hay Magazine* you need to write about hay growing, processing and marketing. Narrow your focus to as small a segment of the industry as possible. It will be easier to learn everything you need to know to qualify as an expert!

You may also want to specialize in a particular type of article. Most trade magazines use one of the following types of articles:

- profile (of successful owners, managers, businesses)

- how to (cut costs, increase production, stop shoplifters)

- forecast (technical trends, industry changes)

- product report (what's new, what it does, and who is using it)

- history (profiles of those who helped shape the industry)

- health and safety (tips on increasing worker productivity through healthy habits and accident prevention)

Once you decide on the area of expertise you wish to develop you have several options. Of course you'll do the reading and research you would for any writing topic. However, for the trades you'll also need to follow these steps to becoming an expert:

• Develop contacts within the industry. Talk to real people. See how they work. Talk to them about their problems. Develop a list of technical people you can call on for information. You may even wish to have someone proof-read technical material for you.

• In addition to general magazines and books, read technical reports, manuals, and trade journals. You don't have to understand everything, but you need to know where your knowledge and your writing fit in the "big picture" of the industry.

• Attend workshops and conferences. You'll pick up useful information, see new products, meet new people.

• Visit stores, manufacturing plants, farms, whatever is connected to your interest.

OK, now you're an expert. You're ready to write. But first you have to study the trade publications market. This is one area of writing where you can't fake it. You *must* know and understand your audience. Readers of trade publications have very specific expectations. The *Writer's Handbook* and the *Writer's Market* both list trade magazines, but you'll find the most extensive list in the *Encyclopedia of Associations*, published by Gale Research. It lists trade, business, and commercial organizations, educational organizations, hobby and avocational organizations, and others. You'll find the address, year founded, name of publication, circulation, staff, and interesting bits of information. The *Encyclopedia* is available in the reference department of most large libraries. *The American Directory of Writer's Guidelines: More than 1700 Magazine Editors and Book Publishers Explain What They Are Looking for from Freelancers* contains over 1,100 magazine guidelines, many of them trades. Since these guidelines are written by the periodicals' editors, they do an excellent job of providing clues to writers interested in submitting work. You'll also glean useful information from reading *Folio, Bacon's Publicity Checker*, and *Advertising Age*.

You can find copies of several trade publications at your nearest university library, or you can order sample copies. Study at least six for your area of interest. Read as many issues as you can. Examine the contents. What is the purpose of the magazine? Study the style and format. Does the magazine use second or third person, active or passive voice? How is technical information handled? What about buzzwords, jargon? Every occupation has a certain amount of "industry-specific language." How does the magazine use graphics, photos? Read the advertising. What is being sold? Who is the target customer?

In particular, study the departments. This is often the area where it is easiest for a newcomer to break in. Departments cover more general topics and are more concise than features.

When considering topics, don't forget the basics: management, employee training, bookkeeping, advertising, delegation, safety, education, etc. There are basic issues of concern for every industry and occupation. Just be sure to give them the correct slant and focus.

Write a brief letter of introduction to each editor detailing your knowledge and background in the industry. Include your resume and published clips if they are pertinent. Ask for a copy of their writer's guidelines, and an editorial calendar if one is available.

Once you receive the publication's guidelines, study and *follow* them. Remember that editors of trade magazines are looking for the same things every editor wants: new ideas, good writing, clean copy. Don't submit sloppy work or save your best writing for the "big markets."

Your work, and your chances of being published regularly, will also be enhanced by photos, charts, sidebars, etc. Trade magazines often have small staffs, and editors are thrilled to find writers who are handy with a camera. Also, give your article visual impact by breaking it into clearly defined sections with bullets, headings, etc.

Editors of trade magazines are eager for new trends, the latest discoveries, the next "great idea." The best way to be successful in the trades is to find your niche and be knowledgeable and dependable! Once you are established as a dependable writer, be prepared to accept assignments, even multiple assignments.

And even if you don't become famous, you'll be working too much to notice.

Mary Maurer is a freelance writer and kindergarten teacher who specializes in childcare and education topics. She has three children and three grandchildren. Her writing has appeared in The Writer, Writer's Journal, Byline, Parenting, Miniatures Dealer, True Story, The Dallas Morning News, Instructor, Mature Living, Flower and Garden, The Durant Daily Democrat, The Daily Oklahoman, *and* Birds and Blooms. *She is currently working on an historical novel and also maintains a history and genealogy weblog at http://mem55.typepad.com/caddo_my_home_town/.*

Listen!

How to use dialogue to light up your characters
until they attract readers like moths to a flame

By Parke Godwin

"NARRATIVE IS NO PROBLEM, BUT I HAVE AN AWFUL time with dialogue." Of all the writers I know, only one ever said dialogue was easy for her. She then added that she couldn't plot worth a damn. For far more writers, by admission or demonstration, the opposite seems to be true.

Good dialogue convinces the reader, depicts the characters clearly and moves the plot. After I decided to throw some light on this subject, I found myself worrying at the root of the problem like a pup at a slipper. Why is dialogue a common stumbling block? Why should something writers hear and speak every day suddenly freeze them up when they try to capture it on the page?

Hearing is one key. We all hear English differently as the words sift through our experience of and meanings for them. In the positive sense this makes for diversity of style; in the negative the writers aren't hearing conversation at all, they're writing for the eye and mind, not the ear.

Why? I'll give it a shot: Their education gets in the way.

Trying to nail down this insight, I thought back through the whole uninspired educational process America foists on children. We're taught to write in complete sentences with punctuation in the right places, and we're graded on the relative success of our results. We are necessarily writing for a judicial eye. "This has got to be the best I can do, gotta be right or I won't get a good mark, get the job, impress the person I'm writing to." Small wonder that when we try to put words into fictional mouths, we restimulate these memories and freeze up, even to an avoidance of letter writing. The words come stiff and awkward because habit is working dead against talent and instinct, so you don't get the ring of truth—and remember, ring is a sound, not a word on paper. Unconsciously the writer strives by habit to be correct, putting down not how they would sound but how they should.

Granted, professional fiction requires a certain literacy. More than this it takes a supple facility with language, but don't let grammar lessons or the layered habits of school get in the way; they can be ruinous inhibitors. There are legions of highly educated people (and, God knows, educators) unable to write or even converse without putting you to sleep. Their graduate and doctoral theses molder undisturbed in university libraries.

The first rule in writing "natural" dialogue—hey, like someone's saying it for real—is to forget your grammar and education and *hear* it.

People don't usually think or speak in complete sentences. A person with a grammatical tic may annoy purists, but such verbal habits can illuminate the character and bring him to life. You've heard the guy who buttonholes his listener by adding "know what I mean?" to so many sentences. Or the speaker who makes a redundant sentence out of what should be a subordinate clause: "...a love affair between two men, which she didn't approve of that at all."

You hear this often in conversation, if you listen like a writer, and I wonder if the person isn't compulsively honoring the moss-grown rule about not dangling a preposition at the end of a sentence. But people *do* when they speak naturally. I've used both of the above tics to good advantage in fiction.

Given that good dialogue lights up the character with his own spontaneous words, you should have a clear idea of that person's "sound"—which is compounded of his background, education and experience, and his emotional makeup, all within the work's chosen style. People don't talk in any consistent style all the time, but in fiction dialogue must be appropriate to the story setting, tone and characters. Let's consider four basic types.

Informal dialogue

Naturalistic or "kitchen sink" dialogue is people expressing themselves informally and the hell with grammar, if the characters knew it to begin with. A classic example is the famous taxi scene from *On the Waterfront*:

> "You don't understand, Charley. I coulda been a contender. I coulda been somebody. Instead of a bum which is what I am, let's face it."

The Brando character, Terry Molloy, probably never went beyond the tenth grade or his own neighborhood and sounds like it. The ear again. The advantage of good naturalistic dialogue is that it moves like a shot, carries the reader along with it. Also the short conversational lines leave a good deal of white space on the page, much more attractive and restful to the reader's eye than long, thick paragraphs.

Here's a good technique that's worked well for me. When I have to talk about a character in narrative, whenever suitable, I like to have him or her break in to the narrative, often in the middle of a sentence, with their own typical comments, like this passage from my *Lord of Sunset*:

> Mother was everywhere, badgering the cooks, fretting over supplies not arrived, upstairs and down...counting linens twice over, seeing to the hanging of holly ropes—
>
> "Don't put it there; it goes *there*. And use smaller nails. It's holly you're putting up, not a gallows."
>
> —and finding time that afternoon before the wedding to bathe and dress me herself.

The above example is a very long single sentence, giving the sense of a mother's perpetual motion preparing for Christmas and her daughter's wedding all at once. I made it more palatable and vivid by breaking in with the mother's harried line of dialogue.

One of my major gripes in naturalistic dialogue, one which dulls much modern fiction and too many films, is excessive profanity or obscenity. This seems to be a pitfall for very young writers or those who never have or never will grow up. "Look at me being gritty and street smart." Come on, we're all big people, we know all the nasty words. Beyond a certain point—very quickly reached—this verbal grime doesn't move the story or illuminate character. It's a lazy copout that no longer frightens horses in the street, merely annoys and ultimately bores an intelligent reader. Sure, people use pungent language and always have, but art cannot imitate life completely and remain art. In this case, "wherein a little more than a little is by much too much"—trust me, less is more.

Then again, if it's right for the character to be salty, make sure you and the reader know why. Justify the choice. In *Limbo Search*, my science fiction novel, the burnout fighter pilot Janice Tyne is a woman at the end of her career and psychological rope at twenty-seven. She can't be what she's been anymore, but she's terrified of the future. Her X-rated dialogue is a symptom of fear and tension; otherwise she'd be an unattractive character with no more than a habitually dirty mouth, and that's never very interesting.

Realistic dialogue

Realistic dialogue, while appearing deceptively natural, is more organized. The vast bulk of modern plays and fiction employ this style combined with naturalistic. Classic examples are Miller's *Death of a Salesman*, Chayefsky's screenplay for *Network*, or William Goldman's piquant tongue-in-cheek dialogue for *Butch Cassidy and the Sundance Kid* or *The Princess Bride*. From the last:

> "You seem a good fellow. I hate to kill you."
> "You seem a good fellow. I hate to die."

Pitfalls in realistic lines are the lack of accurate ear and the old bugaboo of educational freeze-up. One can be so organized, correct and formal that the lines go flat and lose the sound of people talking to each other. Read it aloud and *listen*, please. Your reader will thank you. If that reader is I, I'll thank you profusely and maybe buy your next book as well.

Another dangerous copout in realistic is putting quote marks around what is obviously pure plot exposition and passing it off as dialogue. This needs little explanation; we've all seen examples. The following horror is not from any published source, but one I made up during a lecture to demonstrate:

> "Meanwhile, alarmed by the growth of the Protestant Reformation in the north, Rome's answer was to found the Jesuit order."

Writers who call this dialogue should be restricted to occasional postcards. They haven't taken the trouble to put exposition where it belongs, and they don't fool anyone.

Heightened realism

Here we come to a style I've loved since discovering the riches of Anouilh, Shaw, Dylan Thomas and others of that silver-tongued ilk. Heightened realism is realism with music and the lights turned up high. The language shimmers with wit and a cutting edge. Your ear *and* your syntax are vital here because of the economy and crispness the style demands. Nothing dulls a lucid passage more than too many words. Nothing kills a good line deader than one word too many or in the wrong place. More than once I've winced at my own finished work on the printed page and moaned, "Why didn't I cut that word? Why didn't I invert the whole line?" Never mind how well it reads; how does it *play*?

In *Robin and the King*, a son of William the Conqueror is speaking of his royal father. I could have given him the line thus:

"My father is very devout. He wants to understand the will of
God and the English people but cannot comprehend either."

Historically and hopelessly correct with none of the tart flavor of bluff,
rowdy Rossel who became William II. The line carried the same meaning with
far more bite and economy this way:

"Father is fascinated by things he can't understand. Like God
and England."

And in *Camelot*, Arthur wonders of Guinevere:

"Why is Jenny in that castle? How did we come to this agoniz-
ing absurdity? Where did I stumble?...Should I not have loved her?
Then I should not have been born."

Read that line again. Taste the flavor and the lean muscularity of "ago-
nizing absurdity." Not a phrase you'd hear in realistic dialogue, but so beautifully expressive and precise, a bonus HR affords to those who work for it.
Another favorite example is Eleanor of Acquitaine to her sons in *The Lion in
Winter*:

"Good, good Louis. If I'd managed sons for him instead of all
those little girls, I'd still be stuck with being queen of France and
we should not have known each other. Such, my angels, is the role
of sex in history."

The last two examples are from stage works, true, but there's no reason
why such supple language won't work as HR in prose. Because in HR you're
going a little beyond realism, slightly
larger than life. The style is more suited
to fantasy and historical fiction than a
contemporary setting. The main danger
here is going too far, falling in love with
verbal agility and cleverness for its own
sake (said one of the guilty), but there's
a sturdy cure. In rewrite be a hanging
judge with an honest ear and a long blue
pencil.

> "Good
> dialogue
> convinces,
> bad does
> not."

For a moment let's consider that
honest ear, so necessary to any style from "kitchen sink" to the transcendent
lines of Shakespeare. Good dialogue convinces, bad does not. The magic difference is human truth, which we achieve by living and listening for what makes
humans tick. "The players cannot keep counsel; they'll tell all." So they will,

but you have to listen in depth. Bearing this in mind, let's come to the last category.

Larger than life

Call it lyrical or poetic if you will. In LTL you're presenting truth in a big way. The nature of this style pretty much limits its use in prose to works of high fantasy or magic realism, although Ray Bradbury's early and middle period work made brilliant use of LTL and HR combined. Since the dumbing-down of media-addicted America, many people might find this hard to read, if they read at all, so economy, concision and truth are all-important. You have to be secure in your ear, cadence and command of language. Nothing falls flatter than lyrical language that doesn't sing or soar. So put this down in large letters over your word processor: *High language does not mean highflown.*

Highflown is what you get when words for their own effect inflate beyond the emotional truth they're charged to convey. Put another way, you can take the language as high as the emotional truth is real. When you no longer bear the reader along with language—that labored point where he is simply slogging through *words*: "Look at me writing pretty"—you've lost him.

In LTL you present the pure thought or emotion, all meat and muscle. There's little or no room for the vagaries or digressions of naturalism/realism in which the character may honestly grope for a meaning or even try to conceal it for personal reasons. Try a good modern translation of *Oedipus Rex, Antigone* or *Medea*; better, see them staged and hear them. The action develops like a taut thriller.

The anonymous eighth-century tale of Beowulf plays on a poetic stage as vast and dark as any envisioned by Richard Wagner in his *Ring* cycle. In my novel adaptation, *The Tower of Beowulf,* Grendel and his mother, Sigyn, are hideous creatures, halfling children of gods and giants, but a merciful spell gives them the illusion of beauty. While Sigyn has long known the truth, young Grendel can't bear the horrible revelation of his true appearance. When Sigyn comforts him, to give her a realistic tone would be ludicrously flat and wrong, as perhaps something like this:

> "I don't know, I can't say why we're this way. It seemed kinder
> to let you believe a lie. I would make it different if I could, believe
> me. Because I love you. I am so sorry."

Sure, honest enough, but not *big* enough for LTL. The speech doesn't fill the scene at all or do justice to creatures trapped between two worlds and larger than life themselves. Their joy or sorrow needs far richer orchestration:

"We are (men's) nightmares. If there were more of us than them, I suppose they would be ours. Surely they have been mine. Loki was not unkind. He gave me a little beauty for a little time...oh, Grendel, I would be beautiful for you if I could. I would have all women and all worlds fair for you—and for myself while the wishing. But I am a god's get in the body of a beast. Pity, but can Hrothgar and his kind say more? Deal with what you are, my son."

Never easy, the balancing of high language with emotional truth, so find the truth first and always trust instinct before intellect. Emotional truth is different and more elusive than the cerebral kind, which may intrigue and entertain as it does so effervescently in the works of G. B. Shaw, but rarely invokes deep emotional response. Remember that intellect proceeds from the simple to the complex, wisdom from the complex to the profoundly simple, which is where you'll find the truth of any dialogue, whatever the style.

Parke Godwin has been a published novelist since 1973. His work has been published in England, France, Germany, Holland and Poland. He is best known for his Arthurian novels Firelord *and* Beloved Exile *and for his novels of* Robin Hood, Sherwood *and* Robin and the King.

He is the author of the satires Waiting for the Galactic Bus *and* The Snake Oil Wars *and the historical novel* Lord of Sunset, *a novel of the Norman Conquest and prequel to* Sherwood. *This was followed by* The Lovers, *his first Arthurian novel in twelve years, and* Watch By Moonlight, *a novel based on the popular poem* "The Highwayman" *by Alfred Noyes.*

Godwin has sold film rights to Sherwood *and the black-humor short story* "A Matter of Taste," *plus posting all his work for film possibilities. In recent years, he has turned his attention to short stories.*

Romancing an Editor's Eye

How to pen the splendiferous,
salable romance novel

By Patricia McAllister

S O YOU WANT TO WRITE A ROMANCE NOVEL. Perhaps you've heard it's easy to "dash one off" over the weekend, and earn some quick and easy cash, or maybe you're a devoted reader of the romance genre, and truly believe in the power of love and relationships. I hope it's the latter. You see, nothing is more obvious to a romance editor (or a romance reader) than a writer's real passion. Your views and opinions of the love relationship between a man and a woman, whether enthusiastic or scornful, will be readily apparent in your writing. Just like the characters you create, your writing must be properly motivated. Are you simply a hack, or has a genuine love for the genre prompted you to pick up the pen?

Would-be hacks take heed: Editors can tell if an author has never read a romance.

While it's true some common elements exist in romance novels, just as in westerns or mysteries, it's too simplistic to say there is a "formula" to writing a salable romance novel. Yes, the man and woman will overcome their challenges and be united in the end. Likewise, the murder will be solved in a mystery, and the "guy in the black hat gets his" in the traditional western. Few genre readers expect otherwise. Thus, romance fans faithfully buy romance novels not because they want to discover if it ends happily (of course, it will), but because they want to enjoy a great adventure along the way.

Along with the common misconception that a romance novel is simple to write, also toss out the "quick and easy cash." I'm sorry to say it's the exception, not the rule. Many excellent, highly productive writers still have second jobs. This applies to other genres, as well as romance. You may be the next Margaret Mitchell waiting in the wings, but far more likely you'll work your way up the "corporate ladder" at a publishing house, just as you did at work. Don't be discouraged. The gems found along the way, ranging from lifelong friendships to fan mail, are priceless.

Still interested in writing a romance novel? Good. While romance is still one of the easier markets for a fledgling author to "break into," over the last few years it's become increasingly competitive. Therefore, your book must stand out. It's not enough to be "average" any more—always strive for the exceptional, and you will eventually impress an editor.

Here are few general pointers for preparing to write a romance:

Do your research

Not just for the book, though it's certainly critical to have dates and places accurately researched, but thoroughly research your market before you ever send out a manuscript. Many beginning writers aren't aware of the fact most publishing houses provide free "tip sheets," usually called writer's guidelines. Check *The American Directory of Writer's Guidelines: More than 1700 Magazine Editors and Book Publishers Explain What They Are Looking for from Freelancers*, available at bookstores or your library, or request guidelines by mail. You can obtain publishers' addresses from the latest issue of *Writer's Market*, or various other writing books and magazines. Always include an SASE (self-addressed, stamped envelope) when requesting guidelines.

You'll save yourself a lot of effort by reading tip sheets before you ever submit a manuscript. Some houses are very specific about what their editors are looking for; others are more generalized. But even as you review the tip sheets, keep in mind they are only that: guidelines. There are few hard and fast rules. (Yes, for the curious, some houses do offer suggestions on how to handle a physical relationship between your main characters—and whether they prefer the passionate scenes sweet, spicy, or sizzling. Many leave it up to the author). Also if a particular house accepts only agented submissions, and you are unagented, you will have saved yourself money and time by reading the guidelines and not sending in your manuscript.

Beware of "trends"

Don't comb a bookstore and assume what you see on the shelves is what's selling now. Otherwise, one might suppose tossing an angel and time-travel into a romance makes for a surefire best-seller. "Current" releases on the shelves sold anywhere from six months to several years ago. Likewise, editors are buying books now for release dates down the road.

Unless you have personal knowledge of what a particular editor is looking for (see Attend writing conferences, below), it's safer to stick with a more traditional plot and story line when writing romance. By traditional, I don't mean "conservative." You can certainly have a 1990s heroine who hates to cook and drives stock car on the weekends. Likewise, your hero doesn't have to be what's termed an "alpha" male in the industry—tall, dark, brooding, with pecs the size of footballs. But when trying to break into the romance field, I also wouldn't distort the plot or characters too much. You can afford to take more risks when you're established. Right now, you're aiming for that very first sale.

Read, read, and read some more

If you aren't an avid reader already, start now. Buy and read as many recent romances as you can afford. I do stress the word *recent* here. It may come as a shock to some, but doctor/nurse romances waltzed out the door in the 1940s. (So have 600-page sagas, thanks to skyrocketing paper costs.) Today's topics range from modern, single-father heroes struggling to raise a brood of six, to female warriors in ancient Gaul.

> "Buy and read as many recent romances as you can afford."

You'll probably determine rather quickly if you prefer historical or contemporary settings and characters. This makes a difference in the submission target of your book. Just as you wouldn't send an engineering article to *Vogue* magazine, sending a sprawling, 100,000-word historical to a *Harlequin Presents* editor is a waste of time. If you've done your research on the publishing houses, you should have a good idea of your target house(s) long before you put the stamps on your mailer.

Consider joining a writers' group

It's a practical investment in your writing career. You will gain invaluable feedback and insight into the business. Believe it or not, all those glossy writers' journals and magazines can't keep up with the incredibly fast-paced publishing world. Nine times out of ten, you'll hear of changes in editors, agents, or houses through the grapevine long before you'll ever see them in print. And in this business, time is of the essence.

I believe the right critique group can improve your chances of success. Sure, it's scary letting another person read your work, or reading it aloud yourself, but remember you're aiming for the mass market, and it's a little late to be shy when your book's on display at the supermarket. Many writers have a terror of public speaking (me included). So if an open critique session isn't your style, consider exchanging chapters via mail with another author. Where critiques are concerned, be honest with one another, but tactful. You don't want to create a mutual admiration society, but neither do you want to provoke hard feelings. Egos are sensitive; especially authors'.

Attend writing conferences

I try to work in a minimum of two a year, whether local or national. Yes, there are costs involved, and expenses are a consideration for any aspiring author, but without some minimal investment in your career, your road will be longer and harder. Start off small. Many states have community colleges which offer writing classes or extension courses. Scan the local papers for events where other writers might be present. Writers' leagues are a wonderful way to make new friends with similar interests. I belong to Romance Writers of America, both the national organization and a local chapter, and acquired my agent and sold projects through contacts made at RWA conferences.

Besides the obvious benefits of hands-on workshops, you will meet a variety of writers at conferences, both struggling and accomplished. Best of all, editors from major houses often attend the larger conferences, as well as literary agents, and if you have a completed project, you may be able to "pitch" your idea during a group or individual session with an editor or agent. Don't bring your manuscript and expect a busy editor or agent to take it or read it there, but you may make a valuable contact and be invited to submit your work at a later date. If the editor or agent is interested, they will let you know, and likewise if they aren't. Often, rehearsing with an author friend beforehand helps ease those pre-session jitters.

It sounds impossible to sum up a book in three or five rushed minutes, but most editors can detect a core of promise even in a brief summary. If you are asked to submit your work, don't forget to send it to the particular editor who invited the submission. Include a polite letter reminding him or her of the invitation, enclose a large SASE with sufficient return postage, and cultivate enormous patience. The benefit of conferences is obvious; you can circumvent the so-called "slush pile" by targeting an editor who is already interested in your idea, and greatly increase your chances of selling.

Okay, so you've researched your market. You've attended a conference or two, perhaps even solicited a pearl or two of wisdom from a published author. You're fired up, ready to get started on that best-selling romance. Great! Here are some more specific pointers in "romancing an editor's eye":

Pick your plot before you pick up the pen

The successful romance novel combines appealing characters with an engaging plot and convincing obstacles. This is harder to accomplish than it sounds. The plot in a romance revolves around the conflicts between the main characters, the hero and heroine, but there are many variables which can affect their relationship. It's true there are only so many plots under the sun. All have been used at one time or another, and thus have a familiar ring to readers. Your challenge, then, is not to invent a new plot, but to take a tried and true one and make it unique.

Draw upon your own interests whenever possible. You'll find the research more interesting, and the writing more fun. For instance, I've always loved the sea. There's something primal and compelling about those frothing, blue-green depths. Coupled with my soft spot for the British isles, the Elizabethan era in particular, and my admiration for strong women, *Sea Raven*, my Zebra historical, was a natural evolution.

When developing a plot, I love to play "what if" with my characters. What if my Irish heroine in *Sea Raven*, Bryony O'Neill, was not a helpless female, but rather a match for Elizabeth Tudor with her intelligence, wit, and derring-do? What if my English hero, Slade Tanner, was torn between the desires of his heart and the demands of his queen, faced with courtly intrigue and treachery at every turn; a prisoner to tradition and age-old prejudice? What if his entire family stood to suffer for his forbidden love for the "enemy"?

You can see how I decided to stir the pot (and plot) a bit in *Sea Raven*. Rather than serve up yet another male pirate, I made my *heroine* the scourge of the high seas. Traditional plot; unconventional twist. Throwing readers a curve now and then helps keep your writing fresh.

Know your characters inside and out

This includes secondary characters. It helps to develop a psychological as well as a physical profile of your entire cast. Their actions and reactions to the circumstances in their lives must be logical. Just as in real life, fictional characters shouldn't react to every event the same way. Even their dialogue should reflect their upbringing, social class, education and emotion.

Make your dialogue sparkle

Dialogue is often a challenge for beginning writers. But dialogue plays a pivotal role in pacing the romance novel, and helps to break up long passages of prose. Strive to keep it tight, crisp, and informative. If your book is set in Greece, describe the scenery through your heroine's eyes and speech, rather than resorting to dry, rambling "travelogue" descriptions plucked from an encyclopedia. Let us see the wonder and awe with which she regards these relics, through her comments to the hero. Dialogue should always advance a scene, and thus the plot. Pages and pages of inane chatter will drive an editor mad (not to mention a reader) and quickly bog down a book.

Caution: It's easy to go overboard on authentic dialect when writing an historical. Everyone knows "ye olde" English of several centuries ago bears scant resemblance to today's, but reading endless dialect is tiring and difficult. For example, to lend a Cockney character's speech an authentic ring, you can have him say "Guvnor" now and again, or drop an occasional "h," but use such dialect sparingly, like a strong spice. Just enough to flavor the scene, and offer your reader a glimpse into another world.

Think conflict, conflict, conflict

Don't confuse "conflict" with fighting, however. One of the common problems I come across when judging our RWA chapter's contest entries are characters who argue without purpose. "Married, With Children" should not serve as your inspiration. There is nothing romantic about characters exchanging endless insults, merely for the sake of fighting. Your hero may exhibit a touch of swinish behavior, with proper motivation, but he shouldn't be a pig.

Genuine conflict comes in two basic forms, internal and external. *Internal conflict* usually deals with emotions, e.g., a heroine torn between choosing a career or marriage; the hero haunted by his dead wife's memory. Internal conflict must be strong and serious enough to involve your readers so deeply they are concerned about your characters. Having your heroine agonize for six pages over which dress to wear on her first date with the hero is *not* internal conflict; it is called "irritating the editor."

Any novel is seriously weakened by a trivial or unconvincing misunderstanding. Let's take a contemporary couple called Brad and Susan. If you attempt to sustain a 400-page romance on the "misunderstanding" that Brad is engaged to another woman, and Susan's insecurity and jealousy besiege her throughout the book, this is certainly conflict, but it is unconvincing. A weak conflict is usually one which can be settled simply by communication occurring between the characters. For instance, Susan could end the agony with a single question: "Brad, honey, are you engaged to Holly, or not?"

Readers will feel impatient with a heroine like Susan, for darn good reason. First, she doesn't come across as too bright, and second, she appears to obsess over the hero in an unhealthy way. In a contemporary romance, the heroine should be reasonably intelligent, self-sufficient, and have other interests beside the hero. So, too, should an historical heroine, although her life choices might be severely limited or nonexistent, depending upon the time frame and era you've placed her in. Regardless, the age of the "simpering ninny" is long gone. Most readers like and respect strong, capable women. This doesn't mean the hero can't save her from absolute peril, but it's hard to feel sympathy for a whiny, helpless heroine.

External conflict is influence from an outside force which often drastically alters the plot or your characters' lives. A raging flood threatens the heroine's beloved childhood home (thus tying it into possible internal conflict, as well), or the villain makes yet another dastardly attempt to kill the hero.

Searching for sources of external conflict can really get your creative juices flowing. It's also easy to go overboard here. More is not necessarily better. One major event is exciting; tossing in a tornado, hurricane, and volcano on top of the flood would be downright unbelievable, even laughable.

So you've finally hammered out your first chapter. Congratulations. What's next for the aspiring romance novelist?

Finish the book

I can't stress this enough. Some aspiring authors believe they can cut corners—concentrate on producing a fantastic opening, two or three tightly-written chapters, and call it good.

While I've heard of new authors selling on a partial submission or synopsis alone, it's rare. Most publishers request a finished book from an unknown author. And as any writer knows, the Muse takes us down some pretty unexpected paths. Imagine a romance editor's consternation when the "happy ending in Disneyland" you promised in the synopsis ends up a "blood bath in Savannah," or some such plot quirk. It's happened before. Editors are less willing to be burned these days, and far less forgiving when they are. Trim and polish and rewrite until *every* chapter gleams with promise.

Send in the book

This sounds obvious, but some authors are so leery of rejection they find endless excuses not to send out their manuscript. Remember, no matter how good it is, it can't sell if it's sitting on your desk. Yes, rejection is a cold, hard fact in this business, but so is selling. Both still happen on a regular basis. Think of the odds in terms of thirds. Yes, or no, or maybe. And a "maybe" is not too bad in this industry. "Maybe" means an editor might be willing to buy, if you are willing to do a thorough rewrite. Even a rejection doesn't necessarily signal doom. You'll know you're getting close to the target when you start receiving personalized rejection letters, rather than preprinted forms.

Persist, persist, persist

If there is one "secret" I've learned from selling romance, it's this little jewel: The authors who succeed are those who persevere, whether they're just starting out, or are old hands in the industry. The shining stars of tomorrow doggedly submit their books, over and over, while absorbing and learning from various sources. They never give up. Likewise, the successful, established authors in this business never, ever become complacent.

Don't let anybody mislead you. Writing and selling romance is hard work. But it's great fun, too, and the rewards, when they come, are immeasurable.

Patricia McAllister writes for Kensington Publishing and is the author of five historical romances and one novella. Recent and upcoming Zebra titles include Gypsy Jewel, Mountain Angel, Sea Raven, Absolute Angels, Zebra "Angel Love" Collection *and* Fire Raven. *She is also one half of the writing team of up-and-coming historical romance author Brit Darby. Patricia currently serves as president of the Southern Idaho chapter of Romance Writers of America. She lives in Idaho.*

Selling Yourself in a Query Letter

Not the time to be modest

By Betsy Mitchell

THE NEXT TIME YOU'RE READY to offer a manuscript, take time to create a query or cover letter that will help make that sale. Editors need a reason to buy your manuscript. You may have a terrific story to tell, an interesting new writing style, a nonfiction topic that nobody's hit on yet...but your manuscript still must do battle with a pile of others sitting on the editor's desk. Clinch that sale in your cover letter, with every personal "selling point" you can think of.

Whether they work on fiction or nonfiction books, editors must create what are called "fact sheets" or "tip sheets" for every manuscript they acquire. These are quick guides to both the book and the author that go from the editor's desk to every department in the publishing house. They are a key reference tool for sales representatives during sales conference—and the reps' primary source of information for selling the book into stores. The advertising department uses fact sheets as the basis for writing catalog copy and advertisements. Publicists rely on them to create accurate press releases and letters that accompany advance galleys.

Your manuscript's selling points will help every step of the way toward getting your book into the stores. But most important, a list of strong selling points helps an editor obtain the OK to buy your manuscript. So the more you can present to an editor, the better your chances of making that sale.

Not every selling point listed here will apply to every author. For example, an author's sales history on his or her previous titles is the most important selling point on any fact sheet—but naturally a first novelist or beginning nonfiction writer has no previous sales. If that's your situation, then concentrate on making the most of your other qualifications.

Here are the most important selling points, with explanations of each:

Best-selling track record

Give the latest sales figures for your previous titles; sell-thru percentage (the number of copies sold out of the total shipped—but mention only if this is 65 percent or better); copies in print and average monthly reorder; any appearances on best-seller lists.

First-timers naturally will have no previous sales history—but remember, every author was at this point once in his or her career. If that's your situation, list several "comparative titles" to what you've written: successful books already in print that have similar appeal to yours in terms of audience and author qualification. For example, a female mystery novelist offering a quirky new character who might do well as the centerpiece of a long-running series can say that she is hoping to click with fans of Sue Grafton and Sara Paretsky. Or a pediatrician writing about his theory of child-rearing could list his qualifications as a doctor and compare his approach to that of Penelope Leach or T. Berry Brazelton.

> "Your manuscript must do battle with a pile of others sitting on the editor's desk."

Upward sales trend

If each of your books is selling better than the last, that proves your audience of readers is growing.

Awards received

Awards for your writing come first. Awards in other fields, if they are pertinent to the manuscript you're offering, should be mentioned. For example, if you're a prize dog breeder writing an exposé on puppy farms, tell how many ribbons and titles your dogs have received.

Subsidiary rights sales on previous titles

Foreign rights, book club sales, first serial rights, movie rights, etc. Once again, first-timers will probably have nothing to offer here, but if you feel your book will have appeal to certain subsidiary rights markets, point them out. For example, a book on the Russian mafia would be of interest in a number of other countries.

Quotes and reviews

Comments for the current manuscript should come first, then quotes from print reviews or well-known readers of your previous books. If you know any established writers who might be willing to read and comment on your manuscript, now is the time to ask a favor. In nonfiction writing, quotes from experts in whatever field you're covering are often as useful as those from established writers. Advance quotes supplied at time of submission can definitely help your manuscript's chances, since it gives the editor a ready-made quote to put on the book cover.

Proven or potential audience

If you've sold short fiction to magazines, cite these credits. These readers can be a foundation audience for your novels. In nonfiction, do a little research on how big your potential audience might be—for example, if you're working on a book dealing with a new arthritis treatment, tell how many sufferers of arthritis there are across the U.S.

Success of genre

Give examples of similar titles and their sales figures—especially if yours is a first book. It can be difficult to obtain sales figures, since most publishers are unwilling to release them. Your best source may be *Publishers Weekly*, which runs periodic articles on best-sellers. *PW* also publishes numerous articles analyzing trends in the various genres (mysteries, romance, SF and fantasy, etc.) throughout the year which can be valuable sources of hard information. The periodicals librarian at your local branch should be able to track those down. If you're writing in a genre such as romance, mystery or science fiction, subscribe to one of the newsletters and magazines that cover those fields; they are a wealth of information in a specialized area.

Compelling or unique topic

If your book is tilling fresh earth, point that out. As an example, the 1990s spate of books about near-death experiences and angel visitations began with a manuscript or two that seemed altogether fresh and new when first seen by New York publishers.

Author qualifications

For a fiction writer, if your story revolves around an area where you hold special knowledge (raising dogs, rocket science, international espionage, for example), mention your background. For a nonfiction writer, it's vital to have a strong grounding in your subject. People want to read books by experts.

Miscellaneous—author visibility, highly promotable author

Do you lead workshops, appear on infomercials, write a column for a newspaper syndicate, host a local talk show or do anything else that puts you frequently in the public eye? Are you the president of a large organization, a rock singer, or otherwise well-known to large groups of people? If so, include this information in your query letter.

Every writer has his or her personal selling points. Craft your own list now—and happy selling!

Betsy Mitchell is editor-in-chief of Warner Books' science fiction/fantasy line, Aspect. Her authors include such names as astronaut Buzz Aldrin writing with John Barnes, New York Times best-sellers Kevin J. Anderson and R. A. Salvatore, award winners Octavia Butler, C. J. Cherryh, and Joan D. Vinge, exciting new discoveries David Feintuch and J. V. Jones, and many more. She received a World Fantasy Award for Best Editor for her work on the original anthology Full Spectrum 4, and has written a number of articles on how to market one's writing.

Write from Your Roots

Creating fiction from genealogy

By Marilyn Meredith

CREATING EXCITING FICTION FROM YOUR GENEALOGY, fiction that other people besides your family will want to read, is similar to writing any historical fiction, except you have an edge on other writers: You already know who your characters are, the historical settings, and the outline of the story.

Concentrate on one family line when planning your book. Choose the one you know the most about or that has the most intriguing characters or incidents. When you finish with the first novel you can always write another.

While working on your genealogy you probably discovered some amazing facts about your ancestors, found out about relatives you didn't know existed, and perhaps even uncovered tantalizing secrets. My sister did our genealogy and while I was reading it I discovered one of our ancestors had disappeared when she was sixteen. Though no one knew what became of her, I decided to write a book and solve the mystery. After doing the necessary research, I concluded, because of the time period, mid-1800s, and the place, Wisconsin, probably my heroine had been kidnapped by renegade Indians. I based my assumption on a paragraph in a history book about gangs comprised of Native Americans who had been kicked out of various tribes and roamed around terrorizing the settlers. I wrote a whole section on how Wilhemena was stolen by renegades and rescued by the Menomenee. She lived the rest of her life with them. My information about the Menomenee came from a *Na-*

tional Geographic. Besides being fun to write, many readers reported that this was their favorite part of the book.

Find a theme for the book

As you do more research to fill in the blanks, an obvious thread may emerge that runs through the entire story. In *Trail to Glory* I chose to write about the women of the family who, because of circumstances, had to make it on their own. A thread that appeared throughout the book was the Indian Paintbrush flower. It appears in many different ways, including the Indian name given to Wilhemena by the Menomenees.

Another book I wrote, *Two Ways West,* is based upon the different manner and route two families chose to make their way west. A secondary theme is that despite adversity both families achieved their goals.

You'll want to incorporate all your family legends into your novel...even if you can't find historical evidence to support them. In *Two Ways West,* Newt Crabtree is the man hired by Clarence King to lead the California Geological Survey Party to Mount Whitney, the highest peak on the Sierra Nevada range. He was paid thirty dollars. This is a family legend, and though I found many references to Clarence King's trip, I couldn't locate the name of the guide. However, because King gave a creek, lake and meadow the name of Crabtree, it seems highly likely this particular legend is true. Whether it is or not, I incorporated the incident into the book.

Another important task is to research what was going on historically at the time and place where your ancestors lived. Use the obvious sources: encyclopedias and history books, copies of old newspapers. Check in the library for books written by local people about the period you are interested in. Other published family histories may be helpful too.

Contact the historical society in the place or places you are writing about; they may have invaluable information to share. When I was writing *Two Ways West,* I discovered the Crabtree family lived in Brownsville, Texas, on two different occasions, from 1818 to 1830 and 1842 to 1851, so it was vital that I learn something about the area and what was going on there during those time periods. I wrote to the Brownsville Historical Society and explained what I was doing, and they loaned me a marvelous book filled with facts, people, and anecdotes. Much of this information found its way into the pages of the book.

Organize all the information that you gather, legends and historical facts, in any manner that works for you. Put dates on every piece of information so that you can keep it in the right order. I like to write each historical fact on a separate three-by-five card and also make a time-line that states what's happening when.

Incorporate history into your story

Let your characters be involved with what was actually going on; have them interact with real-life historical characters. Be sure you get the facts right, then embroider them as much as you like. In *Trail to Glory*, some of my family passed through Deadwood City at the same time Calamity Jane lived there. Of course they had a colorful encounter with her. Write about actual historical incidents and include your people in what was going on.

Character motivation

As you gather the historical events, you'll begin to figure out what may have motivated your ancestors to do what they did. If, for instance, they came to California at the height of the gold discovery and settled in Grass Valley, no doubt gold was the motivator. However, if they came later, as the Crabtree family did, ending up in the more southern foothills of the Sierra, the motivation was probably something far different.

You won't have to worry about getting something wrong if you do your research and write only about those people who are no longer living. But don't let the truth get in the way of telling a good story. After all, you are writing historical fiction.

Each character must come alive for the reader. Besides knowing what they look like, you must give them individual personalities. Perhaps you are fortunate enough to know something about their traits from older family members. But it's more likely you'll have to create your characters from scratch.

> "Don't let the truth get in the way of telling a good story."

As you did with the historical facts, you should have a card or page written about each of your major and minor characters to remind you who they are, how they would react in certain situations because of what happened to them previously and their own unique traits, made-up or true.

Your genealogical and historical research gave you clues as to your ancestors' motivations for doing certain things, and the personality traits you give them will provide the way they handle situations that occur in their lives. Make the reader care about your characters. Don't make them perfect; give them a quirk or minor defect, something that makes them vulnerable.

As in any book, they need problems to solve. The problems your characters face should be easily found in your research. Your heroes and heroines must grow and mature along the way.

Make up the villains (unless you know that one of your ancestors was a blackguard). They should be so bad the readers will hate them.

Put other people in the book for your family members to interact with. Think of them as the supporting cast. We don't have to know as much about them but give them identifying character tags such as a limp, a swooping mustache, a hawk-like nose. If you're fortunate enough to find a local history about the area you are researching, you'll have a myriad of characters to add to your story.

Use the real family names. But if some have the same name, create a nickname, or use the first and last together so the reader can keep track of all the characters. For the supporting cast, use names appropriate for the era.

It is important for the reader to visualize the scenery. Do enough research so you can describe what the places looked like when your family lived there or were passing through.

Plan ahead so you know where your story is going. If you see it like a movie in your head, you must be able to put it down on paper in a manner that the reader will see the same movie.

Always let the readers see what's happening while it's happening—don't tell us about it after the fact. Describe the action while it's going on—or have someone tell about it in dialogue. Don't write long, boring narratives. Keep a nice balance of dialogue, action and narrative.

Weave all description into the story so that it isn't intrusive. The description should be part of what's going on.

Dialogue should sound like people talk. Use the slang of the era. Break up long speeches with action. Or have the other person interrupt with questions or comments.

From whom are we going to learn about the story? The hero, the heroine? Don't change the viewpoint character too often. Let the readers see the story unfold through the viewpoint character's eyes. Let us know what he or she is seeing, feeling, smelling, tasting, hearing. Don't forget to add color.

When you change the point-of-view character, either change scenes or have a good transition.

Begin your story with something that's already happening, an exciting event that will cause the reader to want to continue reading. If you have to tell us what's gone on before, do it later with flashbacks or through dialogue. End each chapter with a cliff-hanger. Make it hard for the reader to put the book down. End in the middle of a scene and start the new chapter where you left off.

Use the exact verb that will describe the action, eliminating the need for too many adverbs. Instead of "he ran," use "he galloped, trotted, gamboled, jogged" or whatever word best describes what you mean. Use your thesaurus. Be careful about using the same words over and over. Change the length of your sentences. Don't always write a sentence beginning with a noun followed by a verb.

Don't forget the romance

No matter the genre, every book should have romance in it. People fall in love, get married and have children...that's what genealogy is all about. Your reader will want to know the details of how all this came about. Unless you are fortunate enough to have heard stories about how people met one another, you will have to put your imagination to work.

Write the whole book before trying to edit it. Use your spell-checker. Print the book out. You can't edit properly on the computer. If you don't have a critique group to read it to, read it out loud to yourself. You'll catch mistakes you wouldn't by just going over it.

Turning your family history or genealogy into fiction isn't much different from writing any other kind of fiction, except that you already have a good beginning. It's up to you to create something family, friends and even the general public will enjoy reading.

Marilyn Meredith is the author of the award–winning Deputy Tempe Crabtree mystery series, the latest, Calling the Dead, *from Mundania Press, as well as* Wishing Makes It So, *a psychological thriller awarded best thriller of 2006 by the American Authors Association. She is a member of Sisters in Crime, Mystery Writers of America, EPIC and Public Safety Writers of America. She was an instructor for Writer's Digest School for ten years, served as an instructor at the Maui Writer's Retreat and other writers' conferences and is a popular speaker at libraries and other venues. She makes her home in a small foothill community much like Bear Creek where Deputy Tempe Crabtree lives. http://fictionforyou.com*

Write Nonfiction— Using Fiction

In the tradition of Capote, Mailer and Wolfe, dare to blend fiction with nonfiction and create prose with both substance and verve

By William Noble

ANY OF US LEARN TO WRITE, mindful of demarcations: magazines and newspapers expect different writing, authors and editors do different things, professional and nonprofessional authors expect different treatment.

But let's ask ourselves...why can't magazines and newspapers interchange copy, or editors write and authors edit, or nonprofessional and professional authors expect the same treatment? How roiled would our writing world really be?

The answer's pretty clear: Those "demarcations" don't have much relevance in the current literary world. Crossovers are happening with regularity, and nowhere is this more apparent than with that most basic of all demarcations: fiction and nonfiction. It used to be one wrote fiction or one wrote nonfiction. The idea that the forms could be blended, yet each retain its essential character, was left to those writers carrying the "experimental" label: small audience, small number of reviews, small amount of money finding its way into the author's pocket.

Old ideas about nonfiction focused on reality and truth: If the writing was factual, it was nonfiction. Period. The journalistic approach was the pole star: who, when, where, what, why and how. No one imagined facts manipulated so drama might explode beyond simple recitation of what happened. A couple of generations ago nonfiction meant factual representation (with emphasis on "factual"), and that meant limits not only on content, but on style of writing as well.

Occasionally, someone tried to blend nonfiction and fiction writing. Ernest Hemingway was one; in *The Green Hills of Africa,* written in the 1930s, his foreword read: "The writer has attempted to write an absolutely true book to see whether the shape of a country and the pattern of a month's action can, if truly presented, compete with a work of imagination..."

It didn't work, and the critics were unmerciful. Yet, now, sixty years after Hemingway, we find the artful blending of fiction technique with nonfiction subject well-developed, and our common pool of literature is the better for it.

Extended dialogue

Take dialogue, for example. Most writers know dialogue is more than just conversation; it's conversation *with drama*! What we search for is that excerpt of dialogue that presents dramatic implication. With the old journalism, quoted dialogue was short, relevant but not necessarily dramatic. Eyewitness accounts gave credibility to recitation of facts, and if there was dramatic fallout, so much the better. But now, we change emphasis: We search for dialogue that will add drama, that will build excitement while staying glued to facts. Often, it's extended dialogue, long passages or a series of shorter, uninterrupted passages that tell a story in the characters' own words. We use the dialogue, not to modify the facts but to present the facts. The characters tell us the story (or a significant portion of it) in their own words, and the result is building drama.

Fiction writers use extended dialogue to develop motivation, explain away (or create) uncertainties, offer new conflict potential. Why can't nonfiction writers do the same thing? Issac Singer, Nobel Laureate and recounter of the Jewish immigrant experience, says in *Lost in America* that he skipped dates as well as places and disguised characterization because many of the people were still alive. Then, in the foreword, he writes: "I consider this work no more than fiction set against a background of truth..."

Is it fiction, is it nonfiction? Perhaps the better question is: Why bother categorizing? Isn't it accurate—and useful—to say the story blends fact with drama and produces very readable prose?

See how he handles extended dialogue: He depicts a telephone conversation in Warsaw, Poland, before the war with a young woman he calls Sheba Leah and who calls him Yitzchok.

> "Yitzchok, if you called me a minute before no one would have answered! I went down to buy a paper."

"What's the news?"...

The dialogue continues uninterrupted for thirteen passages, ending with:

"Sheba Leah, you're terrible!"
"That's what I am."

Are the quoted passages exactly what was said? Probably not (in those days tape recorders didn't exist, and it's a cinch Singer didn't copy down every conversation). But Singer gives us the *gist* of the dialogue, and he has given us writing which will dramatize the facts. Remember, he lets us know at the beginning: He's fictionalizing things against a *background of truth*. So we know what to expect, don't we? A true story offered with fictionalized technique.

One caution, however: Singer made his approach clear at the outset, he didn't lead the reader to assume this was pristine nonfiction. He described where he fictionalized, so the reader understood the dramatic license he took. Otherwise the reader could properly question how he remembered facts and dialogue so perfectly, and once a reader questions a writer's veracity, the bond between them is broken.

Interior monologue

Years ago the nonfiction writer kept a proper distance from characters, and the idea that one could get into characters' heads was pooh-poohed. "What'd he *say*?" editors demanded. It was the writer quoting the character or the writer describing the character—never how the character saw the writer or how the character *thought* but never spoke about things generally. Fiction writers, on the other hand, routinely get into the heads of their characters, writing from any number of points of view. If the fiction writer wants to portray a character's growing unease or review facts leading to some conclusion, the character's thought processes, his or her *subjective* point of view, is presented:

What do I do now, the guy's got the gun, I got Laurie in the other room, it's eight degrees outside...? Think, man, think!...

If the fiction writer wants to show the character on an emotional roller coaster, he or she could write:

Black little poppies, yellow middles, dead eyes and flowery strings pulling me, oh God... I can't do it!...

The technique is, of course, interior monologue (also known as stream of consciousness), and it's widely used. Its value lies in character development and dramatic impact because it provides the reader with insights more objective writing could never accomplish.

But what about the nonfiction writer? Since we're dealing with facts and truth, how much, if anything, is permissible? The answer—as with dialogue—is that things have come a long way in the last couple of generations, and interior monologue is appropriate with nonfiction, *provided* there's fact to back it up. We can't get into a character's head because we suppose, or imagine, or deduce that's what he or she would be thinking. We have to *know*!

See how Tom Wolfe does it in his book about the space program, *The Right Stuff*. At the outset he explained that his style was developed to grab readers' attention, to absorb them. What he wanted was to "capture the spontaneity of thought, not just speech..." He wanted to get into the heads of his characters, even if this was nonfiction. And so, at an astronauts' press conference, he quotes a reporter's question on who was confident about coming back from space. He describes the astronauts looking at one another and hoisting their hands in the air. Then, he's into their heads:

> It really made you feel like an idiot, raising your hand this way.
> If you didn't think you were "coming back," then you would really
> have to be a fool or a nut to have volunteered at all...

He goes on for a full page, and in writing this way Wolfe has transcended usual nonfiction style; he's offered characterization and motivation, two fiction writing techniques that can bring the reader in lockstep with the writer. Interior monologue provides a chance to "see inside" the heads of characters, and we know that the more familiar a reader is with a character, the more the reader embraces that character.

Interior monologue is about feelings, emotions, desires, fears, plans, reactions, anything, in fact, that a character might have thoughts about during the story. We reproduce it, and it provides an additional point of view that turns nonfiction away from straight reportage and onto a more creative path.

But...we must know the interior monologue is accurate, that the character whose head we are in actually thought these thoughts. Tom Wolfe would not have written about what the astronauts thought at the press conference unless he was sure they felt this way. He did his research to confirm it, and we should do no less. Remember his guiding principle: "...spontaneity of thought, not just speech..." Here, he let us know what they thought.

Composite characterization

When fiction writers develop characterization, they often use a model, at least at the outset. Then they mold the character to fit their story. Why can't nonfiction writers do this, also? Why can't nonfiction writers use molded characterization, while maintaining allegiance to fact and truth? It used to be that characters in nonfiction had limited roles because emphasis was on "the facts," and a character was only useful if he or she moved the facts along. Now, characterization not only modifies facts, it develops them, too. In fiction writing, a character can be a blend of the author's experiences; in nonfiction it must be a blend of actual people.

We call it "composite characterization," and it allows us to remain true to the facts while going beyond one character's limits. Composite characterization works well with nonfiction so long as we remember that each element of the character be honestly reproduced from our research. We use the composite for more flexibility with the story, and the way we present it is no different from the fiction writer's approach. The composite allows us to remain with the one character through varied situations, and the reader's familiarity with the character will grow.

How's it work? A few years ago I coauthored a nonfiction book on classical ballet, and one chapter deals with the way teenage dancers combine life and art. I decided to use a composite character for the portrayal. I began this way:

> While other parents contend with the blasting cacophony of the current rage in rock groups, a young dancer's parents will hear the strains of Tchaikovsky, Stravinsky, Vivaldi...over and over...

A page and a half later I'd added a bit of dialogue, but mostly I'd described the composite dancer's room (a mess), leotards (cut up and reused), ballet bag (containing everything, including rotten apple cores), and eating habits. I gave my composite dancer no name, but she became "everydancer" in the sense that readers could—and did—identify with the character. Each of her traits was based on solid research, and those familiar with the ballet world empathized easily.

When are composites appropriate? They work especially well when characterization is needed to give life to facts. If the story is bizarre enough or lively enough, composite characterization probably won't be needed. But where composites are used, make sure there's an accurate trace to those who make up the composite. Fiction writers have the luxury of feasting on their imaginations for character development; nonfiction writers must rely on reality.

The move to use fiction technique with nonfiction writing got a big push in the early 1960s with publication of Truman Capote's *In Cold Blood*, the murder of a Kansas farm family and the hunt for the killers. Capote didn't write this as straight journalism; he developed it into what he called a "nonfiction novel," adding that he applied "imaginative narrative reporting." Note his careful word selection here: it was reporting, *but* it was imaginative; it was nonfiction, *but* it was a novel. Clearly, he refused to be bound by the old categories, and the result was a blend of both. This book was nonfiction in the sense that the events actually happened, the characters actually lived (and died), the settings actually existed, the dialogue and thoughts actually occurred. But he applied fiction technique to give the story added life and drama. In this sense he novelized and employed his imagination.

Scene intercuts

> "Perhaps the most useful fiction technique for developing suspense is foreshadowing, the *hinting* of something sinister to come."

Capote used extended dialogue and lengthy interior monologue (most likely from interviews with the characters, where he asked for specific recollections), and out of all this character and motivation developed. But he went further, too. He intercut scenes by moving back and forth, sometimes rapidly, between two settings or time periods, and this had the effect of building drama and interest (it isn't hard to do; keep the scenes short, their endings suspenseful, their relationship to one another clear). Some scenes lasted half a page, but the intercutting, the back and forth, served to keep the reader on the edge of the chair.

Scene intercutting is a frequently used fiction technique. Many adventure, suspense, mystery writers employ it to ratchet up drama and keep the reader tuned in. The key is to use the device only occasionally because no reader—or writer—can cope with a constant dose of high pitched drama. But as a drama-building device, scene intercutting—whether nonfiction or fiction—will give positive results.

Foreshadowing

Perhaps the most useful fiction technique for developing suspense is foreshadowing, the *hinting* of something sinister to come. Can it be used with nonfiction? Norman Mailer, in *The Executioner's Song*, his 1970s story of the life and death of murderer Gary Gilmore, calls his work "a factual account, a true life story." It's nonfiction because it's fact-based, true to life, yet he uses several fiction techniques: extended dialogue, interior monologue, scene intercutting. He also uses foreshadowing, and he does it subtly and smoothly. For example, he has a scene where the murder victim leaves home for the last time to go to work. Mailer has him realize he hasn't kissed his wife goodbye. He goes back and kisses her, gives her a "really good hug and looked into her eyes, things were just going well..." Then his wife says, "I'll see you tonight"... In the next paragraph (the last paragraph in the chapter) Mailer writes the victim "was a very conscientious driver, never broke the speed limit..." Hours later he was dead.

Here again, Mailer must have done his research to be able to create the dialogue; but note the dramatic effect of his foreshadowing. He hints at disaster by painting a rosy portrait of the victim's life. We know something is going to happen because life is rarely this sweet for long. By foreshadowing, Mailer has provided suspense, drama and a reason for the reader to stay interested.

With nonfiction, foreshadowing works well, so long as we stay with the facts and not impute motivation or circumstance that never happened. We can style our writing to highlight certain facts (such as dialogue recollections) so they portray foreshadowing, but it must be a factual representation. No "he should have thought..." or "she might have expected..." unless we back it up factually.

Blending nonfiction with fiction gives writers a wonderful opportunity to build a story with substance and verve. Even the most factually based account can now be livened by extended dialogue, interior monologue, composite characters, scene intercuts and foreshadowing. These fictional techniques have but one purpose: to make a story more exciting, more dramatic and more telling on the reader. No one need groan about writing—or reading—nonfiction any longer; it could be the best game in town.

> ***William Noble*** *is a freelance writer and lecturer, as well as a retired member of the Pennsylvania bar. William has published almost two hundred nonfiction articles and twenty books:* Bookbanning in America; The Twenty-eight Biggest Writing Blunders; Conflict, Action & Suspense; Steal This Plot; Show, Don't Tell; "Shut Up!" He Explained; Make That Scene; *and* The Complete Guide to Writers' Conferences and Workshops. *His latest are* Three Rules for Writing a Novel; Writing Dramatic Nonfiction; *and* The Nutcracker Backstage *(with Angela Whitehill.)*

Your Publishing Options

Why you should consider self-publishing

By Dan Poynter

Nearly everyone wants to write a book. Most people have the ability, some have the drive, but few have the organization. Therefore, the greatest need is for a simple system, a road map. The basic plan in this workshop will not only provide you with direction, it will also promote the needed drive and expose abilities in you which may never have been recognized.

Magazines devoted to businesspeople, sales reps and opportunity seekers are littered with full-page advertisements featuring people with fabulous offers. Usually, these people discovered a successful system of business in sales, real estate or mail order, and for a price, they are willing to let the reader in on their "secret." To distribute this information, they have written a book. Upon close inspection, one often finds that the author is making more money from the *book* than from the original enterprise. The irony is that purchasers get the wrong information; what they need is a book on how to write, produce and sell a *book!*

Writing a book is probably easier than you think. If you can voice an opinion and think logically, you can write a book. If you can *say it*, you can *write it*. Most people have to work for a living and therefore can spend only a few minutes of each day on their book. Consequently, they can't keep the whole manuscript in their head. They become overwhelmed and confused, and find it easy to quit the project. The solution is to break up the manuscript into many small, easy-to-attack chunks (and never start at page one, where the hill looks steepest). Then concentrate on one section at a time and do a thorough job on each part.

People want to know "how to" and "where to," and they will pay well to find out. The information industry–the production and distribution of ideas and knowledge as opposed to goods and services–now amounts to more than one-half of the U.S. gross national product. *There is money in information.* To see how books are tapping this market, check the best-seller lists in *Publishers Weekly, USA Today, The Wall Street Journal* or *The New York Times.*

Your best sources for this salable information are your own experiences, plus research. Write what you know. Whether you already have a completed manuscript, have a great idea for one, or need help in locating a suitable subject, this book will point the way.

Since poetry and fiction are very difficult to sell, we will concern ourselves with nonfiction. Writing nonfiction doesn't require any great literary style; it is simply a matter of producing well-researched, reorganized, updated and, most important, repackaged information. Some of the recommendations here can be applied to fiction. However, all the recommendations are written toward, and for, the reader who wishes to become an author or an author-publisher of useful information.

> *"Writing ranks among the top 10 percent of professions in terms of prestige."*
> —Jean Strouse, as quoted in *Newsweek*

Becoming a celebrity author

The prestige enjoyed by the published author is unparalleled in our society. A book can bring recognition, wealth and acceleration in one's career. People have always held books in high regard, possibly because in past centuries books were expensive and were, therefore, purchased only by the rich. Just 250 years ago, many people could not read or write. To be an author then was to be an educated person.

> *"Books through the ages have earned humanity's high regard as semi-sacred objects."*
> —Richard Kluger, author and editor

Many enterprising people are using books to establish themselves in the ultimate business of being a celebrity information provider. Usually starting with a series of nonpaying magazine articles, they develop a name and make themselves visible. Then they expand the series of articles into a book. Now with their credibility established, they operate seminars in their field of expertise, command high speaking-fees and issue a high-priced newsletter. From there, they teach a course at the local college and become a consultant, advising individuals, businesses and/or others. They find they are in great demand. People want their information or simply want them around. Clubs and corporations fly them in to consult, because it is more economical than sending all their people to the expert.

Achieving this dream begins with the packaging and marketing of information. Starting with a field you know, then researching it further and putting it on paper will establish you as an expert. Then your expert standing can be pyramided with interviews, articles, TV appearances, talks at local clubs, etc. Of course, most of this activity will promote your book sales.

> *"Recognition is everything you write for: it's much more than money. You want your books to be valued. It's the basic aspiration of a serious writer."*
> —William Kennedy

In turn, all this publicity not only sells books, but also opens more doors and produces more invitations, leading to more opportunities to prove your expert status and make even more money for yourself. People seek experts whose opinions, advice and ideas are quoted in the media. Becoming an expert doesn't require a great education or a college degree. You can become an expert in one small area if you're willing to search the Internet (the world's largest library), read up on your subject elsewhere too, and write down the important information.

Sample expert bio

Dan Poynter is a parachute expert who advises attorneys, judges and juries about what happened or what should have happened in skydiving accidents. He is not a lawyer or even an engineer, but has written seven books on related subjects. His technical books on parachutes and popular books on skydiving give him the expertise to be hired and the credibility to be believed.

A book lasts forever

A book is similar to a new product design or an invention, but is usually much, much better. A patent on a device or process runs only seventeen years, whereas a copyright runs for the author's life plus seventy years. Patents cost thousands of dollars to secure and normally require a lot of legal help. By contrast, an author with a simple two-page form and thirty dollars can file a copyright. Once you write a book, it's yours. You have a monopoly on your book and there is often little direct competition.

Many people work hard at a job for forty years and have nothing to show for it but memories and pay stubs. However, others take their knowledge and write a book; the result is a tangible product for all to see. A book lasts forever, like a painting or a sculpture, but there are many copies of the book—not just one. While a sculpture can only be admired by a limited number of persons at any one time in the place where it is displayed, books come in multiple copies for the entire world to use and admire simultaneously.

Another success secret is to cut out the *intermediaries* who are the commercial publishers and produce and sell the book yourself. You can take the author's royalty and the publisher's profit. You get all the rewards because you are both the author and the publisher. Now, in addition to achieving the wealth and prestige of a published author, you have propelled yourself into your own lucrative business—a publishing house. This shortcut not only makes you more money (why share it?), it also saves you the frustration, trouble and time required to sell your manuscript to a publisher. You know the subject and market better than some distant corporation anyway.

> *"It circulated for five years, through the halls of fifteen publishers, and finally ended up with Vanguard Press, which you can see is rather deep in the alphabet."*
> —Patrick Dennis

To clarify for those readers who might misunderstand, publishing doesn't mean purchasing a printing press and actually putting the ink on the paper yourself. Nearly all publishers leave the production to an experienced book printer.

Your own publishing business

A business of your own is the great American dream, and it is still attainable. In your own business, you make the decisions to meet only those challenges you find interesting. This is not goofing off; it is making more effective use of your time by working smarter, not harder. After all, there are only twenty-four hours in a day. You have to concentrate on what will bring the most return if you are to prosper.

Running your own enterprise will provide you with many satisfying advantages. You should earn more money because you are working for yourself rather than splitting your efforts with someone else. You never have to worry about a surprise pink slip. If you keep your regular job and moonlight your own enterprise as recreation, it will always be there to fall back on should you need it. You start at the top, not the bottom, in your own company, and you work at your own pace and schedule.

In your own small business, you may work when and where you wish; you don't have to go where the job is. You can work till dawn, sleep till noon, rush off to Hawaii without asking permission. This is flexibility not available to the time-clock punchers.

Being an author-publisher will sound like a good life, and it can be. However, working for yourself requires organization and discipline. Yet work won't seem so hard when you are counting your own money.

The book publishing industry

To help you understand what's ahead, here are some definitions and background on the book publishing industry:

• **To Publish** means to prepare and issue material for public distribution or sale or "to place before the public." The book doesn't have to be beautiful, it doesn't even have to *sell*; it needs only to be *issued*. Salability will depend upon the content, the packaging, and the book's promotion.

• **A Publisher** is the one who puts up the *money*, the one who takes the risk. He or she has the book assembled for the printer, printed and then marketed, hoping to make back more money than has been spent to produce it. The publisher might be a big New York firm or a first-time author, but he or she is almost always the investor.

• **A Book** by International Standards is a publication with at least forty-nine pages, not counting the covers. Books should not be confused with "pamphlets," which have less than forty-nine pages, or "periodicals," such as magazines and newspapers. Periodicals are published regularly and usually carry advertising.

The book publishing industry in the U.S. consists of some 82,000 firms (up from 3,000 in 1970), according to the R.R. Bowker Co., but there are many more thousands of publishers. Altogether, they publish more than 200,000 titles every year. The large publishers, based in New York, are consolidating, downsizing and going out of business; there are just six left. There are perhaps 300 medium-sized publishers and more than 81,000 small/self-publishers. Some 8,000-11,000 new publishing companies are established each year. Currently, 2.8 million titles are available or "in print" in the U.S.

Your publishing choices

An author who wishes to get into print has many choices. You can approach a large (New York) general publisher or a medium-sized niche publisher. You can work with an agent, deal with a vanity press (a bad choice), or publish yourself. And there are also choices when it comes to printing.

If you publish other authors as you expand your list of titles, you may graduate to the ranks of the medium-sized publisher. You could one day even become a large general publisher. Here are the choices.

1. Large publishing firms are like department stores; they have something for everyone. They publish in many different fields and concentrate on books that anticipate audiences in the millions. A look at the numbers in big publishing will help us to better understand their challenges.

It has been estimated that more than two million book-length manuscripts are circulated to publishers each year, and many of the large publishers receive 3,000-5,000 unsolicited manuscripts each week. Reading all these manuscripts would take an enormous amount of time, and a high percentage of the submissions do not even fit the publisher's line. They are a waste of editorial time. Consequently, many of the publishers refuse delivery of unsolicited manuscripts by rubber-stamping the packages "Return to Sender"; writers are being rejected without being read!

> "Authors do detailed research on the subject matter but seldom do any on which publishing house is appropriate for their work."
> —Walter W. Powell, *Getting Into Print*

"Most initial print runs are for 5,000 books."

The 12,000 bookstores in the U.S. don't have enough space to display all the 200,000 titles published each year, so they concentrate on the books that move the best in their neighborhoods. Consequently, most publishers figure that even after selecting the best manuscripts and pouring in the promotion money, only three books out of ten will sell well, four will break even, and three will be losers. Only 10 percent of the New York-published books sell enough copies to pay off the author advance before royalties are paid.

Have you ever wondered why books in bookstores tend to have very recent copyright dates? They are seldom more than a year old because the store replaces them very quickly. Shelf space is expensive and in short supply. The books either sell in a couple of months or they go back to the publisher as "returns."

Large publishers have three selling seasons per year. They keep books in bookstores for four months and then replace them. Most initial print runs are for 5,000 books. Then the title remains in print (available for sale) for about a year. If the book sells out quickly, it is reprinted and the publisher dumps in more promotion money. If the book does not catch on, it is pulled off the market and remaindered (sold off very cheaply) to make room for new titles.

The financial demands cause publishers to be terribly objective about the bottom line. To many publishers, in fact, a book is just a "product." They are not interested in whether it is a good book; all they want to know is whether it will sell. Therefore, they concentrate on well-known authors with good track records, or Hollywood and political personalities who can move a book with their name. Only occasionally will they accept a well-written manuscript by an unknown, and then it must be on a topic with a ready and massive audience. A published writer has a much better chance of selling than an unpublished one, regardless of the quality of the work.

> *"Few of the major trade publishers will take a chance on a manuscript from someone whose name is not known."*
> —Walter W. Powell, *Getting Into Print*

Publishers, like most business people, seem to follow the 80/20 principle: they spend 80 percent of their effort on the top 20 percent of their books. The remaining 20 percent of their effort goes to the bottom 80 percent of their line. Most books have to sell themselves to induce the publisher to allocate more promotion money.

Many publishers today suggest that their authors hire their own PR firm (at the author's expense) to promote the book.

A savvy success story

There is a story about one author who sent her relatives around to bookstores to buy up every copy of her new book. The sudden spurt in sales excited the publisher, who increased the ad budget. The increase in promotion produced greater sales and her book became a success.

Royalties: The author will get a royalty from the large publisher of 6 percent to 10 percent of the net receipts (what the publisher receives), usually on a sliding scale, and the economics here are not encouraging. For example, a print-run of 5,000 copies of a book selling for twenty dollars could gross $100,000 if all were sold by the publisher at the full retail list-price, but an 8 percent royalty on the net (most books are sold at a discount) may come to just $4,000. That isn't enough money to pay for all the time you spent at the computer. The chances of selling more than 5,000 copies are highly remote; because after a few months, the publisher takes the book out of print. In fact, the publisher will probably sell less than the number of copies printed, because some books will be used for promotion and unsold books will be returned by bookstores.

Your publisher will put up the money, have the book produced, and use sales reps to get it into bookstores. However, they will not extensively promote the book, contrary to what most first-time authors think. Authors must do the bulk of the promotion. Once authors figure out that very little promotion is being done, it is often too late; the book is no longer new (it has a quickly ticking copyright date in it) and is about to be remaindered. They also can discover, to their dismay, that their contract dictates that they must submit their next two manuscripts to this same publisher.

> Whether you sell to a publisher or publish yourself, the author must do the promotion.

Big publishing houses provide a needed service; however, for many first-time authors, they are unapproachable. And once in, an author doesn't get the best deal, and getting out may be difficult. In addition, these publishers often chop the book up editorially, change the title, and take a year and a half to publish it. Authors lose artistic control of their delayed book.

Their publishing approach might be more acceptable if the big commercial publishers were great financial successes. They aren't, or at least they haven't been so far. One publishing house even admits that it would have made more money last year if it had vacated its New York office and rented out the floor space!

But there is a brighter side for the small publisher who understands who his or her readers are and where they can be found. Since the old-line, *big department store-like* publishers only know how to sell through bookstores, there's a lot of room left for the smaller *boutique-like* publishing house and self-publisher.

Be careful if you hang around with people from the traditional book industry. Learn, but don't let their ways rub off. Study the big New York publishing firms, but don't copy them. You can do a lot better.

> To the smaller publisher, there is no front list or back list; it is an only list.

2. Medium-sized (niche/specialized) publishers are the smaller and newer firms that serve specific technical fields, geographic regions, categories of people, or other specialized markets (business, hiking, boating, etc.). Some of these publishers are very small, some are fairly large, but the most successful ones concentrate on a single genre or subject area.

The owners and staff are usually *participants* in their books' subject matter. For example, I publish parachute books with a sense of mission—because I like to jump out of airplanes. Participants at these firms know their subject matter and where to find their reader/buyer because they join the same associations, read the same magazines, and attend the same conventions as the readers and buyers do.

The secret to effective book distribution is to make the title available in places with a high concentration of your potential buyers. When a niche publisher takes on your book, they can plug it right into their existing distribution system. For example, while some parachute books are sold in bookstores, more than 90 percent are sold through parachute stores, skydiving catalogs, jump schools and through the U.S. Parachute Association for resale to its members. Usually three or four calls to major dealers can sell enough books to pay the printing billbefore the book is even printed!

Some writers may think a large New York publisher is more prestigious (good for impressing people at cocktail parties), but a small to medium-sized publisher will usually sell more books because they sell to non-book trade accounts as well as to bookstores. Remember, most book buyers are interested in the subject matter of the book and want to know if the author is credible. Rarely does anyone ask who the publisher is.

> *"Professionals sell then write, while amateurs write then try*
> *to sell."*
> —Gordon Burgett

Contacting a niche publisher: If you decide you want your book published by someone else, the secret is to match the manuscript to the publisher. To find the right publisher, check your own bookshelf or go to your nearby bookstore and consult the shelves where your book will be. Check the listings at an online bookstore such as Amazon.com. Look for smaller publishers who do good work. When you contact a niche publisher, you will often get through to the top person. They know and like the subject, and they are usually very helpful. They will be able to tell you instantly whether the proposed book will fit into their line.

Niche book publishers tend to be helpful and friendly. No two niche books are exactly alike; it is rare if two books on the same niche subject are published in the same year. Consequently, these publishers do not feel threatened by other publishers. In fact, publishers often promote other books and each other. This is why when you contact a publisher and they decide that your manuscript is not for them, they are eager to recommend another publisher. They know of lots of other publishing companies, and most relish being able to help you and the other publisher get together.

3. Vanity or subsidy publishers produce around 6,000 titles each year; roughly twenty firms produce about 70 percent of the subsidized books. Subsidy publishers offer regular publishing services, but the author invests all the money. Under a typical arrangement, the author pays the full publishing costs (more than just the printing bill) and receives 40 percent of the retail price of the books sold and 80 percent of the subsidiary rights, if sold. Many vanity publishers charge $10,000 to $30,000 to publish a book, depending on its length.

Vanity publishers claim that they will furnish all the regular publishing services including promotion and distribution. All this might not be so bad if they had a good track record for delivery. But according to *Writer's Digest*, vanity publishers usually do not deliver the promotion they promise, and the books rarely return one-quarter of the author's investment.

A cautionary tale

Soma Vira, Ph.D., paid $44,000 to have three of her books produced by a well-known subsidy publisher. She received 250 books but could not verify how many were printed and suspects they made very few for stock. The books were not properly edited, typeset, proofed or manufactured. Distributors, bookstores and reviewers refuse to consider books from this and other vanity presses. The books she received cost her $176 each and she had to start over.

> *"Legitimate publishers don't have to look for manuscripts."*
> —L. M. Hasselstrom

Since binding is expensive, the subsidy publisher often binds just a few hundred copies; the rest of the printed sheets remain unbound unless needed. The "advertising" promised in the contract normally turns out to be only a tombstone ad that lists many titles in *The New York Times*. Sales from this feeble promotion are extremely rare.

Print On Demand publishers also provide a subsidy service; *the author pays*. Most of them make more money selling books to the author than to the public. Most of their marketing efforts are aimed toward the author.

The ads reading, "To the author..." or "Manuscripts wanted by..." easily catch the eye of the writer with a book-length manuscript. Vanity presses almost always accept a manuscript for publication and usually do so with a glowing review letter. They don't make any promises regarding sales, and usually the book sells fewer than a hundred copies. Vanity publishers don't have to sell any books because the author has already paid them for their work. Therefore, subsidy publishers are interested in manufacturing the book (as few copies as possible), not in editing, high-quality cover design and typesetting, promotion, sales or distribution. Since they are paid to publish, they are really selling printing contracts, not books. They are simply taking a large fee to print unedited and poorly reproduced manuscripts.

Review copies of the book sent to columnists by a subsidy publisher usually go straight into the circular file (trash can). The reviewer's time is valuable, and they do not like vanity presses because they know that very little editing has been done to the book. They also realize that there will be little promotional effort, that the book has not been distributed to bookstores, and that the title will not be available to their readers. The name of a subsidy publisher on the spine of the book is a kiss of death.

One major vanity press lost a large class-action suit a few years ago, but they are still advertising in the *Yellow Pages*; they are still in business.

4. Literary agents match manuscripts with the right publisher and negotiate the contract; 80 percent of the new material comes to the larger publishers through them. The agent has to serve the publisher well; for if he or she submits an inappropriate or poor manuscript, the publisher will be reluctant to consider anything more from that agent in the future. Therefore, agents like "sure bets" too, and many are disinclined to even consider an unpublished writer. Their normal commission is 15 percent.

Agents are 85 percent hope and 15 percent commission.

According to *Literary Marketplace*, about 40 percent of the literary agents will not read manuscripts by unpublished authors, and a good 15 percent will not even answer query letters from them. Of those agents who will read the manuscript of an unpublished author, 80 percent will charge for the service. Eighty percent of the agents will not represent professional books; 93 percent will not touch reference works; 99 percent will not handle technical books; 98 percent will not represent regional books, satire, musicals and other specialized manuscripts. Although most agents will handle novel-length fiction, only 20 percent are willing to take on either novellas or short stories, and only 2 percent have a special interest in literature or quality fiction.

"It's harder for a new writer to get an agent than a publisher."
—Roger Straus, president, Farrar, Straus & Giroux

On the fringe, there are people who call themselves agents who charge a reading fee and then pay students to read and critique the manuscript. They make their money on these fees, not from placing the manuscripts. For a list of literary agents, see *Writer's Market, Literary Agents of North America* and *Literary Market Place*. Also see the directory of agents on the Writers Net Web site at http://www.writers.net and the Association of Authors Representatives, Inc., an organization of independent literary and dramatic agents, at http://www.publishersweekly.com.

5. Self-publishing is where the author bypasses all the intermediaries, deals directly with the editor, cover artist, book designer and printer, and then handles the distribution and promotion. If you publish yourself, you'll make more money, get to press sooner, and keep control of your book. You'll invest your time as well as your money, but the reward will be greater.

Self-publishing is not new. In fact, it has solid early American roots; it is almost a tradition. Well-known self-publishers include Mark Twain, Zane Grey, Upton Sinclair, Carl Sandburg, James Joyce, D. H. Lawrence, Ezra Pound, Edgar Rice Burroughs, Stephen Crane, Mary Baker Eddy, George Bernard Shaw, Edgar Allan Poe, Rudyard Kipling, Henry David Thoreau, Walt Whitman, Robert Ringer, Spencer Johnson, Richard Nixon, John Grisham, Tom Peters, Stephen King, Ken Blanchard, L. Ron Hubbard and many, many more. These people were self-publishers, though today the vanity presses claim their books were "subsidy" published. Years ago, authors might have elected to go their own way and self-publish after being turned down by regular publishers. However, today, most self-publishers make an educated decision to take control of their book—often after reading my book The Self-Publishing Manual.

Do self-publishers ever sell many books? Here are some numbers (at last count): *What Color Is Your Parachute*, twenty-two revised editions and 5 million copies; *Fifty Simple Things You Can Do to Save the Earth*, 4.5 million copies; *How to Keep Your Volkswagen Alive*, 2.2 million copies; *Leadership Secrets of Attila the Hun*, over 0.5 million copies, and *Final Exit*, over 0.5 million copies. These authors took control and made it big. For an expanded self-publishing success list, see Document 155 at http://parapublishing.com/sites/para/resources/allproducts.cfm.

Self-publishing is not difficult. In fact, it may even be easier than dealing with a publisher. The job of the self-publisher is not to perform every task, but to see that every task gets done. Self-publishers deal directly with the printer and handle as many of the editing, proofing, cover and page production, promotion and distribution jobs as they can. What they can't do, they farm out. Therefore, self-publishing may take on many forms, depending on the author-publisher's interests, assets and abilities. It allows them to concentrate on those areas they find most appealing and use outside services for the rest.

Properly planned, there is little monetary risk in self-publishing. If you follow the plan, the only variable is the subject of the book. Unlike poetry and fiction, most nonfiction topics sell relatively easily, especially to their target markets.

Because the big publisher only tests a book for a few months and then lets sales dictate its fate (reprint or remainder), the first four months are the most important to them. The self-publisher, on the other hand, uses the first year to build a solid market-base for a future of sustained sales. While a big publisher may sell only 5,000 copies total, the self-publisher can often count on 5,000 or more each year, year after year.

Para Publishing's *Is There a Book Inside You?* has a self-paced quiz to help you decide between a large publisher, a medium-sized niche publisher, an agent, a book producer, a vanity press and self-publishing.

> *Do you realize what would happen if Moses were alive today?*
> *He'd go up to Mount Sinai, come back with the Ten Commandments,*
> *and spend the next eight years trying to get them published.*
> —Robert Orben, humorist

Eight good reasons to self-publish

1. To make more money. Why accept 6 percent to 10 percent in royalties from a publisher when you can have 35 percent from your bookstore distributor (or 100 percent if you sell direct to the reader)? You know your subject and you know the people in your field. Certainly you know more than some distant publisher who might buy your book. Although trade publishers can get your book into bookstores, they don't know the non-bookstore possibilities as well as you do, and they aren't going to expend as much focused promotional effort. Ask yourself this question: Will the trade publisher be able to sell four times as many books as I can?

2. Speed. Most publishers work on an eighteen-month production cycle. Can you wait that long to get into print? Will you miss your market? The eighteen months don't even begin until after the contract negotiations and contract signing. Publication could be three years away! Why waste time shipping your manuscript around to see if there is an agent or publisher out there who likes it?

Nixon & the speed of self-publishing

Richard Nixon self-published *Real Peace* in 1983 because he felt his message was urgent; he couldn't wait for a publisher's slow machinery to grind out the book.

Typically, bookstores buy the first book published on a popular subject. Later books may be better, but the store buyer may pass on them since the store already has the subject covered.

3. To keep control of your book. According to *Writer's Digest*, 60 percent of the big publishers do not give the author final approval on copyediting; 23 percent never give the author the right to select the title; 20 percent do not consult the author on the jacket design; and 36 percent rarely involve the author in the book's promotion.

The big New York trade publishers probably have more promotional connections than you do. But with a huge stable of books to push, your book will most likely get lost in the shuffle. The big publishers are good at getting books into bookstores, yet fail miserably at approaching other outlets or doing specialized promotion. Give the book to someone who has a personal interest in it you: as the author.

4. No one will read your manuscript. Many publishers receive hundreds of unsolicited manuscripts for consideration each day. They do not have time to unwrap, review, rewrap and ship all those submissions, so they return them unopened. Unless you are a movie star, noted politician, or have a recognizable name, it is nearly impossible to attract a publisher. Many publishers work with their existing stable of authors and accept new authors only through agents.

5. Self-publishing is good business. There are many more tax advantages for an author-publisher than there are for just authors. Self-publishers can deduct their lifestyle.

6. Self-publishing will help you think like a publisher. A book is a product that comes from you, somewhat like your own child. You are very protective of your book and naturally feel that it's terrific. When someone else publishes you, you think the book would sell better if only the publisher would pump in more promotion money. The publisher will respond that they are not anxious to dump more money into a book that isn't selling. So if you self-publish, you gain a better understanding of the arguments on both sides. It is your money and your choice.

7. You'll gain self-confidence and self-esteem. You will be proud to be the author of a published book. Compare this to pleading with people to read your manuscript.

8. Finally, you may have no other choice. There are more manuscripts than can be read. Most publishers don't have time to even look at your manuscript.

The greatest challenge facing the smaller and newer publisher today is finding a system for *managing the excitement*. Nonfiction book publishers in their how-to books provide valuable information that readers willingly buy because it is going to save them time and money. We send out review copies, draft articles, make email solicitations, and circulate news releases on our books—and customers respond. That is exciting! Publishing is an easy business, a profitable business, and a fun business. The publishing business is truly *excitement driven*.

Should you self-publisih?

Would-be author-publishers should be cautioned that self-publishing is not for everyone. Writing is an *art*, whereas publishing is a *business*, and some people are unable to do both well. If you are a lovely, creative flower who is repelled by the crass commercialism of selling your own product, you should stick to the creative side and let someone else handle the business end.

On the other hand, some people are terribly independent. They will not be happy with the performance of any publisher, no matter how much time and effort is spent creating and promoting the book. These people should save the publisher from all this grief by becoming their own publisher and making their own decisions. Fortunately, most of us fall somewhere in between and can handle both the creative and promotion sides of publishing.

Selling out to a big publisher: Many self-publishers find that once they have proven their books with good sales, they're approached by larger publishing houses with offers to print a new edition. For a short list of them, see Document 155 at http://DanSentMe.com/sites/para/resources/allproducts.cfm.

$4.2 million paid!

Richard Paul Evans took six weeks to write the eighty-seven-page *Christmas Box*. He did so well selling it for two holiday seasons that Simon & Schuster paid him $4.2 million for it. Now it is in thirteen languages. Sometimes authors begin as self-publishers, get attention, and then sell to a larger publisher.

The future of publishing

Packaged information is becoming increasingly specialized. More and more books are being printed in smaller quantities. The information in books is going out of date faster. Books are being produced more rapidly. Computerized equipment allows people to rapidly write, edit, lay out, print and deliver books. The customer wants more condensed and targeted information, faster.

The self-publishing route will enable you to get your book into print at minimum cost. This book could be your second chance. It will show you the way to publication, fame and extra income—a new life.

Obviously, your success cannot be guaranteed, but many people are doing very well in the writing/publishing business. This isn't a get-rich-quick scheme; there is work involved. Even though you are working for yourself, at your own pace, it is still *work*. You won't get rich overnight. Building a sound business-venture takes several years.

Make effective use of your most valuable asset: your time.

The secret is to invest your labor. Your time is precious. Like gold, there is a finite quantity. You have only twenty-four hours of time each day. You can use your time in several ways: you can throw it away, sell it, or invest it. For instance, you can waste your valuable time in front of the television set; time is easy to lose that way.

Most people spend their lives punching a clock, going to work, and getting a check. They trade their labor for money on a one-to-one basis. If you don't punch in, you don't get paid. But isn't it better to invest your time in a book that will sell and generate income while you are away doing something else? Your labor becomes an investment that pays dividends for years while you are playing or working on another investment. Don't throw away your time; invest it. It is up to you.

You have all the ingredients it takes to be a successful published author. Your recipe is at http://parapublishing.com/sites/para/resources/infokit.cfm.

> *"I never said writing your book would be easy. But I do promise the work will be worth it."*

—Dan Poynter

Dan Poynter *is an author of more than 120 books, has been a publisher since 1969 and is a Certified Speaking Professional (CSP).*

He is an evangelist for books, an ombudsman for authors, an advocate for publishers and the godfather to thousands of successfully-published books. His seminars have been featured on CNN, his books have been pictured in the Wall Street Journal *and his story has been told in* US News & World Report.

The media come to Dan because he is the leading authority on book publishing.

Dan travels more than 4,000 miles each week to share, inspire and empower writers, publishers and professional speakers through keynotes and seminars.

Some of his books are Writing Nonfiction, The Self-Publishing Manual, The Skydiver's Handbook, The Expert Witness Handbook *and* The Older Cat.

Dan shows people how to make a difference while making a living by coaching them on the writing, publishing and promoting of their book. He has turned thousands of people into successful authors.

His mission is to see that people do not die with a book still inside them. See his website at http://ParaPublishing.com.

How to Write a Nonfiction Book Proposal

Sell Your Book Before You Write It

By Stephen Blake Mettee

Selling a nonfiction book to a publisher isn't rocket science. If you pitch the right book to the right publisher, getting a "Yes!" is nearly inevitable. Of course your pitch must be taken seriously, and to accomplish this, you need to make it professional. This is where a nonfiction book proposal comes into play.

What is a book proposal?

A book proposal is a ten- to fifty-page document designed to give an acquisitions editor enough information about your proposed book and enough confidence in you as the author to agree to publish it. The proposal must also convince him or her that the book will sell enough copies and make enough profit to repay his company for its investment of time and money.

Even if you have already written your book, you will likely need to write a book proposal to gain the attention of an editor. This is for two reasons: 1) A proposal contains information that your manuscript doesn't, and 2) acquisitions editors don't have the time to read every full-length manuscript that comes across their desks.

The same well-wrought proposal can be used to attract the attention of a literary agent if you plan to use one to secure a publisher for you.

The nonfiction author's advantage

One of the great things about writing nonfiction books, in contrast to novels, is that most nonfiction books are sold to a publisher on the basis of the proposal—before the book has been written. This means that if you can't find a publisher, you won't need to waste your time writing the book. With novels, a first-time author is, almost without exception, required to write the whole book before going to contract.

The anatomy of a book proposal

Your book proposals should have five parts:

- The synopsis
- A table of contents
- A chapter-by-chapter outline
- Sample chapters
- Supporting material

Let's take a quick look at each of these proposal parts.

The synopsis

This is the gist of the proposal. Use as many words as you need to concisely outline the project. Don't skip any essential details, but don't include any extraneous material. Most synopsis will run from one to ten pages. In the synopsis you should:

- State your book's proposed title and subtitle. Titles and subtitles are important; give both a great deal of thought.

- Describe the basic premise of your book. Will it be an irreverent biography of a famous person? An overview of discount shopping opportunities in Southern Florida? A guide for parents with autistic children?

- Define who makes up the market for such a book. Will the tens of thousands of CPAs in the United States be your main market? Or, is your book for teenage girls? Is it a hiking guide for nature lovers? The size of the market and how easy it will be to alert the people in this market of your book are key considerations for a publisher. Quote figures and suggest ways your target market can be reached. Don't fall into the novice's trap of saying it's a book for everyone. There is no such animal.

• Explain how your book will benefit the reader.

• Outline the main points you will cover and explain the depth to which they will be covered.

• Let the editor know your intended style. Will your tone be academic or warm and fuzzy? Authoritative but approachable? Humorous?

• Explain special features you'll include. Will you have frequent side-bars? Quotes from famous people? Charts and lists? Photographs and/or graphics?

• List competing titles and explain why yours will be better or different. Another newbie trap to avoid is saying there are no competing titles. Even if your book will be the first on the elusive black scorpion of Madagascar, there will be other books on scorpions or at least other books on arachnids.

• Tell why you are the person to write this book and how you will help to market it. The two most impressive things you can say are that you are an expert on your subject and that you have a "platform" to help you sell the book. Speaking regularly at industry conferences, authoring a popular Internet blog, or hosting a radio show are examples of author platforms.

If you aren't a expert on your subject, explain what research you will do and which experts you'll interview. If you don't have a platform, develop one. Surely, you can write a blog or put up a website or speak to churches or organizations in your state. This may sound a bit harsh, but publishers of all sizes, with fewer and fewer dollars to spend on promotion, are looking to the author to help make the book a break-out success. Yes, you can sell a book to a publisher without a platform, but it'll be tougher.

• List prepublication endorsements you can obtain and, if you will have a well-known person write the foreword, mention it.

• Include your anticipated word count. This will have to be an educated guess. Don't say how many "pages" your manuscript will be; publishers need word counts.

• Give the publisher an idea of the time and resources you'll need to complete the project.

Table of contents

List the chapters and other parts of the book in the order they will appear. This will look just like a standard table of contents, except devoid of page numbers.

Chapter-by-chapter outline

Use one to three paragraphs to describe what each chapter will include. I find this is the part most writers want to skimp on or skip entirely. Do so at your own peril. If the editor doesn't get a clear conviction that you have thought out your project, he or she is much more likely to take a pass on it.

Sample chapters

Include a couple of sample chapters. These don't have to be the first two chapters in the book, so make them the ones you find most interesting. The editor probably will too.

I find lots of authors send the book's introduction in lieu of a chapter. I imagine this is because they have already written it, but the introduction usually covers information previously given in the proposal and often doesn't exemplify the book as well. It is far better to include real chapters.

Supporting materials

Supporting materials include anything that will help an editor better grasp the project and its chances of success. Among other things, these may include photocopies of pictures or examples of charts that will be in the book, a complete list of all of your publication credits, or newspaper clippings that attest to the public's interest in your subject.

A final bit of advice: Throughout your proposal, try to convey how excited you are about this project and how committed you are to it. Publishers like these qualities in authors because authors who are passionate and dedicated do the best job of writing and promoting their book.

Stephen Blake Mettee is founder and publisher of Quill Driver Books, author of The Fast-Track Course on How to Write a Nonfiction Book Proposal *and coeditor of* The American Directory of Writer's Guidelines. *He is a frequent speaker at writer's conferences.*

Bring Her On and Let Her Scream

*Use colorful description
to enliven your nonfiction*

By Thomas Hunter

WHAT IF YOU GAVE A PARTY AND NO ONE CAME? What if you wrote an article but no one read it? We can fill pages with copy but, if it's not being read, it doesn't do anyone any good—including ourselves. As Henry Luce of Time-Life said, the trick is to get the information off the page and into the reader's mind. To do this, use color to keep your reader reading.

What is color? Color is the sounds, the sights, the smells, the texture, and the feelings of a place or an event. Color takes readers and places them at the scene. You add color by using descriptive words—not just adjectives and adverbs but verbs and nouns—that evoke an image in the reader's mind.

Color for the sake of color is garish, but used properly:

• It can get readers to read even if the basic subject matter doesn't appeal to them, by making a piece of writing an entertainment to read.

• It lets you plant ideas more firmly in the readers' minds, because you're coming at them through the senses and not just feeding them abstract information.

• It lends far greater credibility to writing because, to capture the scene you have to be on the scene. Sensing that, readers are more inclined to feel they are getting hard, straight facts.

As you gather facts and conduct interviews, be alert for descriptive material with which to enliven your writing.

Here's a masterful example.

Bill Reynolds, as associate editor of *TWA Ambassador*, the inflight magazine, wrote a lengthy profile on Alvin Toffler, shortly after Toffler's second book came out. This is the way the article ends.

> He pauses, sits forward in his chocolate-brown and chrome chair and clasps the hands that ordinarily are in almost constant motion. When he speaks, the carefully paced voice is even softer: "I have one great sadness, and that is that my father didn't live to see *Future Shock*. He died a year before I finished writing it."
>
> It is a few minutes before he will speak again. For the time being, Alvin Toffler, who made his name and fortune by writing about possible futures, is caught up in the past.

That's not only powerful writing; chances are we'll never forget Alvin Toffler's one great sadness in life. Had it been presented as an abstract piece of information, we'd most likely eventually lose it. But we can practically hear him say it. We see him as he says it. We feel what he was feeling. And it's all because of the way Reynolds describes the scene. With color you plant ideas more firmly in readers' minds because you're coming at them through the senses, hooking them in a number of different ways.

Here's another example.

Andrew Malcolm wrote an article for the *New York Times'* Sunday magazine section about the effect of federal deregulation on the airlines. He spent twenty-one hours with one American Airlines jumbo jet, fourteen of those hours in the air, flying from city to city. This is how he opens his piece:

> It was 1:00 a.m. and black in the other world outside.
>
> The two men sat in their safety harnesses, softly speaking in codes by the eerie green light of computer controlled dials. At times, a voice from outside read numbers and directions and speeds into their ears, but nothing happened until the final approval came.
>
> Allen Amsbaugh answered, "American 98 heavy, rolling." He looked at Tom Seiger on his right and nodded. Each put one hand on the beige metal knuckles of the throttles between them. They pushed forward.
>
> Instantly there came a powerful deep rumble from behind. Twin furies of fumes shot hot out across the cement, bending the grass and blasting some scraps of paper high in the air over the roadway just south of San Francisco. The rumblings billowed down deserted Millbrae Avenue past a bank and a used car lot and the stoplights winking to no one. They bounced off the darkened storefronts of Burlingame Plaza and rattled the windows of a dry cleaner. And then,

> 35 seconds after it began, the thunder was gone. And so was the
> airplane, a brand new Boeing 767, now just a blinking light cutting
> through the clouds, heading East.

I haven't the slightest bit of interest in the effect of federal deregulation on the airlines. My interest level is absolute zero. But Malcolm's one-sentence lead paragraph was exciting to read, like page one of a Robert Ludlum or Tom Clancy novel. It pulled me into the second paragraph. Then I had to go into the third. By then, he had me fully hooked, and he held my interest by sprinkling color and descriptive material throughout the piece. With color, you entice people to read even when the basic subject matter doesn't appeal to them.

These two examples are lengthy. We need a long feature story to sustain the weight of that much color. A short piece won't, but with short pieces, we don't need that much. A brief opening vignette can work just as well.

Lindsay Smith with US West, based in Denver, wrote an article for the company's employee publication about repair crews putting phone lines back together. A contractor installing sewer lines had ripped through them. Smith opened his article with the lightest touch of color:

> You could see tired written on their faces, the stubble of beard,
> dust and dirt that the wind had etched on, a look in the eyes.

Halfway into the article, he described a lunch break:

> It was not a relaxed lunch. Chicken on paper plates on the hood
> of a truck. The wind whipped one plate off, sending half-eaten
> chicken pieces into the dirt.

Talking with Smith about the article, I told him I loved the way he described the lunch break. He said, "Everybody who has spoken with me about that article has mentioned that exact same scene. What most of them tell me is that it let them know I was there; that it wasn't just a bunch of secondhand reporting they were getting."

To get this kind of material you have to be on the scene, with your powers of observation set at the highest level possible. Connect with everything you hear, smell, see, touch, and taste. It's all potential material. The use of this material is powerful, too, because it follows the maxim "show don't tell"— one of the most basic rules of writing.

If you merely tell readers what happened, you're keeping them distant from the story. When you show them, you pull them into the story. It practically makes them participants in the story and there's a better chance they'll stay. Mark Twain put it this way: "Don't say the old lady screamed. Bring her on and let her scream."

Here's the way Geraldine Brooks does it with an article in *The Wall Street Journal*:

> AKRON OHIO—Richard Misanko punctuates his sentences with the snap of breaking rubber bands.
>
> "This," he says, selecting a yellow rubber band from a spaghetti-tangle of specimens and stretching it between his forefingers, "is a cheapie from Malaysia." The band snaps and a shred of rubber flies across the room. He reaches into the tangle for another. "This is a band (snap) made by a major domestic competitor. Here's another (snap) import. And (snap) another. I could (snap) do this all day."

She puts us right into the story. It's as though we're there in the man's office. You can almost feel the sting in your fingers when a rubber band snaps on you.

Try this article lead by Bev Dotter in *Sun Chemical Magazine*:

> John Ryan likes a challenge. Right now he is testing the laws of balance. Periodically while talking he tilts his office chair backward at an ever more precarious angle. The odds seems clearly in favor of a somersault.
>
> But he doesn't fall. He's weighed the risk and found it acceptable. He knows just how far he can go, and he knows when to stop.
>
> In the three years he has been president of Sun Information Services, John Ryan has relied heavily on that sense of balance to help him meet the challenge of turning SIS into a profitable new business.

That's brilliant. First of all, Dotter alertly makes note of this simple action of the fellow tilting on his chair. Then she uses it so that the reader can visualize an abstract theme she carries throughout the article. Had she not used it for that reason, she shouldn't have used it all. Then it would have been color just for the sake of color. It has to be relevant.

It's like the Lindsay Smith scene. The main point he wanted to get across in his article was that the repair crews didn't waste time. They worked as quickly as they could to see to it that service was restored to customers as quickly as possible. And that lunch scene—"not a relaxed lunch, chicken on paper plates on the hood of a truck"—let him show not tell.

To recap, this kind of writing works on several levels:

• It is a kind of entertainment. You let the reader watch something unfold right while it's happening. It takes a past event and lends a sense of immediacy to it.

- By thrusting readers into a scene, you give them a sense of being participants in the story, and there's a much better chance they'll stay.

- It plants ideas more firmly in readers' minds because we're coming at them through the senses. In doing so, we enliven the story and make abstracts concrete.

If you're doing an article about a trucker, you ought to get out and ride with the trucker and absorb all the sights and sounds and feelings of trucking. How does the trucker check the rearview mirror, the sideview mirror, before pulling out on the road? What's hanging around the cab to personalize it? If there's a stop at a diner for a cup of coffee, what's the conversation between the trucker and the counter attendant; between the trucker and other truckers? How many spoons of sugar does he put in his coffee? What does the lunch counter look like? Is it scratched? If there's a jukebox playing, what are the songs on the jukebox; what are the lyrics? Back out on the road, check the billboards and the other signs along the highway.

Later, you decide what you're going to use. Use only what's relevant. Maybe there's a snippet of song lyric that perfectly underscores the main theme of the article. By putting it into the article, you let the reader practically hear the theme. Maybe a slogan on a billboard succinctly sums up the trucker's view of who he is, what he does. You might sign off the article with a description of that billboard and its slogan in the last paragraph, letting the reader see the trucker as he sees himself.

Go easy with color at first. Too much color is sickening. It's like three inches of icing on a cake.

Irene Pave at *Business Week* did an article about increasing insurance rates and how those increasing rates probably were going to put a lot of small day-care centers out of business. This is her lead sentence:

> Anxiety is sweeping the world of finger paints and afternoon naps.

A simple, lovely lead that both intrigues and captures the essence of the story with visual language. Colorful description doesn't have to be a big block of writing. Search out those words that appeal to the senses, that involve more than just the reader's intellect. Choose vivid, lively words. Don't have someone just "walk" out of a room. Not if they storm out, charge out, sidle out. Don't have someone just "say" something, not when they blurt, mumble, whisper, shout. Words with texture, words that let the reader *sense* what's going on. But, again, we must be sure that the words are relevant, that they reinforce or add to meaning. Most often someone will just walk out of a room; someone will just say something. But if they storm out, there's a reason and the word is relevant. If someone mumbles, there's a reason and it's appropriate to use the word.

If there are no people and no action to describe, use good action words.

• Before David Souter was appointed to the U.S. Supreme Court and was going through the congressional hearings, one of the days of those hearings was his birthday. That evening on NBC television in New York, the newscaster, talking about what took place at the hearings that day, said, "David Souter chose his birthday to unwrap his opinions about a number of legal issues." What a wonderful use of the word *unwrap*, tying it into his birthday.

• An Associated Press story about the demise of the spacecraft Magellan as it plunged into Venus noted, "A final experiment designed to wring the last bits of information from Magellan drained its power to the point where it could no longer transmit data or perform other functions." A wonderful use of *wring*.

As you read, note how the best nonfiction writers always seem able to come up with the visual metaphor or simile to convey an abstract thought and bring it alive. Consider this by Benjamin Stein in *The Wall Street Journal*. The metaphor he uses in an op-ed piece entitled "I'm Having a Wonderful Time" conveys the depth of a disappointment he's experiencing:

> Six years ago this month, I wrote an article for *The Wall Street Journal*'s editorial page, about how I was leaving the nine-to-five life of a columnist at the Journal and heading for Hollywood to seek fame and fortune as a freelance writer. Quoting the immortal Joan Didion, I wrote, "You can't win if you're not at the table," and then I headed for the table. My thought was that if I won at the table I would have the house in Beverly Hills with the pool, the house in Aspen, the meetings at lunch at Ma Maison where producers would eagerly press thousands of dollars upon me, and the attention of adoring starlets as I cruised the strip in my Mercedes convertible.
>
> It is hard to believe that anyone could have been so young and so stupid, but I am here to tell you that I was that stupid and that I still am. There has been a great freight train of disappointment regularly running through my home since I moved here...

You *feel* how enormous, how oppressive the disappointment, more than had he written, "Have I been disappointed."

In an interview with the *Times*' Malcolm about his writing of the federal deregulation article, I told him that I found his article so much more interesting to read than just a recitation of dry facts about cost-cutting, competition, and the rest of it. He said, "Hey, I wouldn't want to read that. So I wouldn't want to write it either."

That's another big plus of color: it works for the writer, too. It can make writing easier. Instead of sitting at the word processor trying to find writer's words for abstract ideas, we have concrete scenes and images to describe and work with. It also makes writing nonfiction more fun, like writing a short story.

In a profile in *the New Yorker*, Pulitzer Prize winning journalist Murray Kempton, referring to his four-day-a-week column in *Newsday*, explained why, before beginning to write, he spends a good part of the day roaming. He said, "I like to get around. I need a scene, something to look at. I'd rather die than try to write out of my head four days a week."

And when you do get out, you never know what surprises, what moments, you'll stumble onto.

An editor of an employee magazine—sorry to say, I forget her name—told me of an article she wrote about six employees at her company who competed in a local marathon. She could have written the story from after-the-fact interviews with the runners. Instead, she got out there and stayed from the snap of the starting gun until the very end. With the sun gone, two runners still had not finished. The next to last was an employee with her company. His family was waiting for him and, as he crossed the line, his three-year-old daughter started to jump up and down, clapping and yelling, "Daddy, you won. You won." There's a moment for you, and here's the editor's lead:

> You don't always have to be the first across the line to be a winner.

A moment like that, a lead like that—and the story almost writes itself.

Thomas Hunter *is a former print and broadcast journalist. His freelance articles have appeared in national magazines and major daily newspapers. He is founder of Effective Communications Group, based in Ridgewood, NJ.*

The King Is Dead; Long Live the King

Your therapist and confidant:
The cathartic value of the small press

By Frederick A. Raborg, Jr.

A S WRITERS, WE HAVE A GREAT DEAL in common with clowns. Even well-known writers are handicapped by the "baggage" they bring to the craft from childhood, the angst of maturation and the "skeletons" most of us store not so neatly in our mental closets.

Unwittingly or not, when a writer turns to the small press it is to purge the tonnage. Clowns, each unique, cover grief and regret with well-designed makeup and "punish" themselves with slapstick, inviting the public to point and laugh at let's-pretend debacles and shortcomings. Writers use the small audiences of litmags as a confessional of sorts, an arena in which the darkest secrets can be revealed with a minimum of taunt and little need to flagellate.

It begins in high school where those creative writing magazines which still are funded (and they are getting pathetically fewer) are filled with discovery poems and stories of death and first loves, usually unrequited. Surprisingly, however, most true future writers shy away from the high school magazines, especially in matters sexual or dysfunctional, probably because maturity has not allowed the acknowledgment and release of such strong insights. The cathartic need is there; the epiphanal machinery is not. Enter the small press.

When I began writing in the mid-fifties, there was no small press as such—a few university journals, and such magazines as the long-defunct *Circle*. Len Fulton's *International Directory of Little Magazines & Small Presses* would not come along until 1964 when it appeared as a small, saddle-stitched periodical of 48 pages. Today, that bible of litmags carries 1,040 pages crammed with general guidelines for more than 4,000 small magazines. What we did have in the fifties was a fairly large number of pulp magazines hanging on from a Victorian heyday and paying ¼ cent to two cents per word, but already dying swans on the newsstands. A few science fiction and detective magazines still struggle to survive in that publishing genre, but even they, like Algis Budrys' fine *Tomorrow*, printed on newsprint, attempt to give a slicker image on the stands.

I've wondered often if small press, as we know it today, might have prevented Ernest Hemingway's suicide. Certainly he had *The Transatlantic Review*, but few other outlets because he already was a man of great reputation both for machismo as well as for the creation of new literary devices and economies. He was never allowed the snobbery of a Ford Maddox Ford, a T. S. Eliot or Virginia Wolfe, though, like Virginia Wolfe, he did have his feminine versions of Dashiell Hammett to serve as levelers. He was allowed to suckle at the teat of Gertrude Stein's salon, but the fact of her lifestyle with Alice Toklas probably drove any inner admissions on his part deeper underground.

> "Almost without exception, each of us comes to writing with high aspirations."

I'm sure he did the best he could with the avenues open to his immense talent and acclaim, but a more active small press may have given him the opportunity to purge his father's suicide and the effects of a dominating mother. Perhaps a stronger small press would have kept Sylvia Plath from the oven and Wendell Keyes from his strange disappearance. Unfortunately, these and other writers akin to them developed reputations which fed strongly on their souls and gave little vent to their emotional needs.

Almost without exception, each of us comes to writing with high aspirations. Many movies of the thirties and forties had storylines in which a romantic character—usually female—sent off the protagonist's novel or story without his knowledge, "to save him from himself," and, of course, the work was instantly accepted, the surprise check changed the path of the writer's life and love, and the work was an instant best-seller surging the protagonist into glory. God, Loretta Young beside the point, it was never so.

True, it was easy to get work into local newspapers. I began my first professional writing at the age of twelve by writing a weekly column titled "The Bowers Hill News" for the old *Portsmouth Star*, long since merged with the *Norfolk Ledger-Dispatch* and the *Norfolk Virginian-Pilot* in Tidewater, Virginia. Newspapers routinely published poetry, good and bad...and they sometimes paid a small stipend. I wrote book and drama reviews for more than a decade, for no other reason than to heighten my education. Newspapers succored our Erato. Newspapers today have disallowed the personal side of their issue; most have lost sight of and touch with their readership, which is why so many are folding.

The same is true of major slick magazines. Their publishers and editors have forgotten that it was their choices in fiction and poetry, not articles about jogging and nouveau riche dining, which established the long-lasting voices for which they are noted. Today, most popular magazines look alike, contain identical articles, and are not attractive at all. How I miss stories illustrated with double-truck illustrations by the likes of Joe Bowler. How proud I was when the first several of my short stories appeared in that manner. They were gorgeous and fed my ego with ambrosia.

When I began to write, we had hundreds of religious magazines, men's magazines, women's magazines and general interest magazines, such as the *Saturday Evening Post* and *Collier's*. Every magazine, many appearing weekly, published three to four short stories and an equal number of poems in every issue. As a young male writer, I could sail the seven seas and climb the highest mountains by writing stories for *Argosy* or *True Adventures*. The women's magazines published male writers and allowed us to imagine incredible love affairs. I could write a story for a men's magazine on Monday and be pious for a religious outlet on Tuesday. Of course, men's magazines contained quality tales in those days instead of *only* tails, if you will pardon the pun. Mythic or not, the opportunities for publication seemed endless.

Perhaps the demise came with the first mergers of literature with peanut butter and cigarettes. New high speed presses, computers and cameras made excellent photography readily available and affordable, which meant the demise of much fine illustration; to make room for cartoons, the poetry went; and finally many of the cartoons disappeared in favor of computerized sidebars and other generally inane and superfluous fillers. The folding of most major general interest magazines, and the format downsizing due to rapidly rising paper costs and poor editorial/advertising ratios, capped the abundance of opportunities for writers.

Was it actually easier to become published during the plethora of outlets? Not really. When I began writing, there were more than a half million writers trying to fill the five or six hundred major monthly literary spaces for which large checks could be expected when successful. (At one time, *Playboy* was paying up to $5,000 for a first short story sale. Similar checks were not uncommon among the women's markets. Even *True* paid a grand.)

I became friends with the late Georgie Starbuck Galbraith, one of the few poets who could make a living at her craft even then. She managed that by writing under more than 125 pseudonyms. Four poets—Galbraith, Phyllis McGinley, Richard Armour and Suzanne Douglas—claimed virtually all of the major poetry space each month. It was no different in prose. Most writers, even today, are familiar with the two hats worn by Evan Hunter—his real name for "better" prose such as *The Blackboard Jungle* and the pseudonym Ed McBain for his detective series. He was successful under both hats. Nevertheless, excellence would always rise and gain acceptance. Multiple hats brought about something much more sinister—the preplanned best-seller.

Perhaps it began with the enormous financial support *Reader's Digest* gave to the writing of *The Longest Day.* The complete services of that company's vast research department was given to Cornelius Ryan's use.

Many publishers bought storylines from unknown writers to be reworked by best-selling authors and published under the well-known byline (many still do). One well-known series author was not an author at all; he advertised in the *Writer's Digest* for storylines and paid a small fee for novels which would bring thousands once the Jakes byline was added.

I remember, as a budding writer, visiting the offices of Dietz Press in Richmond, Virginia. They published cookbooks and Virginia history for the most part, but wandering their musty stacks was awesomely comfortable, and I felt much the way I did when, as a youngster, I sat down in the dark, murky stacks of the Portsmouth, Virginia, library to read the Oz books, and when, at age nine, I got my first adult library card in the Egyptian decor of the Richmond, Virginia, main branch. I got the same feeling in the late sixties when, in New York to see an agent, I rode that somewhat rickety elevator in the Charles Scribner's building to offices that reminded me of Dickens.

All of those are gone now, or have been severely redesigned for the nineties, I'm sure...traded for the stainless steel and glass of modern Gotham. Such places fed my writing hunger, however, and in Scribner's I could feel the presence of Hemingway, Wolfe and Steinbeck. Oh, yes, at age sixty-two I am still very much the literary romantic. I like to think I bring that same awe still to my editing for *Amelia.* Technology stands against me, however, like the Roman legions against Carthage or Gaul.

Computers and faxes beside the point, submission procedures were very different then as well. Stamps were never glued to return envelopes, they were paperclipped...just in case there was a sale. It was Naomi Lewis of *Good Housekeeping* who campaigned to stop that practice because it seemed to have occupied two young readers' time simply pasting on stamps for manuscripts returned from a slush pile which, even then, produced only 1 percent of the magazine's fiction. Novels were sent back and forth by Railway Express, the return trip always collect. All book publishers were open to unsolicited, complete scripts; today, very few are willing to expend the high costs needed to maintain a "slush pile," and most want to see only sample chapters and outlines except from agents.

As I said, I got my start by writing men's fiction and religious stories. It was an era during which *Playboy* was discovering writers such as Ian Fleming and Charles Beaumont, a time when I shared contents pages with the likes of Ed McBain and Harlan Ellison. Harlan and I cut our literary teeth in Greenleaf Classics' *Rogue* among others. He became rich and vibrantly gregarious. I became...well, hopefully a good editor whose own writing isn't quite over.

In many ways, the transition from newsstand literature to today's apery, not unlike the sameness of television talk shows, was as exciting as the lost and beat generations. For instance, I remember when *Cosmopolitan* was one of the finest literary magazines around, having discovered such writers as Kit Reed; however, sadly, with the advent of Helen Gurley Brown's editorship the magazine slipped from richness of content to richness of purse. I remember writing a long letter to Ms. Brown when she published a series of very short tales by John Lennon. She agreed that the stories were poorly written, but she pointed out it was what the youthful readers wanted at the time. As we know so painfully in the nineties, creative artists cannot beat the spin numbers. Reputations and careers turn on them.

Yet, today, thanks to small press, writers still can create in every genre, still can pursue any theme and still can aspire to become well-known, even stellar artists. A case in point would be Tobias Wolff, who published dozens of short stories in small press before being picked up by such magazines as *Vanity Fair* and *Esquire* and made a literary star.

Another writer comes to mind chiefly because I rejected so many of his stories for *Amelia*. Rick Bass made every effort to sell to me; he even sent me postcards from his travels. Now I couldn't afford him even if he wished to send me something new. As editors, we all have our nightmares about such successes. I cannot explain why Rick's work didn't hit me between the eyes. I justify such oversights as Rick Bass by assuming that what he offered was too close to something we already had published or for one of the hundreds of reasons there are for rejection. Nevertheless, there remains a personal embarrassment for not having brought Bass into my creel.

There is another aspect of the golden age of publishing which small press since has picked up and, frequently, turned into an art form—the personal rejection letter. Perhaps editors, who no longer have the time to edit, still empathize with writers trying to break into major publishing. When I began, my juices continually were stirred by often lengthy letters from editors. I used to judge my degree of success with a rejected story by how far up the staff it had gone. If the note was signed by someone not listed on the masthead, the story didn't score very well; if, on the other hand, it was signed by an editorial assistant, an assistant editor (oh, yes, there's a difference), or an executive editor (the rarefied atmosphere of the publishing house), I knew someone may even have argued in favor of the piece at a weekly editorial meeting. Lee Quarfoot, who replaced Naomi Lewis at *Good Housekeeping*, calls it "going down the hall."

In my early years, I owed a great deal of thanks to editors such as Ann Bayer of *Saturday Evening Post*, who had me convinced each new story would be the one that scored. Barbara Husted of *Cosmopolitan* was equally encouraging, to the point I visited her one day at the Cosmo offices. When the elevator opened, there was Barbara in the mooning position before me as she selected a sweet roll from the coffee cart. She had a fascinating array of sketches on the walls of her office cubicle—drawings by Noel Coward signed personally to her, along with a few more erotic sketches.

At least three editors made acceptances of my work part of their last duties with a magazine. It happened at the *Horn Book*, at *Cuisine*, and at *Ladies' Home Journal*, and I thank those editors profusely.

Small press editors continue that personal-touch tradition. Most of us try to get to know our regular contributors, and we try to say something positive on all rejections. There are times when it becomes difficult, because too much encouragement causes some writers to feel free to telephone at all hours of the night and on weekends and holidays for advice of one kind or another. Because most small press editors have their offices in their homes, such late night calls can be unnerving, especially when the editor has widely scattered children. One doesn't like to hear the phone ring at two in the a.m. There's something quite sinister to it. And, I must say, usually the writer on the other end has had a snootful.

Small press also can handle almost any subject or treatment, and we take chances still not allowed by the majors. For instance, because approximately 15 percent of our readership is gay, we allow at least that much space in every issue for such themes. We try to use material which in some way helps the movement and try never to be pejorative. We are becoming more daring with our illustrations, too. In a recent issue we ran three male frontal nude photographs as well as some similar drawings to accompany both fiction and poetry. The skies did not crack open; the earth did not swallow us; we had three complaints, much praise, and one lost subscription. We use fewer female nudes than in the past because NOW and other feminist groups object vehemently and, to a great extent I agree with them—it's the male's turn to be sexually exploited.

"Exploited" is an awful word, yet accurate, and writers—especially beginning writers and others who do not study their craft—are among the most exploited. As an editor, nothing breaks my heart quicker than to receive a cover letter from a writer, usually stuck in Victorian language and syntax, boasting about the many poems he or she has published in anthologies from *World of Poetry*, *National Library of Poetry* and other similar organizations. They undoubtedly have been awarded all sorts of Silver Poet of the Year or Golden Poet of the Year certificates, and one lady comes to mind who actually won $1,000 for a hideous piece of poorly rhymed and metered doggerel. If the truth were known, she had spent enough with the organization in question to have made it "her turn" to win.

Beware, while most small press contests are completely legitimate and afford stipends for excellence, groups that purchase display ads touting their "contests" in national magazines or large newspapers' funnies sections, publish anything by anyone willing to purchase a copy of

> "There is, among the small press today, an opening for virtually any theme or statement a writer may wish to evoke or emote."

the anthology. Because such an organization also tries to sell the poet bio and photo space, a person can spend nearly $200 to publish a small poem, perhaps a sonnet, on a page with ten to twelve other poems. It is not an honor to appear in those terrible hardcover anthologies, and no editors pay any attention whatsoever to those credits. Still such offers persist until the company feigns bankruptcy, only to rise again with a different name...much the same way as do furniture and jewelry stores.

I understand the "need" to publish. As an editor, I would never tell a poet or writer he was wasting his time. All I have to do is to look back on my own early work. Egad! Yet much of it was published eventually. It was published because I studied the press listings and tried to submit my work to magazines which indicated needs for particular themes and which professed a preference for new writers.

There is, among the small press today, an opening for virtually any theme or statement a writer may wish to evoke or emote. Chew the scenery...there's a place for you. Write a poem to a drop of blood on a slice of radish...there's a place for you. I once wrote a lengthy rhymed piece of humor on gourmet dining which I questioned, especially after a half dozen rejections. I still liked it, and ultimately *Tendril*, that fabulous magazine, now defunct, accepted it.

Not all excellent magazines can last a century, but some have. Most fold within two to five years. Use them while you can. Your work is not lost, because most such quality small press magazines are indexed and copied by a multitude of references and shelved in most universities.

True, we small press publishers have no *Reader's Guide to Periodical Literature* as do the major magazines, but thanks to Harvard and Cambridge such an encompassing index cannot be far down the pike.

You are never too old to purge. Literary bulimia is not the same as the physical disorder; it works in the opposite manner: The writer gorges himself on exempla and sources while purging his emotions. Eventually he will gain literary weight, and the purging will become much more judicious.

Oddly, once all of the clutter has been written from the writer's system, the atelier of creation becomes a clean, well-lighted place and no longer a sagging tent of clowns. The writer is allowed his focus, and it is focus which makes great literature.

Frederick A. Raborg, Jr. edited Amelia, Cicada *and* SPSM&H *magazines. His own stories and poems have appeared in hundreds of periodicals, among them* Sports Afield, Ladies' Home Journal, Cuisine, Spy!, Prairie Schooner, Cimarron Review, Dramatics, Cavalier, Chic *and* Catholic Home. *His many awards include the U.S.A./The Netherlands 200 Foundation Award, The Guideposts Award and many poetry awards.*

Atmosphere, Imagery & Figures of Speech

Delight your reader
with singular images and compelling moods

By Ardath Mayhar

OFTEN THE EVOCATION OF A TIME, A PLACE, a mood, or an atmosphere is the element that makes a book or a story work.

What would Daphne DuMaurier's *Rebecca* be without that overpowering sense of foreboding, of mist and fear and madness permeating this novel? What would Georgette Heyer's Regency England be without her sure instinct for recreating the images, the speech patterns, and the mind-set of that era through terms suitable to its time?

Employ figures of speech

Perhaps the most effective tool for creating such effects is the use of figures of speech. While not often mentioned with much emphasis in writing courses or books on writing, this tool, which is the backbone of poetry, is equally useful to the writer of prose. The principal figures of speech follow, together with examples.

Simile—The common root with the word *similar* gives the definition of this term nicely... Similes say that this is *like* that.

> *She* was *like* a *kitten*, purring and cozy but with sharp claws concealed in her neat little paws.
>
> The *night* was *like* a black *curtain*, shining with cold rain and streaked with rips where the lightning tore it apart.

Metaphor—This says that one thing *is* another, totally dissimilar, thing.

> *She was a kitten*, purring and cozy, her sharp claws concealed in velvet paws.
> *The night was a curtain*, shining with rain, ripped with streaks of silver lightning.

This can also be used as a sort of adjectival device, in which a noun forms the adjective for a dissimilar noun:

> The *pewter cloud* spat rain and intermittent sleet.
> Across the *beaten-copper desert*, the sun set amid a tangle of crimson clouds.

Metonymy—This uses a universally understood proper name to denote characteristics of an individual.

> "I'd better go before *King Kong* catches me," said the timid little man, with a glance at his *large and overbearing wife*.
> "*Fort Knox* called today," she said, taking out her checkbook and frowning at the balance.

Onomatopoeia—This device imitates the sounds of things through the use of specific words.

> The bait *plunked* into the water, and the small waves *lapped* against the bank.

Many words are directly derived from the thing they describe: swish, thump, flap, flutter, lisp, whisper, growl, purr, clank, grumble, buzz, hiss, rumble, rip, zip, clatter, and hundreds more echo phenomena they represent.

Anthropomorphize

Personification is something we use constantly without realizing it. This makes an inanimate object or force behave as if it were alive:

> The tornado dipped lazily and *stuck its dark toe* into Mr. Johnson's hay barn, which whirled away amid dust and loose hay.
> The automobile veered out of line and headed straight for me, *its bumper sneering at me as it took aim* for my cringing body.

Stay in bounds

The use of such unusual elements gives life and originality to your work, but used to excess can clutter your style. A restrained approach is best, such phrases dropped in at important points at which sensory elements are needed to make the scene or the background come to life. Here's a well-written example:

> Marilyn clung to the porch railing, feeling the greasy damp of the wood slip between her cramped fingers. *Like a shipwrecked sailor clinging to a lifeline,* she held on, praying that no one would come out of the house and look up to find her, *an unlikely ornament,* hanging against the vine-laced lattice. If someone did come and see her—she shuddered, her teeth *clacking* in the chill—the *Godfather* would soon know of it, and she might as well loose her grip now and die a clean death.

This is, of course, a mood of suspense and fear, complicated by chill and danger. But other moods can be evoked just as easily:

> Ellen bounced along the path *like a red and white striped ball,* her small bare feet displacing shells and pebbles as she made her way to the wavelets where her mother let her play. Behind came the *Elephant,* her nanny, with a large basket of lunch for her small charge and the *flock* of instant acquaintances that she inevitably gathered about her on the beach.

Frequent repetition of any element becomes monotonous, of course. A mixture of several, as in the first example, makes for liveliness without repetitiveness. One or two, as with the second example, create color and action.

Match the right noun with the right adjective

Mood and atmosphere can, of course, be created without the use of such figures of speech. A judicious use of nouns and verbs, together with carefully selected adjectives, can do just what you want. Here is an example:

> The Baroness *posed* at the top of the *curving* steps, the *dark* lace of her gown accenting her *slender* shape, which *belied* her 70 years. The *antique ivory* of her hands moved outward as she *greeted* her host with, "Eh, Paolo, che bello!"
>
> About her, the *marble* columns and the *sweep* of steps became a stage, which she *commanded* with practiced ease. Below, the guests already *assembled* in the *loggia* looked up at the spotlighted pair and almost applauded, so dramatic was the gesture with which Paolo Benedetti took the arm of the *venerable* actress and led her down in *triumph* to join the others.

Equally useful are charged nouns and verbs when dealing with a mood of action and suspense:

> Derek *dropped* the last six feet, to land with a *crunch* in the soft soil of a flower bed. The low voices of the watchmen *cursed* and *muttered* beyond the high stone wall, while before him the *asylum shimmered* in fitful moonlight. The first dangerous step was behind him.

Choose the definite and the specific

Nouns and verbs can do wonderful things. Common ones like walked and ran, sat and said, are the mainstays of ordinary writing, and we use them constantly. But there are magical ones that can instantly create mood and atmosphere.

Instead of *walked* we can use other verbs, each of which evokes a different picture. He *trudged* home in the evening, his head bowed with weariness. The child *pranced* at the end of her leash, held out of traffic only by the desperate grip of her mother on the thin strip of leather. She *crept* from the room, shaken with sobs, and *fled* to her study. The small boy *slipped* through the woods, his slingshot at the ready. She *waddled* confidently forward, her skirts held in one pudgy hand, her basket in the other, waiting for the fishmonger to *produce* for her the best of his catch.

Use nouns that portray

Nouns can contain a thumbnail sketch of the character, if you find just the right one.

> The *hag* grinned, her wrinkles gleaming in the early light.
> I caught a glimpse of the *behemoth* as he skulked behind a pillar.
> The *mansion* loomed over the *hut* as if to emphasize the difference in their status.
> "I was attacked by a *berserker*!" she shrieked. "He took my purse and almost caught me in the alley."
> The *warrior* bent over the fallen *shepherd*, a hint of regret in his eyes.

Each of these not only mentions a person or a thing, it also brings into focus a host of connotations inherent in the noun used, thus creating the individual atmosphere of each.

Never wander far from your thesaurus

A thesaurus is filled with scintillating words just waiting to be discovered and used to make your prose sparkle. The best writers' thesauruses are dog-eared and worn with use. The ever-important lead—the opening sentence or paragraph of your book, chapter or story—should combine these elements in order to grab the reader at once with both mental and sensory appeals.

George R. R. Martin's *Dying of the Light* presents a visual effect and a dark mood with its use of poetic imagery. It begins thus:

> Beyond the window, water slapped against the pilings of the wooden sidewalk along the canal. Dirk t'Larien looked up and saw a low black barge drift slowly past in the moonlight. A solitary figure stood at the stern, leaning on a thin dark pole. Everything was etched quite clearly, for Braque's moon was riding overhead, big as a fist and very bright.

> "The best writers' thesauruses are dog-eared and worn with use."

Fritz Leiber begins his wonderful fantasy, *Ill Met in Lankhmar*, with a combination of consonance, unusual hyphenated adjectives, and exotic names:

> Silent as specters, the tall and the fat thief edged past the dead, noose-strangled watch-leopard, out the thick lock-picked door of Jengao the Gem Merchant, and strolled east on Cash Street through the thin black night-smog of Lankhmar, City of Sevenscore Thousand Smokes.

If you are not smiling after that, yours is a very dark mood, indeed.

Anya Seton's *The Hearth and the Eagle* begins with a storm, and she sets the mood deftly:

> On the night of the great storm, the taproom at the Hearth and Eagle was deserted. Earlier that evening men had wandered in for beers or rum flip ... They had drunk uneasily, the pewter mugs shaking in their vein-corded hands, while they listened to the rising wind ...In the Great Harbor...the mounting breakers roared up the shingle, muffling the clink of mugs on the table and the men's sparse comments.

The tension here, as men wait out the violence of the storm, comes through with brevity and impact, and the noise of the storm is a character in the scene.

Kathleen Snow's *Night Walking*, a mystery, has an equally evocative beginning:

> Wednesday, June 16, 1976
> 11:59 p.m.
> The car eased off Long Island's Highway 27, homing in on the sound of surf. The tires drilled upon asphalt, turned right, crackled onto a hard-sand roadbed. Hollies, then the mittens and gloves of sassafras flogged the car's sides. It burrowed deeper. The roadbed became a path, engulfed by masses of catbrier and twisted lianas of grape and poison ivy.

Without a single obvious word of warning, Snow has created a sense of tension and dread. The word flogged has a dire connotation. The car burrows deeper (personification) and is entangled with poison ivy, a bad omen, indeed.

A wide-ranging vocabulary, a sense of rhythm and the flow of language, and a crisp picture in your own mind to be conveyed to the mind of your reader, these are the basic elements needed for masterful writing.

How do you develop a feel for this evocative prose? One good way is to read excellent poetry—good old stuff like *Dover Beach* by Matthew Arnold that creates its own reality as it sings to you. Language can be used with the accuracy and skill of a scalpel, as the best poetry uses it, and second-best words never do the job.

Ardath Mayhar has written almost all her life—first poetry, then science fiction novels, westerns and children's books, and most lately books of fiction that recreate the worlds of prehistoric Indian cultures. She began writing novels when she was forty-three. She has written close to five dozen books, plus hundreds of short stories. She continues to write, and even sell, poetry.

Ardath has changed genders, becoming Frank Cannon for three western novels published by Zebra Books, and John Kildeer for a sequence of Mountain Man novels published by Bantam Domain (although someone else has taken over as "John Kildeer" for more novels). Her prehistoric Indian novels, written under her own name, include People of the Mesa, Island in the Lake, Towers of the Earth, *and* Hunters of the Plains.

Can These Bones Live?

Writing good period dialogue

By Leonard Tourney

GOOD STORIES REQUIRE MOVEMENT, dramatic action in which characters experience conflict, deal with it, and change for better or worse. Action includes literal, or metaphorical, car chases and fist fights, scenes of angry confrontation and passionate lovemaking, struggle and the uncertainty that creates suspense. But of course you already know all that.

Dialogue is also a kind of action. When it's good it gives us the impression of real talk, grounding the scene in its own kind of reality, defining character, and advancing the story. In historical, or *period* fiction, dialogue has an added job. While accomplishing all the things that dialogue does in any story, period dialogue must also reinforce the historical setting. Placing your story in ancient Rome, Regency England, or the Wild American West isn't merely a matter of furnishing your story or novel with togas, fancy hats, and wigwams. You must give your characters a language that will seem to the reader to be compatible with that setting, thus making the magic that allows your readers to feel they are not *here* and *now*, but *there* and *then*.

Recently at a live writer's conference I participated in a panel of historical novelists discussing period dialogue. While we agreed that there was, unfortunately, no divine legislation on the issue of creating good talk for historical characters, we did conclude it was possible to offer some insights to help beginners and published writers in their struggle to succeed in this difficult area. To the common wisdom emerging from our discussion, I have added some insights of my own. (You know, the kind of thing one thinks of the day after the conference).

With the warning that what follows is not the Ten Commandments of Period Dialogue, I offer the suggestions below. In fact, I have deliberately confined myself to eight points, just to dispel the heavy-handed authoritarianism that inevitably comes with the number ten. These are not commandments, only observations. Take them for what they're worth.

Know the language of thy period

Don't make the job of creating period dialogue a matter of simple intuition or conjecture. Read around in the authentic texts of the period—the plays, poetry, and novels. Read diaries, journals, letters. Soak up the flavor of the speech. Listen for its peculiar rhythms, characteristic expressions, its name for common objects, its terms of endearment, its exclamations, oaths, and curses. Of course it's writing you're experiencing, not speech, but unless you have a time machine in your garage or know a competent transmedium, a written text is the best, indeed only, evidence of how the people of your chosen period talked.

> "Read around in the authentic texts of the period— the plays, poetry, and novels."

Knowing the language of the period is as important as getting the names of kings, the dates of famous victories, and the location of public monuments and streets right. In some ways, it is more important. Getting a historical fact wrong may distract the knowledgeable reader (assuming it isn't a major blunder like placing Queen Victoria on the throne of France or locating Kansas in New England), but failing to make dialogue convincing will turn off just about everybody who reads your story or book.

Remember that good dialogue isn't real talk

Only the naive believe that the way to write realistic dialogue is to hide a tape recorder in the office water cooler and record what people actually say.

Let's face it, real talk is frequently incoherent, repetitious, desultory, colorless, and trivial—and that's been the case since people first began to blabber.

While real talk may indeed reveal character, it does not necessarily advance a story, show conflict or emotion, or move us to laughter, pity, or fear. That is, it does not automatically do all the things that effective dialogue does in fiction. It's not the replication of talk that the writer is interested in, but the suggestion—even the illusion—of talk. All good dialogue writers recreate not the real thing, but a working and plausible semblance. They want the apparent spontaneity of real talk without the inarticulateness (except in the case of characters who are just plain stupid!). They want purposeful, directed, and dramatic speech, not just rambling.

They know that for dialogue to work for them it must work for the story.

Now this is even truer for period dialogue. Let's suppose, for example, that you are writing a novel set in England in the Middle Ages. You might be hard put to replicate the language (let alone the various dialects of English) prevalent when knighthood was still in flower and might find a pleasing substitute by cribbing phrases from Chaucer or the *Paston Letters*. Yet all such filching would accomplish is putting your reader to the work of keeping at hand a dictionary of lexical dinosaurs and obscure topical allusions. The story would surrender its primary role to the language, which would be so opaque as to defeat the good intentions of even scholars of the period—perhaps even of your mother who reads every golden word you've ever inscribed.

Keep it simple, keep it "spoken"; garnish as needed

Simple English, in any period after Geoffrey Chaucer, pretty much follows the same syntactical formulas. When spoken, sentences generally start with the subject, continue with the verb, and build on modifiers from there—a pattern that reflects spontaneously generated thought in Will Shakespeare's time and our own. But be careful. Despite the proverbial wisdom to the contrary, spoken sentences are not necessarily shorter than written sentences, although in the mouths of ordinary folk the elements of the sentences are usually strung together more loosely (i.e. with ands and buts), with fewer conspicuous conjunctive adverbs (therefore, moreover, however, nevertheless, etc.), and rare instances of sentences with elaborate parallelism or long introductory dependent clauses—both structures that suggest at premeditation or revision. Remember, although you may have revised a passage of dialogue a hundred times, the sentences you labor over are supposed to reflect spontaneity, not the polish of a professional speech writer.

As far as words are concerned, keep them simple and, if possible, Anglo-Saxon. For periods earlier than the 1500s, when Old or Middle English makes translation a practical necessity, keep the diction simple. Consider, for example, this poignant and convincing exchange between Edgar and Catherine in Sharan Newman's medieval mystery, *The Devil's Door*:

> "Could you move a bit, Edgar?" Catherine asked. "There's a very sharp bit of this hay sticking straight into my back."
>
> Obligingly, but with reluctance, Edgar lifted himself up and waited while she wriggled herself away from the offending fodder.
>
> "This isn't exactly the wedding night I'd planned," he told her. "I had thought we'd have a feather bed and silken sheets."
>
> "And all the relatives snickering at the door? I've heard enough about those to be glad we didn't," she said as she put her hands around his neck. "A blanket on straw is really more practical, considering."

Simple, straightforward, convincingly "medieval" because it is clearly not something later.

If your setting is the 1500s or 1600s, remember that we think of this period as being one that reveled in metaphor and verbal cleverness. For the Elizabethans, a man of few words is a man of few brains. Look for vivid verbs, adjectives with punch, similes and metaphors that draw upon the life of the time. Elizabethans lived intimately with disease, fleas, dogs, cats, farm animals, nature, war. Their metaphors are drawn naturally from this pool of experience. Their humor was raucous, crude, sometimes cruel, and frequently obscene and bawdy. And of course their oaths, epithets, curses, and insults were colorful and incisive.

Here, for example, is a speech from Leon Rooke's delightful comic novel, *Shakespeare's Dog*, in which the Bard, speaking candidly to his canine companion Hooker, complains about the dullness of Stratford:

> "Hooker," he said, "they would have me behived here, with no more spin to my life than a windmill's feeble blade. They would have me leak out my life in driblets and sink down into Holy Trinity's dust with no more honor to my name than a hare's hind leg. Here he lies, they will say, old William Shagspeer, the puke, said to be a glover's son. Well, I will not have it, Hooker. I will run."

Or consider, as a pungent illustration of early nineteenth-century nautical talk, this passage from Patrick O'Brian's *Desolation Island*. Speaking is Jack Aubrey, captain of a British man-of-war:

> "I will tell you what," said Jack heavily. "I respect the cloth, of course, and learning; but I cannot feel that a man-of-war is the proper place for a parson. Just take this morning...On Sunday, when

we rig church, I dare say he will tell us to treat one another like brethren, and to do unto others, you know. We will all say Amen, and the *Leopard* will sail on with all those people in irons in the filthy hole forward, just the same. But that is only what occurred to me this morning; in a larger way, it seems to me uncommon odd, and precious near to cant, to tell the ship's company of a man-of-war with loaded guns to love your enemy and to turn the other cheek, when you know damned well that the ship and every man jack aboard her is there to blow the enemy out of the water if he possibly can."

Avoid the verbal clichés of the period

We've all seen costume dramas in which buccaneers go around saying "Avast, me hearties." or Westerns in which cowboys sprinkle their conversation with "howdies" and express their gratitude with the inevitable "much obliged." The question is not whether real westerners actually used such terms but whether such language hasn't been tainted for use by an intelligent writer trying to recreate a historical setting without ghosts of old melodramas haunting the scene. In sum, then, be fresh, creative. Remember that you're writing a superior book or story, not the script for a B movie.

> "Look for vivid verbs, adjectives with punch, similes and metaphors that draw upon the life of the time."

Avoid even the appearance of the anachronism

Obviously, you should not use slang expressions, technical terms, or metaphors that are associated with a later time period or name things, experiences, or attitudes that did not exist in your period. You can find some authors who would disagree with me on this principle and "modernize" the historical scene to underscore the relevance of the story to modern readers. Sometimes it works; usually it doesn't. I do know that such blunders—or artifices, if they are that—are distracting to readers if not laughable and will do more than anything to undermine the credibility of your historical setting.

But be also aware that even if you can prove to a skeptical copyeditor that the word you have chosen is to be found on the lips of an Elizabethan courtier or a Victorian lady, the choice may still be inappropriate if it evokes a more modern setting. I once was criticized in one of my Elizabethan books for using the phrase "property in the suburbs." Now suburbs is a word we use a lot in modern America but the fact is that it was current in Elizabethan times when it meant the same thing. It can even be found in the King James (1611) version of the Bible!

Nonetheless, upon reflection I realized, somewhat reluctantly, I admit, that the copyeditor was correct. The issue wasn't the historical accuracy of the word but its connotation. Since to modern readers it would probably evoke images of subdivisions, swimming pools, and paved tree-lined streets it did nothing to reinforce the historical setting I was elsewhere at pains to create and sustain.

Avoid lengthy speeches

This is good advice to any writer, not just the writer of period fiction. In a historical setting, the lengthy speech with all its mannerisms is sleep-inducing, almost regardless of its content. If dialogue is indeed dramatic, it is so because it represents the conflict of characters in a fair exchange of views, butting heads so to speak. Windbags suck up the vitality of a story, turn drama into a lecture.

How to avoid such wordy stuff? Have your character's speech interrupted with questions from another character; turn the lengthy report into a dramatic exchange. Or try narrative summary as an alternative to dialogue, especially on the less-quotable material.

Of course, you should consider these alternatives only after you have ruthlessly pruned and trimmed the offensive discourse. Sometimes all that information we felt the reader just had to know isn't that essential after all.

Avoid phonetic spelling

Just because you've found out how a word was pronounced in 1775, doesn't mean you have to distract the reader with phonetic spelling. Remember, if the dialogue is to be a real asset to the story, it should not try the reader's patience or phonetic skills. Besides, once you've committed yourself to phonetic accuracy, you're stuck. And you better not make a mistake, or you'll be getting letters from outraged linguists and amateur historians in Bakersfield and Sarasota assuring you that they loved your book—until page 235 when it was ruined for them by a mistake in pronunciation. Yes, I know that's a silly reason for not liking the book. You'll still get complaints. Why make trouble for yourself?

Learn from other writers

Writers have been learning their craft by the example of other writers for generations, so there's no reason you can't learn much about writing period dialogue in your time and place of choice by studying the methods of successful practitioners. The novels of George Garrett (*Death of a Fox, The Succession*) or Anthony Burgess (*Nothing Like the Sun, A Dead Man in Deptford*) have a lot to teach the novice about presenting the talk of Elizabethan and Jacobean England to contemporary readers. For eighteenth-century Ireland, read the novels of Thomas Flannagan. For lovers of the Victorian era, the mystery novelist Anne Perry is a good model, as is that excellent chronicler of the great days of the English navy, Patrick O'Brian, quoted above. For those setting their books in the American West, don't miss the opportunity of examining Larry McMurtry's popular westerns or the classic work of A. B. Guthrie, another fine writer of period dialogue.

For medievalists, I like to recommend Robert Bolt's play, *A Man for All Seasons*, as an outstanding example of expressive and credible period speech. And those seeking to resuscitate the ancient world should not overlook the monumental books of Mary Renault.

Find out who's publishing historical fiction and being praised for the effort. But be careful, just because a book gets published doesn't mean it's worth imitating. There's lots of junk around. Use good judgment. But when you discover a master, make yourself into an apprentice. Writing workshops can provide valuable instruction, and some textbooks are worth their price, but nothing compares to the master-apprentice relationship as a way to bring your writing to where you want it to be.

A final word

In the Book of Ezekiel, the prophet is whisked away by the spirit of God to a valley full of dead men's bones. The bones were very dry, we're told, and God asked Ezekiel: Can these bones live? It's a question all writers of historical fiction should ask of the characters who populate their stories. Are these dead bones, or are they endowed with sinews, and flesh, and the breath of life?

Writing convincing and expressive dialogue is one of the great challenges of writing historical fiction. It challenges the writer's knowledge of the distant past and its language and, more, it assumes the author's exact knowledge of the speech of his or her own day and age too. But, like almost every aspect of good writing, success requires effort and practice. In my own books, I have sometimes spent days and even weeks trying to get a passage to have a certain lilt, tone, or syntactical wrinkle, only to realize later—usually after the novel has been published—that I didn't quite get it "right" after all.

Perhaps, when all is said and done, there's a mysterious something about capturing the speech of the past that requires more than imitation or effort or luck—something that demands of the writer an instinctive and passionate empathy with a historical period, something bred in us by our unique life experiences and the profound and remote parts of ourselves.

Am I talking about something metaphysical like a reincarnation of souls or a spiritual kinship? No, not really. Am I claiming that this mysterious and ineffable something—like "talent" or "genius"—we either have or do not? Perhaps. But whatever magic, skill, or art enables a writer of today to summon from distant yesterdays vibrant voices of power and conviction, how can we know whether we have that art until we put ourselves to the test, until we steep ourselves in that distant time and try our skills to make it breathe and speak again?

Leonard Tourney has written nine novels set in the period of Elizabeth I, the most recent of which is Times Fool *(Forge). He is currently a professor of English at Brigham Young University in Provo, Utah. Leonard also is a staff member of the respected Santa Barbara Writer's Conference where he teaches a workshop in mystery writing.*

KEYNOTE

Quit Your Day Job?

*Fifteen secrets to running a successful
home-based writing business*

By Terri Lonier

A HOME-BASED ENTREPRENEUR WEARS MANY HATS: receptionist, bookkeeper, shipping clerk, sales manager, janitor—and, oh yes, CEO. No day is ever the same, and it's always an adventure.

What does it take to run a successful writing business from home? Many things, including flexibility, skill, grace, and humor. The following collection of tips is based on my two decades of work as an author, editor and publisher, as well as insights from thousands of entrepreneurs I've encountered along the way. Each contains a kernel of truth that will help you build a successful home-based writing business.

Think business

Writing may be your passion, but to create a successful career, you must learn the "business of making it a business." Even if you are only making a small amount of income from writing at this time, your intention and focus must be professional if you want to create a successful enterprise.

While being a freelance writer is a noble career, the term *freelance* often implies an "I'm doing this until something better comes along" attitude to many people outside the writing field. In dealing with individuals unfamiliar with the world of publishing, consider replacing the word *freelance* with the word *independent*. Yes, they mean nearly the same thing. But they can convey a world of difference about how you—and others—view your work.

As writers, we make our living by knowing the subtleties behind words. When presenting your business, choose carefully the words that describe you and your company best. Soloists often find value in performing an exercise conducted by many successful firms, both large and small: Write a mission statement about your business. You'd be surprised at how challenging—and worthwhile—it can be to summarize your company's values and goals in a sentence or two. It does not have to be crafted in lofty language; in fact, simplicity is often more powerful. The process will clarify your thinking and bring focus to your efforts.

Image matters

Home-based businesses of all types are susceptible to misconceptions by outsiders. Because of the primarily intangible nature of a writing business—we don't have physical "widgets" to produce, only thoughts that appear on paper—writers are often highly suspect. Common myths are that we really don't work, we have all the free time in the world, and we don't take our work very seriously.

To succeed as an independent writer, you must combat these perceptions in every way you can. Invest in well-designed business cards and letterhead. If your business warrants it, create a brochure. Make your online presence professional, both in email and on the web. Practice your telephone and presentation abilities until you can easily and effortlessly talk about yourself and your business without feeling self-conscious. Polish your communication skills so that you can engage in conversation with editors comfortably.

There are two corollaries to this tip:

• If the Client Doesn't See It, Don't Spend Money on It.

Avoid the impulse to invest in fancy office furniture, equipment or other items when you're setting up your business. Keeping your overhead costs low is crucial in the early days of any business, when income may be tight. Clients don't care if you're using plastic crates for filing cabinets, or if your office is tucked away in a back bedroom. On the other hand...

• If the Client Does See It, Sweat the Small Stuff.

It pays to invest in those things that will represent you and your work. An editor will be making judgments about many aspects of your abilities as a writer that go beyond your talent for putting words on paper. Initial impressions count. Mentally put yourself behind a client or editor's desk and judge how your materials appear. Crisp letterhead with a concise cover letter, free of typos or grammatical errors? Clean photocopies of writing samples? A website with appropriate information and clear contact details? Voice mail so that there's never a worry about getting a busy signal or an annoying call-waiting beep? Success lies in attention to details.

Make your office a silent partner

When setting up your home office, be aware of the physical layout. When designed well, your office can become a valuable partner, enhancing your efforts and enabling you to be more productive. An L-shaped or U-shaped desk configuration allows easy access to computer, phone, fax, and plenty of surface space to spread out papers.

Some seasoned home-based entrepreneurs intentionally set up their office spaces so they must get out of their chairs every so often. They'll place a printer or photocopier on an opposite wall so that they avoid the sedentary habits that can lead to discomfort or chronic health issues.

Don't overlook the psychological issues in designing your workspace. Make your office as cheery and inviting as you can, so that you'll enjoy spending time there. Also be sure to establish some kind of barrier between your work and living space. If it can't be a door, invest in a row of plants, a curtain, or some other visual divide so that you can clearly make the distinction between your office and living space.

It's not how big you are, it's how big you work

Today's home-based entrepreneurs are able to compete with businesses many times their size through the use of digital technology and the Internet. Invest in the best technology you can afford, then don't panic when you look in the paper the next day and see it cheaper, faster, or better. Think of technology as a fast-moving train—you have to jump on at some point. Smart entrepreneurs invest business profits into technology that can increase a company's earning potential.

Keeping current with technological advances can be an all-consuming task, so take heart if you find yourself frustrated or overwhelmed at times. Most experienced home-based entrepreneurs recognize that it often takes a while to find the appropriate combination of technology that suits their needs best. It's important to find technology that enhances your productivity, rather than having the latest techno-toy. For example, some writers can't imagine not having two monitors—one for active work, the other for a digital desktop—while others shudder at the thought of anything larger than their trusty laptop screen. Some prefer a dedicated fax line; others use their computer's fax capabilities. Experiment to see what works best for you. At the end of the day, you want your home office technology to support your effort, not add to it.

Working solo is not working alone

Successful independent entrepreneurs understand the value of staying connected. As home-based writers, we spend major parts of our days having only internal conversations as we create our work. It's important to combat this isolation by scheduling get-togethers with friends and colleagues. You might consider setting up a regular lunch date with fellow writers or other home-based business professionals. It's a refreshing way to replenish your energies and get feedback on what you're doing. Professional peers can also keep you on target toward a deadline.

Another valuable technique is to create a "Power Partner" alliance with a like-minded individual who also is committed to achieving a specific personal goal. Agree to be accountable to each other, and establish regular appointments to discuss your individual progress toward your goals. Knowing you've made the commitment to someone else—and that he or she has now signed on as your advocate and cheerleader—gives an added boost to your efforts.

With today's digital communications, Power Partners can be located anywhere in the world. It may be that you share a monthly hour-long telephone call with your colleague. (It's about the same cost as lunch in a good restaurant, and much less fattening!) What's important is that you reach out and stay connected. For if you crave your solitude, you'll probably have your poverty as well.

Forget the muse

Successful home-based writers are self-starters who don't hit the snooze alarm of life. Abandon the notion of waiting to be inspired to be productive. Most seasoned writers understand that finished work comes from putting fingers to keyboard and keester to chair on a regular basis. Find your personal motivators. A certain time of day? Music? Silence? For some, looming deadlines are the ultimate inspiration.

It's also important to weed out distractions that diminish your focus or motivation. For example, turn off the telephone ringer if you're the type who just can't bear not to answer, and let voice mail pick up your messages. Watch your refrigerator stocking, too. Choose your groceries carefully if you know you'll be tempted to polish off a pint of double fudge ice cream instead of re-writing that draft.

Pebbles in the pond

Whether it's a 150-word sidebar for the local newspaper or a major article commissioned by a national publication, treat every assignment with importance as you develop your writing career. Think of each piece as a pebble in a pond, sending out ripples that may take a long time to reach shore.

Remember, words in print live on. It's not unusual for an editor to refer to something you've written months or years before. Powerful electronic databases such as Lexis/Nexis and online archives mean that a collection of your past writings may be only a few keystrokes away from anyone in the world.

Make life easy for editors and others

In working with editors and other professional contacts, think about building relationships for the long term. Publications come and go, and editors bounce from job to job. Often, they'll stay in contact with their favorite writers. If you're on that list, your chances of getting published can multiply quickly. How can you make the preferred roster? It's actually quite easy: Make life easy for them.

The key quality is being reliable. This means turning assignments in on time, with no factual or spelling errors. Be as helpful as you can. Track down or offer ideas on accompanying visuals. Give suggestions on how an article might be expanded or slanted to fit their readers' interests. Send in materials clearly marked, all at one time, so editors don't have to scramble to locate all the pieces of your work. Put yourself in his or her seat, behind the editorial desk. Would you like to do business with a writer like you?

Last, but not least, show appreciation. This may mean sending a simple e-mail, a handwritten note, or another modest gift once in a while to say "thanks." It's not the expense of the item, but the thought. Small niceties add up, and make you stand out from the crowd. You'll be remembered—and called upon again and again.

Never forget: Cash is king

You may be a talented writer, have a four-color letterhead, an impressive website, and the latest computer or technological marvel—but if you don't have cash regularly flowing into your business, you won't survive. Monitor your accounts receivable on a regular basis, and take a proactive stance toward your finances. Some writers I know make up an invoice before they even put a single word on paper. They hang it on the wall in front of them so they can stare at it every day—a wonderful motivation for completing the work!

Don't be shy about asking questions to clarify payment details. If a check hasn't arrived on the intended day, pick up the phone and inquire about its status. Many times invoices get buried on an editor's desk or in some accounting department—and if you don't call, payment may be delayed for weeks longer.

Editors run their publications as professional businesses, and you should take the same attitude. They need your talent, and you expect to be paid in full, on time.

Time is more valuable than money

Most new business owners do everything by themselves, from answering the phone to long-range planning to sweeping the floor. This is natural and provides a solid grounding in all aspects of business operations. As a company develops, however, there usually comes a time when the owner realizes that the best way to grow is by delegating tasks and working with others.

For example, if you can generate more income from writing than doing administrative chores, it pays to hire someone else to do those activities. Whether these workers are employees or independent contractors is your choice (but the IRS has guidelines on the distinction between the two). What's important is that you value your time and make the most of it.

Time is our most precious asset. It's a finite gift, and we can't make or buy any more. Smart entrepreneurs learn how to leverage it by working with others, and focus on what they do best.

Polish your craft

No writer ever reaches the pinnacle of the craft. We all have things to learn. Take time out to stretch your mind and talents by participating in workshops or reading books on writing, editing, or style. Sometimes the change of pace can burst the doldrums or initiate a new breakthrough.

Concert-level musicians spend hours in practice. Elite athletes employ coaches and trainers to help them reach the next level of achievement. As a writer, take your work seriously and invest in yourself. Consider setting aside a percentage of each check you receive from a writing assignment and designating it for professional development.

Even the great literary masters believed that their best work was yet to come. Always strive to improve.

Have dual focus

If you've known how to drive a car for many years, you probably take for granted the many skills it requires. Traveling down the road, you intuitively keep a dual focus. You concentrate on things close at hand, yet remain aware of hazards or shifts in the road ahead, always prepared to react if something happens.

Successful entrepreneurs are those who are able to maintain a similar dual focus on short-term goals and long-term vision. They keep their sights on what's at the end of the road, all the while dealing with the traffic of day-to-day details right in front of them.

As your writing business develops, never lose sight of your primary goals while battling daily distractions. By focusing on your personal and professional mission, you can fill your days with valuable achievement, not just activity.

Give to get

Seasoned entrepreneurs understand the abundance that comes from giving to others. Develop a generous attitude. Share your writings, your books, your sources, your insights, your praise. Is this a Pollyanna attitude? Perhaps. But more than two decades of this approach have shown me that the power of connecting will pay you back many times over—and that you'll be the one who reaps the greatest rewards.

Give of your time to help others who may be starting a writing career. Offer encouragement and support—and acknowledge those who did the same for you in earlier years.

Most of all, learn to celebrate the successes of others. Their win is not your loss. Be genuine in expressing your delight at their accomplishments. Then, when it comes time to celebrate your own achievements, you will be surrounded by a multitude of friends—and your satisfaction will be even greater.

> "Share your writings, your books, your sources, your insights, your praise."

Self-confidence is the currency of self-employment

The longer I'm in business, the more I recognize that this is one of the most important factors for solo success. As you build your business, do everything you can to develop your self-esteem. Celebrate your accomplishments and place the inevitable stumbles in perspective. Connect with peers who can offer "reality checks" on issues that concern you. Learn the wisdom of protecting your confidence: Be aware of situations that can undermine your sense of self and avoid (or transform) the environments in which you feel particularly vulnerable. When you're working on your own, you are your business. Recognize that self-esteem builds confidence, which leads to a powerful upward spiral of entrepreneurial achievement.

Designing a life is more than making a living

As your home-based writing business blossoms, it's important to take time to enjoy the journey. Learn to take care of yourself, and try to find a balance between the many deadlines and obligations you'll likely juggle. Step back every so often so you can catch a perspective on all that you've accomplished.

One day, the delight of working as a home-based writer will sneak up on you. It may come after friends comment how lucky you are to be on your own. Or someone may say they sure admire your guts and determination—and someday they'd like to do what you're doing. Then you'll stop, take a breath, and realize, "Hey, I'm doing this! And it feels *great!*"

The satisfaction of that moment will erase all struggles and frustration, and you'll celebrate your arrival as a successful solo professional. You will have discovered that you're doing more than just make a living—you're designing your life.

***Terri Lonier** is one of America's most respected experts on entrepreneurship and self-employment. An author, speaker, and consultant, she has been working solo since 1978 in the fields of art, design, marketing, and high technology. She is the author of five books, three audio programs, and hundreds of articles, including the classic business startup guide,* Working Solo, *named the "#1 choice for independent entrepreneurs" in an* Inc. *magazine cover story, and "the free agent's Bible" in* Fast Company.

Ms. Lonier also consults with Fortune 500 and high-tech firms on how to access and communicate with the booming SOHO (small office/home office) market. Her research on workplace trends and the impact of technology make her a frequent media guest, and her work has been featured in the New York Times, Wall Street Journal, Fortune, Business Week, USA Today *and other leading publications as well as on CNBC, CNN/fn, the BBC, and radio programs nationwide.*

Ms. Lonier is the founder of WorkingSolo.com, the original online clearinghouse for information on self-employment. The website (http://www.workingsolo.com) has guided millions of individuals in their quest for successful self-employment since its debut in 1995.

Working Solo *is a registered trademark of Working Solo, Inc.*

Alternative Presses

Or: Why am I lying here with a tulip sticking out of my ass?

By Patrick LoBrutto

I'LL EXPLAIN ABOUT THE TULIP, I PROMISE.

The wide world is getting tougher by the minute. If you're a writer—especially if you're a writer...and *especially* if you're an unpublished writer—you don't want to see it get any worse.

I don't think anyone could look you straight in the eye and tell you that it's getting easier than ever before to get your novel published...by a big New York publisher. Indeed, for the new or budding writer, it's harder, I think, than ever before. Publishing companies, like predators gone amok, have gobbled each other up. Where there used to be a great many publishers of all shapes and sizes and specialties on the New York scene, there are now a few publishers each with a number of imprints.

You could say that there are really only seven major publishers...well, okay, give or take a few, but I like the sound of the seven secret masters. Now, of course, the major houses have many imprints, but you can bet your padooki that the overall number of titles is down—most publishers are trying to cut their lists. And, I predict that the number of titles overall is going to fall even further in the future.

Plus, current marketing dictates dictate that—just like the movies and TV—you give the customer more of what he liked before (I'm waiting for Hollywood to remake the first *Rocky* movie so they can call it *Rocky I II*). You can hear the jaws of Catch-22 snapping shut here: If you haven't been published before, how can you get published in the first damn place? Good question.

In addition, many major publishers won't accept unsolicited manuscripts, meaning manuscripts not directed to a specific editor, or requested by someone in the house. That means you have to get an agent before you can even submit to a major publisher. And *that* means that you have to go through *two* long, involved and difficult submission processes. At least.

Well, given the above, you're a dope to try, even. Publishers and editors and agents have writers they've been working with, writers with proven track records. They'll go to those writers when a project comes along or when they need books. For Pete's sake! Why would they want *you*? Even if you could get them to read your manuscript.

Ahhh. But there *is* hope for the wretched.

Everything that has been published has been written by *some*body.

You just aren't looking at the right publishers.

I know, I know, the previous two lines sound suspiciously like Zen.

But consider, just for a moment, that you haven't been looking at this in the right way. You're seeing best-sellers, you're seeing hype, you're seeing books distributed by *mass market* publishers. Look behind that screen of major and blockbuster titles, behind the big-name-author books and the books that have been lucky enough to get the marketing attention. If you make the effort, you'll see a huge number of books from regional, university and independent presses (like this independent press that has published my workshop. Hey! I'm getting published!). Some of these presses do scholarly or academic material, some specialize in one or two areas, some are generalists.

Okay, having gotten this far, thus far, I should tell you two things: Keep the day job. And quality control is important.

Money. Well this *is* America and we all want to get paid. But. But writing is a most difficult and insecure profession. If you like your three squares and a roof, you'll stay a wage slave. Even writers who are regularly published by major publishers are hard-pressed to make a living from their scribbling. And, believe me, independent publishers do not generally pay well. What you want is to have your ideas and dreams and tales out there, eagerly devoured by legions of hungry fans. Yeah, but if money is the major factor, you'd better have stupendous talent, exceptional luck, unfailing persistence, and a damn good agent.

Ninety-nine percent of us have to contend with the fact that it is virtually impossible to make a living by our writing alone. Get used to the idea.

So *caveat author*, or something like that. I'm not even going to think about telling anybody how to make a living from writing. Your reward has to come from what you write and how you write it. (Well, not you. I can tell by how you're reading this that you're the exception and *you* will make millions.)

And, actually, that's what's known as quality control. Here, you're on your own. In this most lonely of professions, that's as it should be. You have to get it out there often enough and well enough to give you a shot at a career. You *must* always bring the best you can to the table. That means you must constantly learn your profession in every way you can. You must be persistent.

There was an article in *the New York Times* about senior citizens—unpublished senior citizens—attending critique groups and practicing their craft. My favorite was a woman who came to New York City when she was nineteen; she had grand dreams of becoming a writer. That was sevetny-five years and three unpublished novels ago. She has *just* gotten an agent. *That's* persistence. I hope, gentle reader, that we all are like her—too stupid or too dreamy to know what's impossible. We'll find out, won't we?

And don't pay anybody to have your work published. That is...unless, of course, you have a sound business plan, a surefire and well-crafted book and a realistic distribution channel. And about $20,000 to gamble with—I *don't* mean the rent, grocery or college money, either.

Okay. You live in East G-string township, far, far from the make-believe, *tres chic* world of big-time publishing. You don't know anybody, or anybody who knows anybody, who can help you. All you've got is a pretty fair book. You don't even know where the publishers *are*. What do you do?

You do your homework is what. You hike your fanny to the bookstore and look for books that are roughly in the same category as yours. This will be easier, I know, if we're talking about nonfiction (like a cheese repair manual, or how to hunt the mighty snark) or even if your book falls into one of the recognizable fiction categories—like science fiction, mysteries, westerns, romances, etcetera, etcetera, etcetera. If wurst comes to wurst (as they say in the deli business) you look under General Fiction. You'll see, generally, all the secret masters—a lot from them, too. Look harder and you'll see a bunch of publishers you don't recognize. And for Pete's sake, don't just take fifteen minutes or a half hour to do this—take two or three hours. Because if you study this you'll find the regional, university and independent publishers. There'll be more than you'd realized.

Of course, you should always submit your manuscript to the big New York publishers and the literary agents who work with them, but if that fails you should always (*I said always*) do the whole list. You should give everybody a chance to say no...or yes.

And yes, you might actually be better served by one of the little guys. A small publisher will have a smaller list than your average secret master, and might well take more time and effort to market your book. A small publisher might consider you a bigger deal—maybe even a *big deal*—where a big publisher might ignore the book, even if it is on their list.

See what I'm getting at?

Okay. You've done the bookstore thing. Now you go to the library and get the very latest edition of the *LMP*—the *Literary Market Place*. This is a nice thick tome that lists agents, printers, editorial services, foreign trade associations, book clubs, artists' representatives, paper merchants and mills, reference books and like that. Oh, and Book Publishers. Xerox the entire Book Publishers section. Have a bunch of change handy. This will give you telephone numbers, fax numbers, addresses, number of books in print, and all sorts of useful information like that. Also check out *The American Directory of Writer's Guidelines* and *Writer's Market*, two handy quicks. In one swell foop, you can come by your plan of attack. And don't think you won't need an oil tanker's worth of patience, because you most certainly will. This is a long-term project. Then, what you do is call the publishers that might work for you. Get a catalog—pay for it if you have to.

Get lots of postage. Start submitting. Don't get discouraged. I could regale you with oodles of stories about great and successful books that collected a veritable slew of rejections before finally being accepted. Don't make me do that. Take my word for it.

Once you get it *there*, it's up to you to razzle-dazzle 'em with your skill. Choose your words, compare your work to the competition. Work *hard*; revise as often as necessary. Always look for ways to improve. You are on a training course in a kind of surreal triathlon...and there's no real finish line.

Oh, yeah, I lied about the tulip. I just did that to get your attention...unless you consider that, when you write, you *expose* yourself. You can fail, and fail over and over again. In point of fact, in order to write well you must expose your skill and imagination and intellect and knowledge in a very public way. You have to have something to say. And, although you have to say it in your own way...it must *connect* somehow with other people.

Now, run along. Go and be wonderful.

Patrick LoBrutto is an editor, author, anthologist and a recipient of the World Fantasy Award for editing in 1986. He has worked for Ace Books, Bantam Books, Doubleday, M. Evans, Stealth Press, and Kensington among other publishing houses. He has held the position of editor, senior editor and editor-in-chief, working with authors like Isaac Asimov, Stephen King, Eric Van Lustbader, Spider Robinson, Walter Tevis (the author of The Hustler and The Color of Money), the Louis L'Amour Estate, the Star Wars novelizations and the Dune Novels of Brian Herbert and Kevin Anderson. He is presently an editorial consultant to publishers, agents and authors. His website address is www.patricklobrutto.com.*

Good Writing + Self-Promotion = Best-Seller

Thirteen things you can do to help yourself become a best-selling author

By John Kremer

E VEN WITH THE BIGGER PUBLISHERS, unless you're a Stephen King or a Danielle Steel, much of the promotion for your book will be left to you. But don't despair, there's plenty you can do on your own. Always, of course, keep your publisher informed—with sufficient lead time—about what you're doing so they can tie their promotions into your own.

1. Become a speaker

There are a good number of ways to use speaking engagements to sell books. Here are just a few of them:

• Simply mention your books in any talks you give, whether to the Ladies' Auxiliary, Rotary Club, or an association meeting. Integrate the subject of your book into the subject of your talk so you can mention your book as a natural part of the talk. Then let the audience know they can buy copies of your book in the back of the room after the talk (these sales are known in the speaking trade as back-of-the-room sales) or from their local bookstore.

I know of at least one speaker who earns over $1,000 per talk from sales of his books.

Sir Edmond Hillary used to sell at least two books for every person who attended his lectures.

At one of his Super Seminars in Los Angeles, A. L. Williams sold 7,600 copies of his book, *All You Can Do Is All You Can Do, But All You Can Do Is Enough*, in just two hours and fifteen minutes.

Here are a few other places you might want to give a talk: libraries (especially meetings of the Friends of the Library), bookstores, clubs, churches, civic groups, chambers of commerce, schools, colleges, PTAs, writers' clubs, garden parties, business luncheons, workshops, seminars, professional meetings, cruise ships, museum shows, conferences, ski lodges, and anywhere else that welcomes speakers and entertainers.

The Indiana Chamber of Commerce has set up its own speakers bureau. Check to see if your own local or state Chamber has a similar program.

Your local Rotary group (and other service groups such as the Lions, Kiwanis, etc.) needs a new speaker every week. They are hungry for speakers.

The program chairs of your local Toastmasters Speakers Bureau meet monthly to pass on names of good speakers and to hear presentations from new speakers. Why not track down your local Toastmasters group to see if you can speak to them?

• Give something free to everyone who attends your lectures. Art Fettig of Growth Unlimited offers everyone a free copy of one of his verses, illustrated and ready for framing. Each verse has his name, address, and phone number. He gets many bookings and book sales through this means alone.

• Give everyone a brochure and order blank. Hand them out free during the lecture, or just afterwards. If you include some points from your talk or a list of resources that the audience can follow up on after the talk, they are more likely to take your brochure home with them.

• Offer to accept MasterCard and VISA orders (if you are set up to do so).

Again, when Art Fettig offers one of his higher priced book/tape combos, he tells members of the audience to just write their charge card number on the back of their business card. In this way, he often gets over $1,000 in orders each lecture.

• If you are giving a seminar to a corporation or a talk to a professional association, you might try preselling your books to the program planner so that each attendee receives a free copy of your book as part of the program. If your books will make the meeting that much more effective, the corporation will probably jump at the chance.

One speaker raised his fee from $325 per person for each seminar he gave to $495 and then included his book as part of the materials for the seminar. He met no price resistance when he raised the price of his seminar.

• Have the toastmaster announce that you will be available after your talk to autograph books and to speak to anyone with any additional questions. Of course, those people who do not already have a copy of your book will want to buy one from you so they can get your autograph at the same time.

• If you are speaking at a newsworthy event, let the media know about your speech. Also, send them an advance copy of your talk so they can quote accurately from your talk if they do decide to cover the event.

• Remember, as a professional you should also charge for speaking to any major seminars, conferences, clubs, and so on. These fees will help to pay your way to other speaking engagements and help to keep your promotional show on the road.

On the other hand, Bruce Sievers does not charge for his poetry readings, but he does insist on his right to sell his books after the readings. And does he sell! In one year alone he sold over 25,000 books just as a result of his poetry readings.

• If the topic of your book is of interest to a specific national association with local chapters, why not set up a speaking tour with these local chapters? Linda Salzer, author of *Infertility: How Couples Can Cope*, funded her lecture tour by visiting local chapters of Resolve, the national support group for infertile couples.

• As you travel, plan ahead. Try to arrange speaking engagements wherever you travel.

Beverly Nye, self-publisher of *A Family Raised on Sunshine*, bought a thirty-day bus pass to tour five cities where she had previously lived. In each city she arranged with Mormon church groups and homemaking classes to give lectures where she talked about her own methods of homemaking. Not only did she make money on the admission fees charged for the lectures, but she also sold over 1,500 copies in thirty days.

• Finally, remember that it was through such speaking engagements that Wayne Dyer, Leo Buscaglia, and Robert Allen all became best-selling authors. Robert Allen traveled to different cities, offered "A Free Evening with Robert Allen" seminars, got people excited about his ideas for creating wealth, and sold loads of books.

2. Become a teacher

A good number of self-publishers and writers have found that lecturing at colleges and adult education classes is a superb way to market books.

• Melvin Powers, publisher of Wilshire Books and author of *How to Get Rich in Mail Order*, has been teaching for many years in the California college system. Not only does a description of his course get mailed to over a million potential students, but in the course description he recommends that his own book be bought and read ahead of time. He suggests that students buy the book at a local bookstore or check it out of their library. As he notes, "The result was phenomenal from a standpoint of sales."

3. Write articles

Besides selling first or second serial rights to your books, you might also consider adapting chapters of your book or writing related articles for magazines.

• Tom and Marilyn Ross did this for their *Encyclopedia of Self-Publishing*, selling short articles about self-publishing to such diverse magazines as *Southwest Airlines Magazine, Toastmaster Magazine, Pro-Comm Newsletter,* and others. In each case, they insisted that the magazine include an endnote telling readers where they could order the book.

If you can sell these articles, all the better; but even if you don't, you should try to place articles in any magazine whose readers might be interested in the topic of your book. Be sure to coordinate any such freelance writing with your publisher (who may already have approached the magazine about second serial rights).

4. Write a column

To gain greater visibility, write a regular column for an appropriate trade journal or newsletter.

• Luther Brock, a direct mail copywriter, wrote regular columns for *Direct Marketing Magazine, Mail Order Connection,* and *Information Marketing Newsletter*. He did no advertising because these columns brought him all the business he could handle.

• While I was writing the first edition of my book, *1001 Ways to Market Your Books*, I also wrote a regular column for an association of independent publishers' newsletter. Not only did the column help members of the association, but it also provided additional visibility for my publishing activities. Moreover, many of the columns were taken straight from books I was about to publish. Of course, I mentioned the books at the end of each article.

5. Become a joiner

Do anything you can to become visible. This means joining appropriate trade and social associations related to your topic (if you don't already belong). But don't just join, become active in the association's activities. If you were interested enough to write a book about the subject, you should be interested enough to become active in working with a related association.

• That's why I joined the publishers' association and also why I was a member of its board of directors for four years—not just because it's good for business, but because I really am concerned about the problems and possibilities of smaller book publishers.

6. Become an expert

As a published author, you automatically become an expert in the subject area of your book. To become recognized, however, as an expert, you must also establish yourself as a reliable source of news or information. Hence, do not respond to a reporter's question if you do not know the answer. Admit the limits of your expertise if you want to become quoted as "a reliable source."

• As an author of a number of books about publishing, I am often called upon to consult with smaller publishers and nonprofit associations about book production and marketing. I help where I can, and when I don't know the answer I send them to people who can help them. In the same way, many editors and publishers have sent people my way because they knew I could answer the questions from their readers. I've received many book orders from these referrals.

7. Become a talker

The subhead above means just what it says. Talk to anyone and everyone you meet. As a self-promoting author, you should not hesitate to talk about your book and your writing. Let people know you are an author. Naturally, they will then ask what you've written. Don't just tell them; show them the book (especially when your book is first published, be sure to carry a copy around with you at all times so you can show people the actual book). Be sure to let them know where they can order the book.

• One author of a guidebook for handicapped travelers happened to sit next to Abigail van Buren on an airplane flight. Of course, during their conversation the author mentioned her book. Some time later, Abigail found an opportunity to write about the book in her syndicated column, "Dear Abby." Over two sackfuls of mail—all orders—resulted from that one little mention.

8. Leave parts of yourself behind

Besides carrying around a copy of your book, you should also carry extra copies of any promotional brochures, bookmarks, and news releases about your book. Give these away to people you meet. Leave some lying around the doctor's office, in the laundromat, on the bulletin board at your local grocery store, at the airport, and wherever else you go—especially places where other people have to wait and are, therefore, likely to be looking for some reading material to pass the time.

Nice looking bookmarks (printed with the title of your book, the publication date, the name of the publisher, the retail price, your name and address, and an illustration from the book cover) have proven to be an effective way to keep an author's name before potential readers. Give these to people you meet during your day-to-day activity. Bookmarks work especially well in casual social occasions where giving out a business card would be inappropriate.

Here are a few other parts of yourself which you can leave behind:

• If your books are stocked by your local retailers (and they should be!), print up some stickers or cards that point out that you are a local author. Ask the stores if they would mind if you placed these stickers on the copies of your books in stock. Ninety percent of the stores will appreciate this bit of help.

• Offer to autograph the books as well. That makes the books more valuable—and more likely to be bought. Again, provide a sticker or card that points out that these copies have been autographed. Note that bookstores cannot return to the wholesaler books that have been autographed. Whenever I am in a different city, I always visit at least one bookstore. When I do, of course, I check to see if they have any copies of my books. If they do, I offer to autograph my books. When I did this at the main Kroch's and Brentano's store in Chicago, they placed a band around the autographed copies that announced that the books were autographed—and then placed the books on a special table up front.

• Give bookmarks, copies of the book's cover, or autographed copies of the book itself to the people at the cash register—or the person in the store most likely to have contact with potential buyers.

• Above all, leave a good impression. Wherever you go, dress well, speak well, and act with good manners.

9. Work with bookstores and distributors

Bookstores and distributors are generally happy to work with local authors. As mentioned above, most will appreciate any copies you have time to autograph. But they also respond to visits from authors. Indeed, some actively pursue continued contact with authors.

• Not only was Jacqueline Susann a superb interview subject for TV shows, but she was also a tireless self-promoter, going so far as to get up at six in the morning just to meet the drivers for mass-market paperback jobbers and encourage them to place her books in the prime spots. And they responded to her personal attention. Wouldn't you?

• Ron Hickman, book buyer for Florida East Coast News, actively seeks contact with authors. Not only does he attend the Florida Writers Conference, but he also regularly invites authors to speak to his monthly sales meetings with the drivers. He even supplies copies of the book for the author to autograph. When Maggie Davis, author of the novel *Satin Doll*, spoke at one of these monthly meetings, sales of her book in that region were much greater than in areas where she had not spoken to the drivers.

• When you send promotional material to bookstores and wholesalers, send them a personal note as well. Such personal touches help to get your material to the top of the stack—and read! Indeed, Dan Berger, book buyer for the Raleigh News Company, has said as much. He definitely pays more attention to writers' own promotional material, especially if it's newsy and interesting.

• As an author, you might want to publish your own small promotional newsletter (two or four pages), which could be sent to major chain buyers, wholesalers, jobbers, and other buyers and opinion leaders. Keep them up to date on any new promotions, publicity, and sales that might encourage them to take a second look at your book. If you have a fan club, send your club newsletter to these buyers. That will save you from having to write two newsletters.

10. Knock on doors or set up tables on the street to sell your book

Don't laugh. Direct selling can be one of the most effective ways to sell your books. People love to meet and talk with authors—and they love reading books by people they've met personally. Who wouldn't buy and cherish a personally autographed copy?

• Gary Provost, author/publisher of *The Dorchester Gas Tank* and many other books, began his career this way. He'd take a suitcase of books to downtown Boston every day, settle down at some busy corner (around City Hall, the public library, a subway entrance, or plaza), and begin peddling his books to anyone who'd listen. He'd sell twenty to twenty-five books a day. That's more sales than most books make per day.

• Another author sold his novel, *A War Ends*, door to door. While knocking on doors one day, he met a reporter for a Los Angeles newspaper. The reporter was so taken by the author's approach to selling books that he featured him in a story. That story not only brought the author many local sales, but it also inspired a number of other feature stories nationwide, thus bringing more attention to the novel...and more sales.

• Peter Gault sold 5,000 copies of his self-published novel, *Goldenrod*, by traveling across Canada setting up tables and selling books to anyone he met. At one point, he even sold books on the street in front of the offices of Canada's major newspapers. Not only did he get lots of attention there, but he also received many reviews for his book from the major book critics.

Later, while selling his books in front of Lincoln Center in New York, he met another writer, Richard Kalish, who bought his book, liked it, and introduced Gault to Martin Shepard of The Permanent Press. In the spring of 1988, The Permanent Press published a hardcover edition of Gault's book for the U.S. market.

11. Form alliances with other authors

Besides joining organizations for writers, you should also try to work out arrangements with writers in other parts of the country to promote each other's work in your home areas.

• When visiting bookstores and distributors, you can check to see if they stock not only your own books but also the books of the other authors with whom you are working.

• You can leave promotional material for each other wherever you go.

• You might even co-publish a newsletter that carries news and features about you and the other authors.

• And, if you go on tour, you can stay with your friends across the country (and they with you). That alone would make an author tour more cost-effective for your publisher.

12. Set a record

One way to get publicity for your book is to set a world record (a record that can somehow be related to your book). Note that you don't have to set a world record to gain publicity, you only have to attempt it. Actually, if you're not into setting world records, you could sponsor an attempt or announce a contest and prize for such an attempt—anything at all that associates you and your book with the world record.

For more details on how to go about getting in the record books, read Clint Kelly's self-published book, *The Fame Game*, available from Performance Press, 504 51st Street SW, Everett, WA 98203; 206-252-7660.

13. Do it for charity

While you are attempting the world record or, for that matter, while you are doing other promotions for your book, do them for a charitable cause. Not only will this help you in getting publicity for your book, but at the same time you will be doing a good turn for the charitable cause by bringing publicity (and money) to it as well.

• Kathryn Leigh Scott has sold her book, *My Scrapbook Memories of Dark Shadows*, to several PBS stations to use as a premium in their annual pledge drives. As part of the deal, she spent several days shooting generic spots for pledge drives across the country.

14. Do everything

If you have the time, you can be your own best salesperson. Sharon Scott is responsible for selling thousands of copies of her two books, *Peer Pressure Reversal* and *How to Say No and Keep Your Friends*. Here are just a few of her activities that have helped to sell her books:

• She conducts in-service training programs for teachers, counselors, and parents.

• Through seminars and workshops, she has trained 25,000 students.

• She speaks at many conferences, both regional and national, for professionals working with youth.

• She writes a "Positive Parenting" column which appears in many school newsletters.

• She is a frequent guest on local and national TV and radio shows.

• She is now producing several videos based on her work.

And now a word of caution:
Be careful not to overcommit yourself to the promotion of your books. Do what you can, but be sure to save time to write new books. That's what you do best.

John Kremer is an acknowledged expert on book publishing and marketing. Besides being the owner of his own publishing company (Open Horizons Publishing Company in Fairfield, Iowa, 515-472-6130), he is the editor of the Book Marketing Update *newsletter.*

John is the author of a number of books on publishing and marketing, including 1001 Ways to Market Your Books: For Authors and Publishers (6th Edition), Book Marketing Made Easier (3rd Edition), The Complete Direct Marketing Sourcebook *and* Celebrate Today.

In addition, John is the developer of the Mail Order Worksheet Kit, *the* Mail Order Spreadsheet Kit, *and the* Publicity and Promotional Events Data File. *He was the original developer of the* Directory of Book Printers, Book Publishing Resource Guide, PR ProfitCenter *database,* Book Marketing No-Frills *database, and four special reports on publicity and specialty marketing.*

Finally, John is the author of Tinseltowns, U.S.A., *a trivia quiz book and* Turntable Illusions: Kinetic Optical Illusions for Your Record Turntable, *which features 101 uses for your obsolete turntable.*

John is a member of Mid-America Publishers Association, Publishers Marketing Association, Book Publicists of Southern California, Midwest Independent Publishers Association and Marin Small Publishers Association. He often speaks at book publishing and marketing seminars throughout the nation.

Show, Don't Tell

It's not nice to tell tales! Unless you show them too

<hr />

By Marsh Cassady

I F YOUR MOTHER TOLD YOU NOT TO TELL TALES, she was absolutely right, as moms often are. She probably also cautioned you against showing all in public. Right again.

Mom probably didn't mean what she said as writing advice, but it is. She should have added, however, that at times it is fine to tell a little and show a lot. But if you show too much, you are going to lose your reader.

What does it mean to show, not tell? Allow me the immodesty of using some samples from my own published works. This is telling:

> I'd quit my job and gone to graduate school, so we had little money. After my wife and I finished Christmas shopping, Bobbie, the younger of our two daughters, said she needed a dress for the eighth-grade dance. We bought her one, but she said she wouldn't wear it. I followed her to the bedroom she shared with her sister and told her she had to. She insisted that the other kids would make fun of her. I tried to make her see that she was behaving childishly. She screamed that she hated me and ran outside. Upset and frustrated, I tore the dress into shreds. Bobbie came back and said she'd go to the dance. Then she saw the dress.

This is showing:

"Bobbie!"

"Yes?"

In that single word I read vulnerability, longing, a need for comfort. I ignored them. "Open the door!"

It swung slowly open. Bobbie stood there, a wild look in her eyes. Nearly as tall as her sister, she'd always been timid, unsure of herself. I was like that at her age.

"What, Dad?" she said, her tone defiant, yet still with a hint of that terrible vulnerability.

"What is this about not going to the dance!"

"I can't."

I pushed on into the room. On the dresser, arranged from biggest to smallest, stood Andrea's stuffed animals. Bobbie's lay heaped in the corner, along with dolls made from coke bottles and scraps of clothing, half-finished drawings and partially knit sweaters beginning to ravel.

"Your mom and I spent good money on this. Money we didn't have." I picked up the dress. "What's wrong with it?"

"Everyone will make fun of me."

"Put it on!"

"I can't. I won't. You can't make me!"

I grabbed her arm and turned her toward the mirror. "Look at you. Behaving like you're five years old."

She twisted free and raced downstairs.

"Come back here!"

"I hate you, Daddy." She grabbed her coat from the hook by the door.

"Where do you think you're going?" I pounded down the steps in time to hear shoes clicking on ice. The door slammed.

What had I done by quitting my job and going back to school? A person tries to do his best, I thought... I sank into my desk chair, the dress in both hands. I grabbed it on either side of the neck and jerked with all my strength. The fabric resisted, then split to the waist. A second time I yanked, then again and again.

I buried my face in the dress, the dress that was now only rags.

The front door opened, and Bobbie came in. "Daddy? I'll go to the dance," she said. "I want to go to the dance."

Then she saw the dress in my hands, the beautiful dress in my hands.

Why show, not tell?

Why is the second example more effective than the first? There are many reasons.

1. A writer needs to involve the audience emotionally. In the scene from "The Beautiful Dress," readers are more likely to identify with both the father and Bobbie if they feel a part of the action.

2. Showing can provide a sense of time and place, particularly if the story is set in an unfamiliar world. Shortly before the following, Willie, one of two central characters, has been whisked back to the summer of 1887.

> Women passed by wearing shoes with pointed toes; most carried silk parasols with bows on the handles. All wore hats with feathers. Trailing feathers, feathers that stuck straight up or fluted out in all directions. And bustles. My God, Willie thought, did women really wear those things? The men were just as bad, with stiff collars and wool vests. Most carried canes....
>
> Occasional cyclists coasted along, dressed in straw hats, two-toned shoes and black spats. Some wore suits, others linen shirts that laced to the neck and tied. An assortment of horse-drawn vehicles passed—milk and produce wagons, hansom cabs, carriages, carts.

"A writer needs to involve the audience emotionally."

3. Showing creates suspense. Why is Willie, a man from the latter part of the twentieth century, suddenly back in time? Who brought him there? How? Why?

4. Showing reveals relationships more exactly than telling does. It's easy to see the relationship between the two characters in "The Beautiful Dress," or in this scene:

> John asked if she'd like to go for a bit of a ride. "Thought I might show you the farm."
> "Out Old Town Road?" she asked.

"How did you know?"

She couldn't tell him she'd always known. Since she'd first seen him in church and asked who he was.

He started the motor. "It's not a big farm. Eighty-some acres. It used to be more, but I sold to the strip miners." He glanced toward her and then eased out into traffic.

"Why did you sell?"

"For the future. For Mary and the kids. For our dreams. They'd be somebodies, those kids. Not dumb farmers like me. Doctors or architects. Teachers or professors." He shrugged. "The older you get, the more you think of the past."

"Beautiful country," she said. "I don't often get out this way."

Rolling fields and hills stretched into the distance, bare-limbed trees scattered here and there.

John clutched the wheel with knobby hands. Thick wrists protruded from the sleeves of his pin-striped suit.

"Here we are," he said as they passed over a one-lane bridge. A square-shaped house squatted at the end of a driveway opposite a faded red barn.

"Can I confess something?" He pulled over and stopped. His hands still gripped the wheel. Hers, in fur-lined gloves, lay one in the palm of the other on her lap. "I've wanted to ask you out for a long, long time. Near worried myself to death about it."

"I don't understand."

"You have so much education, what would people think?"

"I don't give a hoot what people think!"

He chuckled. "Looks like I provoked a storm."

She folded her hands. "May I confess something as well?" She gave him a sideways glance. "You'll think me terribly immodest."

"I doubt it."

"I've been attracted to you for thirty-three years."

5. Showing helps limit the story. A writer can immediately point out what is typical, and what is unusual. Here's an example of each sort of scene.

Dennis trotted and ran for what he knew to be just under seven miles, winding in and out around the coves and crannies of the beach, doubling back upon his own trail several times. Stocky, his body hard like a boxer's, he wore faded running shorts and a torn T-shirt, not as a reverse kind of snobbery as people were wont to do in a place like the Village, but because they were comfortable. He looked up to see the sun still young and white in the sky.

Knowing he's run seven miles, the clothing he wears, and his physical condition tell the reader that Dennis jogs regularly.

A store in Ravenna had begun to stock black walnut ice cream, Lou's favorite as a boy. On his way home from the theatre, he stopped and bought a half gallon.

He'd arranged to have the evening free, his first in months. It was his and Sally's seventeenth wedding anniversary.

He pulled into the driveway, got out, reached back for the ice cream and ran to the landing. He saw that the front door stood open, the storm door swayed in a gentle breeze.

"Sally," he called. "Sally?" They planned a cookout. Maybe afterwards he could talk Sally and the kids into a game of Monopoly.

He poked his head inside the door. The living room was deserted, the house silent. "Sally. Tommy. Diane!" Tommy was fifteen, Diane sixteen. In a few more years, they'd be off to college.

He hurried into the dining room and on out to the kitchen. And oh, my God, the blood. The floors, the walls, the table, the counters! Everything was covered with blood. Sally's blood. He screamed till he was hoarse, then forced himself to look once more.

She lay in a heap by the kitchen sink, a metal mixing bowl trailing lettuce and radishes over her chest, her head attached in back by a narrow strip of flesh. Then the smell hit him, a smell of the stockyards where his grandfather used to work. He choked on bile and something sour. He sank to his knees, forced himself to crawl to the table, pulled himself up by grasping the edge. Diane sprawled across the top, her long brown hair flung over her head, her arms jutting out at angles. A butcher knife stuck from her back.

Tommy! he thought "Tommy?" His voice was that of a stranger. An actor in a play. "Tommy! Tommy, Tommy, Tommy!" He raced outside to the patio. "Tommy! To ..." Tommy lay on his back, arms and legs and head forming a five-point star, his stomach ripped and torn, insides trailing across his belly.

Lou pulled a handkerchief from his pocket and brushed off a wrought iron chair. He perched on the edge, watching the sun as it slowly described its arc and dipped beyond the horizon. The phone rang, once, twice. Lou didn't understand what that meant, and so he ignored it.

The world seemed far away. He stood and moved his feet toward the kitchen, but they seemed not to touch the floor. He stepped around the body; he didn't look.

He was thirsty, so terribly thirsty. He opened the refrigerator, took out a pitcher of iced tea. He pulled off the lid and drank. The tea dribbled over his chin, down his neck, into his shirt.

He finished and replaced the lid. He looked down. He hadn't realized the gigantic height to which he'd grown.

He set the pitcher on the counter. It was Tommy's job to do the dishes. He picked it up again. He'd wash it himself, save Tommy the trouble.

He flung the pitcher into the wall, pounded the cupboard. He split one door and then another, his knuckles ripping, bursting, adding to the blood. The world became red and then blue and then white. He stumbled into the living room, smashing furniture, ripping pictures off walls, and then he thought of the ice cream. He walked to the kitchen, and there it sat, melting, running into the silverware drawer.

6. Showing foreshadows future events. Almost immediately, a person reading the preceding scene senses that something is terribly wrong—the references to the barbecue and playing Monopoly, the open front door, the swinging storm door, Sally's not answering. The certainty of disaster is foretold in Lou's thinking that Tommy and Diane will soon be off to college.

7. Showing makes the writing explicit. The reader knows that Lou loves his family and treasures the time he can spend with them. He buys the ice cream, his favorite as a boy, because he wants to share a part of himself.

The detail about the bodies is important, not for shock value, but rather to show that in extreme situations, part of a person's mind is likely to stand aloof and observe. Still, there is a reserve. It would be too painful to say the word "intestines." Instead, Lou sees Tommy's "insides" trailing across his belly. The characters and situation dictate the word choice.

Lou owns a theatre and for years has been an actor, hence he's even more prone to be aware of his behavior and the way he thinks.

After finding Sally and Diane, Lou has a slight hope that Tommy somehow escaped. "Tommy!" Then he questions. "Tommy?" When he lets the boy's name trail off, the reader knows that Tommy is dead.

8. Often unique or unusual details give a scene a feeling of depth and reality. An example is Willie's noticing that all the women's hats have feathers, a small observation that suggests the setting is not the world we know.

Lou's thinking is clear and yet muddled, an unusual contradiction. He carefully brushes dust from the wrought iron chair, sits, and watches the sun go down. Even saying he watched the "sun sink" would be too mundane since the moment is unique. Yet at the same time he watches the sun "describing its arc," he cannot comprehend the ringing of a phone.

All this shows he's in shock, further intensified by the feeling that he's floating. Then he's so thirsty he cannot wait to pour tea into a glass. For a moment he forgets or blocks out the murders, deciding to wash the pitcher, which normally is Tommy's job. Then reality strikes full force, enraging Lou to the point of smashing doors, furniture, and his knuckles. Finally, physically spent, he notices the melting ice cream. All the horror centers on one tiny detail.

The reader perceives all these details and understands what they mean, much more than if any part of them were told.

9. As already implied, showing is to reveal the motives behind an action.

What to show

It's usually better to describe a person's emotions than to state them. The narrator's ripping the dress shows frustration; Lou's screaming "till he was hoarse" is more effective that saying he was overwhelmed by despair.

Sensory details involve the reader—seeing, hearing, smelling, touching, and tasting, as well as movement, balance, and temperature. We see John's knobby hands and feel their grip on the steering wheel. We hear the ripping of the dress. We smell the blood, taste the bile, and feel Lou's sensation of floating.

Showing means describing such things as places, objects, people, clothing, seasons of the year, time periods, and socioeconomic conditions. It means mixing the ordinary—the salad bowl, the wrought iron chair, the melting ice cream—with the rare—the condition of the bodies, the smell of the blood.

Some don'ts of showing

1. A sentence or paragraph with few adjectives and adverbs is more powerful than one with many. A good rule, though sometimes legitimately breakable, is: Never use an adjective or adverb unless it's necessary, and then use no more than one. Compare the following:

> "I remembered the stream, icy cold, that meandered behind the
> barn; the fields of wheat and corn; and, past these fields, the cool-
> ness of the sugar woods with its soft carpet of leaves."

Or:

"In the eye of my mind, I visualized the silt-laden stream, always icy cold, that flowed slowly in a seemingly random pattern behind the rotted, half-fallen, unpainted barn; the vast, sun-drenched fields of tawny wheat and ripe corn; and once past these rolling fields, the welcoming coolness of the maple sugar woods with its soft, plush carpet of brown, fallen leaves.

2. Don't use generic words like "frustration," "hatred," "beautiful," or "ugly."

"How was your evening."
"Wonderful, lovely."

That doesn't mean anything. The following are somewhat better:

"How was your evening?" I asked
"Wonderful, lovely." Linda, my forty-year-old sister, giggled like an eleven-year-old, the first time I'd heard her laugh since Paul's death.

Or:

"Wonderful, lovely." Her voice was as hard as the fake diamond embedded in her thumbnail.

Yet the reader still knows nothing about the evening. Did the character win a state lottery, ask for and receive a raise? There's no way of knowing. Bobbie's father does refer to the "beautiful dress," but earlier on the readers actually saw it. The woman in the car—her name is Odelle Whiffin—says "beautiful country" but then goes on to think of the fields, the hills, and the trees.

3. Don't over-describe. The amount of detail depends somewhat on the genre. There are exceptions, but literary novels generally have much more description than mainstream or genre novels.

The fiction writer and the reader make a contract with each other. The writer says:

"I agree to provide entertainment (and maybe knowledge and new ideas). I'll give you enough detail to enjoy my work, but you'll have to fill in the rest. If I tried to show the things a camera does, you'd be bored and probably would skip large sections."

The reader says: "I agree to use my imagination to visualize the ruined barn, the upper-class mansion, the character's appearance beyond the few hints that you give me. I realize, due to background and experience, that I won't imagine it in the same way anyone else will."

In other words, a description consists of a somewhat "vague" outline. Yet with "the willing suspension of disbelief," readers see a completeness if the piece is well-written or the genre and style to their liking.

4. Don't go on about unimportant elements. If you fully describe a minor character, the reader will expect the person to play a role later in the story. A mailman who appears once to deliver a letter is only a device, deserving of no more than a few words of description.

Some background is important to the reader's understanding of the story but not important enough to show in detail. In "The Beautiful Dress," there are these two narrative sections. The first opens the story:

> The kids were already twelve and thirteen before I finished graduate school and took a job at a little college in New Jersey. So what with paying back student loans and finance companies to whom we'd gone into hock, things were awfully tight those first few years.
> "Don't blame yourself," she said. "You weren't getting anywhere at the paper writing obits."

These explain why the prof's daughters are older than might be expected for a man in his first year of college teaching and why he went back to school. Yet they are merely background needed to explain the scenes that are shown.

5. Don't slow down a fast-paced scene with long descriptive passages.

6. On the other hand, don't suddenly refer to a character by name without an introduction. Unless Bob has been previously mentioned, you can't say: As Raphael and Susan carried out the dead body, Bob went to pick up the RV with the oversized freezer. Who on earth is Bob? the reader will wonder.

7. Most rules can be broken, maybe even this one. But that would be rare. Don't show transitions in detail. Suppose your central character Louellen receives a message to meet an old college prof whom she hasn't seen in years. Further, suppose that the prof called and told the receptionist at Louellen's office that the meeting is vitally important. Of course, it's fine to show that Louellen is intrigued or apprehensive. Don't, however, show her going through the rest of her workday, leaving the office, driving home, entering her apartment, cooking dinner, *ad nauseam*. Instead, go immediately to the next important scene. A simple way of doing this is to skip down a couple of extra spaces on the manuscript page and pick up with, "Louellen patted her hair and opened the car door. It was nearly one o'clock, and she knew how Dr. Philburn hated tardiness." Or use a bridge like "that evening," "the next day," or "a week later." These are akin to invisible words like "the," "an," or "said" in not calling attention to themselves.

8. Don't over sentimentalize emotions: Tears streaming down her face, Rosie Fleming clutched the letter to her breast. "Oh, no." Her piteous sobs echoed through the empty house.

The example is exaggerated. Yet do avoid clichés like "tears streaming down her face" and "clutched the letter to her breast." Try to find a new way of expressing the emotion. Yet this new way should not stand out or call undue attention to itself. However—and some may consider this heretical—it is better to use a trite phrase than one that comes across as bizarre or awkward, unless that is your intention.

Three types of scenes

The confrontation between Bobbie and her father is nearly pure portrayal, while the "bridge" between the scenes is narration. Many times, however, a scene is neither all showing nor all telling. Lou's scene is a combination. The first few sentences are expository; they tell things that already have happened. Soon, however, the reader is brought to the present. Whether each scene is pure telling or showing doesn't matter. What does is that it accomplishes its goal.

So what do you think? If your mom had known you were going to follow her advice, would she have given it? What if she had known you someday would write about grisly murders or illicit sex, or that you'd have your characters curse and use obscenity? Would she still have given you the same advice? I suppose that depends on your mom.

Marsh Cassady is the author of more than fifty published books including novels, short story and drama collections, humor, haiku, true crime, and books on theatre and storytelling. His plays have been produced across the United States, including Off-Broadway, and in Mexico.

In the nineties Cassady and his partner, Jim Kitchen, operated Los Hombres Press which published novels, nonfiction and haiku. He has served as editor of two magazines and a couple of literary journals. A former columnist for two writer's magazines, he has had close to 1,000 short pieces published.

A former actor/director and university theatre professor, Cassady has a Ph.D. in theatre and has taught creative writing classes at UCSD and elsewhere. His digital art and ceramic sculptures are on exhibit in several galleries in Baja California, Mexico where he has lived since 1997. He shares his home with his partner and five members of the feline persuasion. Cassady presently writes a column, the editorials and occasional articles for The Baja Times and leads a writing workshop. Email: marshcassady@yahoo.com.

Keys to Crafting Your Nonfiction Book

By far, most books published are nonfiction. Learn how to join the ranks of successful nonfiction book authors from a pro.

By JoAnn Roe

WRITING A NONFICTION BOOK IS LIKE CREATING a human being. The central theme of the book is the skeleton, the details flesh out the body, and the paragraphs of illustration, anecdotes and quotes—like specialized organs and nerves—make the skeletal theme come to life and move forward.

Focus on a central theme

Finding that central theme is not always easy. I remember an assignment from *Canadian Geographic* magazine, where the editor simply said, "What makes the Okanagan Valley of Canada tick?" My unspoken reaction was, "How would I know!" But I knew my job was to find out and that, by looking and talking and researching, the theme would emerge strong and true. And so it did: snow melt, the control of which affected ranching, lake levels, fish runs, irrigation, tree growth, and all the human economics that accompanied these factors.

On being asked to write a book about what happened in a particular mountain range of Washington, I chose man's 100-year effort to build a trail or road through the rugged range as the clothesline or skeleton on which I could hang tales of mining, dam building, freighting, dog sled rescues, and the people who came to the mountains. The central theme acted as a vehicle for the passage from the opening attention-getter to the wrap-up.

The theme for a biography may be the person's lifelong love of poetry or, for a how-to book, the secrets of New England woodcrafters.

Most nonfiction books fall into the following categories: how-to (including the perennial self-help tome), biography, adventure, or history.

How-to

You don't always have to be an expert on the subject you're writing about when you start a how-to book—but you had better be one when you finish.

These books necessarily are written in straightforward fashion. Here is the problem. Here are the answers. Clarity is paramount. Use short sentences and uncomplicated words. Lead your reader step by step through the solution to the problem, deviating only briefly to illustrate some important point.

Do not assume your reader knows anything about the topic—some will, some won't. Your reader is seeking specific instructions on how-to, how to build a house, train a horse, fix a car, replace lost self-esteem.

How-to books run the danger of being too dry, too technical. The best writers add a touch of human warmth with anecdotes about people involved in the subject, quotes from these same people, or touches of humor. A word of warning though: Keep your humor spare and subtle; when humor appears forced, it works against the author.

Biography

Biographies are fact but should read like novels. The central theme is simple: birth, school, marriage, children, work, illness, death. A narrative style works well for biographies. Pretend that you are telling your best friend about a fascinating person you met last year. Include personal stories that give insights into the personality or character of the subject. Begin with the subject's achievements or reason for fame, working in the statistics of his life later. For example:

> It was a surprise to almost everyone in Podunk when Joe Doakes became an astronaut. He almost flunked physics in Podunk High School. All that changed when...

It is essential in telling of the personal life of anyone that you are totally accurate and can document your statements and sources.

It is often best to obtain a release from the subject or subject's family to avoid problems. Naturally, if you are writing an unauthorized biography, perhaps about a nefarious person, the family is not likely to cooperate. In this case, you will be limited to material that you can glean from other sources.

The material that is public record must be documented thoroughly. It is wise to work with an attorney whose specialty is intellectual properties (see *Literary Market Place*, available at most libraries, for a list of names), especially if you are writing about matters that portray a still-living subject in an unfavorable light. Consult a book (Jonathan Kirsch's *Handbook of Publishing Law* is a good choice) on your legal responsibilities and rights as an author.

Let's say that the subject is a willing one. Nothing enlivens a biography more than quotes from the subject, personal glimpses into his or her life, and personal takes on events or incidents that have been central to this person's career, adventure, or whatever.

Adventure

Leap right into the adventure tale. Make it impossible for the reader to put the book down. Use active verbs and gripping development. For example, a sailing trip around Cape Horn:

> The wave seemed to rise forever from the depths of the sea, towering above our forty-five foot schooner. Lashed to the boat, Jim and I did not realize until the sea subsided that our hands were bleeding from merely hanging on. Whatever possessed us to take such a dangerous journey! It all began...

Early in the adventure story you should work in descriptive material, not tired narration but words that enable the reader to have a sense of place—where are you? On a ship? Are the sails up or reefed? Is it raining? Are you terrified or confident? Are objects sliding off the decks? Your reader should be vicariously in your shoes.

Know when to quit. The story is complete, the danger past, the dawn comes, your subject survives and goes on. Stop. Leave your reader glued to the tale and wishing to read more rather than bumbling off into dull explanations after the adventure is over.

> "Know when to quit... Leave your reader glued to the tale and wishing to read more..."

History

I write on historical topics frequently—living, breathing history for the general public. For a magazine article you would bracket a specific topic, an incident, a battle, a place or, say, five nineteenth-century hotels. For a book, the bracket is broader but still should contain a manageable theme. Attempting to cover too much ground in a single historical or other nonfiction book will result in a style of writing that is staccato and without an even flow. Nonfiction books should read as smoothly as fiction.

Let's use an actual book of mine, *Stevens Pass*, as an example. I had no personal knowledge of the place prior to my publisher suggesting it to me as a book topic. The first thing I did was to drive through the Stevens Pass area, taking very few notes, soaking up impressions, developing an emotional reaction to the topic, and assessing the scope of the project.

Because the suggestion came from the publisher, I hadn't prepared a list of references. But, if you plan to propose a topic to a publisher, you'll need first to peruse book lists like *Books in Print* (available at most libraries) or search one of the more complete Internet bookstores such as Amazon.com to see what other books have been written on the topic. Bibliographies of books written about subjects similar to your own provide other leads to useful sources. Scan all the books you find, assembling background information. Most will be available either in your regional library or through interlibrary loans. Check out your state library. State libraries collect virtually every book written about the state. Use the information you ferret out to prepare a formal nonfiction book proposal to present to the publisher. (See How to Write a Nonfiction Book Proposal: Sell Your Book Before Your Write It, page 141.)

> "Nonfiction books should read as smoothly as fiction."

If the publisher says yes to your proposal, and it's a history book you've tackled, travel to the site or sites you are writing about. List towns, roads, trains, mines, events, terrain features, weather, economics of the place, and unusual occurrences that come to light through conversations with locals. (Join the local coffee shop crowd some morning and ask, "Whatever happened around here, anyway?")

Research

Research materials take many forms beyond books: county and state real estate and title records, plats of towns, collections of personal papers donated to a research facility by an individual, lists of corporations filed with the state and lists of defunct corporations (which give you names of officers), even school records. The United States Forest Service stations maintain clipping and data files about their specific areas, material often not duplicated elsewhere. You can "mine" these files and those of local and regional museums.

Interest groups have newsletters. For my project on Stevens Pass (closely tied to the Great Northern Railroad), I contacted the Great Northern Historical Society at Saint Paul, Minnesota, which issues a newsletter. Several editions featured Stevens Pass. The articles were authored by keen rail buffs—sticklers for accuracy. In trying to ferret out information on a sawmill for another book, I found newsletters from the defunct company in a logging museum.

Of course, locate the names of all the newspapers or magazines published presently or in the past for your area of interest. Today many are on microfilm, which you can order for use on the premises of your regional library.

For my history books, I like to scan weekly newspapers because anything of importance will be on the front pages. In the process, I will come up with names of key people in the area. I also look in the phone book for possible descendants of the same name.

Make photocopies of pertinent material for your files; it's much faster than taking copious notes. Occasionally I have used a tape recorder or laptop computer to copy data at archives, where old materials are never released nor can they be photocopied—e.g., old letters, legal documents, diaries, etc. The more notes you can bring home for assimilation the better.

Pursue details on key topics as you progress. Set up computer files, three-by-five cards and/or manila folders by topic as they develop.

Interviewing

From here on, the research becomes a detective story, with one source leading you to another and another. Keep an eye peeled for experts and other interesting people you would like to interview. Intriguing "people" stories come from such rolling research, the stories that make your nonfiction tale come alive and become a human saga, the organs and nerves of your story, not just a dull recitation of facts.

Most people will be flattered that you wish to interview them. Approach them as a professional, calling ahead and making an appointment for the interview even if you will be conducting the interview over the phone.

How do you extract useful information from people you will interview? With patience. Prepare for each interview by outlining specific questions for the interviewee. If, in a face-to-face interview, you use a tape recorder, use one with a conference feature—one that you can lay on a central table to pick up conversation. Many interviewees clam up if faced with a hand-held microphone but tend to forget a stationary recorder.

Assure the interviewee that he need not worry about your quoting something he wishes he hadn't said, that you will check with him before using any revelation that seems sensitive. Then ask a leading question and sit back. Let the interviewee ramble on, even as you try to keep on track with specific questions, because you never know when he will launch into some tale that is of critical interest. You can pick and choose material from the tape and your notes later on. When the interviewee seems to be rehashing the same old stories, or covering the same ground twice, stop, thank him, and end the interview.

Sometimes two people provide sharply differing versions of the same information; if you include this information, you should attempt to uncover the true facts from hard copy such as books, newspapers or documents. If this isn't possible, credit such information to the source, e.g., "Old-timer Will Jones remembers that..." or "According to CEO Fred Smith..." This holds true with any facts an interviewee has given you: Verify the facts independently or if you're unable to and still wish to use them, attribute them to your source.

Start writing

When you find that interviewees or other sources are producing nothing new and you have bulging file folders of data, perhaps your research on a topic is sufficient and it's time to start writing.

Decide if you will write from a time line, a topical line, a directional line such as east to west, or another organizational structure? Ask yourself: How does the action develop naturally?

Create a chapter outline, which acts as a guide for the rest of the book. Don't worry; you can always add or subtract material or blend in a late discovery.

Assemble all your notes and photocopies that touch on the topic for chapter one, two, etc. Before writing anything, saturate your memory with this pertinent data, reading it over and over with concentration, so that the diverse source material homogenizes in your mind. Then sit down and start writing. Don't worry about grammar, sentence structure, forgotten dates or fragments of data (leave spaces and add later). Just put down everything you know about the subject matter for that chapter. When you have completed this "brain dump," you will clearly see where the holes are in your chapter—what you do know and what is missing.

Go back to the research to fill in the missing gaps, then polish the grammar and structure, and work in your human interest stories. Be sure to think about "ties"—sentences that logically lead the reader into the next chapter's topic.

Be sure you understand "fair use" of material taken from other writings. Ask for written clearance if you use—even rewritten—significant segments of information from another book. Keep one copy of this permission slip in your office; one copy should go with the manuscript to your publisher.

One way of acknowledging sources in an informal writing is to say, "According to Joe Doakes in his 1989 book, *Mysteries*, such and such happened." Another, more specific way, is to use numbers after the data, placing all the source notes by number at the bottom of the page, end of each chapter or the end of the book. Since I write for the general public, I seldom use source notes or footnotes as scholarly writers do. I find them distracting and alarming to the general reader.

The choice is up to you and your publisher; however, in your own files you should always make notes as to where you obtained the material for a given chapter, enabling you to "defend" yourself if someone later questions the accuracy of some statement.

You must control the length of your book to conform to the publisher's specifications, or you will be required to do laborious rewriting and addition or reduction later. I write until I have completed my thoughts, not worrying unduly about length. After the first draft is complete, I return to sharply tighten the material, eliminating deadwood, and even entire incidents, to meet the length required. In the process, the book is always improved.

Supposing you have tightened the manuscript until you cannot imagine further elimination. If you still must chop, say, 3,000 words from the script of 300 typed pages, try pulling a mere ten words from each page.

Ask an expert to review sections you feel the least bit uncomfortable about. In the process of amalgamating diverse information, you may have made some obvious error or drawn a skewed conclusion. Most experts will be pleased to do this for a mention in your acknowledgments at the front of the book. But, even if you offer the expert a fee for checking such material, the key factor for nonfiction books is accuracy, and your reputation rests on making as few errors as possible.

Photos and other illustrations

While you deal with the cleanup operations of your manuscript—the fact checking, the clearances, etc.—you can assemble the illustrations. You, the author, are expected (unless it is spelled out differently in your contract) to furnish any reproducible photos and illustrations at your cost. If your book requires maps, you must create rough drafts from which a professional map maker—at your expense—can complete maps to be included in the book.

Generally, you first provide photocopies or electronic copies of suggested illustrations to the publisher, who retains the right to choose the ones included in the book. Beware of potential costs for use of materials. Use fees per photo or illustration can run from nothing to hundreds of dollars. If your publisher is a nonprofit corporation, often use is free. Yet you, the writer, still must absorb the cost of obtaining the image from the source's files.

Discuss the above expenses with your publisher—some negotiation may be possible—before signing your contract. It is a good idea to place in your contract a ceiling on the total use fees for illustrations that you are willing to absorb.

Identify illustrations by using numbers that correspond to a separate sheet of typed captions.

Make a floppy disk, CD and a printout of your final draft, keeping a copies for yourself. Mark your backup material clearly, because you should make *no* alterations to this disk or CD thereafter. Your disk or CD and the publisher's disk *must* match, in the event of requested changes later on.

Protect any photos and other illustrations with cardboard on both sides. Mail the whole package off, perhaps by certified mail to protect your investment in photo/illustration production costs, and sink back into your easy chair to breathlessly await the publisher's comments.

JoAnn Roe is especially known for her lively, readable books on historical and travel subjects, though she's not limited to these topics. She is the author of several hundred articles for national and regional magazines. Among her many awards for writing are the Society of American Travel Writers (SATW), Frank Riley Award, the National Federation of Press Women's top national award for feature writing (three times), the Pacific Northwest Booksellers Award and the Mayor's Award for Arts and for Tourism. JoAnn also gives seminars, workshops, and young authors' programs.

Solving the
Protagonist Puzzle

Just sit down at your computer,
open a vein, and let your character flow out

By Lesley Kellas Payne

DURING MY TEN YEARS OF WORKING as a freelance editor of adult fiction, the deepest challenge with which I have observed writers struggle is the creation of fully developed and consistent protagonists. Yet, the protagonist, your story's main character, is the character with whom the reader must identify to find satisfaction, the kind of satisfaction that leaves the reader wanting more, the kind of satisfaction that makes the reader recommend your book to friends.

The inspiration for a story can come from an image glimpsed or imagined, a unique human quality experienced, a philosophical conclusion formed, a belief abandoned, or any of a myriad of other things. However, if your story does not derive from the protagonist's goals and motivations, if his character is not deeply and consistently developed, if he is not inspirational and credible to the reader, if he lacks heroic qualities or fails to complete the hero's journey, the reader will simply not care how beautiful the image, how unique the human quality, how fascinating the philosophical conclusion, or how profound the change in beliefs.

The specificity of *protagonist* here is intentional. Secondary and minor characters are not so problematic for the fiction writer. This is in part because they can be less fully developed. They can be villainous or funny or wildly eccentric, but they have no heroic burden; the story does not rest upon their motivations and goals, their consistency or their depth of characterization.

They are also less of a problem because a protagonist is more likely than a secondary or minor character to be created with the weight of the writer's own psychological baggage—though this process may not be conscious to the writer.

For example, in an early draft written by one of my clients, severely depressed at the time, the hero was shot in a gunfight and settled into bed, where he remained for close to a third of the novel. Since I was depressed myself at the time, I found this rather charming. It was, however, neither charming nor heroic; the man had to get up—long before a third of the book dribbled by—and become the hero of his own story.

Conceive characters larger than life

Readers want their story heroes and heroines to be bigger than life, to be inspiring—to be heroic. In contrast, it is more often the concern of the beginning writer to remain *realistic* or *true to life*. The reader expects certain qualities in the protagonist, anticipates that he will be worthy of admiration and respect, that he will be a role model or inspiration. (Let me note that I am speaking here of mainstream and genre fiction; the literary fiction reader has her own quite discrete set of expectations and standards, including a willingness to embrace depression for hundreds of pages. The reader of popular fiction is not willing to do so. She reads for escape, for relief, for hope.)

Create consistent characters

Verisimilitude is the essential goal of fiction, the achievement of what is written *appearing* to be real or true. The great irony is that the sense of *reality* in fiction is achieved through *artifice*. You will achieve effective dialogue, for instance, not by copying everyday conversation but through artfully crafting it.

Credible characterization is accomplished by techniques and with guidelines that do not apply to people in real life. Real folks are not consistent; they are erratic and unpredictable, up emotionally one day, down the next, often for reasons inexplicable to themselves and those around them. An individual can be lazy or ambitious depending upon his or her whim, the day of the month or the specific situation; can change beliefs about critical life decisions; can embrace and then discard ideas and feelings by the score daily.

However, to create the illusion of realness in a story character, consistency is a critical element. Characters may change throughout the course of the story; in fact it is the happiest of all reading experiences when the protagonist experiences life, learns, and changes, but he must grow and change in ways that are both emotionally logical and credible to the reader within the parameters of the basic characterization established. And the growth achieved must be proportionate to the scope of the story. It might be stretching for the protagonist to transform from wimp to warrior though he might reasonably evolve from student to teacher.

Real people, then, must be fictionalized to become dramatic and thus effective fictional characters. Real people or psychological types and archetypes can be used to inspire characters in stories, but the effective fictional character takes on a consistent individuality of his own. It is, in part, this unrealistic aspect of consistency that makes the fictional character credible.

Know your protagonist

As a writer you must know your protagonist inside and out.

Henry James said, "We care what happens to people only in proportion as we know what people are." As readers, we care about a fictional character only to the extent you make us care by showing us how that character acts upon his own positive qualities and how he deals honestly and courageously with his fears and negative qualities. According to Dean Koontz, successful protagonists have virtue, competence, courage, likability, and imperfection. You cannot convey all this to us without knowing your protagonist intimately.

You must understand your protagonist in great specificity and depth. You must know everything from what is in her refrigerator and on top of her dresser to her family background and her greatest hopes and fears, what she believes, supports, denies, and yearns for, consciously and unconsciously. You will not use everything you know about your protagonist in the story, but the more you know, the more fully the character will come alive in your mind, the more carefully you can select the specific details that contribute meaningfully to the story's plot as well as to the character's development.

It can be effective to organize what you know about a character into three major categories, as follows:

Physical
    appearance
    health
    genetic heritage
    appetites
    body type
    body language
    physical habits
    defects or limitations

assets or skills
fitness/training
posture

Socio-cultural

racial heritage
socio-economic class
education
religious heritage
national heritage
habits/manners
environments that are comfortable/uncomfortable
political affiliation
group affiliations
cultural values/activities
peers and friends
specialized training

Psychological

needs and goals
fears and complexes
motivations
archetypes
emotional wounds
personal/self-image
capacity for intimacy
greatest failure
greatest success
moral and ethical values/standards
introversion/extroversion
talent
humor: dry/earthy
intelligence: intellectual/instinctual
way of knowing: thinking, feeling, intuition, or sensation
way of perceiving: visual, auditory, or kinesthetic

Integrate into this the following key back-story questions:

• What is most important to the protagonist during the time frame of
the story?

• What does he fear most?

- What critical events happened for him at seven, fourteen, twenty-one and twenty-eight years of age, as applicable?

- What ties the character inextricably to the current situation, making the problem an inevitable source of conflict for him, an issue he is compelled to resolve?

- What is the character's relationship to his environment? How does it tie him to the story problem?

- What are the protagonist's weaknesses and strengths in facing this challenge? Are they flip sides of the same coin of character?

- What is his internal conflict? How does it relate to the primary story conflict?

- What does he risk in accepting the call to adventure, the challenge of the heroic journey at the heart of the story? What can he gain by reaching his goal, through resolving his internal conflict and the story conflict?

Give your protagonist a goal and compelling motivation

You must give your protagonist a goal to strive for and a compelling reason to achieve that goal despite conflicts strong enough that they are not easily resolved. If the protagonist has no goal, no compelling motivation to step onto the path of the heroic journey, there is no story, only ideas and events that will inevitably become episodic. The protagonist's motivation and goal, carefully integrated with deeply and consistently developed characterization, is the fertile ground for story, the ridge line along which plot must develop.

> "Successful fiction is just one damned thing after another."

When one conflict is resolved, its resolution best leads into the next conflict, increasing the protagonist's high personal stake in the outcome of the primary conflict. Because successful fiction is just *one damned thing after another*, it is the writer's duty to throw every obstacle conceivable and credible in the way of the protagonist's achieving her goal.

Allow your protagonist to grow and develop, to be affected by the events of the story in much the same ways as you want the reader to be affected, but remember your protagonist must have personal empowerment sufficient to drive her own story. The protagonist can have allies and a mentor along the way, but in the end it must be because of her own drives and motivations and through her own inner resources and talents as well as acquired skills that she learns her particular life-lessons and accomplishes her goal. In the best of stories, the protagonist achieves reward for the successful completion of her goal within herself, undergoing her own transformation, becoming more whole.

Use tough love

You need to love your characters, perhaps, but never make it easy for them to be less than they can be, never coddle them, allow them to take a pass or to become passive. This is another of the reasons protagonists are so puzzling. Having conscious and/or unconscious identification with the protagonist, you may have difficulty in allowing him to suffer. It's hard to be hard on those we love, even when it is best. In writing the protagonist, tough love is the only kind that works. You must challenge your protagonist with obstacles and enemies, with trials in the external world through which he can learn about himself and life; to complicate his internal life with conflicts with which he must grapple. It is appropriately said that a novel needs three things: *conflict, conflict, conflict*, the external conflict reflecting the internal conflict of the character himself.

Avoid happy coincidences

Coincidences must always, or as always as anything can be, operate against the protagonist. Protagonists need to have an abundance of obstacles and numerous opportunities to make mistakes through the owning of which they can change and grow. They need to have the kind of challenges that force them to rise to the occasion of becoming truly heroic so they may triumph. Lucky coincidences dilute these challenges and disappoint your reader.

Endow a special quality

A key ingredient that mythologist Joseph Campbell points to as critical to the heroic character is that of a special quality. The protagonist must be very good at whatever her life work, whether she is a spy or a surgeon, a hacker or an attorney, but beyond that competence she must also have a unique ability or quality. It can be a psychic gift, such as ESP; physical prowess, such as a rare ability in martial arts; a unique creative talent, such as the ability not only to sculpt but to define a new medium or style; an emotional dimension, such as a rare sensitivity that allows perception of things others miss. Campbell says this special quality is key to the connection between reader and protagonist.

Open your own consciousness

All of this sounds fine theoretically, but when it comes to putting it in practice, you will bring all of yourself to the process, the known and the unknown, including the rejected, projected, and repressed parts of the self. Such parts of the self tend to sneak into the characterization of the protagonist and undermine the successful characterization of an heroic figure. This is particularly true with the same-sex protagonist, with whom the writer is most apt to identify.

Examples make the point best. I have observed the following in first-draft manuscripts: a romance writer whose sexuality was so blocked her female protagonists were denied full orgasm and orgastic release; a male thriller writer, a powerful man in his own life, whose male protagonist was so passive he was eclipsed not only by the villain and the secondary characters but by his own dog; a male action-adventure writer whose protagonist was such a misogynist he couldn't have found print any later than the mid-fifties, and even then would have needed "politically correct" guidelines; a woman writer who, alienated from her own father, depicted a female protagonist's grief at her father's death flatly, despite otherwise rich characterization.

> "A novel needs three things: *conflict, conflict, conflict.*"

These writers were surprised to discover that such things were occurring, but they recognized what was happening and redeemed their protagonists and, perhaps at some level, unknown parts of themselves.

Hemingway is reputed to have said it is not difficult to write a novel, that all a writer had to do was sit down at a typewriter and cut open a vein. I think this is the key to the protagonist puzzle. It takes discipline to sit down at a computer or typewriter to write, talent to string words together artfully, inspiration and creativity to come up with good characters and stories, an analytical and objective mind to revise and rewrite, but to achieve the creation of a protagonist of any depth takes the consciousness and courage to cut open that emotional vein to which Hemingway refers.

Paul Valéry has been credited with saying if you want to go down into the self, you'd better go armed to the teeth. This is another way of saying that to create an heroic protagonist the writer must be willing to go to heroic lengths within herself in reaching depth and uniqueness of feeling and vision and, even more difficult, in confronting shadow parts of the self. In this way the writer becomes more conscious, more able to creatively use all parts of the self rather than allowing these elements to undermine her creative work. Absent this conscious attention in creating a protagonist, there is an enormously high likelihood the protagonist will be constricted by the limitations and denials of the writer.

The committed writer picks up the knife and cuts deeply, in whatever way or ways work for her; she is willing to grapple with her own limitations and demons. Writing *will* bring them up. So why not seek them out and use them? The alternative is that they will stalk and limit your creativity and cripple your protagonist, puzzle yourself, and create even greater confusion for the reader.

You have resources for cutting the vein, some internal, some external. The serious writer, at least by my definition, has or develops most of the necessary inner resources—courage, a commitment to the process of writing, a willingness to face what needs to be faced to bring creative work to fulfillment. External resources include teachers and books that help develop introspection and understanding of the human psyche, counseling and therapy, astrology and archetypal analysis and editors or *book doctors*, who, at their best, offer direct and clear counsel.

The single most important book I have discovered for getting fictional structure right in itself and in regard to the development of the protagonist is *The Writer's Journey, Mythic Structure for Storytellers and Screenwriters*, written by Christopher Vogler and based on the work of Joseph Campbell. If you can buy only one book on story development, this is the one I recommend. It has proven invaluable to my clients, both published and unpublished. It addresses necessary novel structure and the essential relationship of the writer's process with protagonist and story development in an accessible, practical, and profound manner.

If you attend to the concept of the heroic journey, make your own heroic journey, honor the unique relationship of writer and protagonist, and risk Hemingway's cut, you will shorten the learning curve necessary for becoming a successful fiction writer, bring more of your authentic self to your writing process and gain solid footing on that ridge from which the protagonist puzzle can be perceived and solved.

Lesley Kellas Payne *is an independent editor of adult fiction, memoirs, and occasional nonfiction projects with more than twenty years experience in assisting writers to attain publication and to further their careers once published. She has presented classes and workshops on writing through university extension programs, at writer's conferences, and for community writers groups.*

Lesley studied literature and creative writing at Stanford University, Scripps College, and California State University, Fresno. Ongoing study of the craft of fiction, the editorial process, and archetypal psychologies and mythology deepen her editorial skills, particularly regarding the creation of credible, consistent ,and compelling characters and their appropriate relationship to story development. She has a particular interest in projects with a mystical theme or thread, whether fiction or nonfiction.

Slice Yourself a Piece of Mud Pie

Writing for the children's book market

By Andrea Brown

WHEN I WORKED AS AN EDITORIAL ASSISTANT in children's books at Dell Publishing Company (now part of Bantam Doubleday Dell and owned by Bertelsman) in the late seventies, we were called the "Bunny Department." It didn't matter that we made more money for the company than the adult mass market division. We got no respect.

Yet in those days children's book editors were able to buy a manuscript just because they liked it, even knowing it might only sell a few thousand copies. Editors just wanted to get good books into the hands of children everywhere. That's what made the children's book business so wonderful to work in compared to other parts of publishing.

Now things are quite different in children's books. It's more of a "bunny eat bunny" world, with relatively few big conglomerates controlling many book imprints. And, like big business everywhere, money and the bottom line is all that matters. Editors must show that a profit will be made before a manuscript is approved for purchase. Marketing and sales people influence greatly most of the buying decisions. Editors now worry about their jobs—as well as their favorite authors—if their projects don't show big sales.

The children of the twenty-first century are more sophisticated, smart, and savvy than we all were as children. It is a big responsibility that writers of children's books have, to provide sophisticated and enlightening books for today's kids. Or we will lose them forever as readers and they will spend more time on the computer.

J. K. Rowling is a perfect example of what every children's book writer needs to do to be successful. The reason her Harry Potter series is a phenomenon is that she does everything right: She makes kids the heroes, provides lots of action and sets her books in the most normal setting for kids—school. Don't you think every child reading a Harry Potter book wishes their school was the Hogwarts School? And she takes normal kids and makes them extraordinary. Reading Rowling is like a perfect class in writing for the children's book market.

And, thanks to Rowling, getting kids to read who never did before, then wanting to read other books, the children's book business is booming, and many first-time writers are getting published and making nice, five- and six-figure deals. In my over thirty years in the business, this is the strongest market I've seen for children's books.

The biggest mistake new children's book writers make is that they think they have to conjure up unique settings—or set books in weird, imaginative universes. The most successful children's books are those that revolve around what is actually in a child's universe; school, camp, first time at the doctor, siblings, pets and friendships. Stick to the universe.

Good concise writing

The truth is, writing a wonderful children's book—especially a picture book—is probably the toughest format to write within all of publishing. With a picture book, you get to use only about 1,500 words, sometimes fewer, and every single one must be absolutely *the* perfect word. Your book must also tell a simple story that both kids and parents will like and understand, especially if it is to be read over and over. And that's the test of a successful picture book: Is it one a child wants to read many times?

Look at the simplicity of a book like *Goodnight Moon* by Margaret Wise Brown, which has become a classic. Every word is perfect. It is simple elegance. What the words don't say, the pictures do. And the repetitious language helps make it a winner. Young children love hearing "Goodnight moon, goodnight kittens, goodnight nobody."

Illustrations

There may be a surprise in store for the new children's author: Picture book writers usually have little or no control over how their book will eventually look. They may visualize the book differently than the illustrator who has been chosen. It is usually the editor and/or the art director at the publishing house who chooses the artist. If the author is established, or lucky, he or she might have artist approval. The same book can look totally different given two different artists, or two different publishers. And the right mix is what makes a successful children's book.

Rhyming? Beware

A mistake I see all too often is the idea that a good children's book must rhyme. Writing in verse is truly the hardest kind of writing of all. It must all fit snugly—in cadence, word usage, rhythm and style, and nothing about it can be forced. One off-word makes it too easy for an editor to reject a manuscript. Editors like to edit. They cannot edit rhyme. It either works perfectly or it is off.

Find a fresh voice

I was lucky enough to work with Dr. Seuss on some of his "Bright and Early" books while at Random House. Part of my job was to look for the next Dr. Seuss. I never did find one and neither has Random House.

"Editors are looking for that fresh voice..."

It's a mistake to try to copy another author's forte—especially in children's books. Editors are looking for that fresh voice that will speak to a child. Nothing too didactic, and nothing condescending. And many people use an old-fashioned voice that would have sold in the seventies and eighties but won't work for the more sophisticated kid of today.

Nonfiction is healthy

Luckily, many teachers are now using trade books to tie in with their curricula in subjects such as science, geography, history and the social sciences. This has helped the nonfiction book market and certain types of chapter books and middle-grade readers. Some publishers won't buy a nonfiction title unless they know it is a subject taught at a certain grade.

For this reason, anyone who has training in the sciences and also can write for kids can find a future in the children's book field today. At a time when many of my fiction authors, even those with a large number of published books, are having a tough go at signing up new books, my nonfiction authors are more in demand than ever.

One is a physicist at a major university in the east. He writes books for the middle-grade reader on subjects such as plastics, artificial intelligence, engineering failures and scientists' work. I wish he could write faster because I can sell as many books as he can produce. His books are getting good reviews and good sales, even though they are mostly institutional sales, meaning schools and libraries. So there are opportunities for good nonfiction writers, especially with a science background.

Early-readers

Another hot category is in the area of early-readers or chapter books. Lines such as Harper's "I Can Read" and Random House's "Stepping Stones" are selling well. Scholastic, Dutton, Troll, Dial and many other publishers have similar lines and new ones are always starting up. There are three reasons for the need for new authors in this category. First, due to preschool and other factors, kids are reading on their own at a younger age. In many families, both parents work, leaving less time for the parent to read to the child. So kids from ages five to eight need books that are easy to read by themselves.

Second, this type of book is often used to teach reading in schools. And, third, these are difficult books to write. There are not enough authors out there who can write well for the kindergarten through third grade reader. Writers are limited on vocabulary and subject matter. How many topics can a writer use for a seven-year-old? The child's spheres of experience are limited to school, friends, family, pets and playing. So, you must have a story—with a beginning, a middle and an end—as in any other good book, but you only have forty-eight to sixty-four pages and a limited vocabulary to work with.

There are many different lines within this category, and your job, as the writer, is to study and read a lot of the different formats.

Since chapter books are a booming area, it is easier to break into. Perhaps you can revise your picture book manuscript into a chapter book. Try making the story break up into four or five short chapters. Editors are always telling me that they need more manuscripts in this category, and I am always looking for good writers.

Funny middle grades

Another category I can usually sell quickly is the funny middle-grade novel. Judy Blume's *Blubber* and *Tales of a Fourth Grade Nothing* and Beverly Cleary's Ramona books are classic examples of this genre. They are written for the eight- to twelve-year-old, and are usually 72-128 pages in format. As in the case of the early readers, the topics revolve mostly around school, friends and family, but also camp, vacations, relationships and varied situations. I recently sold one to the first editor who saw it. The title is *The World's Greatest Toe Show*, by Nancy Lamb and Muff Singer, published by Troll. It's about a school contest to raise money, and one team is certain that their unusual booth at the fair will win them the grand prize. Rather than a boring bake sale, they are showing the toe of one of the kids' dads in a matchbox. It had been cut off in a lawn mower accident and the kid found it and saved it. It came in handy for the fair! Yes, it is gross, but funny, and kids love that sort of story. Look at the success of the book *Everyone Poops* by Taro Gomi, and *Grossology: the Science of Really Gross Things* by Sylvia Branzei.

> "The secret to writing a successful children's book is not to think like a child or to try to remember what it was like to be a child, but to still *be* a child within."

The secret to writing a successful children's book is not to think like a child or to try to remember what it was like to be a child, but to still *be* a child within.

Young adult

My personal favorite children's book category is the young adult market, or YA's, as they are known in the business. Some of the best written and best written and best edited books in all of publishing are in the young adult area. And, again, thanks to J. K. Rowling, more kids ten and over want to read other books after they finish the Harry Potter series and they are looking for young adult books of all kinds, especially the edgy, issue-oriented ones that deal with teen angst, peer pressure, social taboos, sex and coming-of-age. The darker the theme, the better.

There is also more "crossover" publishing going on, with the publishers finding that young adults in their early twenties will also will also read the more sophisticated YA titles, so we are seeing main characters who are seventeen and eighteen and even up to the early twenties. Primarily YA characters are fourteen to seventeen with the average reader being twelve to fifteen, as kids like to read up. Many adult fiction writers have been turning to the young adult market as the money has gotten better, with many six-figure deals, and the books are well-published. Voice and character development are crucial in writing successfully for this hot market.

What's the future hold?

In the past, children's books have always been able to weather any recessions and turns in the past. Children will always have to read. Schools and libraries will always need books. Parents will always want to have that special quality reading time with there children. But, the market gets glutted and the pendulum swings up and down. Don't write to the trends—write what your passion is and what age group you relate to best. If you don't remember what it feels like to be six, don't write for the young age group. If you can't relate to teen angst, don't write YA's.

Money matters

As a writer entering the field for the first time, you must not only write the most polished manuscript you can, but you must think more commercially than ever before.

I became an agent in 1981 because I saw that most children's book authors and illustrators didn't have representation—and needed it. The average advance was $1,000. Contracts were only three or four pages long, and now they are thirty in some cases.

I am glad to say that advances have increased a lot for children's book writing since I left editing and became an agent. Five and six figure deals are happening more and more and children's book writers can now make nice livings doing what they love—writing for children. Authors spend more time on the road, visiting schools, getting paid for talking to children at schools, and selling books at the same time.

Generally speaking, advances range from $2,500 to $10,000 for the average children's book. If it is a picture book, royalties and advances are split equally between the writer and the illustrator, unless the illustrator is quite well-known, in which case the illustrator might receive 60 percent. Standard royalties are still 10 percent for hardcovers, and 6 percent and 8 percent escalating for paperbacks, but these numbers are changing. Depending on the publishing house and the type of books they sell, royalties can also be paid on net sales. And there are more clauses than ever, reducing royalties for remainders, higher discounts, returns, foreign sales and a whole host of creative accounting procedures.

Most authors don't have a clue about these clauses. It is more important than ever to work with either an agent or an intellectual property rights lawyer. I used to tell writers that they didn't need an agent if they were just planning to write one or two books, or if they would mind the idea of not knowing where their manuscripts were at all times, or if they would begrudge the agent her 15 percent commission.

Now when I speak at conferences, I tell writers that if they are serious at all about their writing careers, to get an agent they can work with for the long haul. Unfortunately, it's not easy to find an agent these days, because most agents who have been in the business a while are taking on very few, if any, new clients. But, the publishers are depending more and more on agents to ferret out the good manuscripts to the point that most of the large publishing houses do not even accept unsolicited material any longer. In other words, you must have an agent submit your work.

Here are some more suggestions to speed you along on your children's book writing career:

• Study the formats and the age group you wish to write for, and read lots of those types of books.

• Join the Society of Children's Book Writers and Illustrators (SCBWI) at 8271 Beverly Blvd., Los Angeles, CA 90048, www.scbwi.org.

• Consider writing nonfiction first as it is easier to break into this segment of the market.

• Study *Children's Books in Print* for subjects and talk to teachers and librarians for ideas needed.

• Get ideas from the children in your life, as well as from magazines, TV, and the natural world around you.

• Write a lot, revise a lot and read your work out loud.

• Don't test the stories out on children. It is not a true test, as kids will like anything read to them in person.

• Join writing critique groups.

• *Submit, submit, submit.*

Despite the problems in the business these days, the children's book field is one of the most satisfying and creative businesses you could ever be a part of, so keep writing!

Andrea Brown has spent more than thirty years in the children's books field, at Dell, Random House and as an editor at Alfred A. Knopf in New York City. In 1981, she was the first to form a literary agency specializing in representing both children's book authors and illustrators. In 1990, she moved her agency to Northern California and currently has five agents all specializing in children's books as well as some adult titles. Check out the website at www.andreabrownlit.com.

A graduate of the Newhouse School at Syracuse University, Andrea has taught publishing classes at UCLA, UC Santa Cruz, Dominican College in New York and the Learning Annex in San Francisco. She speaks at many conferences including the SCBWI conference, the Maui Writers Conference, San Diego, Willamette, Whidbey Island Pacific Northwest, Yosemite, Florida Writer's Association, Georgia, Pike's Peak, Amarillo, Texas Writer's League, Maple Woods and numerous others. She has been president of the San Francisco Chapter of the Women's National Book Association and is executive director of the Big Sur Writing Workshops, www.henrymiller.org.

Andrea has published numerous articles in Writer's Digest Magazine *and been quoted in* Forbes, Good Housekeeping, *and* CNN *and is the author of the Quill Driver book,* Writers' and Artists' Hideouts: Great Getaways for Seducing the Muse, *half a travel guide and half a writer's guide.*

How to Earn $50,000 from Your First Book

Niche publishing

By Gordon Burgett

THERE ARE THREE WAYS TO GET YOUR BOOK profitably in print. One, let an established publisher put your words on the bookstore shelves. Two, put it on the bookstore shelves yourself through self-publishing. Three, well, we'll talk about that in a bit.

The first is likely to take forever and make you a pittance, even if you can get that big-city editor to dig into her pile of manuscripts and find, in yours, the company's answer to its red-ink woes. The second is risky because bookstores aren't clamoring for self-published tomes. It's also a quick way to shift the red ink to your own hands.

The third way is to forget the bookstore shelves altogether, self-publish, sell by mail, and test your book and the potential profits with readers before you write the first word. This third category is called niche publishing.

I like the third path so much I wrote a book called *Publishing to Niche Markets* to tell others precisely how it's done. I really wanted to call it by the seminar title I use to reveal its magic: "How to Earn $50,000 Profit from Your First Book—Then Double It!" "Too much hype," others, and my inner voice, cried. You decide.

You need three things to successfully self-publish: preparation, production, and promotion. (Some suggest two more: patience and prayer.)

In standard self-publishing, you ideally begin by finding an idea so broad and compelling that anybody seeing a book about it in a bookstore would grab it off the shelf and instantly buy it. (Alas, your biggest problem will be getting the bookstore to put the book on the shelf in the first place, while you fan up the secondary promotional fires.) Then you write those magic words (or get somebody else to write them) and put them into salable book form.

Niche publishers also start with the promotion, but practitioners of this service think narrow to earn big. They find some critical, unmet need of a specific buying public, design a book that meets that need, then test that specific market's desire to buy their book before they write the words. The difference is dramatic: the risk is infinitely smaller, the potential profit much greater, and the cost—well, that's the rub; it is much greater too. Read on.

Applying the TCE process

Three steps give continuity and flow to the creation of a niche-marketed book. I call them the "TCE Process." T is for targeting, C for customizing, and E for expanding.

First you find a target market, one composed not of everybody but very specific bodies. Probably 35,000 of them at a minimum, better if it's 65,000 plus.

Let's use dentists as our example. There are 150,000 of them currently in practice.

You must qualify your target market. The two most important qualifications of five are the number of people in your market and their accessibility through an affordable mailing list. To see if such a list exists, check the *SRDS Direct Mail List* in your library. Not listed? Find another market, since as many as 98 percent of your sales will be made by mail.

Once you've found a large enough listed target market, find a problem that most of those in that market have and would rush to buy a book to solve. Thus niche publishing won't work for poetry, autobiographies, or novels. Stick to nonfiction how-to.

Let's use a live example, a book about a problem my publishing firm is attempting to solve for dentists as this is being written. It concerns standard operating procedures.

Dentists are trained to work on teeth. They are skilled crafts folk and technicians often able to perform dental miracles. But they learn virtually nothing about business in dental school—and are expected to graduate, open an office, and somehow create and nurture a dedicated, efficient staff; control overhead; play a civic role in the community; turn a profit, and still treat a certain number of patients daily, all with grace and an attractive smile.

Somewhere in the hustle the key elements of effective office administration get lost—or are never created in the first place. That's where standard operating procedures, and a procedural manual to keep them together and accessible, fit in. They define the arenas of operation: front office, back office, and management. They include job descriptions and task lists, means for consistent employee evaluation, even procedures for conflict resolution. But mostly they break down the key operations by description—opening the office, answering the telephone, cleaning the traps, laying out the operation trays, etc. Then if an employee is ill or leaves, not only can others follow the SOPs and fill in, a new employee will become fully functional twice as fast with guidelines already in place.

How did we know there was a market for this book? By asking dentists what was most needed in their field. Then by asking dental consultants the same question. Who knows better what they will buy than those in need unable to find help?

We then had two choices: write the book or find somebody else to write it, then publish it. I knew nothing about dentistry—beyond flossing when I remembered. So I hunted for the person best qualified to write the book.

Marsha Freeman had been active in the field for seventeen years, starting out chairside and advancing through office administration. She had also been a consulter to dentists for six years, earned a degree in psychology and a master's in organizational management, and for her thesis she had written a procedural manual for a pediatric dentist! We looked no further. Together we published *Standard Operating Procedures for Dentists*.

But I'm jumping ahead of myself. Many hours were spent pounding out the promotional structure of the book before a penny was spent, a word was written, or a contract was signed.

You must determine what flyer you must put in the potential book buyers' hands to get them to fill in the form, write out the check, and put it in today's mail, *or*, better yet, have the office manager call your 800 number with a credit card in hand!

What promises must you make? What benefits must your book bring? We designed a rough flyer with every promise clearly stated, every need our book would meet, every benefit it would bring. The rest—the table of contents, the author's photo and bio, perhaps a mock book cover, some short examples or scenarios, the ordering information and process—can be added later as the book takes shape. First you must know the promises you must make so you can design the research and writing so those promises are, in fact, kept in the text. And you must know it so you can test your premise before you invest more time or money.

The critical test

After finding your market and qualifying it, the third and most important element of the targeting is the testing. Before investing hundreds of hours and thousands of dollars in meeting your target's needs, get them to tell you if they will pay enough money to make it worth your while.

First determine what kind of profit you want. State that in absolute financial terms: so many dollars. Let's use $50,000 here, though our goal was much higher.

What would you have to sell to earn $50,000 profit? If you sell your book for $15, and if, after costs of production and marketing, half of that is profit, and if ten percent of your target market buys it, you'll need a target market of 67,000 people. ($15.00 x .5 x 6,700 = $50,250) In this scenario, because production and marketing costs are half of the retail price of the book, you would need $50,000 working capital to make $50,000.

If you sell your book for $150, and if the production and marketing cost $35 a book, and if two percent of your market buys it, you'll need a target market of 21,750 to sell 435 books. In this case you would need $15,225 ($35 x 435 = $15,225) working capital to generate $65,000 in sales and earn $50,000 in profit. ($150 x 435 = $65,250 - $15,225 = $50,025.)

Playing with ratios like these will give you a rough operating guesstimate against which you can develop the essentials for your test. What you need to measure, beyond the percentage of recipients who state that they would buy the book, is the price. A quick way to test your market is to select a solid mailing list, rent 500-1,000 names (or a small set percentage) selected at random, and send them a three-part mailing: (1) an introductory note explaining what you are doing and asking them to please respond, (2) an information sheet, one- or two-sided, with the promises and benefits of the book, an abbreviated table of contents, photo and short bio of the author, explanatory copy, approximate length and binding form, and cost, and (3) a response postcard with actual stamps and your name/address on one side and at least two questions with yes/no checkoff lines or boxes or something on the order of: "I would be interested in buying __(the book)__" and "I would pay __(the amount)__."

If you had three prices you wanted to test, divide the addresses into three equal sets and put the same price on the information sheet and postcard for each set, i.e., one set might say $39.95; the second, $49.95; the third, $59.95.

Or if you want to test three different titles, keep the price the same but change titles for each set.

Send them out and see how many respond affirmatively. If for your $15 book you get back 6 percent for one set, 9 percent for another, and 11 percent for the third, only the third will bring you $50,000 profit, if in fact your market buys as the test shows. If you simply test the other book at $150 and 2.1 percent say yes, bingo. But if 1 percent says yes, you have questions to ask: will I accept $25,000 profit? Is the price too high? Is the book as shown on the information sheet not what the buyer wants? Does it need a better title? Are you offering the wrong promises? Do more tests, take the lower profit, or drop the idea altogether. Just be thankful you didn't produce a garageful of unwanted books!

Customizing the book

Those in the target market will buy your book because they think it is for them. The best way to make that immediate identity is to put them in the title: *Standard Operating Procedures for Dentists; The Chicago Cubs: Where They Are Today,* for Cubs fans; *The Fifth Grade Teachers' Handbook.*

Then fashion a book so the buyer is comfortable with its contents. Determine the gender ratio and median age of the target market, then stick close to them in selecting the photos and interviews.

Use the language they use. If their books are hard cover, 6" x 9", full of charts and graphs but utterly devoid of frills, as much as possible stick to their expectations. You're not out to change their lifestyle, just elevate their understanding about a particular subject.

Do they buy by phone? Then install an 800 number. Would they rather fax? Then a dedicated fax is necessary. Would they prefer to use airmile credit cards? Better have a way of converting their wishes into sales and cash.

The bottom line: Dentists buy dental books to learn something about dentistry. Make your book fit like a comfortable glove.

Creating the book

Once you know there are enough potential buyers to earn the profit you wish, you must create and publish the book.

There isn't space here to do what it took Dan Poynter and Marilyn and Tom Ross hundreds of first-rate pages to explain, so read their self-publishing manuals. Just remember that what goes on your book's pages must fulfill the promises you made in your promotional material. How well you do that will determine whether the buyer will believe you or buy from you in the future.

The funding

When you are simply publishing, then selling the books to libraries and through distributors and bookstores, you might produce 2,000 copies 200 pages long for less than $6,000.

But when you must not only produce the book but find the mailing list, create a strong flyer, mail the fliers, then fulfill the orders, the costs rise quickly. With a mailing to a target market of 67,000, you might spend $47,000-$50,000—60 percent of it before the book appears and the first sale is made!

There are three strategic funding approaches, with a dozen variations: (1) the "fat cat" approach, sending a flyer to the entire mailing list, printing 7,000 books, and relying on the industry standard of 50 percent of your sales being made in four weeks and 98 percent in 13 to get your heavy investment back fast; (2) the "skinny cat" approach, where you cut your outlay in half by mailing to 20,000 and printing just 2,000 books, with subsequent printings and mailings paid from the sales, and (3) the "alley cat" approach, where you print 2,000 books and finance the direct mail costs from books you sell directly, which usually means to local friends. John Kremer's *1001 Ways to Market Your Books* will suggest other ways to make those first sales quickly and inexpensively. This alley cat approach will still cost at least $6,000 for the books and some start-up expenses.

What makes any niche marketed risk worth taking is the thoroughness and reliability of the test you made earlier. If those in the target market responded loudly and clearly that they want your book, they and others like them will probably buy it. And more than half of each purchase is profit: yours, since you are also the middleperson.

The real profit in niche publishing

What those in the niche are really buying isn't a book but expertise. In our case, yes, on the surface dentists are buying Marsha Freeman's book *Standard Operating Procedures for Dentists*. But in fact they are paying its cost because her years of direct dental experience and skill at creating SOP systems have been converted to paper, and the dentists correctly perceive that on those pages they will find information, a step-by-step process, and a solid example that will bring them benefits far in excess of the cost and the time to read and apply what the book says.

They are buying Marsha Freeman's expert knowledge, plus her ability to make it readily understandable and usable. And they are buying us as a publisher that brings valuable information in that field.

So if Marsha speaks at regional and national dental gatherings, those aware of her books—presuming their contents to be valuable and unique—will want to hear her. And will want to buy more good things from that source. They will pay to attend her workshops or seminars. They will buy her audio and video cassettes, case studies, and reports. This is the "E" of the TCE—expanding.

And when she creates a newsletter to update the older SOPs and introduce new ones, they will continue to purchase it as long as it is as valuable in keeping the dentist abreast of the newest changes as the book was in creating a way to convert operational knowledge into simple, accessible, straightforward action guidelines.

Finally, if the concept works in dentistry, it will probably work in related fields. Which is why we are currently publishing similar SOPs books in six other fields.

In other words, from one concept come many products, often in other formats. Once you have convinced the niche that you have knowledge they need, it is easier to convince them a second time, and far easier and less expensive the third, fifth, and tenth time—as long as it is true each time! That's the golden rainbow of niche publishing, with a new pot every time you have a new product.

The future caught up to niche publishing

Until computers made camera-ready or disk-ready book creation possible in every home and printers could likewise reproduce books faster and cheaper, we were limited to big volume bookstore offerings. But the future is now: A book for 300 people can be printed in a few days or a month, be affordable, and earn the publisher (who may be the writer) a handsome return.

Simply substitute your area of expertise for dentistry and Marsha Freeman, find the need, do the test, and produce the text.

Niche publishing requires plenty of work, promotion before preparation and production, and an amount of up-front risk capital. But nowhere are you in such command of your product and your profits. And every time there is a serious need or problem, a book begs to be written.

Novels, textbooks, and volumes for children will be the province of the big publishers. By the year 2010, if not well before, most of the rest of the publishers will be small niche houses moving from need into every new glen of information dissemination, from a book core into a new digital world. TCE is the path from here to there.

Gordon Burgett has been a publisher since 1981. In addition, he has had 1,700 articles in print, written thirty-one books, and offers up to 100 seminars and speeches nationwide annually. Included in his books are Publishing to Standard Marketing, Standard Operating Procedures for Dentists, Sell and Resell Your Magazine Articles, *and* Publishing to Niche Markets. *He can be reached at Communication Unlimited: gordonburgett.com, 800-563-1454.*

Writing Self-Help Books

A 12-step plan for the non-Ph.D.

By Eric Maisel

SELF-HELP NONFICTION SELLS. I made more money from the *advance* for my first self-help book than from all the literary fiction I wrote and published during a twenty-year career.

Self-help nonfiction pinpoints a human problem or challenge, takes into account the psychology of the matter, and offers strategies to solve the problem or meet the challenge. Self-help books help readers land jobs, lead more spiritually or psychologically healthful lives, deal with gender differences, or wrestle with any of an almost limitless array of issues—from improving verbal skills to recovery from alcoholism, from motivation in the workplace to dying with dignity.

Because we live in a society that's fraught with such problems, people continually look for solutions and coping mechanisms. And let's face it: A twenty-dollar hardcover that promises to keep you out of destructive relationships is a lot more affordable than a year of psychoanalysis.

Yet relatively few freelancers jump into this lucrative market.

Why? I suspect the major stumbling block is a psychological one. We might not feel like experts in the self-help field. After all, we reason, aren't editors interested in hearing only from experts? Aren't credentials what really matter, not research or writing skills?

The answer is yes...but only to a point. Publishers *are* interested in authors' credentials and naturally would love to publish the leading experts in their fields. But they also look at proposals from nonexperts.

What you must do is make yourself an expert, through research, talking to people already established in the field, and finding a niche that hasn't been done to death. By following my 12-step plan, you can become an expert—and a self-help author.

Getting ready

1. *Identify a workable, compelling issue.*

Your idea should be compact enough to be captured in a book title, robust and large enough to attract a wide audience, and defined and confined enough to let you do it justice. If it's also controversial or brand new, that's a plus.

You'll get workable ideas from a myriad of places: life experiences, research, alert reading of newspapers and magazines, alert TV viewing, and casual conversations with friends, family members and coworkers.

There may be questions in your life that have puzzled you. You may have wondered, as writer Tina Tessina did, if long-term membership in Alcoholics Anonymous fosters sobriety or dependency. Out of her puzzlement came *The Real Thirteenth Step*. You may have wondered how people can use mythology in today's society. Out of such wondering came David Feinstein and Stanley Krippner's *Personal Mythology*. It may have struck you that men and women who work together and are sexually attracted to each other could benefit from some sensible office ground rules. Out of such a notion came David Eyler and Andrea Baridon's *More Than Friends, Less Than Lovers: Managing Sexual Attraction in the Workplace*.

You may want to do active research in order to come up with a compelling, workable topic. In that case, read both specialized and general self-help books. You own ideas will soon percolate.

Your daily newspaper can also provide food for thought. Here's one recent Sunday edition's article lineup: the incidence of depression among artists, the growing number of young adults too poor to maintain their own apartments, and changes in the divorce rate. Any one of those topics could provide the basis for a self-help book.

Talk shows such as *Geraldo at Large*, *Larry King Live* and *Oprah*, as well as such news shows at the *News Hour with Jim Lehrer*, are also excellent sources. Pay attention, too, to local radio shows hosted by psychologists or psychiatrists. Callers will let you eavesdrop on all kinds of problems.

Listen to conversations around you. What are your friends and coworkers complaining about? What confuses them or piques their curiosity? What problems do they encounter? What challenges do they find surprisingly hard to manage—money, time, allergies, persistent ex-boyfriends? If many people complain about similar problems, aren't those areas worth investigating?

Do enough digging, and the just-right issue will come to you.

Next, you'll need to find out if your idea has been tackled before. Chat with a reference librarian or bookstore clerk about your topic. The bibliography in the first article you look up may point the way to all the relevant material in the field. (But go the extra step: You should do enough research to at least be *aware of* all the material out there.)

In researching my self-help book, *A Life in the Arts*, I came to the happy conclusion that no one had yet attempted to describe the range of emotional challenges that creative and performing artists regularly face. Keep your fingers crossed that the same luck holds true for you.

Even if your idea *has* been tackled before, you may want to pursue it. Did the writer reach only a small, professional audience with her book? Was it written in stiff academic style or in jargon only an insider could decipher? Is its information out of date? When queried, editors want to know what *recent* books might compete with yours. They won't be terribly concerned if a writer tackled your topic twenty years ago—or even five years ago if new research has changed the field.

2. *Turn the idea around.*

The idea you come up with may be more like an image or a feeling than an idea. Imagine, for example, that your starting point is the image of a husband striking his wife. You find the image intriguing and compelling, but you haven't a clue yet what a book based on this image might be about.

First begin by "turning the idea around." The following ten are such twists.

• You see in your mind's eye that the man was beaten by his father, that he identifies with aggressors, and that he manifests that aggression against his wife. The book title that comes to you is *Fathers and Sons: The Violence Cycle and its Effects on Women*.

• You see that she is the daughter of an alcoholic father whom she could not change, that she determined to change some other weak man, and that she attempts to change her husband by criticizing him, which provokes him. The book title that comes to you is *I Only Called Him a Stupid Coward: What Women Say and How Men React*.

• You see that he really enjoys seeing someone scared of him. The book title that comes to you is *Everyday Sadism: When Hurting Others Feels Good*.

• You see that they both have poor impulse control. She speaks impulsively, he hits impulsively. The book title that comes to you is *Hair Triggers: Impulse Control Disorders in Men and Women.*

• You see that he doesn't respect women and that hitting her is no more significant an action for him than kicking a can down the street. The book title that come to you is *It Wasn't Like I Hit the Boss: Why Husbands Batter Their Wives.*

• You see that she is depressed and craves drama, and that she values being hit because it wakes her up and lifts her depression. The book title that comes to you is *Violent Wake-up Calls: When Getting Hit is Better Than Depression.*

• You see that she hates him but that she needs her hatred of him to be periodically reinforced by concrete actions. The book title that comes to you is *If He Hits Me I Can Hate Him: Why Women Provoke Their Abusive Mates.*

• You see that hitting her arouses him. The book title that comes to you is *Beating as Foreplay: The Dance of Sex and Violence.*

• You see that she considers being hit by him the appropriate punishment for the mismanagement of her life. The book title that comes to you is *Don't I Deserve It?: Low Self-esteem and Victimization.*

• You see that both of them are anxious and depressed but that neither of them has much self-knowledge. The book title that comes to you is *Two Blind Mice: Lack of Insight and the Path to Violence.*

Before you commit to the self-help book you mean to write, give yourself a chance to turn the idea around. It may be a much more compelling idea to you—and to your readers—configured one way rather than another.

3. *Frame appropriate questions.*

A solid piece of self-help nonfiction provides compelling answers to an appropriately framed series of questions.

• Whom am I writing about? When planning *A Life in the Arts*, I determined that I wasn't writing about writers, painters, dancers, actors or musicians *specifically*, but about creative and performing artists in *all* disciplines. This defined the scope of the book for me and widened its market.

• What *exactly* is the issue that the book will address? Is it a single problem or several interrelated issues? In my book I pinpointed eight challenges that artists regularly face. How many interrelated issues might you find if you were mapping, say, the territory traveled by single professional parents, by people afraid of public speaking, by children of divorce living in newly blended families, or by anorexic women abused by their fathers?

• Is this a recent issue? Is it one we've only started coming to grips with? Are the sources or causes of the problem rooted in another time and place? For adults molested as children, for example, or Vietnam vets suffering from post-traumatic stress disorders, the pain has roots in the past, but it must be treated in the present.

• What must readers know so they can help themselves to grow, to heal, to deal more effectively with a challenge? What appears to cause the problem? Do the experts know? Do they agree or disagree among themselves?

The better your handle on the directions your book will take—which is what your answers to these questions will reveal—the easier the researching and writing will be. And well-defined projects always face better chances of acceptance by editors and publishers.

4. Serve the reader as "mapmaker," not "expert."

Judge Roderic Duncan says he wrote *Everybody's Guide to Municipal Court: Sue and Defend Cases of up to $25,000* for "the people struggling with the procedure. I thought, 'If they just had a road map, it would be so much easier.'"

Sure, Judge Duncan is an expert, and you probably are not. You haven't been counseling alcoholics for twenty years, you don't have a doctorate in psychology, you haven't done intake interviews at a mental health hospital. You can't quote Jung or Freud from memory.

But you do have life experiences and common sense. You possess writing, researching, interviewing and organizational skills. You know how to look at an issue from many sides, how to see the big picture, how to present diverse opinions and how to engage in controversy. In short, you possess the personal qualities that allow you to *examine* any important issue and *present* it fairly to the reading public.

If you do a thorough job studying the available research, interviewing experts, preparing and compiling questionnaires, writing letters and talking with people who've wrestled with "your" issue, you'll *become* an expert. You'll be ready to present readers with a detailed, useful map.

5. Reframe "problems" as "challenges."

A *problem* may be difficult—even insoluble—but by referring to it as a *challenge*, you'll give readers the hope and motivation to tackle it. While self-help nonfiction writers must not sugarcoat issues or gloss over real problems, they're obligated to encourage their readers.

Building the book

6. Decide on a structure.

The self-help writer must balance three major components: general information, individuals' stories and self-help strategies (more on these later). You have, however, significant latitude in how you interweave these elements and in how much attention you pay to each.

One example is found in Mary Beth McClure's *Reclaiming the Heart: A Handbook of Help and Hope for Survivors of Incest.* Each chapter begins with a single topic, such as beginning the recovery process, seeking help or feeling the feelings. Then readers are offered fill-in-the-blank exercises to help them work on amnesia, identify themselves as survivors, choose a therapist, etc. Each chapter ends with a single, substantial first-person account.

Another structure gives greater weight to general ideas and strategies and less to vignettes. Christopher Mc-Cullough divided his book *Managing Your Anxiety* into two roughly equal parts—the first beginning with a series of brief vignettes that personalize the issues. It then goes on to present many general ideas about anxiety, with only a sprinkling of additional vignettes included along the way.

> "A good self-help book deals with human beings, not just issues."

The book's second half is devoted to an elaborate seven-level self-care program that encourages readers to keep a journal, coping checklists, a nutrition and medication log, an assertiveness log, a negative thoughts inventory, and many other self-help logs, checklists, and inventories.

Ruth Maxwell's *The Booze Battle* takes a third approach. She highlights vignettes and general information and offers fewer strategies. Individual case study chapters are interspersed with general information chapters on the experiences of relatives and friends of alcoholics. Information on strategies and resources is reserved for a brief last chapter.

So what's the best structure? That's up to you, the nature of your material—and your editor.

Self-help books vary greatly in length. An important book like Ellen Bass and Laura Davis's *The Courage to Heal: A Guide for Women Survivors of Child Sexual Abuse* runs 500 pages. Daniel Sonkin and Michael Durphy's useful *Learning to Live Without Violence: A Handbook for Men* comes in at 150 pages. A double-spaced, typewritten manuscript page usually has about 250 words on it. As a rule of thumb, expect your editor to ask for a manuscript in the 80,000 to 90,000 word range.

Writing the book

7. *Provide examples, vignettes and illustrations.*

A good self-help book deals with human beings, not just issues. These are often real people with real stories, but sometimes they're presented as composites to more clearly illustrate a point.

You have many options in how you present these example "stories." You might introduce several people early on and track their progress throughout the book, or write about different people in every chapter or major section. You might use such examples sparingly, so that only a handful appear, or you might construct the whole book around them. But you must have them. Without examples, your self-help book will be poorly grounded in reality.

In *A Life in the Arts*, I used examples very sparingly. I personalized the book by including quotes from hundreds of celebrated artists, living and dead.

The vignettes you provide will come primarily from four sources. The first will be experts. Such examples will typically appear in your book like this: "Dr. Smith, a noted authority, reports that his client Mary..." A second source will be published first-person accounts from books, magazines and newspapers. ("John, a recently divorced father of three, stated in a *New York Times* article that...") The third source consists of individuals whom you know, with whom you speak directly, or who respond to your questionnaires. ("Bill, in responding to questions about symptoms of performance anxiety, reported...") The final group will be made up of the composite examples you create. ("Jill is an agoraphobic. During the past eight years, since her anxiety condition worsened, she's left home only a handful of times...")

It's okay to either use examples sparingly or make them the core of your book. Be aware that if you include too many vignettes, however, your book will begin to feel like an interview book—a different category. On the other hand, too many strategies will overwhelm readers. And a parade of abstract ideas will tire readers and turn off editors. A commonsense approach is to include no less than 10 to 15 percent each of general exposition, vignettes and strategies, and not more than 50 percent of any one of them.

8. *Make use of available research.*

You don't have to reinvent the wheel as you research and write your book. Give credit where credit is due, get permission to use quoted material as needed, and make full, fair use of existing research.

(As you're researching your topic, pay attention to which publishers have already covered this area. Are three of the books you found published by the same house? That's certainly a publisher to let your agent know about, or to query yourself, once your proposal begins to take shape.)

9. *Create classifications.*

Part of the mapmaking task is identifying and creating classifications that help readers better understand the concepts involved. It's one thing to write a treatise on moral behavior—and another to codify your ideas into the Ten Commandants. Human beings—and human editors—want projects that make use of codification and classification schemes. Some examples:

• Early, middle and late stage alcoholism

• Denial, anger, bargaining, depression and acceptance (the stages through which the dying and grieving pass, according to Elizabeth Kübler-Ross)

• Oral, anal, phallic, latency, and genital stages of human development (according to Freud)

• The 12 steps common to various dependency recovery programs.

As you work and shape your material, look for classification schemes to emerge. Do you see people going through specific stages in recognizing or handling the challenge you're describing? Are young people affected differently from older people, are men and women affected differently? Can the many causes of the problem be grouped together into a succinct, coherent number of categories? Can solutions be grouped together?

10. *Offer strategies for readers.*

To earn its self-help label, your book *must* present a variety of workable strategies that people can employ—and benefit from.

After my editor read the first draft of *A Life in the Arts*, he told me it was well-written, informative, even stimulating—but just not useful enough. "Where's the *self-help*?"

To answer that question, I started asking myself what strategies I used in working with clients. What strategies had I learned in my psychotherapy training? What sorts of strategies were regularly presented in the workshops

I attended and in the self-help books I read? What specific strategies did I use in my own life?

I saw that I could walk readers through the process of starting a journal, so they could see the challenges confronting them. I could describe breathing exercises to help reduce anxiety, guided visualizations, role plays, cognitive restructuring exercises, behavior modification strategies, empty chair techniques from gestalt therapy, subpersonality identification techniques from psychosynthesis, and many more.

If you look carefully at the strategies and tactics self-help books provide, you'll begin to identify the categories they fall into. You'll quickly learn how you can modify existing strategies to suit your purposes, how you can best present the strategies offered by the experts, and how you can create strategies of your own.

11. *Describe the available resources and support services.*

An appendix that lists the pertinent organizations, newsletters, foundations, self-help groups, governmental agencies and private foundations that deal with your issue can become one of the book's most important selling points.

12. *Look to the future.*

Show readers where they may go from here. Your readers have learned how to quit smoking—but what will withdrawal feel like? What challenges will they encounter? Your readers have improved relations with their teenage daughters, but what will happen in a year or two, when the oldest leaves home? What new challenges will readers face? Just sketch these predictable future crises in broad terms to help readers orient themselves—and to prime them for your next book!

Eric Maisel, Ph.D., is the author of Fearless Creating, A Life in the Arts, Affirmations for Artists *and* The Performance Anxiety Workbook. *Eric maintains a private psychotherapy practice in Concord, California.*

Make It Sizzle

How to write great queries without
resorting to threats, bribery or coercion

By Wendy Keller

WHY IS IT THAT SOMEONE BRIGHT AND DEDICATED enough to write a 400-page manuscript cringes in terror when it comes to writing query letters? Why is it that when agents say, "Tell me your book's story (premise) in two sentences," the writer, who knows the book better than anyone, so rarely can?

There's an adage in sales that says, "Sell the sizzle, not the steak," by which we mean that people look closer on allure, but they buy (we hope) on facts. In writing a query letter, you are going to need to include some basic information—what your genre is, what expertise you have, whether the book is fiction or nonfiction, the location and size of the potential market, those all-important two sentences mentioned above—and only this basic information, but dressed up so it sizzles!

Think of it this way (perhaps you already do): An agent staggers into the office after spending the weekend mired in reading—reading submitted manuscripts, reading proposals, reading for pleasure, reading trade magazines. Eyes blurry, the agent sits down at the desk and stares at the big white corrugated plastic post office box full of queries that have come in over the weekend. No exaggeration here. Most of us get boxesful every week!

I, for one, pick up my silver Tower of London souvenir letter opener. The shiny blade catches the morning light and illuminates my evil grin as I slice open the first letter, ready to cut the heart out of some poor person's years of creative endeavor. (Insert haunted-house, derisive background music here). "This better be good..." I grumble.

Some writers envision the other extreme: an agent perched by the mailbox, checking her wristwatch, waiting for the tardy mail truck. Nervously twisting her hands, she finally sees the truck come reeling around the corner, and her heart skips a beat. Perhaps the ideal query letter will come today! The mailman, accustomed to this daily routine, hands her the query letters first, the bills and publishing contracts second. She tosses the latter to the ground and sits down on the curb, eagerly tearing open the first query letter. The mailman shakes his head and drives away as she reads.

Neither one is reality. In reality, agents spend most of their time on the phone and may not even read the queries that come in. That job is often delegated to a junior agent or assistant who has been carefully taught how to screen material. Let me share with you how we screen queries in my office, and perhaps in the telling it will give you some clues as to how to beat the odds—overcome the obstacles that stand between you and attracting the right agent.

My assistant carries in the big white box of mail each day and places it beside his desk. He picks up the first envelope and if it is obviously a query he gives it "the finger test." That is, he slides the envelope between his fingers to feel for an enclosed self-addressed, stamped envelope (SASE). If there is not one, the entire thing goes into the trash, unopened.

Tip No. 1: Always include an SASE if you want an agent, however big or small the agency is, to look at your query. That way, we can respond *and* send you information about all our recent sales. (A good way for you to screen agents!).

If he feels a SASE, he slits open the letter and skims it. If it is handwritten, in shaky handwriting especially, or is full of typographical, spelling, syntax or other errors, he sends a form rejection.

Tip No. 2: *Always* make sure you have spelled everything properly, always type your letter, no matter how much effort that may require and always, always, always use your best English. (Have you noticed we haven't even gotten to what you are supposed to say yet?)

I love agenting and would prefer no other profession. But we get some of the strangest queries one could ever imagine. When I read these bad examples at writers clubs, conferences and university classes, people can hardly believe they are real submissions. Here's a few examples of my all time favorites. (Names have been left out to protect the guilty.)

Some authors are in a hurry:

> My book will show, through symbols, that I am Indiana Jones,
> not the one of movies or television, but a real one. I would like a
> quick recognition of my work and would like to replace Harrison

Ford in the next Indiana Jones movie. Time is of the essence, because I have no idea what will happen to me regarding that aspect. I must obtain prompt publication because I am insecure.

This one needs help with capitalization, punctuation, spelling and sentence structure:

> enclosed are some chapters of the story of a girl and her adventures on stage
> if you are interested in this story i can send you the complete stry if you are not interested please retuen the chapters
> to me thank you

Some are confused about the necessary qualifications of an author:

> My Dear Ms. Keller:
> As can see, I do not have a typewriter at present. I did have a 12 year marriage, ending in a Mexican divorce. Would you say Katherine Hepburn married Spencer Tracy?
> Must I be married in order to get my book published? I could easily arrange that, even with an ad.

And my all-time favorite:

> Dear Madam/Sir:
> If you are one of those agents who charges reading fees, use my SASE to keep in touch with the head of your witches' coven. However, if you are not, I have written a book guaranteed to be a best-seller..."

Obviously, not one of these books ever got represented by anyone, and therefore never sold, until the writers figured out what was wrong. (They would have profited from this book!) We sent each one of these kind folks a form rejection. Too bad, because some of this may have been wonderful stuff, but somehow I don't think so.

Agents also tend to disregard queries that include the word "best-seller," as in, "My book is the next best-seller." Now, after many years in this business, sometimes I get hunches about what is going to be a best-seller, and sometimes I am right. But I have a hard time understanding how some "outsider," some writer in Butte, Montana, knows that his or her book is what the world has been waiting for. It's a little too much self-confidence.

Tip No. 3 : Be appropriate—neither vain nor overly humble and shy.

We get queries from folks who have done some market testing. They write: "My Mother read it and she said it was the best book she's ever read!"

Grown adults tell us this! Or, "I read it to all the children in my first grade class and they loved it!" (Of course they did! They like Barney, too, which shows their level of discrimination!) These people are NOT qualified to give you an expert opinion, even though they may really like the book and be well-read. Their opinion, sadly, except in groups of 5,000 or more, means almost nothing in the publishing world. So don't mention their recommendation.

Tip No. 4: If you have an endorsement from a professional or an author in a field related to your book, mention it in the query by all means.

While we are discussing qualifications, there are a few more tips that can make your query terrific. Know your subject. If you are writing nonfiction, your knowledge of your subject will be the single largest determinant in whether your book sells, closely followed by "Can you write?" People who are *not* millionaires should not write books about how to become one. People who do not have children should *not* write books about how to parent. If you have decided to become a children's author and your art has never been published, you've never taken an art class or been paid for any drawing you have done, *do not* include your sketches with the query. If you are writing fiction, set your story in cities you have *actually been to* and know well. If you are a guy, it's really hard to write a book with a female protagonist, and vice versa.

> "Agents also tend to disregard queries that include the word 'best-seller...'"

Tip No. 5: Write what you know, research what you don't know and write it well. Only when you have done this will you have a book worth querying!

Sometimes people decide that writing a book is a quick way to make lots of money. It is not. To be a real writer takes dedication, not just to sit down typing, but to research, plan, think, organize and edit ruthlessly. There is a saying, "There is no great writing, only great rewriting." Remember this if you think your book was typed letter-perfect the first time.

So once you have written this marvelous book, and completed it (never query fiction that is not yet complete), it is time to actually write the query. Get yourself a copy of the *Insider's Guide to Literary Agents, Literary Market Place* or *Writer's Digest's Guide to Literary Agents*. All of these books, available at your library or bookstore, will list agents. Look for agents who expressly handle the type of book you have written (known as genre). Note: If you don't know your own genre, go to the local bookstore, stop a clerk, describe your book and ask where it will be shelved when it comes out.

When you have identified your genre, select thirty agents who specialize in that genre. For instance, my agency does not handle horror, gore, erotica, sci-fi or fantasy, and that is clearly stated in our listings, yet people constantly send us queries for it. (Don't imagine you are such a great writer that you will convince the agent to get into a new genre. You may be, but the amount of work it takes to establish oneself as an agent in a new genre is enormous, and you will be waiting for a sale while the agent does this.)

When you have handpicked thirty of the most-appropriate agents—those who have sold books similar to yours, have an interest in books like yours, or who say something in their ad that appeals to you otherwise—split the list in two. I call it The Rule of 30. Take the top fifteen agents and query them. That means write each one a personal letter. Don't address it To Whom It May Concern or Dear Sir/Madam. Make it personal—it's only fifteen letters—and don't photocopy the letter fifteen times. You will look extremely unprofessional.

Mail the queries to each agent simultaneously, with whatever other materials they request in their listing. Then wait. Wait a whole six weeks. Don't give anyone an exclusive anything, don't jump at the first one who bites. Wait until you have heard from everyone. If a bunch of agents want you, you are on to something. If no one wants you, try the next fifteen. If thirty agents have been queried and no one will even look at your material,

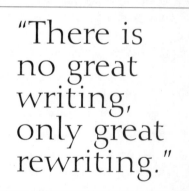

"There is no great writing, only great rewriting."

something is drastically wrong with your concept and/or your query letter.

Writing a query letter may sound intimidating, but using the tips above and by following the simple procedure outlined below, you will create compelling, interesting queries that make agents stand up and listen.

1. Personalize it. If you must, call ahead to verify the agent is still there, the address and the spelling of the name.

2. Get to the point right away. Think about the sizzle and the steak again. If the biggest feature of your book is the fact that you are a millionaire and are writing a book to share your secrets, the first line needs to read something like:

> "I have written a nonfiction business book called 'Millionaire's Secrets.' I am the President of XYZ Corporation, with holdings in 12 countries and assets over $3 billion. I started this company on my dining room table a year ago..."

If you are a doctor, a lawyer or a Ph.D., and that is relevant to your book (fiction or nonfiction, e.g., Grisham being an attorney), put that up front:

> "I have been an EMT for the last ten years in the Bronx. I have written a fiction novel about an EMT in the Bronx who..."

If you have an endorsement that means something, say it:

> "Norman Vincent Peale's widow has endorsed my devotional book."
> "Wayne Dyer has endorsed my self-help book "Flowers for Anastasia"..."

Did you notice that I use genre in the first line? Most of the book queries I receive are returned because they are outside my genre. If you have done your homework, prove it to the agent by putting your genre in the first sentence or two. Use our jargon to get inside.

Once you have grabbed attention by using your book's greatest strengths...oops! I hear some readers crying, "But I don't have any of those strengths! It's just a plain old fiction book." What then? Then the first line reads:

> "I have won two local awards for my writing."
> "I published an article in my local paper in 1989 from which the idea for this novel sprouted."

There has to be something. If there isn't *anything* special about you or your book, perhaps that's the problem right there. You, the author, should be able to come up with something wonderful to say—whether it is your research, your previous credits, the fact you really lived through the events that transpire (depression, incest, robbery), or you work in the field. If you don't, really don't, have *anything*, you probably should not be writing on that subject.

For the second paragraph and *maybe* (only maybe) the third, describe your story. This is where writers bog down and get mired in fear and write awful queries. We truly are not overly worried about what your heroine's name is, and which city she was born in. All you have to say is something like:

> On a blustery day in 1890, an old miser sat shivering in his elegant home. The scant heat from one lump of coal barely warmed the old man's feet. Yet he drifted off to sleep and as he slept, he was visited by three ghosts. The Ghost of Christmas Past, who showed him what his life had been, The Ghost of Christmas Present...

You have the idea? It doesn't have to be particularly long because it is to writing what an appetizer is to dinner. The point of the query is merely to make me want to read more. (Ideally, this is also the point of every single paragraph in your entire book.)

That accomplished, you move on to the final paragraph, which does not need to contain threats, bribes, coercion, deadlines, exposes, or other useless and common drivel—I have been offered money, certain death, evil curses, chocolate, flowers, even lingerie(!) as bribery to represent a manuscript. It needs to be professional, please, and say something like:

> Thank you for taking time to consider my manuscript. It is complete at 346 pages, double-spaced, 12 pt type. I look forward to sending you a copy at your request.
>
> Sincerely,
> The author

That's it. That's all you have to say. It isn't hard, it isn't even scary anymore, is it? Remember, in query writing *less* can be more—sell us on your sizzle first, then we'll want the "steak."

Wendy Keller won her first writing contest at age ten, and landed her first job as a newspaper reporter at sixteen. Her continual passion for writing and fascination with the power of the written word drove her to work for PR Newswire, the Knight-Ridder newspaper chain, as managing editor of Dateline magazine and associate publisher of Los Angeles' then-second-largest Spanish language newspaper, La Gaceta.

In 1989, Ms. Keller envisioned ForthWrite Literary Agency, founded in integrity, honesty and compassion for the writer.

Today, ForthWrite Literary Agency has closed more than 540 rights deals worldwide for clients. She is the author of twenty-nine published books under eight pseudonyms, and has been a featured guest on forty-seven television programs, including Dateline NBC, CBS The Early Show, Rosie, Crosstalk, Fox, ABC, Politically Incorrect and other programs. She and her books have been featured on more than 300 radio shows worldwide and has been written up in seventy-nine magazine and newspaper articles, including The Wall Street Journal, Arizona Republic, Dallas Morning News, Chicago Tribune, Playboy, The Scotsman, Maxim, Parenting *and the* Miami Herald.

Today, she teaches other writers and speakers how to market, promote, and profit from their idea.

Paradise Beckons

How to overcome cutthroat competition,
absurdly low pay, greedy publishers, and other
impossible obstacles and actually sell your travel writing

By Lan Sluder

YOU'RE ON A BEACH IN THE SOUTH PACIFIC. The sand is like talcum powder under your toes. The water of the lagoon, ridiculously transparent, looks like the cover of *Condé Nast Traveler.* Roberto has just brought you an ice-cold something-and-tonic. In a moment you'll go back to your thatch cabaña for a siesta. Later, after dinner under the stars of the Southern Cross, you'll type up your day's notes on your MacBook Pro. If this isn't paradise, it's as close as you or Jimmy Buffett will ever get.

Best of all, it's free. Your airfare was comped by the airline, eager to have you write about their new PrimoFirst service. The hotel is picking up the tab for your room and meals, hopeful of getting a plug in your upcoming article. The island's tourism officials have wined and dined you, no less than your due as a—tah-dah!—Travel Writer.

That's the dream.

The reality, of course, is different. Much different.

Travel writing's harsh reality

Travel writing, in fact, is one of the most competitive fields in all of journalism. The supply of travel writers and wannabes so outweighs demand that some publications have stopped accepting freelance submissions. The pay is absurdly low: Guidebook authors often end up making minimum wage, or worse.

Slick airline magazines offer $100 for a short piece. Large newspapers such as the *Chicago Tribune* may pay only $250 for a lengthy feature article. The one to two dollars-a-word goal that serious freelancers strive for is a pipe dream in travel writing. Fifteen cents a word (equivalent in today's dollar to less than the penny a word paid by the pulps in the 1930s) is much more common.

Easier it is to get a loan from your stingiest cousin than to get a free night at a resort or a comp meal at a restaurant. And less demeaning to ask for the loan. Which is just as well, because the most prestigious outlets for travel articles, such as the *New York Times* Travel Section and *National Geographic Traveler*, won't take your article if you accept a single freebie.

It's so difficult to crack the travel market that one veteran travel writer, Harry Pariser, author of numerous guidebooks to the Caribbean and Central America, advises, "Don't bother. The market is oversaturated, and the stuff desired by the larger magazines and newspapers is largely pap."

For those lucky enough to get assignments, expenses are seldom paid, and the actual workday of a travel writer is, more often than not, long and absorbed in mundane details, such as double-checking fax and telephone numbers (the leading complaint of travel guide readers is incorrect phone numbers) or writing detailed directions on how to get to an isolated beach long after the writer has forgotten where the beach was.

The glories of travel? How about this reality check from Kit Snedaker, a long-time travel writer and former travel editor at the now-defunct *Los Angeles Herald-Examiner*:

"When I was green I took a press trip to Togo. We went up country in three days on a trip that normally took six. The local photog got sick with malaria and vomited out the front window of the bus as the wind blew this in the back. We arrived at government hotels too late to see anything, but the locals would still dance for us—in total darkness. All we could hear was the thump of their feet and the jingle of the bells on their feet. We weren't even sure where they were. Engines failed as the plane home went up the coast. We spent 24 hours on the floor of the Dakar airport, were put in a filthy hotel, fed, but charged for water. I never want to see or hear of Togo again."

Despite all the reasons not to bother with travel writing, chances are you'll try it anyway. After all, who wouldn't rather write about a wonderful little bistro in Paris than about the latest line of faucets for *Bathroom World Today*?

If you're going to travel, why not try to cover at least part of the cost through freelancing? You may just be the next Pico Iyer or Paul Theroux. Indubitably, there's a market out there for travel-related materials. *1000 Places to See Before You Die* by Patricia Shultz, from Workman Publishing, has sold more than a million copies and consistently ranks in the top 100 of book sales on Amazon.com.

Here, to help you avoid mistakes and max your chances for success, are suggestions, tips, and advice from travel writing pros and semipros on markets for travel, on how to break in, on winning strategies for making sales, and on helpful resources for the travel writer.

Paying markets for travel writing

The market for travel writing is, at once, shrinking and growing. It is shrinking, because one of the traditional ace markets for travel prose and pictures, the Sunday newspaper travel section, is buying less and less. The news hole for travel in newspapers is getting smaller, and more wire service and syndicated copy is available to newspaper travel editors at low cost. Why should the editor buy your piece on London, when she's got, at little or no incremental charge to her section's budget, a ready-to-go piece from AP, complete with maps, sidebars, and digitized color photos?

The travel market is growing, however, because of the number of new publications and publishing options. More travel guides are being published than ever before, and guides are becoming more segmented. Instead of a single regional guide, for example, publishers now are doing country-by-country guides, city guides, adventure guides, shopping guides, dining guides, beach guides, and nature guides.

The revolution in desktop publishing and the World Wide Web means that more writers are churning out self-published guides, Internet e-zines and blogs, and electronic travel articles. The pay may not be much, and the quality sometimes may be slap-dash, but there's more travel information being created today than ever before.

Here's how the markets for travel writing look today:

Newspapers

Although the space available for freelance travel articles in daily papers is shrinking, travel section editors still buy. The average metro daily travel section has about three destination stories, and perhaps 30 to 50 percent of travel features are freelance-written. For a major feature, expect to get anywhere from $50 (in small-city dailies) to around $500 or more (in the *New York Times*). The good news is that, with the exception of a few large papers with a national audience, including the *Times* and the *Washington Post*, newspapers expect exclusivity only in their local coverage areas. You can market the same story to newspapers all over the country. You'll have to provide photos to sell to most papers.

Guidebooks

If you're willing to work hard, doing a guidebook can be a good way to break into travel writing. Never in history have more guides been published, or guides of higher quality. Paul Glassman, author of several pioneering guides to Central America, points out: "If you can find a guidebook in the library from 20 years back, you'll find it woefully inadequate by today's standards—basic maps, a quick once-over on food, recommendations that you take a tour rather than giving instructions for doing it on your own."

Today's market, led by the Lonely Planet, Fodor's, Moon, Frommer's, DK, Michelin and Eyewitness imprints but with scores of specialized and small press titles, is saturated with city guides, and with guides to heavily traveled countries such as France and England or to currently hot destinations such as Costa Rica and Thailand. Frommer's publishes some 300 different guidebooks, Fodor's publishes about the same number, and Lonely Planet claims to publish about 500 different titles.

Country guides to less-well-known destinations in Africa, Asia, and South America, such as Bulgaria, Morocco, Dubai, Cuba, and South Africa, may interest a publisher. Also, state and local guides to destinations in the United States, or special-interest guides such as those targeting divers, hikers, climbers, kayakers, or antique shoppers, may also sell.

However, mainstream guides to U.S. destinations can also do well. Frommer's best-selling guide is *The Official Guide to Walt Disney World*, and it sells around 100,000 copies annually.

The typical guide takes at least six months to a year of work to complete, and the amount of detail involved—touring hundreds of hotels, for example—can be staggering. Although compensation and royalty arrangements vary tremendously, guidebook writers may get a small advance, a few thousand dollars, against future royalties. Royalties might range from 5 to 12 percent—averaging 10 percent—of the wholesale price of the book, which is typically 40 to 50 percent of cover price, after discounts. Thus, a $20 title that eventually sells 15,000 copies at a 10 percent wholesale royalty might gross the author $12,000, less the advance. In practice the royalties actually paid may well be lower, the world of publishing accounting being what it is.

Writers typically do not get travel expenses paid, or at most get a few thousand to defray costs. Avalon Travel Publishing (which was merged into Perseus Books Group in 2007), publishers of the Moon Handbook series, for example, pays advances starting at around $3,000 against royalties but pays no expenses. It accepts detailed queries, with author's credentials, competition analysis, proposed outline, and sample photos from freelancers and expects delivery of the manuscript in nine to twelve months from contract signing.

Increasingly, travel publishers are requiring that their authors write on a work-for-hire basis, with the copyright held by the publishing company. Fodor's, a unit of Random House, has long operated this way, and more recently Lonely Planet has gone this work-for-hire route. In this case, the writer gets a flat fee, typically in the range of $10,000 to $25,000 for a destination title, with a small advance up front and the balance paid on completion. Usually, but not always, the author of a work-for-hire guide will get first dibs on updating the guide. The fee for an update might be one-third of the fee for the original book.

With guidebooks on a short economic leash, some publishers are turning to young, inexperienced writers. They can pay them a pittance, with more experienced editors checking their work. Frommer's and MTV are working together to publish a new series of budget guides to Europe, and their young writers get as little as $1,500 for 150 pages. Let's Go, owned and run by Harvard Student Agencies, employs Harvard students exclusively. It sends some seventy-five researchers on low-budget travel guide assignments during the summer.

Some publishers, such as Fodor's, prefer to use writers who live in the areas they cover, while others simply expect their authors to spend enough time at the destination to write knowledgeably about it.

In any case, most guides sell less than 15,000 copies, so you won't get rich as a guidebook writer, but if you enjoy the destination you're writing about, the project may be a labor of love, and your credentials as a published expert may help you sell spin-off articles.

You can also dream about hitting the big time. Rick Steves' forty guidebooks, published by Avalon, have sold a total of more than two million copies, and Steves spends five months a year traveling in Europe. Steves himself is now virtually a travel brand.

Travel magazines

When trying to sell their travel stuff, many would-be travel writers immediately think of the slick national travel magazines such as *Condé Nast Traveler, Travel + Leisure,* and *National Geographic Traveler.* These pubs pay fairly well—in the range of $1 a word and up, or $500 to $5,000 an article, or more, and sometimes with expenses paid—but they get dozens of submissions and queries for each piece they accept. Most assignments are made to established writers known to the editors. The top mags don't accept articles when the writer's trip was subsidized.

You'll have a better shot at getting published in the smaller circulation magazines, such as *Caribbean Travel and Life* or *Islands*. It's easier to break into the columns and short features rather than with a destination piece. *International Travel News*, a monthly printed on newsprint, is a reader-written magazine that's easy to break into—it's open to all submissions on travel anywhere except the U.S. and the Caribbean, as long as you're an *ITN* subscriber. The pay, however, is lousy—under $25 for most pieces.

Other consumer magazines

The best magazine market for travel articles isn't in the travel mags, but in general-interest or specialty pubs that may buy one or two travel-related features for each issue. Women's magazines, men's magazines, outdoors pubs, RV and trailer magazines, and golf magazines are among the literally hundreds of outlets for good travel writing. And there's more good news: Many of these magazines pay more than travel pubs.

> "You'll have a better shot at getting published in the smaller circulation magazines"

Travel trade magazines

Pros who write for money know that while the glory may be in the slick consumer magazines, the cash often is in the trade publications. The same holds true for trade pubs in the travel industry. Trade periodicals put more emphasis on solid reporting and industry knowledge than on flashy writing. If you prove yourself as a dependable writer who can deliver on time, you may be able to sell regularly to *Travel Weekly*, *Travel Agent*, and other trade magazines.

eBooks

With the growth of the Internet, eBooks have become a way to do inexpensive publishing and self-publishing of travel writing. In fact, eBooks are an ideal medium for travel writing, as guides and other travel books can be inexpensively produced and frequently updated. Practical, factual, how-to books, such as tips on retiring in a foreign country, seem to do best.

Although there are a number of proprietary eBook formats and eBook readers, the simplest and arguably best way to do an eBook is simply to convert your Word or other file to Adobe Acrobat Portable Document Format (PDF). A pdf file can be read on any Windows or Mac computer, or printed out in hard copy. Adobe also offers free eBook Reader software and has its own eBook, *How to Create Adobe PDF EBooks*, downloadable free from www.adobe.com.

For the author looking to actually make money from an eBook, the key is finding a high-traffic Web site to sell the book. You can create your own site, of course, but you probably won't be able to generate enough traffic to sell more than a few copies. Web sites such as Escape Artist (www.escapeartist.com) and Expats eBooks (www.expatsebooks.com) can be good options. Typically, these sites sell eBooks on a commission basis, taking 50 to 60 percent of the total revenue, so the sale of a $20 eBook would net the author $8 to $10. Usually, commissions are paid quarterly. Popular eBooks on these sites can sell briskly, and some authors report earning $1000 to $2000 per quarter, revenue that compares favorably with royalties from hardcover books. Amazon.com now also sells eBooks, including self-published eBooks, though you'll have to convert your book to proprietary eBook software.

How to Write and Publish Your Own eBook in as Little as 7 Days, by Jim Edwards and Joe Vitale (Morgan James Publishing) is one of several books out to help you create your own eBooks.

Other digital publishing

No one can be sure exactly what the future of electronic publishing is, but almost everyone agrees it *is* the future. Travel CD-ROMs were hot for a couple of years, but publishers found most CD titles sold poorly. Podcasting currently is at the leading edge of digital travel publishing. Lonely Planet, Frommer's and other guidebook publishers now offer travel podcasts that you can listen to on your MP3 player. Travel guides, maps and hotel, dining and shopping recommendations also are becoming available for cell phone and PDA users.

The Internet, of course, is still today's 800-pound gorilla. All of the leading travel publishers have Web sites. Some, including Frommer's, Fodor's and Rough Guides, put part or all of selected guidebooks online. Increasingly, publishers view offering their guides on the Internet as comparable to having their books in public libraries—free distribution boosts awareness for the guides and ultimately results in bookstore sales.

Publishers, mostly of the shoestring variety, have launched a number of travel e-zines on the Web. Most offer nothing for contributions, except the promise of seeing your story on the screen and hot links to your own home page. A few say they pay writers.

Electronic rights are a touchy issue for both publishers and writers. Many publishers, claiming they are at present making no money in electronic channels, may offer nothing extra for e-rights. Writers, and in particular organized groups such as American Society of Journalists and Authors, say they're unwilling to give away future income from what may become the dominant form of publishing.

Foreign publications

Magazines and newspapers outside the U.S. can be good secondary sources for travel articles. Many foreign cities have English-language newspapers and magazines.

Broadcast

Television, especially cable with programming such as the Travel Channel, increasingly offers opportunities for freelance contributions. Streaming video on the Web is becoming very important, and sites such as YouTube are outlets for amateur, and unpaid, travel videos. A recent search found more than 50,000 travel-related videos posted on YouTube alone.

Self-publishing

Whether on the Web, as eBooks, or in traditional books, self-publishing is a viable option. In my own case, over the past twenty years I've made more money from self-published books and eBooks than I have from my books that were published by Avalon, Random House, Macmillan, and other regular publishers.

Even narrowly focused local guidebooks, if well marketed, can have considerable sales. Central America guidebook writer Paul Glassman says his best-paying jobs in travel writing were self-assigned ones. "My guides to Belize and Costa Rica quietly sold very nicely, before these countries were discovered."

Almost without exception, self-publishers recommend Dan Poynter's *The Self-Publishing Manual* as the bible for do-it-yourself publishers.

Pros tell how to break in

Successfully breaking in to travel writing requires the usual blend of moderate ability, immoderate persistence, and a certain amount of luck. "It helps to be good, it helps to be pushy, it helps to be reliable, but I'm not saying that you have to be all three, or that you absolutely must be tops in numerous other traits," says Paul Glassman. "There's a lot of plain, workaday, undistinguished prose that gets published, because the writers kept flinging their stuff at editors, or turned the stuff in on time. Keep at it, and find a niche where you can squeeze through, but don't count on anything, and don't let your happiness depend on it."

Teresa Mears, an editor with the *Miami Herald*, offers this advice for newbies: "Look for stories other people aren't doing, especially from areas you know well. Learn to take good photos. If you're not from a journalism background, learn something about basic journalism and ethics. I would advise novices to start with newspapers and small magazines where what you write carries more weight than whom you know and what clips you have."

Kit Snedaker, former newspaper travel editor and longtime freelancer, has advised would-be travel writers this way: "As a novice, you should...read every travel writer you can get your hands on. Then, start writing sample pieces and submitting them on spec with art. But keep your day job." Novices need to be published, said Snedaker, so try the smaller markets, the weeklies, and the smaller magazines. "But never let your stuff be published free! Always charge something for it and do stories about your own backyard if necessary."

It's always tough to sell mediocre stories, according to veteran Australian travel writer and editor Gareth Powell, but professional writing shows through. "When I was a newspaper travel editor I would get 30 or 40 submissions a day. Most were rubbish. In the end, as a means of self-defense, I had a list of 20 or 30 professional writers I knew I could depend on. They were paid reasonable money and delivered good stories."

Getting good travel assignments is hard work. Josh Berman, who updated the *Moon Handbooks Belize* and co-authored *Living Abroad in Nicaragua* and *Moon Handbooks Nicaragua*, all for Avalon, says he spent many months preparing a proposal for a new travel book. His pitch to publishers included a book outline and several sample chapters.

Ten tips on selling your travel writing

1. **Network.** Get to know travel editors and schmooze public relations people in the hospitality industry. While good writing sells stories, people who know and like you make the plum assignments.

2. **Specialize.** Many successful travel writers combine general travel writing with a specialty in golf, fishing, cooking, technology, or another subject.

3. **Narrowly focus your stories.** Write about the best coffee houses in Sydney instead of your trip to Australia.

4. **Learn to shoot.** Good photos help sell travel writing, and with many

publications, especially smaller newspapers and magazines, they're an absolute necessity. Point-and-shoot digital camera technology makes it easier to snap decent shots. It may also pay to take a course on photography at a local college.

5. **Go beyond destination pieces.** Destination articles are a drug on the market. However, editors much less frequently see stories that rate, compare, contrast, review, or explain. A well-researched piece on the ten best folk art sites in Florida, or the twenty-five best free attractions, likely will sell better than another article on Disney World.

6. **Look professional.** It should go without saying that professional-looking manuscripts and photos are the minimum requirement. Most publications now ask that you submit electronically, via e-mail. Be sure your electronic submissions are in the format requested by the editor.

7. **Repackage.** Don't limit yourself to one article per destination. Each trip you take is fodder for many different stories targeted for different publishing markets. Research once; write many pieces.

8. **Avoid the obvious travel markets.** The travel magazines and newspaper travel sections are swamped with over-the-transom material. Go where the competition ain't, such as in general interest consumer mags, small destination-oriented publications, electronic media, niche publications, and foreign media.

9. **Resell.** Unless you've signed away all rights, every article you write can be sold again and again. Keep it fresh, update it, add new art, try new markets, but resell it.

10. **Don't bug editors.** Editors, even at the large daily newspaper travel sections and at magazines, usually are overworked, underpaid, harried, and harassed. Editors may not have secretaries or assistants. They may get hundreds of letters a day. They hate interruptions. Avoid telephone calls, unless you know a call is welcome and it won't come on deadline day.

Resources

The following may be of value to those interested in travel writing.

Books and publications

Writer's Market, Writer's Digest Books. Updated annually. This is a listing of books, magazines, and other publishing sources that may accept freelance contributions. The only drawback is that everybody uses it, and the travel publications listed get a lot of submissions. Writer's Digest Books also publishes a slew of books for writers, many of which are of value to travel writers. Also, you can access Writer's Market online at www.writersmarket.com, with monthly online subscriptions available. However, I found the online edition nearly worthless and cancelled my subscription.

The American Directory of Writer's Guidelines compiled and edited by Stephen Blake Mettee, Michele Doland, and Doris Hall, Quill Driver Books. This is a compilation of more than 1,700 magazine and book publishers' guidelines for writers. It's a great place to browse for ideas as well as markets.

There are a number of how-to books out on travel writing, most along the lines of "make extra money when you travel." Among the ones currently in print are *The Travel Writer's Handbook: How to Write—and Sell—Your Own Travel Experiences* by Louise Purwin Zobel and Jacqueline Harmon Butler (Surrey Books); *Lonely Planet Guide to Travel Writing* by Don George (Lonely Planet Reference); *The Travel Writer's Guide* by Gordon Burgett (Communications Unlimited); and *Teach Yourself Travel Writing* by Cynthia Dial (McGraw-Hill).

Online resources

Travelwriters.com (www.travelwriters.com) is a community of more than 10,000 travel writers, editors, and public relations and tourism practitioners. Its goal is to connect travel writers with travel marketers and in doing so offers information on press trips, press release distribution and other services.

Transitions Abroad magazine (www.transitionabroad.com) has expanded its coverage of travel writing and travel writers. It provided extensive links to travel writing blogs, lists of the best travel books, and interviews with travel writers.

TravelMole (www.travelmole.com) says it is the largest Internet community of travel professionals, with more than 450,000 registered members worldwide. TravelMole offers email newsletters, searchable archives, and referenced directories.

Professional organizations

Society of American Travel Writers, www.SATW.org. SATW is the largest and most prestigious of the travel writer organizations, with about 1,300 members. Active members are travel editors, writers and freelancers; associate members are those engaged in public relations in the travel industry.

North American Travel Journalists Association, www.natja.org. NATJA has more than 500 members.

American Society of Journalists and Authors. ASJA is for freelancers of all persuasions, but there is a section for travel writers.

A former newspaper editor in New Orleans, **Lan Sluder** *is a travel and retirement writer with credits in newspapers and magazines around the world, including the* Bangkok Post, Caribbean Travel and Life, Chicago Tribune, *the* New York Times, Where to Retire, *and* Country Journal. *He is the author of half a dozen travel guidebooks including* Fodor's Belize 2007, Frommer's Best Beach Vacations: Carolinas and Georgia, *and* San Pedro Cool. *He also has authored two books—*Adapter Kit: Belize *and* Living Abroad in Belize—*and several eBooks on retirement and relocation. Sluder founded and edits* Belize First, *now an online magazine on Belize at www.belizefirst.com.*

A member of the Society of American Travel Writers, Sluder was educated at Duke University and the University of North Carolina, and in the U.S. Army in Vietnam. He lives on a mountain farm near Asheville, NC.

Researching &
Writing History

Or: The money's not important when you're having so much fun!

By William B. Secrest

HAVING WRITTEN CALIFORNIA AND WESTERN HISTORY as a hobby for over thirty years, I have from time to time enjoyed talking with aspiring writers. Writing for me has always been both an avocation and a source of great pleasure, and I have always counseled others to have fun. First and foremost, enjoy your writing. Revel in the research, wallow in the writing, and take pleasure in polishing that text. If you are good enough you will make a little money. If you really enjoy what you're doing, you will discover a hobby with rewards that can be far more gratifying than money.

Read, read, read

Some people have a natural penchant for writing, while others develop their craft through study. However you go about developing your skills, get in the habit of reading. There's no better way to learn than reading the well-versed phrases of a master writer who knows just how long to make a sentence, how to describe a subject with just the appropriate words or how to develop a rhythm that makes reading a distinct pleasure.

In the western genre Stuart Lake's masterful biography of Wyatt Earp flows from page to page like a novel. J. Evetts Haley's *Jeff Milton* is also a skilled piece of writing. Richard Dillon's lively and descriptive prose is a pleasure to read as is John Upton Terrell's *Bunkhouse Papers*. Although distinctly different from modern prose, Mark Twain's work is as enjoyable today as when it first appeared so long ago.

Choose a fresh subject or fresh angle

I have developed my own methods for selecting subject matter over the years. I decided early on that editors would not be interested in material that was well known and being constantly rehashed. Back before it was politically correct to do so, I did articles on African American pioneers in the West and women outlaws—always searching for subjects that hadn't been done before. Western characters such as Wyatt Earp, Billy the Kid or Wild Bill Hickok should only be a subject if you can come up with a previously unexplored aspect of their lives. This might be newly discovered material, or just looking at them from a different direction. Editors are always seeking such material.

> "Revel in the research, wallow in the writing."

For example, years ago I researched the life of Wild Bill Hickok with a view to doing a book one day. I never did the book, but I utilized my research for several articles pertaining to the noted gunman, always seeking a little-known aspect of his life. A particular favorite was my biography of Hickok's wife, a famous circus performer who was one of the first woman circus owners in the country and a fascinating character in her own right. She was one of the first to put a circus on the railroad, and it was while touring the West she met the noted lawman at Abilene, Kansas, in 1871. Her story had never been done before, yet she lived a wonderfully colorful life. Later, Joseph G. Rosa, Hickok's biographer, was able to utilize my material in the second edition of his work.

An excellent method of finding subject matter is to pick an interesting but obscure character in a nonfiction history book. With a little practice, exciting characters will jump out at you and you'll be on your way.

Ben Daniels, one of the early characters of old Dodge City, is mentioned in most if not all of the many books on the subject. No one ever had much to say about him, however, because most writers were more interested in Wyatt Earp or Bat Masterson. When I decided to look into Daniels' life I found a fascinating and controversial character who had been a buffalo hunter, peace officer, horse thief, convict, Rough Rider with Teddy Roosevelt, U.S. marshal of Arizona, and warden of Yuma Prison. Part of one ear was missing as a reminder of his rustling days, and his final years were spent as the husband of a prominent Arizona schoolteacher. I found bits and pieces of his life in books, old magazine articles and in various state historical societies. The National Archives provided material on his controversial appointment as U.S. marshal of Arizona and his military record. His story made a wonderful article about a colorful frontiersman no one had ever taken seriously before.

Another rich source of ideas are footnotes. Often there isn't room to fully explore a minor character in a book, but the author will give intriguing biographical information in a footnote. This is frequently an excellent starting place for further research, and in time you will instinctively know if the subject is worth following up.

Don't lock yourself into writing about people. There are all kinds of subjects out there, so keep your eyes and ears open for ideas. I have done articles on riverboats, the gunfighter's code, bull and bear fights in old California, a history of frontier saloons, and frontier towns. Some old buildings have wonderful histories when you start looking into them and an in-depth account of a little-known incident of frontier history can be fascinating to research and write.

Keep an idea file

As you research your subject in old newspapers, keep an eye open for other interesting articles. When you find something (and you will), make a note or a copy of some kind. You might not want to at first because you are looking for your primary subject. But do it. Over the years you will turn to this "idea" file again and again.

Research in depth

Once you have selected your subject, put together all you can from the readily available sources, then start filling in the holes. If possible, keep your subjects local to begin with; it'll be easier to find sources and research. Descendants are easier to find, also, and you'll feel much more comfortable in describing familiar areas and local color. As soon as possible, start developing an outline of your article.

You'll quickly have to come to grips with locating sources. This shouldn't be a problem for anyone interested in history—you will already have some experience from school or personal projects. As you broaden your approach, the many different libraries, municipal and state archives and state historical societies possessing useful material will become readily apparent. Genealogy can often be an important aspect of your historical work, so familiarize yourself with its methodology and learn to utilize source books on this subject. Likewise, get to know your local librarians, who are often old hands in fields you are just beginning to discover.

Discuss your project with others—frequently, laymen can recommend a source you were unaware of or perhaps had forgotten. I always make a point of mentioning current writing projects to friends and others that I meet for just this reason.

Some years ago I was working on a biography of an early San Francisco police detective. While attending an historical society fund-raiser one weekend, I stopped to chat for a moment with a fellow board member. She asked what I was working on and I told her something about my detective project. I was startled when she mentioned she had recently read the journal of an early police detective. She couldn't remember any names or details, but gave me the name of the owner, whom I contacted immediately. It turned out to be a collection of some twenty years of journals kept by a detective who had actually worked under my detective subject!

It was an incredible discovery. The journals were not only handwritten accounts of all the famous cases of the day, but were filled with photographs, wanted posters, telegrams, notes, letters and newspaper clippings that were an invaluable source of information for my project. I was able to borrow all the volumes over a period of time and I've never forgotten just how serendipitous that chance meeting had been.

Keep more than one ball in the air

Try to research two or three subjects at the same time. As you work on one story, keep busy researching several others, and you'll always have the material for your next article ready when you finish your current project.

One of the big pluses of researching an article is learning. It never stops. In western writing you have to know how long it takes to ride a horse a given distance; how to load a cap and ball pistol; what the medium of exchange was at a given point in history. With history, you are dealing with a finite subject and you must know the details you are writing about. If you don't, some nitpicking reader will complain about your inaccuracy—something editors frown at, to say the least.

While working on a current book project, I was confronted with an incident concerning an early Texas keel boat explorer of the Rio Grande River. I had what seemed to be a valid account of this explorer being involved in an army patrol as a scout, but I knew he had started on his exploring expedition a week or so before the patrol. His orders had been to stop periodically during the trip to look for minerals, flora and fauna and to question settlers he met along the river. It was perfectly natural for him to have stopped at the army post and been roped into a scouting party for a few days. My problem was this: Between his departure date and when the army patrol left, was there time enough to make this scenario feasible?

I had already researched keel boats and knew something of their operation and history, but now I delved into their rate of speed and methods of propulsion. After examining time records of actual keel boat trips, and knowing the state of the river and wind conditions at the time, I concluded there was, indeed, an opportunity for the explorer to have gone on the scouting party. This is a good example of the importance of checking details and never taking anything for granted.

Network

An important and particularly enjoyable aspect of historical writing is making contact with established writers in the field. Most writers will reply to letters, while a few will be curt and some will not respond. Gradually you will build up a network of contacts and before long you will find yourself helping others as you share interests and discoveries. It's important to remember that no one expects you to give away your own research work that you plan to use. At the same time you might have peripheral material or research you can't use that would be vital to another writer. Aside from material, however, these history pals can often suggest sources of research you have overlooked or didn't know existed. This type of networking will pay off time and again. The real value, however, is the fun and enjoyment of meeting writers with the same interests and exchanging ideas and material.

Use strong distinctive prose

Unless you are writing for a stodgy historical journal of some kind, don't be afraid to be creative. That first sentence should be calculated to make the editor raise his eyebrows and want to read more. It can be a strong, quoted statement or a startling disclosure. Likewise, it may merely be some good descriptive prose. And don't be afraid to start out with something that happens in the middle of your story—a flashback. Be careful, though, as you don't want to confuse the reader.

Edit tightly

Once you have a manuscript, it's time to begin editing. Check each paragraph. Make sure you haven't begun succeeding paragraphs with the same word or in the same way. Also check to make sure you haven't used the same word too many times in a paragraph. Be descriptive, but stingy, with words so as to keep your narrative moving. Instead of saying, "Jim Jones was the mayor of Salmon City and liked to carouse in the town's saloons," use the active voice and say "Mayor Jim Jones caroused in Salmon City saloons." Instead of sixteen words, you now have eight, and the sentence reads better.

So what are you waiting for? Put together your research, then get to that computer keyboard and start typing. If you love history and the idea of creating an entertaining and informative story from raw resources you yourself have located, get busy. You may or may not make much money, but you are practically guaranteed to impress your friends while having the time of your life!

William B. Secrest *has been interested in history since his youth in California's great San Joaquin Valley. Beginning as a hobby of comparing western films to what really happened, his avocation grew into serious research and correspondence with noted writers. He soon began researching and writing articles.*

Although at first he wrote on many general western subjects, Bill realized how his home state has been consistently neglected in the western genre, and he concentrated almost exclusively on early California subjects. He has produced hundreds of articles for such publications as Westways, Montana, True West *and* The American West.

His book I Buried Hickok *(Early West Publishing Co.) appeared in 1980, followed by* Lawmen & Desperadoes *(The Arthur H. Clark Co.) in 1994 and* Dangerous Trails *(Barbed Wire Press) in 1995. His most recent projects include* California Desperadoes *(Word Dancer Press, California, 2000),* Perilous Trails *(Word Dancer Press, California, 2002),* When the Great Spirit Died *(Word Dancer Press, California, 2003),* Dark and Tangled Threads of Crime *(Word Dancer Press, California, 2004),* California Feuds *(Word Dancer Press, California, 2005),* The Man from the Rio Grande: a biography of Harry Love, the leader of the rangers who tracked down Joaquin Murrieta, *(The Arthur H. Clark Co.) in 2005,* California Disasters *(Word Dancer Press, California, 2006), and* California Badmen *(Word Dancer Press, 2007).*

Making a List and Checking It Twice?

Ten-point checklist for your screenplay

Kathie Fong Yoneda

YOU'VE READ ALL OF LINDA SEGER'S books. You've probably taken at least one or two workshops or a couple of courses on screenwriting through your local university or college. You've finally mastered the art of proper margin settings and scene headings. And you have typed—at last—those long-awaited words FADE OUT indicating the completion of your script.

Now, take a deep breath and consider your answers to the following important questions before sending off your script to Steven Speilberg.

1. Are my characters well-drawn and interesting?

Your characters are responsible for telling your story. Along the way, it's vital that they also capture our interest and sympathy. Your hero or heroine should be vulnerable and relatable, as well as courageous. This means putting your main character through a series of tests in which he or she may sometimes fail but will ultimately succeed.

These tests can be physical and/or emotional in nature and serve as plot complications.

Examples:

• Tom Hanks' character overcomes both grief and distance in *Sleepless in Seattle.*

- Scarlett O'Hara overcomes her self-centered ways and the horrors of the Civil War in *Gone with the Wind.*

- Lindsay Lohan's character takes a roller coaster ride through high school popularity before she realizes the importance of being herself, thus regaining the respect of her friends and family and winning the heart of the cute guy in *Mean Girls.*

The physical and emotional journey your hero or heroine takes (and the lessons learned along the way) is what is commonly referred to as a "character arc."

And while most writers spend a great deal of time and energy breathing life into their hero or heroine, not nearly enough development goes into their villain and secondary characters. Bad guys are every bit as important as the hero when it comes to giving your story the dramatic texture and tone that can set it apart from all the rest.

Examples:

- Where would Luke Sky-walker be without Darth Vader to put him to the test in *Star Wars?*

- And who can forget the villainy of the Sheriff of Nottingham who vowed to put an end to *Robin Hood?*

- And how about the pompous head of security who refused to show any humanity for Viktor Navorski, the man-without-a-country, who was stuck in an airport in *The Terminal?*

Secondary characters give us important backstory on the hero and the situation at hand. They often provide vital information which helps to advance

> "It's especially important that each character has his or her own voice."

the plot. They help to define the goals of the hero and often times will be involved in a minor subplot which complements and supports the movie's main theme. Secondary characters can also provide comic relief and are a contrast to the hero's personality.

Examples:

- Would Ariel still be voiceless without the loyalty and friendship of Flounder and Sebastian in *The Little Mermaid?*

• Would Alex Foley have rounded up the bad guys without the help and support of straitlaced, by-the-book officers Taggart and Rosewood in *Beverly Hills Cop*?

• Would Frodo have made the long, but successful, journey if Sam, Legolas, Gandalf, Merry, Pippin, and Aragon were not by his side in *Lord of The Rings*?

2. Does my dialogue add to the personality of my characters and support the plot points of my story?

Your dialogue should be meaningful and appropriately "in character" with the personality of each role you've created. It should effectively convey the thoughts and feelings of your characters and reveal any plot points that are key to the progression of the story. All of this should be done, however, in a subtle, natural-sounding way.

Now's the time to go through your script with a mental red pen to make sure each line and each word is absolutely necessary. It's especially important that each character has his or her own voice. Here are three simple, but effective, ways to test your dialogue:

• Cover up the names above the dialogue and see if each of your characters is easy to distinguish from one another. Remember that your dialogue should be consistent with the personality of each individual.

• Ask your major characters the same question and see if you can give each of them answers that readily separate them from one another.

• Ask members of your writing group or close friends to act out a scene or two. Hearing dialogue spoken out loud can be quite an eye opener for a writer and is a very effective method which can quickly pinpoint any dialogue trouble spots.

3. Does my story fall within a general three-act structure?

Many new scriptors are intimidated by the term "three-act structure." Have no fear, writers, all we're talking about is a beginning, middle and ending. All stories (short stories, plays, novels, and motion pictures) have the same classic structure. Let's take a look at the basic three-act structure using the Oscar-winning film *Witness* as an example:

• Your "beginning" should have an attention-getting setup that introduces your characters and their dilemma.

Example: Dedicated POLICE OFFICER finds his life in jeopardy when a young AMISH BOY identifies the officer's BOSS as the man behind a drug-related murder.

• Your "middle" should have character dynamics, action and plot complications that both entertain and involve the audience as the story progresses.

Example: The OFFICER is forced to seek refuge in the peaceful Amish community where he is attracted to the recently-widowed MOTHER of the young AMISH BOY. The OFFICER finds himself at odds, but gradually adapts to the gentle ways of the community. Unfortunately, his BOSS soon discovers his hiding place, putting the Amish community at risk.

• And your "ending" should be compelling and satisfying by wrapping up all major and minor plot points and character relationships in a memorable way.

Example: The OFFICER is confronted at gunpoint by his BOSS and nearly killed, but the Amish community surrounds the two men and "bears witness," forcing the surrender of his BOSS. The OFFICER and the AMISH WIDOW have a bittersweet farewell, knowing their worlds are far too different to compromise.

4. Does each scene have a distinct purpose for being included?

Time to get out that mental red pen again and selectively excise any scenes which are affecting the pace of your story and slowing down your plotline. Many a novice scriptor can be easily identified by a screenplay weighed down by extraneous sequences and conversations which go on a beat or two longer than necessary.

If your script weighs in over the unspoken 120 page "line of demarcation," you might want to combine scenes if possible.

Examples:

• Your script contains a series of scenes in which the hero learns two pieces of information. Would your story be just as effective by merging two of the scenes into one?

• Your screenplay includes a small scene between the heroine and her mother to show they don't get along. Could that information be included in another conversation your heroine has with her best friend, who already plays a more significant role throughout the overall story?

5. Have I paid attention to details by doing proper research?

If your story is set in a specific area, foreign country or unusual environment, please take the time to read about that location before attempting to recreate it on the page. If your story takes place during a particular historical period, go to the library, surf the Internet or speak at length with an authority on that era for detailed information or little-known, but interesting, anecdotes that can add color and atmosphere. Information on such subjects as politics, religion, clothing, music, architecture, modes of transportation, women's roles in society, education, issues of the time, etc. can provide valuable observations on what life was like and can add to the challenges of your characters and the conflicts they are facing.

A word of caution, however—try to suppress the urge to go overboard by showing off too much of your newly-acquired knowledge. Don't allow those descriptive paragraphs to become so heavily detailed that they overshadow your story and bog down the pace.

If your movie project takes place in an unknown or futuristic world, be sure to take the time to map out the geographical, political, cultural, economical, social, and familial details of this new environment in a concise, but stylized manner.

Whether your story takes place in the past, present or future, one of your primary concerns is to immediately immerse your potential buyer or agent into the "world" of your movie project. Familiarizing the reader is what's commonly known as "setting the scene." The sooner your reader becomes comfortably "oriented" with your story's surroundings, the sooner he will be "hooked" into your project.

6. Do I know who my target audience is?

Ideally, all writers would like the whole world to see their movies, but the simple truth remains that not all stories will appeal to everyone. If your goal is to sell your screenplay as a motion picture project, you should find out what other successful films fall into the same category as your script. After finding other movies that fall under the same general genre, you should ask yourself the following:

• What was the predominant age range of the audience viewing those similar films?

• Was it predominantly a male or female audience?

• Did these films have considerable crossover appeal? In other words, did they attract the interest of a wide range of individuals by crossing sexual, socioeconomic, racial, cultural, and age lines?

• Which studio or production company distributed and/or produced those films? Do you remember how those films were promoted, i.e., what was the emphasis, theme or main thrust of the trailers, television promos, and print ads?

It's important to keep in mind that not all movies are meant to be made and distributed by large studios. Many successful films have been made and distributed by smaller independent companies who specialize in less commercial fare. This becomes abundantly apparent around Academy Award time when many critically-acclaimed, more modestly successful independent films are likely to dominate the Oscar nominations, over their action-packed, big-budgeted, studio-released cousins.

By knowing who your target audience is, you'll have a much more realistic idea of which production companies or distributors to target when you are ready to start submitting your material. If you haven't already done so, I urge you to invest in *The Hollywood Creative Directory*. If your local bookstore doesn't have it, you can call them directly: In California, call 310-315-4815; outside California call 800-815-0503. Or you can contact them at their website at: www.hcd.com. It contains the addresses, website, phone, and fax numbers of more than 2,700 production companies, networks, cable entities, and studios in the entertainment industry.

More important, it contains a partial listing of produced credits and the names and titles of each company's executives. From these listings, you can easily eliminate those companies which may not be appropriate for your low-budget horror script or your historical drama, and you'll be able to more effectively pinpoint your query by directing it to the appropriate person in charge (usually a creative exec, director of development, story editor, or vice president of production).

If your goal is to gain agency representation, you may want to invest in the *Hollywood Agents & Managers Directory*, also published by the people who put out HCD. The agents' directory contains the names, addresses, website, phone, and fax numbers of industry agents and managers. Please pay careful attention to the type of clients each agency or manager represents. Some specialize in representing directors and cinematographers, while others "rep" actors only. Be sure your query goes to an agency or manager who specializes in representing writers.

And, it goes without saying, if you have doubts as to the ethics or validity of an agent or manager, don't hesitate to call the Writers Guild of America to ask if the agency is affiliated with the WGA. Just ask for agency verification or log-on to their website at: www.wga.org.

Needless to say, "targeting" can save a writer considerable time and effort, not to mention the costs of phone calls, postage, envelopes, and duplication of scripts.

7. Have I streamlined my storytelling?

Nothing slows down the reading of a script more than extraneous material. Writers should always focus on writing the best story possible…yet many writers become so involved in detailing their film exactly as they've always envisioned it that they clutter up their efforts and end up slowing down the pace of their storytelling. Here are some tips to keep in mind to help you streamline your script:

• Keep camera angles and descriptive paragraphs to a minimum. This is especially difficult for writers who are attempting to faithfully adapt a screenplay from their novel. Screenplays of today are lean. They contain very few specific camera angles and descriptive paragraphs are concise, giving just enough information to set the scene and/or atmosphere.

• Remember to break up any action description so it's not one massive block of words. Describing an action sequence in a series of two or three sentence paragraphs is much easier to read and gives the potential buyer a feeling of anticipation or urgency, as well as movement.

• If possible, eliminate all flashbacks and voiceovers or keep them to an absolute minimum. In addition to the extra expense of more sets, props, costumes, stuntwork, and actors, flashbacks—if overused and not judiciously placed—can be confusing to the audience. Voiceover is a device that's generally ineffective unless it's used in a highly stylized manner. Nostalgic film projects can sometimes benefit from a few well-placed voiceovers.

Examples:

• In the television series *Desperate Housewives*, the voice of a now-dead housewife from Wisteria Lane sets the scene and conveys her personal observations at the start and finish of each episode.

• In the movie *Stand By Me*, Richard Dreyfuss' adult voice is heard as he sets the stage for an important turning point in his adolescent life.

8. Can I summarize my story in one or two sentences?

When queried by agents or execs, the experienced writer can usually summarize his/her script with just a few brief sentences, while writers who are less experienced have been known to go on for more than ten minutes or ten pages "summarizing" their movie. Encapsulating the essence of your story is creating a "logline," and in this time-is-money world, it's often used as a fast, effective, attention-getting selling tool for a movie. It helps if you can think of a logline as a slightly expanded *TV Guide* blurb that summarizes the Movie of the Week or the latest episode of your favorite weekly television series.

It's important that your logline teases the potential buyer, making him or her want to hear more of the story. In the following example for *Beverly Hills Cop*, notice how each succeeding line adds more intrigue and builds in importance:

• Cop investigates killing: We know what the main character will be doing during most of the movie.

• Cop investigates killing of best friend: We now know that the main character will have a personal stake in the investigation.

• Detroit cop travels to Beverly Hills to investigate the death of his best friend: We are aware that the main character, who is from Detroit, will probably be a "fish-out-of-water" during his investigation in Beverly Hills.

• Street-wise Detroit cop turns Beverly Hills upside down to uncover the man responsible for killing his best friend: We have an indication that the main character is not only determined, but probably used to dealing with an investigation in an unorthodox manner. This logline gives us the distinct feeling that there is going to be a lot of "fireworks" as he doggedly pursues this case to avenge the murder of his best friend.

It's often helpful to start out with a skeletal one sentence summation, then build upon it. Don't forget to use those verbs, adjectives, and adverbs to add color, personality, and attitude to help sell your project. Here are two more examples of loglines from successful films:

• An extraterrestrial is accidentally stranded on earth and must depend upon his extraordinary friendship with a young boy to find his way home (*E.T., The Extra-Terrestrial*).

• Following the Civil War, a soldier is assigned to a remote prairie outpost where he forges a deeply spiritual bond with his Sioux neighbors (*Dances With Wolves*).

• A young Japanese girl sheds her impoverished background and ascends the ranks to become the most popular geisha, but soon realizes that love is what is missing in her life (*Memoirs of a Geisha*).

9. Is my screenplay in professional shape for submission?

Much of this information might sound like simple common sense, but form is the one area which can be an overlooked downfall for a novice writer. Here's a checklist:

• All scripts should be cleanly typed or printed. Absolutely no handwritten notations. Remember to use an easy-to-read type face or font, preferably in 12 pitch.

• Your screenplay should be carefully proofread for grammatical errors, improper punctuation, and misspelled words and typos. If you belong to a writing group, offer to trade off proofreading duties with another member or ask a friend who excels in English.

• Be sure your screenplay is copied onto plain white bond. This means absolutely no colored pages, onionskin or parchment.

• It goes without saying that you should always submit a copy and never an original of your script.

• Place your script in three-hole punched card stock covers, fastened with two brads that are long enough to hold the script securely. Most screenplays are submitted without a title on the card stock cover, but if you want to invest in having the title neatly printed onto the front cover, you can do so.

• There should be a title page listing the title of your script and your name as the writer. If you are not represented by an agent, you may put "Registered with the WGA" (if you are) near the bottom. You should also add an address, phone number, and e-mail information so Hollywood knows how to contact you. There's no need to add the registration number or a "warning." If your script is not registered with the Writers Guild of America, I'd suggest doing so. Registration is currently twenty dollars for nonmembers and the WGA can be reached at the numbers listed above for more detailed information on the registration process.

• Be sure you have numbered each page in the top right-hand corner, and again, please do *not* number scenes. After making copies of your screenplay, be sure to check for any missing pages. Nothing is more frustrating or annoying to a potential buyer (and possibly damaging to your chances for a sale) than coming to an important or crucial part of a story only to find a page or two is missing.

If you've followed the checklist above as well as the guidelines for standard screenplay formatting, you should be in good professional-looking shape. One of the most reliable references for screenplay formatting is *Formatting* by David Trottier, which can be ordered through most bookstores. The WGA also puts out a brief, concise pamphlet on formatting. You can contact the WGA for details on obtaining this helpful booklet.

10. Is this a story that I love?

My advice to new writers is to make your script a story that you love. It doesn't have to be a story that's commercial, but it should be well-written. Few writers sell their first script, but it's the first few scripts which can signal an agent that you are a writer who's consistent, determined, and passionate.

In speaking with scores of successful screenwriters through the years, it's interesting to note that it takes an average of seven to eight scripts before a writer obtains his/her first agent or has his/her work optioned or purchased. Only one writer sold her very first script and she was quick to add that it took her five more years before she had another sale. Another screenwriter wrote fifteen scripts before he got an option and he confided, in hindsight, his first ten screenplays are an embarrassment to him, but were necessary practice.

It's also important that new scriptors understand that most potential buyers are looking at screenplays with two key questions in mind:

• Is this a project that's appropriate for my company?

• Is this a writer that warrants a spot on my Writers List for future projects and rewrites?

Many times I've read a screenplay which wasn't appropriate for the studio where I was employed, but the writing was so impressive that I put the writer on a list for upcoming open writing assignments.

Keep in mind that each of your screenplays should be a labor of love that exhibits strong writing and storytelling skills that should translate into a "calling card" script which will open the doors for future work.

Some words of wisdom: Once you've completed a script, immediately suppress the urge to rest on your laurels. After a congratulatory sip of champagne or designer water, get to work on your next screenplay. Agents and production execs just love doing business with fast, prolific, creative talent!

With more than twenty-five years of industry experience, Kathie Fong Yoneda has worked for such prestigious studios as Paramount, Columbia, MGM, Universal, 20th Century Fox, and

Disney, specializing in story analysis and development of live action and animated projects. Her career includes executive positions with Walt Disney, Touchstone, Island Pictures, and Walt Disney TV Animation where she has evaluated more than 18,000 submissions.

Kathie has presented more than 100 workshops and seminars throughout the US, Canada, Europe (Germany, Austria, France, Ireland, England, Italy, Spain) and Australia and has written a popular column on screenwriting and the entertainment industry. She's been published in Writers Aide, Screen Talk, Script Writer, *and* Portable Writer's Conference *and has been interviewed or written articles for dozens of magazines, newspapers, e-zines, radio segments, and television shows. She was a guest of the Soviet Peace Committee for a ground-breaking ten-day media symposium in Moscow and was also a keynote speaker for Asian-Pacific Heritage Month at The Smithsonian Institute.*

Kathie and noted script consultant/author Dr. Linda Seger developed a highly-successful six-day seminar for the training of development executives in Ireland. In addition to seminars with Linda, Kathie also team-teaches with Pamela Wallace (writer-producer, co-writer of Oscar-winning Witness*) and Pamela Jaye Smith (author of* Inner Drives, *creator of* Mythworks*), and is a member of the Writers University on-line faculty.*

Kathie is an independent script consultant whose clientele includes several award-winning writers. She is the author of The Script Selling Game: A Hollywood Insider's Look at Getting Your Script Sold and Produced, *which is in its third printing. She is also a principal in TalkStory Productions with Pamela Wallace and Jason Lau, and they are co-executive producers on the upcoming cable series,* Beyond the Break.

Scoping Out Magazines

*Use a magazine's own pages
to learn how to hear "Yes!" from its editor*

By Ania Savage

THERE ARE CERTAIN PREREQUISITES FOR SELLING your work to magazine markets. The one imperative you probably already know is that you must read the magazines where you want to publish, not occasionally but every issue. Yet, this kind of prepping—although essential— is only the beginning. Does this surprise you?

Where most nascent writers err—and sometimes even those who have been selling for a while—is that they approach a magazine as a reader. What they—and you—need to do is to analyze the magazine as a potential contributor.

Reading back issues is important since such study reveals what subjects a magazine has reported on in the past and what it is likely to cover in the near future. Reading submerges you in the magazine's personality, distinctive voice and editorial point of view. But the writer who wants to sell has to push on beyond this essential knowledge. The writer needs to find answers to these basic questions:

• What is the overall focus of this magazine?

• What is the typical reader's economic situation, education, interests?

• How do I read the editor's mind to discover what he or she is looking for now?

- Are my credentials similar to those of the regular contributors?

- How will my article or story idea fit in this magazine?

Some of this information may be gleaned from *Writer's Market*, an annual compendium of magazines and what they buy from freelancers, or by browsing *The American Directory of Writer's Guidelines*, a collection of writer's guidelines, both available at your library or bookstore. Writer's guidelines may also be obtained from most magazines if you send them a self-addressed, stamped envelope (SASE). But these sources, though necessary and excellent, are not enough.

Writers who succeed in selling articles are often those who supplement this information with information that is readily available but which not many writers use.

So pick up two or three issues of the magazine that you want to write for and together let's scope them out as a seasoned professional would.

Start with the cover

Place the magazines next to each other and study the covers. Yes, that is where you start. Examine the photo or art on each cover. Editors choose cover art with exceeding care. They agonize over it. Why? For two reasons: One, the cover sells the magazine at the checkout counter. Remember the furor when actress Demi Moore appeared naked on the cover of *Vanity Fair*? That issue sold out nationwide.

Two, the cover tells you at a glance what the magazine is all about. One of the most dramatic changes in cover art occurred in 1995 when *Modern Maturity* (new title: *AARP The Magazine,*) the nation's largest circulation magazine, got a facelift. Out went head shots of such venerable "senior citizens" as Dr. Joyce Brothers and in came hard hitting, provocative art. The first "new" cover showed a splayed figure of a woman crushed under a heavy square block. When asked, the editors said that the cover was the "culmination of five years of change" as the magazine, published bimonthly by the American Association of Retired Persons, refocused itself on a new audience—the aging baby-boomers.

Magazines, like people, have a unique personality. The cover gives you the first inkling of a magazine's personality, just as a person's face and hair style do. *Vanity Fair* tries to be provocative, while *People Weekly* is a breathless fan of the latest celebrity and the newest wrinkle in American pop culture.

What do the covers of the magazine you are examining tell you? That this magazine is helpful? Flippant? Highbrow? Outrageous? Service oriented? As you jot down your evaluation, ask yourself: Do the covers share a common denominator? What kind of statement about itself is the magazine making on the covers? Whom would the covers attract?

Study the blurbs

Don't leave the covers just yet. Many magazines have cover blurbs, which are teasers usually printed in bold colors (yellow and red are favorites) aimed at impulse buyers at the newsstand. Ask yourself: How do the blurbs or teasers relate to the cover art or photo? Do they reemphasize what is pictured? Do they stress a particular type of story, or a variety of stories? Are they human interest, personal experience, or how-to stories? Notice the similarities in blurbs from issue to issue. Can you discern a trend? A particular emphasis on a subject, or type of article? A point of view? A story mix?

Jot down what subjects are repeated or stressed in the cover blurbs. Examining blurbs not only reveals trends, but also tells you what the editors think is most important inside the magazine.

Now fast forward to the contents page of each issue and mark in the margin the stories that you saw highlighted in the blurbs or teasers on the covers, then close the magazines.

Check out the advertisers

Whether we, as writers, like it or not, a magazine is a dual product. About half of it is editorial content while the other half is advertising. Too many beginning writers pay attention only to the editorial content. They should also pore over the advertising half. To do so, flip the magazines over to the back covers and examine them. More likely than not the back covers will be full page advertisements. The back cover ad, plus the one inside the front cover and the one on the first page (or pages), sell at a premium, several thousand dollars above the cost of other full-page ads. These "front-of-the-book" and back cover locations are considered prime exposure and are purchased by advertisers who believe that the magazine's readers are likely prospects for the product or service being advertised.

> "Magazines, like people, have a unique personality."

As you study the ads, imagine the person who would buy the product or service being advertised, or the person who would fit easily into the environment pictured in the advertisements. Often, the same advertiser purchases a certain location for several consecutive months. But don't stop with a single advertiser. Get an ad consensus. Examine the ads inside the front covers and inside each issue. Who advertises in this magazine most often? Whom are the advertisers targeting? Is it mostly teenage girls? Female college students? Young professionals? Female *and* male, or just one gender? Magazines are very narrowly focused to appeal to a specific segment of the population. That's what a magazine's "niche" is.

Advertisers know what type of people make up this niche so studying a magazine's advertisements will tell you a great deal about the magazine's readers, their interests, their buying habits, their concerns and, of singular importance to you, what kind of stories would interest them.

Jot down what you discover are the characteristics of the typical reader. List the gender, age group, education level, occupation, place of residence (regional, city or suburban) and hazard a guess at the income level. The trends you have spotted in the blurbs on the cover should dovetail into your readership analysis. Thus, if the cover photo is of a beautiful young model and the cover blurbs emphasize articles on dating and makeup, more likely than not the ads you examined were for cosmetics, perfumes and perhaps for trendy clothing. Now ask yourself: "Would a person who is likely to buy this magazine and the products advertised in it be interested in a story on _____?" If the answer is not a resounding yes, you should do some more thinking and refocusing before you query this publication.

Peruse the editor's own words

Flip through the magazines until you come to the editor's letter or column. Often this page precedes the contents page, but not always. Some magazines have a publisher's letter and an editor's letter. These letters are addressed to readers. Read them.

Some of the best known letters from the editor are those written by retired *Cosmopolitan* chief Helen Gurley Brown, the legendary editor who created the Cosmo Girl. Brown described this woman in her monthly letters—a savvy, fun loving, not too innocent young woman who works and plays hard—and her vision created one of the great successes in publishing in this century.

The letter from the editor highlights what the editor *hopes* will interest the typical reader. Can you see this editor lauding your idea in her monthly letter? Sometimes these letters reveal the personality of the editor, his peeves, her interests. Will your article catch the editor's attention? Since the editor will be the final decision maker on whether your idea is published or not, get to know this editor by studying what he or she writes.

Sift the table of contents

Next, turn to the contents page. It is usually divided into departments and features. The departments remain the same issue to issue, while the features change with trends, seasons of the year, and sometimes even with advertising requirements. For example, if the ad sales department feels several large appliance advertisers could be lured with a special issue on kitchens, a house-and-garden magazine is likely to run an issue that is partially or wholly devoted to features on kitchen design, remodeling and cooking equipment.

Examine the contents page, paying special attention to feature articles, traditionally a freelance market. Focus on the articles you had highlighted as those that were promoted in blurbs or teasers on the cover. Do these articles reveal a trend, a certain kind of story line, a unique way of examining a subject? Is there a "formula" for writing a story for this magazine? If so, add this information to your analysis. What is the mix of personal stories, how-to articles, profiles? Will your idea fit the magazine's story mix? Where will it fit?

Return to the features and read them not for enjoyment, but as an editor would read them. Ask yourself: Why was this article published? How does it serve—or entertain—the magazine's readers? If I were the editor, what other subjects or issues would I address in the coming months? A year from now? Is there a new way of looking at a subject already done by this magazine?

Study the departments

Departments deal with the same topic, such as investing, real estate, dining, etc. Since magazines maintain a certain consistency in editorial content from issue to issue, departments are often written by the same person, who is an expert on the subject covered. There are magazines, however, which welcome freelance material for their departments. Jot down the subjects covered in these columns before proceeding to your next stop, which will tell you whether the departments are open or not to freelancers.

Find the editorial masthead. Often it comes after the contents page and lists the names of the people who write for and edit the magazine, starting with the editor-in-chief. Read down the list and notice if there are special editors for certain subjects, such as real estate, cooking, wine, etc. Then flip back to the contents page and see who wrote the column in each department. Sometimes you have to flip to the page on which the column appears to see who the author is. If the department is written by one of the specialty editors whose name appears on the masthead, you are out of luck. This means that the department is produced by an in-house expert. Also, if a department column is not bylined, that is usually an indication that it is written in-house, probably by several people. As you are reading the masthead, make sure to look for "contributing editors." These are people who are freelancers who regularly write on a particular subject for that magazine. Often, contributing editors are department columnists.

With your thumb marking the masthead page, flip forward to the feature articles. Who is writing them? Check the bylines against the names on the masthead. You may discover that most of the bylines repeat the names on the masthead or the features are not bylined. This means that a good portion of the magazine is written in-house or by part-time contributing editors and the publication is not a good freelance market. Of course, the opposite is true: If the names don't match those on the masthead you probably have stumbled on a good prospect for your freelance work.

Analyze the competition

Let's assume you discover several bylines that do not correspond to any names on the masthead. This is your competition. To find out who these people are, you look in three places. First, study the contents page to see if there is a "contributors" listing. This listing is usually in front of the magazine, near the contents page. Read it carefully. Sometimes, contributors are named in the editor's letter. If you strike out in these places, scan down the columns of the article. Often a small blurb on the contributor appears either on the bottom of the first page of the article or at the conclusion of the piece.

Examine dispassionately these thumbnail biographies. Is yours similar? If you want to write a piece on jogging for a sports magazine, and the contributors are either athletes who excel in the sport or people with doctorates in sports medicine, and you don't share these or similar attributes, then you may be out of your league. Your qualifications need to be similar to those of other contributors in order for your query to be taken seriously and for the editors to feel comfortable in giving you an assignment.

Write down the qualifications of the writers on your analysis sheet. Then do one more thing, check back issues to see if these writers have published in this magazine before. If you find one or two that are regular contributors, read everything—and I do mean everything—these writers have published in this magazine. Obviously they know what sells in this market and you will have a greater chance of selling your work by analyzing their successes.

Contact the marketing department

There is one more thing you can do to increase your chances of contacting the magazine at the right time with the right idea.

Many magazines develop an "editorial calendar" that lists the subjects they will be highlighting during the calendar year. (Remember the example about the large appliance advertisers?)

These calendars are distributed to advertisers to keep them abreast of what subjects a magazine plans to explore in the near future. You can call the marketing department of the magazine and ask that an editorial calendar be sent to you. Sometimes you may be asked if you are interested in placing an ad. You can reply with whatever you feel comfortable saying, but the truth, that you're a freelancer studying your potential markets, should work. Many magazines do demographic surveys of their readers. Some, especially women's magazines, publish these surveys in the magazine. Ask the marketing department if a recent survey of readers or a demographic profile is available and ask that a copy be included in the material they send you.

Sell your work

Study what you have written down. Look at the big picture. Your analysis should have revealed what kind of stories the magazine is publishing right now, who its readers are, their interests, and whether this magazine is a freelance market that uses writers with your qualifications. Use this information to focus the query you'll send to the editor.

Be sure to select a market in which you feel at home, a magazine whose readers are not unlike you. Writers who take the time to find their niche are writers who gain an edge on the competition.

Ania Savage is an award-winning journalist, editor and freelance writer whose work has appeared in a number of national publications, including the New York Times, USA Today and House Beautiful. Ania also teaches nonfiction writing at the University of Denver and Metropolitan State College of Denver.

She has been a writer and editor for such nationally-known companies as Time-Life Books, National Geographic Society's World magazine and National Geographic's books. Among Ania's many awards are first place in the National Writers Club's Novel Writing Contest and finalist in the National Magazine Award competition.

Interviewing & Quoting

"Judge a man, not by his answers, but by his questions." —Voltaire

By Cork Millner

"Madam, Adam."
"Eve."

And so began the world's first "interview." The ensuing question and answer session must have been fascinating. Unfortunately, there wasn't a third party, a writer with a tape recorder, on the scene to record it.

What if Barbara Walters had been on hand to chat with Cleopatra and Mark Antony? What if Mike Wallace had been able to confront Genghis Khan? What if Howard Cosell had been there to interview David and Goliath before their big fight? What if *any* of today's interviewers had been there to question Shakespeare on the opening night of *Hamlet?*

I once asked actor Don Murray this question: "Of all the famous personalities in recorded history, who would you like most to have lunch with?" His quick response was, "Jesus."

Jesus Christ is a fascinating enigma because no one with a list of questions interviewed him. Would Jesus be such a mystery today if he had been interviewed by a newscaster from the CNN Network? Imagine sitting down for a background talk with Moses. How about John the Baptist? Pontius Pilate? A Roman centurion?

Studs Terkel, whose interview books included *Working* and *The Good War* are virtually devoid of famous personalities, once said that his biggest fantasy was to be at the foot of Calvary with a tape recorder. What, he wondered, went through the minds of the masses when Christ was crucified?

Would these people have agreed to an interview? Would Shakespeare? Would Napoleon? Would George Washington?

From the beginning of time people have delighted in talking about themselves. Answering questions gives an individual an air of importance and boosts his or her ego. As journalist/interviewer A. J. Liebling said, "We are an articulate people, pleased by attention, covetous of being singled out." Fortunately for the writer, people love to talk about themselves, their work, and their personal expertise.

Quotes lend credibility

Getting firsthand, expert quotes will beef up any nonfiction work and make it more salable. Learning the interviewing process will enable to writer to add vitality, credibility and an authoritative voice to a manuscript.

A writer can't know everything. You may want to write an article on divorce settlements. Whom to interview? A divorce attorney. Let's say you are writing a story on Columbus' perilous journey across the Atlantic to the New World. Whom do you interview? An historian with expertise in that era. Want to write a piece on Mom and Pop grocery stores? Whom do you interview? Mom and Pop.

A student writer decided to write about ATMs, the automatic tellers that banks use to provide patrons with day-and-night cash and deposit facilities. Whom did the writer interview? Her husband—an ATM repairman! From him she got great quotes—"Look, Sarah, I told you so. There *is* a little man in that machine!"—and wrote the story.

Where do you find these experts? It's as simple as running your fingers through the Yellow Pages or using a search engine the Internet. Anyone, from magicians to marble cutters, from wine consultants to zoologists, can be easily found.

Getting these "experts" to agree to a brief interview, especially a telephone or e-mail interview, is easy. Professionals like to make statements, to show their expertise, to see their name in print. Just explain what you are doing—"I'm writing an article on emergency care centers, called 'The McDonald's of Medicine,' and I'd like to get your opinion of their place in the medical profession." You'll get answers.

Quotes add variety, entertainment and readability

You're in the dentist's office for a checkup. You pick up a magazine, thumb through the pages and come across an article that interests you enough to start reading. After a few minutes your mind wanders and you have to reread paragraphs. Boring stuff. Your concentration trails off and you shake your head to get back on track. Nope, still boring. Like so many other articles you have read, this one can't maintain your interest. What went wrong? The idea was stimulating. The title was intriguing....

The problem was the middle. It was just plain dull.

Capturing the reader's attention with an exciting lead isn't enough. If you do not want your article to stimulate the yawn reflex, then you'll have to write with variety. Monotony in writing is like a paralyzing frost. The Greeks were aware of the value of variety and contrast: They set off the beauty of flowers by planting them next to onions and leeks.

To ensure interest in the "body" of your material here are six techniques that can improve your writing:

- Narrative

- Anecdotes

- Quotes

- Imagery

- Creating a scene

- Character, action, and dialogue

A mix of these attention-grabbing elements throughout the article will add that needed variety—and readability. Call it a writing recipe. Like a master chef, you can spice up your writing by adding enticing ingredients: a pinch of dialogue, a teaspoonful of quotes, a dash of anecdotes, and a cup of imagery. For instance, here's an anecdote that is a quote, and has dialogue and imagery:

> Dame Judith Anderson is standing on the edge of the movie set between takes while the cameras and lighting equipment are being reset. An electrician on a ladder yells down to her: "Hey, Judy, baby, move over a few feet!"
>
> The great dramatic actress slowly swivels her head upward and in her deep resonant voice says, "It's *Dame* Judy Baby!"

Here's a quote that a student writer used to begin an article:

> "Frankly, my dear, I don't give a damn."

By using this familiar line from *Gone with the Wind*, the writer has caught the reader's attention. It has impact because we didn't expect it and wonder how it ties in with the article. (In this case, the piece was about communication and angry, walk-out-the-door scenes in marriages.)

In the beginning (the lead) of an article, quotes can be used in two ways:

1. *Preceding the text.* To do this indent or center the quote on the page below the title and the author's byline, then space and state who said the quote. Double-space and begin the text.

2. *Within the text.* You may want to use the quote as your lead sentence or paragraph. Just start typing.

Styles of quotes

An interview does not have to be a two-hour session for the purpose of writing a personality profile. You may catch a teacher in a hallway, an actor behind stage, a writer on tour, a guide on her bus, and have only time enough for one or two questions. Here are the different styles of quotes you may encounter.

• *The quick quote.* On a trip to Scotland my guide was a Scotsman who wore a kilt. Of course, I had to ask:

> "What do you wear under your kilt?"
> With an impish grin, he answered,
> "Why, nothing's worn. Everything's in perfect working order."

• *The dialogue quote.* If you are involved in a conversation about a subject you are going to write an article on, record the dialogue. I visited Devil's Island, the infamous French penal colony, and wrote an article that sold to *Islands* magazine. It included many dialogue quotes, such as this one:

> "Welcome to *l'Ile Royale, Monsieur*," the Frenchman said, flipping the blackened cigarette into the sea. A whisper of air rushed through the palm trees and the Frenchman squinted suspiciously at the rustling leaves for a moment. He shrugged, then turned back to me and nodded to the neighboring island. "Saint Joseph. The *bagnards*, the prisoners, called it *la mangeuse d'hommes*, the devourer of men. On the island there was a special prison called the Reclusion. It was the place of solitary confinement. Few survived."
> "And Devil's Island?" I asked. I had yet to see the island, hidden from view by the 500-foot-high plateau of Royale.

"Ah, *l'I'le du Diable*," he sighed. "The *bagnards* called it the dry guillotine. Few survived on Devil's Island."

• *The extended interview.* You may want to sit down with a recorder and talk to someone, perhaps an expert on the subject, or simply someone who has something interesting to say. This example is from the article, "The Spirit of the Delta Queen."

> I had the opportunity to interview the Delta Queen's Master, Captain Michael Monaghan, who, at age sixty-four, was on his last cruise. "I've been on the river forty-three years," he told me, his face showing the deep lines that come from living with the ever-changing eccentricities of the Mississippi. "The river has its own smell, its own flow." He paused, scratching at his chin. "Nothing better than a nice clear night going up river to make me feel good. You know, I'd like to have captained a paddlewheeler a hundred years ago, to live back then with a plantation on the Mississippi to come home to." He nodded his head. "I'll miss this old boat."

The complete interview lasted twenty minutes, of which I used about half of the quotes for the story. Note that the mixture of dialogue and narrative make the information more palatable.

Quotes from other sources

Usable quotes don't always come directly from a one-on-one interview. There are many sources to obtain quotes that can be used in adding variety and readability to your writing. Such as:

• *Books and magazines.* Yes, you can quote from the writing or other writers. You must attribute it to that writer and where it was written. Here's an example from my article, "Devil's Island—the Green Hell." I found very little research material on Devil's Island. One of the books I used was *Papillon* by Henri Charriere, a fascinating story about a prisoner's life on the island. The following *quote* not only shows the brutality (which was the slant of the article) of life in the penal colony, but is also strikingly visual.

> In his autobiography, Papillon, the celebrated inmate who spent twelve years imprisoned on the islands and escaped to tell about it, described the burial of a fellow prisoner, a close friend named Matthieu: "Wrapped in flour sacks, Matthieu's body slid from the small boat into

the water. Jesus! He was no sooner in the water—for good, I thought—than he rose above the surface, lifted by, I don't know, seven, ten, maybe twenty sharks. The flour sacks were torn off, and for perhaps two or three seconds Matthieu seemed to be literally standing on the water. His right forearm was already gone. With half his body out of the water he was bearing down on our boat when an eddy caught him and he disappeared ... Everybody, guards included, was terror-stricken."

• *Comic strip quotes.* Why not add a bit of humor to your article? If you are not funny, then quote from another source, perhaps the funny papers. Here's a comic strip quote that fits in nicely with the interviewing process. It's from *Calvin and Hobbes,* created by Bill Watterson:

> Calvin enters the kitchen where his mother is cooking. He says, "Hi mom. I'm making my own newspaper to report the events of our household."
> Mom: "That's nice."
> Calvin, paper and pen in hand: "Now I'm looking for a page one lead story. Can I interview you?"
> Mom: "Sure."
> Calvin: "OK, what are you cutting up there for dinner?"
> Mom: "Fish."
> Calvin, writing furiously: "Knife wielding mother hacks ichthyoid! Grim melee is evening ritual! Suburban family devours victim!"
> Mother: "Out of the kitchen. Out! Out!"

• *Television and radio quotes* from prominent or outspoken people can also attract the reader's attention and add vitality and credibility to a manuscript. I happened to be writing a story for *The Saturday Evening Post* titled "The TV Games People Play," about what it takes to be a game show contestant. Here's a quote I got from watching the *Oprah* show: (Note that it is attributed to the person who said the line, not Oprah.)

> "What kind of contestant are we looking for? It takes a type," says Mark Goodson, TV's godfather of game shows. "We want hype and we want enthusiasm, personality and a little reasoning ability. And you can't fake it. It has to be there!"

• *Quotes from writers:* As a lead for my workshop in this book, I have quoted a line from a famous author which pertains to the craft of writing. Here's another for good measure:

> When asked what it took to be a novelist, author Somerset Maugham replied: "There are three rules for writing the novel. Unfortunately, no one knows what they are."

• *Quotes from experts*. Experts are all over the place, in books, magazines, on television, on-line. Quote them.

Telephone interviewing

Need to interview someone in New York, Los Angeles, perhaps Sedona, Arizona? No problem. Pick up the telephone and say who you are, what you are writing, for whom, and that you'd like five minutes of their time to ask a few questions. (Even better send an advance letter or e-mail to prepare them.) I once interviewed a Hollywood film director on his cell phone while he drove the Los Angeles freeway. Scared *me*.

> "Why not add a bit of humor to your article? If you are not funny, then quote from another source"

Once you've got the interviewee on the telephone, here are a few suggestions to get those succulent quotes:

• Tape-record the interview. Many answering machines have this ability, or you can get a connection to hook up your recorder to the phone from such electronic stores as Radio Shack.

• Inform the interviewee that the session will be recorded (federal law). If you get a "No", then pull out your note pad.

• Keep the questions short, clear and to the point. If you don't understand what is being said, clarify immediately.

• Fifteen minutes for a telephone interview is enough. Call back if you need to ask further questions.

Cork Millner has written over 500 magazine articles and fifteen nonfiction books, including Hollywood Be Thy Name—The Warner Brothers Story *(which has been optioned for a Broadway musical), and a book on creative nonfiction writing titled,* Write from the Start. Portraits *is a collection of twenty interviews with such celebrities as Ronald Reagan, Jimmy Stewart, John Travolta, Sharon Stone, and Jane Seymour. He is the conference coordinator of the Santa Barbara Writers Conference and the annual Santa Barbara Writers Workshop.*

The Hidden Hazards of Being an Author

What they don't tell you in creative writing class

By Persia Woolley

EVERYTHING HAS ITS DOWN SIDE: falling in love, recycling newspapers, eating chocolate for breakfast. And, I suppose, every profession has its pitfalls.

But no one thinks to warn authors and/or their families about the hidden dangers of writing for a living. Quite apart from the obvious threats— hordes of readers waiting to mob you when you step outside your door; TV producers turning your life into a weekly series (if you write mysteries, that is), or irate fans holding you captive to their own plot devices—there are dark and secret aspects of the profession known only to the initiated.

First is the dearth of personal correspondence that descends on a working author. "Why don't you just drop me a line?" my father says, not being computer literate. "I love your e-mails—have saved every one," a friend admits. "Can't wait to check my mail," claims a fan.

And me? Am I whacking out letters at an astonishing clip, flooding cyber space with examples of deathless epistolary art? *No way*. I'm reaching for the telephone, because no matter what it does to my bank account, it's a lot less crazy-making than sitting at the computer when I'm not writing prose.

Dalton Trumbo summed it up pretty well when he told one demanding correspondent, "I do this for a living; how impertinent for you to expect me to write to you gratis."

Probably few authors think of their letters as deathless prose (though it's amusing how many of us save every single scrap just in case some discerning graduate student wants to research us for his or her thesis). Still and all, whether as hard copy or an e-mail, what starts out to be a casual half-hour communiqué can easily turn into a flood of words that go on for pages, must be edited and re-edited, checked for spelling and printed out in draft form for final proofing. The whole morning has gone by and you're lucky to have produced more than a single letter to the hardware store!

So when friends and family grumble that you never write, or worry that you're spending too much money on telephones, tell them it's one of the hidden hazards of authorship.

Second, once you get published everyone wants to share your good fortune. Your kindergarten teacher is thrilled to discover you've become a Book-of-the-Month Club author, and promptly suggests that the two of you collaborate on a book about an elf who lives under a cabbage plant. How do you tell her, nicely and politely, that your horizons have shifted since those good old childhood days and you now specialize in works on serial murderers?

Then there's the classic "I've got this wonderful idea for a novel. I'll give you the story if you'll write the book, and we can split the profits."

It's generally said with a straight face and deep sincerity...they are, after all, offering to share their brain child with you. So it's not fair to double over with hysterical laughter. At least, not the first time they say it. These people want to be taken seriously...and some, God help us, may be important in your life. Surely you don't want to alienate your landlady's cousin, the mayor's wife or the only mechanic in town who can coax another thousand miles out of your old Subaru.

For them—and your own future tranquility—it's worth it to learn how to tactfully explain that lack of ideas are rarely the author's problem. They pop up everywhere: out of the newspaper, over tea with a neighbor or when you're covered with soap in the middle of a shower. (The person who invents a waterproof board on which a writer can scribble priceless notions while the shower is running, then easily erase it before the next bath time, will make a fortune; calling out for the cat to jot down something for you just doesn't work.)

Another of those catch-22s is agreeing to look at a friend's manuscript. Everyone says they're writing a book, but finding someone who's actually produced one is a real rarity, so it's easy to be enthusiastic...until you read the thing. If the work is absolutely awful, you may have to say, "Gee, George, I think you'd better stick with plumbing."

And there's the fan who writes great letters of praise (isn't all praise great?), then mails you not thirty but two hundred pages of her manuscript, most of which are different versions of the same chapter. Even if it's a winner, chances are you never intended to end up playing editor for her.

In the long run, instead of agreeing to look at their work, it's far more humane to tell friends and relatives that in spite of being a writer, you never learned to read.

Speaking of friends, there's a perilously thin line between immortalizing them in your prose and making yourself a pariah. All authors mine their own lives for material and people, but there can be some pretty weird fall-out if your portrait of Jenny is too recognizable. Thomas Wolfe dissected his family in *Look Homeward Angel,* only to discover he'd been disowned. The fact that one of his later books is titled *You Can't Go Home Again* should tell you something.

If you just can't resist using a real person or circumstance in your newest work, better not mention it to anyone. No matter how you present it, they're likely to take umbrage; if you're too accurate they'll deny it vehemently, and if you fictionalize the character or story too much, they'll complain it wasn't that way at all. Worse yet, if your book is very popular and everyone is trying to figure out who is who, feuds may develop between friends all wanting to claim the same role. I live in a small town where three ladies, now in their nineties, haven't spoken to each other for forty years because each is convinced she was the model for the lover in a popular book written by a local author shortly after World War II...and every one of the dears is adamant that the other two are outright imposters. No point in causing bad blood if you don't have to.

The closer you get to home, (as in under the same roof), the more trying the hazards become. Living with a partner is difficult enough without introducing the peculiarities of authorship. Most of us carry around notebooks in which we record bits of inspiration, information and general trivia...including great quotes that we absolutely must save for posterity. Do you wonder if your companion gets a little uneasy during those times when you're looking for a pen all the while muttering scraps of dialogue over and over lest you lose them entirely? Not only strangers but housemates may start looking at you oddly.

Then too, most writers live in a house of paper, surrounded by notes, clippings, articles, magazines, books and all those pages of earlier drafts of your magnum opus. Indeed, many authors are obsessive about hanging on to every scrap, as though printing might suddenly cease and there wouldn't be anything left to read but their own carefully hoarded supply.

A certain amount of saving is worthwhile, though keeping every one of the first nine versions of your book may be taking it to extremes. Yet as soon as you toss out the first five, some editor is going to say "Can't you do so-and-so..." and nothing is worse than realizing you lined last week's garbage pail with exactly what you need now. So you keep it all—at least until the book is off the presses. Call it a kind of security blanket that might prove to be crucial if some mega monster destroys all your electronic files.

Usually these papers pile up in unsightly stacks, get shoved into cardboard boxes or spill dangerously over the edges of bookcases. You know which pile is which, and are sure that letting a stranger loose to tidy it up will make chaos out of an already questionable universe, even if that stranger is your Significant Other. Not only years of research but your whole sense of stability can be demolished by a well-meaning neatnik. So think twice before you let someone else in your writing area; marriages have ended for less, I'm sure.

Even more important, however, is the undeniable fact that if you are a working novelist, you inhabit two worlds, one of which nobody else can see. Makes things a bit awkward from time to time.

Say your partner comes in cheerful from an evening at the bowling alley to find you sitting at the computer in a state of shock. Tears stream down your face, his good mood has to make a sudden adjustment, and while he frantically asks "Is it the children? Did someone run over the dog?" all you can do is shake your head in despair.

> "...if you are a working novelist, you inhabit two worlds, one of which nobody else can see."

That sort of thing is hard enough on you, but you chose to become a novelist, to live inside and care deeply about what happens to your characters. Your partner, on the other hand, comes to it second hand and half the time hasn't a clue what's tearing you up so badly. Eventually you'll be able to tell him one of your favorite characters just got run over by a herd of buffalo and lies dying on the prairie—a sad, cruel ending you didn't even see coming. Until then, however (and certainly the first time it happens), he'll probably go nuts trying to figure out what's upsetting you. No wonder so many authors are single.

So much for interacting with the rest of humanity. Difficult as it is, it's only half the picture; there's all the other stuff that affects you only.

Take the question of lifestyle. Sedentary lifestyle. You just think that's middle-age spread setting in a little early! Whether it's sitting at a keyboard or reading for your research, the author's muscles turn to flab and arteries clog up in direct proportion to the amount of time spent earning the money that puts those calories on the table.

Nor are there any simple solutions to this one. Ever tried typing while jogging in place? Or stopping to do a dozen sit-ups every hour, leaving your heroine to fend off three rabid dogs and a human lunatic without your help? Somehow the need for physical toning is low on the list of priorities at such moments.

It has been said that we use up more calories if we work standing up. Thomas Wolfe is the only author I've ever heard of who did such a thing, using the top of a refrigerator crate as support for the paper on which he hand-scribbled his prose. But Wolfe was a giant of a man who simply didn't fit into common desk chairs back in the twenties, before the word ergonomics was even invented, and he probably stood more for comfort than for health reasons. So if you want to retain your sylph-like shape, and/or stay healthy, best to put aside time for regular sessions at the gym.

Which brings us to the most treacherous hazard of all...time. Time is a very peculiar dimension, assuming different characteristics depending on the circumstances. Most notably, when the words are flowing and your fingers flying, hours—even whole days—can disappear without you being aware of it. Most everyone else notices things like sunrise and sunset, and it probably takes another writer to understand that you missed the whole of Thursday because something wonderful happened in your head. This tendency for writing to eclipse all else may account for why most mothers don't start writing full-time until their youngsters are grown and gone, or at least able to feed, clothe, and transport themselves throughout the community.

But an author's time is seen differently by the rest of the world. Friends are afraid to contact you, imagining that you slave over the computer every waking hour, and they don't want to frighten away your muse. Fans too often imagine that you spend your time lolling by the pool, scheduling cruises or shopping endlessly. (Sounds as if they should try writing fantasy.)

In any event, your time is your own, to do with as you wish, and *oy vey*, what a lot of trouble *that* invites! For the workaholic it's an open invitation to pig-out. What do you mean other professionals only put in twelve-hour days on their job? The compulsive-obsessive writer *never* stops working. One fellow I know generally had two books and a syndicated column going at all times. Finally, after twenty years of this, his long-suffering wife dragged him off on a vacation, threatening to divorce him if he didn't leave his typewriter behind. Afterwards he proclaimed—with a wry grin—that the vacation had been a success; during the week he was in the Bahamas, he only sent home ninety-eight postcards.

It's also the perfect profession for the procrastinator. How many of us have heard a friend or colleague bemoan that they just need another week of research, a bit more tinkering with the plot, or—may the saints protect them—they are "waiting for inspiration" before starting to write?

(For those of you who are novices, Thomas Edison was right when he announced that genius is 1 percent inspiration and 99 percent perspiration. If you wait for the muse to strike, you'll be stuck on Chapter 3 for the rest of your life.)

Lastly, there's the problem of money...you remember, that stuff with Ben Franklin's picture on it, the stuff that motivates other people to do whatever it is that they do instead of writing.

Most authors understand the lack of it—less than 5 percent of us make enough money at writing alone to live on it, though everyone else assumes we're rolling in dough. But like the hazard of time, money's a double-edged sword.

Try applying for a loan when your last check runs out. Sure your credit rating is fine, but that's because you shop at thrift stores and always pay cash. And everyone knows you're a solid citizen in spite of being a writer; haven't run through the streets naked since you came to live here. You think that's going to sway the bank in your favor when you can't show any income for the last ten months? Ha, Gulliver, let me introduce you to a Lilliputian....

The other edge of the sword begins to gleam when you finally do get paid. Because it's usually in a chunk, your money feels like a fortune, whether it's $10,000 or $100,000. So even after you've paid off long-time IOUs to the friends who helped you through the lean times, bought as many frozen dinners as the freezer will hold, and patched up that big, open hole in the roof before the rains come, chances are you're still tempted to order champagne, caviar and dinner for everyone at the best restaurant in town. You do, and they all know you're a spendthrift, wastrel and improvident artist. You don't, and you're chalked up to being a miser, a misanthrope and ingrate. On this one, there's no way to win.

Worse yet is hitting it very big very early. Aside from the pressure to repeat the feat for next year's list, there's the problem of assuming the money will last forever. Who, on receiving a check for six figures, has the foresight to recognize that unless you're careful it can slip through your fingers in an appallingly short time? Whether it's $100,000 or $500,000 it isn't going to last forever and you may find yourself back to looking at the want ads again. Indeed, the bigger it is, the more likely we are to think it won't ever run out.

Since I'm a writer, not a financial consultant, the best advice I can give you is the traditional caution to actors— "Congratulations on getting the part, but don't quit your day job yet."

Considering the peculiarities, pitfalls, and outright hazards of being an author, why do we pursue the calling?

Why, indeed? How else could you achieve such a remarkable lifestyle with little more investment than a notebook and pen? Your time is your own to screw up any way you want. Your sanity is in question much of the time and your finances are sublimely uncomplicated, as long as you don't mind living on nothing. If you're a journalist, you get to go places and ask questions of people you'd never be able to get near otherwise. And if you're a novelist, you get to A) give voice to all those alter-egos and extra personalities that inhabit your head, B) play god and/or immortalize all the people you know, love or hate; and C) get paid for doing all of the above.

When you look at it that way, I can't imagine why anyone would do anything else, no matter what the hazards!

Persia Woolley *made the shift from nonfiction to novels twenty years ago with the publication of her Guinevere trilogy,* Child of the Northern Spring, Queen of the Summer Stars *and* Guinevere, the Legend in Autumn. *Since then Writer's Digest Books has published her* How to Write and Sell Historical Fiction. *Living in a small town, she writes for the weekly paper and several regional magazines, and at the moment she is completing* Ophelia's Story.

Giving Up?

When to toss in the towel
and when to keep trying

By Beverly Engel

I'm a well-known nonfiction writer with eighteen books to my credit, but several years ago I decided to write a novel. For the first time in my writing career I felt desperately in need of help. I decided to go to my first writer's conference, hoping to get some much needed assistance on the mechanics of fiction writing. During the networking sessions I met many other writers and learned that we all shared some common concerns. One of the concerns I heard voiced most often was, "How do I know when to give up on a project and when to keep trying?"

Many of the writers I met had just completed their writing project and had come to the conference hoping to get feedback and to meet agents and editors who might be interested in their work. Others had been trying for some time to sell their project. For example, one woman told me, "This is my last writers' conference. If I don't meet the right agent this time, I'm going to give up."

Marci is a good example of the first group. I met her the first night of the conference at a cocktail mixer. She was quite charming but very self-deprecating about her work, a novel she had just completed. The next time I saw her was the following evening when we had dinner together. She'd had quite an eventful day. She had a one-on-one conference with a famous agent who told her that she was extremely interested in her project and would love to take a look at it. In addition, in one of the workshops she attended, she read from her work and was given extremely positive feedback from the entire group, including the facilitator, an editor at a big publishing house.

Now, if all this had happened to me, you'd have to scrape me off the ceiling. But Marci told her story in a very lackluster way. When I got excited for her and asked her why she wasn't more thrilled she told me she was too frightened to be excited. "What if the agent doesn't like it once she sees it? What if it isn't really very good?" she agonized. Throughout dinner she obsessed over her situation. Ironically, it seemed that the positive feedback she'd received had actually caused her more anxiety than it had given her encouragement. I marveled to myself at how different her responses were than mine would have been.

The very next day I met a gentleman named James who had enthusiasm to burn. He was positive his mystery novel was going to get published. It was just a matter of time. When I asked him how long he'd been trying, he said five years. When I told him that five years seemed like an awfully long time he stated, "I don't care how long it takes. I know I've got a winner. I just have to hang in there."

I was amazed at the differences between these two people. One seemed like she'd given up before she'd even begun to try, and the other wasn't about to give up no matter how many rejection slips he got.

Since then I've met dozens of writers and I've noticed that speaking very generally, writers tend to fall into one of these two categories: 1) those who are insecure about their work and seem to give up easily, and 2) those who, despite numerous rejections, seem undaunted and strongly believe that their work will one day be published.

The first type tends to be shy about their work. They have difficulty showing it to others until it is "perfect," and are never quite sure it is any good, even when they get positive feedback.

The second type tend to believe their work is good, right from the start. They are eager to show it to people and are confident that their work is publishable. Positive feedback just confirms their belief in themselves and their work, negative feedback is rationalized away with, "I'm before my time," "These people don't appreciate my genius," or "She's just envious."

Being a psychotherapist, I couldn't help but wonder why there were these differences and what caused them. This workshop is the result of my research and observations. It is also about learning when to keep trying and when to move on.

Many people hold on to pie-in-the-sky dreams long after they've been given every indication that they need to go on to the next project. Others give up too easily, quit at the first rejection slip. Both types of people need to take a closer look at their attitude and behavior so they can recognize how they hold themselves back from achieving what they really desire.

Your level of self-esteem

What are the differences between these two types aside from their overt behavior? The first and perhaps most important difference seems to be their level of self-esteem. Our self-esteem affects our perception of our work to a tremendous degree. In fact, it can be argued that it affects it more than any other single factor—more than feedback from others, even more than how much actual talent we have.

If you are like Marci and have a difficult time accepting compliments or positive feedback about your work, you have a problem with low self-esteem, and this probably carries over into other aspects of your life. You may have noticed that people become very impatient or even angry with you because you constantly question whether you look okay, whether you said the right thing to someone, whether you are capable of completing a task. Often, people may think you are fishing for compliments when in reality you really have a difficult time believing that you can do anything right.

If you identify with Marci and what I am saying, you may want to spend some time exploring the causes of your low self-esteem (such as negative parental messages or an abusive relationship with someone who constantly put you down). At the very least, you need to be aware of the fact that *no amount of encouragement from others* is going to solve your problem. The problem is inside you and you will only turn people off (including editors and agents) with your self-effacing attitude. If you have low self-esteem it won't matter how talented you are, or how much positive feedback you get from others, because you will constantly question yourself and your work, constantly doubt yourself. In addition, if your self-esteem is low, *negative* feedback or rejection slips will tend to devastate you and consequently lower your self-esteem even further. And more important, if you have low self-esteem you are likely to give up at the first sign of rejection.

There are many books on the market on how to raise your self-esteem and I recommend that you study them closely so that you don't, in essence, give up before you ever get the chance to try.

Perfectionism

Others who give up before they begin to try are the perfectionists. Perfectionism can also be a sign of low self-esteem. Like Marci, perfectionists always have more work to do on their project before it is ready to be seen by others. Unfortunately, if you suffer from this problem, you may never be ready to send your work out. My suggestion to you is that you hire an editor who can give you objective feedback about your work. Then follow their suggestions, and without further ado—send it out!

If you fall in the perfectionist category, know that you cannot trust your perceptions when it comes to your own work and that your work will *never* seem right to you. You have to send it out anyway, *even if it isn't perfect.*

Fear of rejection

If you are so paralyzed with fear and insecurity that you have difficulty mailing out your work or even showing it to someone, you may suffer from a fear of rejection. This too, can be related to your level of self-esteem. Once again, you may have experienced this problem in other aspects of your life (your personal relationships, your job). If you are the type of person who feels devastated by even the slightest rejection, if it takes you months or even years to recover from a rejection, you are going to have a very difficult road ahead with your writing. As you've no doubt heard countless numbers of times, writers get rejected *all the time.* If it is a major blow to your ego every time you receive a rejection slip you are going to be in a great deal of pain a lot of the time.

Sean is a good example. For as long as he could remember he desperately wanted to be an author. He spent all his free time writing and everyone complimented him on how talented he was and encouraged him to try to get his work published. Finally, he sent a short story to a literary magazine.

He had chosen the magazine carefully, feeling that his story was just right for their particular style. When he received a rejection slip a month later, he was devastated. He couldn't eat or sleep for days. Eventually, his friends encouraged him to try another magazine and he finally did. When he didn't hear from them within a month he was certain that they too, had rejected his work.

Six weeks later he received a very nice letter from the publisher telling Sean he liked his writing but that this particular short story was not what they were looking for. Now, many writers would have been absolutely ecstatic over the fact that the editor took the time to write a personal letter and that he'd liked his work. So what that he didn't like this short story? He obviously thought enough of his writing to take the time to encourage him. Therefore, send him more stories, right? Wrong. Sean was so devastated by the rejection of his short story that he stopped writing altogether. When friends and relatives would ask him about it, he just said nonchalantly, "Oh, you know, it's impossible for a writer to make a living nowadays."

While Sean was perhaps right about writers' making a living, that wasn't why he stopped. His fragile ego had been so badly bruised by the rejections he'd received that he had silently vowed that he would never put himself through that kind of pain again. The saddest part of this story is that Sean was a writer at heart. He never really found anything else he liked to do as well and he robbed himself of a great deal of pleasure by not continuing his great passion, even if he did so as a hobby.

It would seem that our second type of person, the one who seems to never give up, who seems to exude self-confidence about his or her projects, has high self-esteem and little or no fear of rejection. For some people, this is the case. But interestingly, this is not always true. Sometimes, those who have low self-esteem defend against it by puffing themselves up, convincing themselves they are fantastic writers and will be successful. And ironically, the reason some people seem to never give up is because they are defending against having to feel rejection. If they don't ever accept defeat, they don't ever have to feel rejected.

Your ability to feel and accept disappointment

For some, feeling disappointment is so painful that they simply cannot tolerate it. When something doesn't go the way they'd planned they use any number of strategies in order to avoid feeling this dreaded emotion. Some maintain a Pollyanna-type attitude, lifting themselves off the ground and dusting themselves off without even noticing their injuries. For these people, there is no such thing as failure. "Well, maybe next time," they say cheerfully, or, "Can't win 'em all." While this optimistic attitude may seem admirable, and certainly keeps them going on to the next challenge, it isn't unless they learn from their mistakes and give themselves time to heal from the last rejection.

"Disappointment serves an important function."

Tom, a friend of mine, had worked on his historic novel for three years and has been trying to sell it for almost four. Although he has boxes of rejection slips, he doesn't let this stop him. He believes that if he keeps trying, someday an editor will appreciate his novel. He listens patiently when friends and other writers suggest he give up and try another project. And at a recent writer's conference a writer he greatly respects bluntly told him that his book is unpublishable. But Tom still holds out hope that someone will see his work for the genius it is.

Disappointment serves an important function. It helps us to process the situation so that we can let it go. If we don't allow ourselves to feel disappointed when things don't work out, we tend to stay stuck and can become disillusioned or bitter.

Sour grapes

Some writers are so good at rationalizing and avoiding feeling disappointment that they can convince themselves they never really wanted something in the first place, the "sour-grapes" attitude. When they don't get their article, short story, or book published, they tell themselves, "You know, maybe this is a blessing in disguise. Look how hard I've been working for the past few months at getting this published. I've been so focused on selling my work that I haven't been able to write." How many times have you heard writers say they never really wanted to be published anyway, that they were just writing for themselves?

Learning to deal with disappointment means allowing yourself to want something even if you can't have it. If Sean had been able to do this he would have at least been able to continue his writing for his own pleasure. Or, perhaps if he would have been able to process the failure and learn from it. This may have meant realizing that he needed to go to school, participate in some writing workshops, or read more books on writing. Or perhaps it meant he needed more time and practice, or he needed to try to get an agent who would sell his work for him, and thus avoid the painful situation of receiving rejection slips.

Admitting that you want something you can't have can be terribly painful, but it is at least being authentic. It is being honest with yourself. Pretending you don't want something when you really do can be crazy-making because soon you may get to the place where you don't know *what* you want.

Andrea is a case in point. Andrea wanted to write children's books. She'd managed to pump out seven of them in only a few months, and was excited about trying to get some of them published. She'd shared them with her friend's children and they all loved them. And so she decided to go to a writer's conference where a children's writer she admired was going to be the guest speaker and where there were going to be several children's publishers and agents.

What she heard at the conference totally discouraged her, however. The publishers and agents who spoke all said that the children's market was saturated and that it was nearly impossible to get your book published nowadays. One agent, who'd heard her work read out loud in a workshop, took her aside and told her, "You're too good a writer to write children's books. You're wasting your time and talent. There's no money in it."

Instead of allowing herself to feel her disappointment in learning that it was going to be harder than she thought to get her stories published, Andrea became so discouraged after the writer's conference that she convinced herself she didn't really want to be a children's writer after all. She put her children's stories away and started writing a novel, which incidentally, she never finished.

Many, many people do as Sean and Andrea did and give up their dream, or quit trying and then convince themselves they never really wanted it after all because they are unable to feel and accept disappointment.

The real quandary

So far we've discussed how your level of self-esteem and your ability to handle rejection and disappointment can affect your chances for success as a writer and I hope this information may have helped you. But I still haven't helped you answer the question, "When do I give up and when do I keep trying?"

It really may depend on which group you fall into. Generally speaking, if you identified with Marci, Sean or Andrea, if you now recognize that you have low self-esteem, tend to be a perfectionist, or have a fear of rejection, you probably need to keep trying as long as your ego can take it.

I say this because I assume you haven't tried hard enough or long enough, you're easily discouraged, and don't have much faith in your talent or your project. If this is true you will need to keep your mind on your goals, allow yourself to feel disappointment but don't let it get the best of you, and remember to get outside feedback.

If, on the other hand, you identified with James or Tom, you may need to recognize that while it appears that you are self-confident, the truth may be that you have puffed yourself up in order to cover up your insecurities. You may in fact, be deathly afraid of rejection or failure and that is why you refuse to accept it. You may need to try to lower your defenses a bit more and listen to the people around you who are encouraging you to try something else. In addition, what appears to be optimism on your part may be a cover to hide your unwillingness to feel and accept disappointment. If this is true, you may need to consider giving up your project and going on to the next, or at least putting it aside for a little bit while you focus on something else.

Another way of deciding whether to give up on a certain writing project or not is to follow these guidelines. It's time to put your project aside and move on when:

You've been told by more than one publisher or agent that there is no market for your work because:

- the market has dried up;

- your work does not fit into the parameters of the genre you have labeled your work (relabel it);

- your work is insulting to the audience you are aiming toward.

Or you are a beginning writer and you've received handfuls of rejection slips, no agent has agreed to represent you (or has encouraged you) and you're writing group tells you you aren't "getting it."

We are constantly being told by magazine articles, "infomercials," and self-help books that we can have anything we want or be anything we want to be if we just set our mind to it and if we try hard enough. But is it really true? While it is great to be positive and optimistic, is it always good to keep trying?

These questions are particularly pertinent to writers. We've all heard stories about famous writers whose stories or novels were rejected by dozens of publishers before one editor finally accepted their work. These stories have kept many a writer going with fantasies of one day connecting with that one special editor who will recognize the genius in their work, of one day being vindicated and "showing" all those nay sayers and doubters in their midst.

But let's discuss for a moment who these legends really were. They were exemplary writers, pioneers charting new territory, rule breakers on the verge of a new genre, or rebels daring to explore and expose heretofore unchartered or forbidden territory.

So for them, persistence paid off because their work was so good or so unique that it was only a matter of time before someone recognized it. But is that true of the average writer?

If you have been given feedback that you too are an exemplary writer (by your agent, by editors, by your writing teacher or your writing group, *not* just by your friends) or if you too are on the cutting edge (again as defined by the above) then you should by all means continue to persevere. Otherwise, it may be time to move on.

Keep your eyes on the horizon

If at this point you are considering giving up on your project, it is important to remember that many new writers talk about how their first book or their first stories were more exercises in learning their craft than anything else. When they look back on their initial works they are often surprised and even appalled by the caliber of their first efforts. Just as you would not presume to know how to build a house without training, most of us need to learn to write. And for most of us, our first efforts are our best learning tools.

It is gratifying and often exhilarating to discover that one can actually create a work out of nothing but the contents of one's imagination. But after the dust settles and we stop being impressed with ourselves, we need to come down to earth and realize that while we may not have known we were capable of such imaginative ramblings they are often in fact, just that—ramblings. Creative, imaginative, fun, but *not* professional, publishable work.

And last, but certainly not least, we need to make a distinction between being a writer and getting a particular project published. Giving up on a project *does not* mean you are giving up on being a writer. In fact, it may be just the thing that sets you free to write the project that is going to get published, or to discover the genre that is just your forte. As spiritual leaders and philosophers have told us for centuries, holding on to something only limits our possibilities. As the old saying goes, "When one door closes another one opens." Letting go of a project may create the opening for your most inspired work. So don't decide that *this* book or *this* story is your best work. Your best work is whatever you are currently working on.

Beverly Engel is an internationally recognized psychotherapist as well as a best-selling author of eighteen books, including Loving Him without Losing You, The Emotionally Abusive Relationship, The Power of Apology, Honor Your Anger *and* Healing Your Emotional Self.

Beverly has shared her expertise on numerous television programs, including Oprah, Ricki Lake, Sally Jesse Raphael *and* Starting Over.

The Book Doctor Is In

The seven most common
first-novel problems and how to avoid them

By Sherry M. Gottlieb

OK, YOU'VE FINALLY FINISHED WRITING YOUR NOVEL, but you've had no luck marketing it, even though your closest friends have all read it and told you they liked it. A lot.

C'mon, what else are they going to say? Even though you swore them to tell you "the truth," you've got your fragile ego invested in a work you spent a significant amount of your life to complete—and no one wants to be the one to burst your balloon, particularly those who are close to you. Besides, they're unable to make any constructive criticism, because they can't figure out why your book doesn't quite work.

But I can, even though I haven't read it. I'm a "book doctor" who teaches new novelists how to rewrite their manuscripts to a publishable level, and I've discovered that most beginning novelists make the same mistakes. I can't guarantee that fixing these problems will get you published, but I can promise that it will improve your novel considerably.

1. A hookless beginning

"There were 117 psychoanalysts on the Pan Am flight to Vienna and I'd been treated by at least six of them. And married a seventh."

That's how Erica Jong began her 1973 bestseller, *Fear of Flying*, and it's a helluva good opening. In two sentences, Jong tells us her narrator has had a lot of problems—but isn't too dysfunctional to have married a psychoanalyst—and she immediately arouses our curiosity by making us wonder what her main character is doing on a Vienna-bound airplane full of shrinks.

Your opening sentence, paragraph, or scene should be a hook to grab the readers' attention and perhaps give them some idea what kind of novel they're getting into. Agents, editors, and book buyers have too many books to peruse, and far too little time to do it in, so if you neglect the hook, readers may lose interest quickly and never find that your book really takes off around the fourth chapter. Just because someone has started reading your novel doesn't mean they're going to finish it—in fact, agents and editors frequently reject books after reading fewer than five pages! How far would you read in a novel that opens with: "Joe woke up when the alarm went off and noticed it was raining"? (Which brings me to a sub-peeve: First-time novelists often open their first chapters with weather reports.)

You may not know what the "hook" is when you start your novel—you might even write the entire first draft before you work on it—but don't neglect it. The beginning of your novel is the most important part.

> "Your opening sentence or paragraph, called the lead, should be a hook to grab the readers' attention..."

2. Multiple or diffuse points of view

Much more than the plot, what readers are most interested in are other people—and this means the main character's thoughts and feelings, and how those relate to, and resonate with, the reader's own experiences. Ideally, a novel should have one major point of view (POV): that of the main character, the protagonist. That means that the entire story should be seen through his eyes, in the same order that he finds out about events, and not including information to which he is not privy —he cannot see into anyone else's mind, so can only guess what others are thinking from visual and verbal clues, and also cannot know what he has neither witnessed nor been told.

Keeping one POV enables the readers to identify with the main character, at least to the extent that he is our eyes and ears. If you switch POV mid-scene, you give the readers a kind of literary whiplash which prevents them from really getting involved in your novel the way they would if they'd gotten to know—and were staying with—one person for the entire ride.

The only viable exceptions to having one clear POV throughout are, generally:

1) If there is one adversary whose mind and motivations are sufficiently juxtaposed to the protagonist's to make a consistent alternation between those two POVs feasible (a common device in serial killer novels, but not much else);

2) Two or more entirely separate plots, each with a different main character, are alternating through the entire novel before coming together at or near the climax; or

3) A single scene from another POV is used as a prologue and/or epilogue, giving the reader a dimension not otherwise available through the hero's POV.

3. Lack of insight

Which tells us more:

"Gina bit her lip" or:

"Gina felt embarrassed, sure that everyone was staring at her"?

The first example is an observation, the second is an insight. Unlike a movie, a novel allows us to see inside the mind of the protagonist, and it is her personality and emotions which make a reader care what happens. Characterization makes a novel come alive, not the plot; a book still can be good with little or no plot if it's got some interesting and multidimensional characters, but a solid plot without well-developed characters might as well be an action movie.

We have to be able to understand what makes the protagonist tick, what are her strengths and weaknesses, hopes and fears. Many beginning writers' heroes are nonentities who lack dimension or depth; their main purpose seems to be to conduct the plot. Remember that everyone has a personal set of quirks and habits, and so should your major characters. Reveal your character's background through her reactions, what she relates to and why; people don't respond in a vacuum—our present reactions are formed by our past experiences.

It is essential that you develop your protagonist's personality from the inside-out, consistently showing us what she thinks and feels as events unravel, keeping us up on how she reacts to the other characters she runs into.

4. Non-realistic dialogue

"I am looking forward to going to the prom with you on Saturday," Karen said.

Bill responded, "We are going to have to take the bus to the prom on Saturday, Karen, because my father will not lend me his car. Is that all right with you?"

While that may be all right with Karen, it's not OK with me. People don't really speak that way—particularly teenagers! Native speakers of American English use contractions (I'm, we're, won't) and shorthand ("OK?" instead of "Is that all right with you?"), seldom speak in complete sentences, and use slang appropriate to their ages and backgrounds.

Each of your characters should have his own syntax and vocabulary, different from the others, rather than all sounding the same...and probably much like the author. Some will swear, others won't. Some are educated, and their speech patterns will show that; others might have limited vocabularies or use regionalisms. The reader should be able to learn about the character from how she expresses herself, as well as from what she is saying.

As an exercise, try removing all external indications of which character is speaking in a written conversation and see if you can still tell who's talking. If you can't, your dialogue needs work.

Listen to the people around you talking; mentally type their sentences as they speak. Notice that in a conversation between two people, the other's name is hardly ever used—and usually only for particular emphasis, as in: "I'm leaving you, Steve."

Check your television's settings menu to activate its closed-captioning capabilities; if you use that in addition to the audio, you can read the same dialogue you're hearing.

Try reading your novel's dialogue aloud—it will help you avoid lines which sound written—in the theater, such dialogue is said to have "printer's ink" in it. Once you develop an ear for dialogue, your characters will seem much more real.

5. Poor research

You know the old adage "Write what you know"? Although it's sound advice, it doesn't mean you have to write your novel about a guy who sits on the couch in his skivvies and channel-surfs. Likewise, you don't have to be a homicide detective to write a police procedural, you just have to be willing to do some research.

I saw one manuscript in which the main character was supposed to be a hospital administrator/psychiatrist, and another in which the protagonist was meant to be a best-selling author, but the novelists obviously knew nothing about hospitals and psychiatry or the publishing business, so their lead characters came off as inept and unbelievable. Fiction should be well-researched because it adds verisimilitude; if you try to fake it, it'll show.

Don't do your research by watching television or movies—the information thus obtained is notoriously incorrect. (For instance, you know the white outline that TV police often leave where a body has been? It's a Hollywood invention; doesn't happen in real police work.) Spend the time and energy to find out what you need to know from a reliable source. Doing research online is easy, but always take into account the source of the information you obtain; there's a lot of misinformation perpetuated on the Net. If you don't have Internet access, libraries and librarians are still excellent sources. Try to talk to people who work in the field you need to investigate. If you need a coroner, diamond merchant, or nurse to "talk shop" with you, look up some in your area, explain that you're writing a novel involving their field of expertise and offer to take them to lunch. Go with a prepared list of questions to cover what you need to know. If you are fortunate enough to be able to interview someone, make sure to write down some of their work-related lingo—for instance, police "clear" a case, rather than "solve" it.

Use only what research is needed to make the characters sound real; throw the rest away—don't show off your research.

6. Redundant repetition

In real life, a trial lawyer tells the jury what she's going to show them (her opening statement), then shows it to them (her examination of witnesses), and finally, tells them what she showed them (her closing argument). However, you can't do that in a novel because you bore the reader by telling them the same thing three times. Most beginning writers tell the reader too much, which can result in a suspense novel without any suspense. They tell the reader what the protagonist thinks, then the protagonist tells another character, who then rephrases it.

A story is a collaboration between writer and reader; please allow readers room to think on their own. If you've already told your readers that the redhead couldn't have killed the doctor because there is no midnight flight on Wednesdays, don't make them read through it again while your detective tells that to his captain. Assume your readers are as intelligent as you are; don't "talk down" to them.

Try to leave things hanging at the ends of scenes and chapters, so the reader will wonder what's going to happen, instead of already knowing—if they know, there's no reason to finish reading the book!

7. A rushed ending

In an early draft of my first novel (*Love Bite*, Warner Books, 1994), I got to the scene where the protagonist and the antagonist have their climactic confrontation, but I was so sure by then that the reader would have guessed the final outcome—and thus found my telling it to be anticlimactic—that I skipped it entirely.

I didn't understand why my editor was so upset about that—I thought I was being subtle!—until I edited someone else's novel with the same problem. My client had led up to all hell breaking loose after one antagonist died, yet he skipped all that hell and went directly to the summing up, depriving his readers of seeing the villain get his come uppance. The readers deserve a big, dramatic scene when they finally get where you've been leading them—don't be stingy with it!

But an author should not end a novel with the climax. After the climax, there should be a denouement, a winding down. It can be an epilogue, or a resolution of a subplot, but without it, any ending will feel terribly rushed and unsatisfactory—and will leave the reader reluctant to ever read any of your books again!

Before I finish here, I'd like to point out that you can't write novels if you don't read them. When you read published fiction, study what you read—ask yourself how the author makes you like, dislike, and/or understand the characters. Figure out how the author makes those characters come alive for the reader. If you find yourself reading rapidly, step back and observe how the author has paced the book. You can even learn from badly written books—if you're bored or otherwise not involved, try to figure out why, and how the author has lost your attention. If you read with a critical eye, you can learn from any novel, by either positive or negative example. I learned how to how to write and edit saleable fiction by being an active and analytical reader.

Don't get discouraged. Not everyone who plays piano will get to Carnegie Hall, and not everyone who writes will get published—but if you don't continue to work at it, you'll have no chance at all.

Sherry Gottlieb is a book doctor who specializes in novels. Several of her clients have sold their books to major publishers, including Knopf, St. Martin's Press, Harper-Collins, and Berkley-Putnam.

A published author herself, her first book was Hell No, No, We Won't Go! Resisting the Draft During the Vietnam War *(Viking, 1991), an oral history which was a nominee for the PEN West Literary Award for nonfiction. Her novel* Love Bite *(Warner, 1994), an erotic police procedural with fangs, was the basis for the abso-*

lutely terrible 1995 TV-movie "Deadly Love,", starring Susan Dey (which bore scant relation to the book). Her sequel, Worse Than Death, *was published in hardcover (Forge Books, 1999) and paperback (Tor Books, 2000). She has also written* Pup Fiction, *the adventures of canine P.I. Sam Spayed, and 2,000 professional résumés for clients of her company, Career Boost Résumés.*

Sherry owned A Change of Hobbit Bookstore in Santa Monica, California; for nearly two decades it was the oldest and largest speculative-fiction bookstore in the world.

Her website is www.wordservices.com.

Copyright

What every author should know

By John D. Zelezny

Copyright law is at the very core of the authorship and publishing professions, though it is often overlooked and much misunderstood. Unfortunately, many authors' first conscious encounter with copyright is in a negative light—as a legal impediment to "borrowing" passages from others' works. But in fact, authors create copyright at the instant they craft original manuscripts, and when authors sell those manuscripts it is actually a copyright interest they are selling.

Copyright law is the author's friend, the author's bread and butter. Therefore, it pays to know and appreciate the basics of copyright.

What is protected?

Copyright is a right of ownership in an "original work of authorship," such as a book manuscript, poem, magazine article or screenplay. Copyright also applies to graphic works, such as photographs and cartoon sketches. The crux of all copyright protection is some original, expressive work. Copyright protects an author's particular manner of expression—the author's creative work product.

This principle is important: Copyright does *not* apply to the underlying *ideas* behind a creative work; it applies only to the author's actual presentation. An *idea* for a novel or article is not protected. Ideas are not "works of authorship" covered by the Copyright Act. For the same reason, underlying facts also are not protected by copyright. An author might spend days or months researching facts upon which to base a book, but regardless of the effort, those facts do not become protected property. Copyright protects only the author's original manner of presenting those facts.

Once an original work of authorship is produced, the owner of the copyright is granted by law extensive property rights to that work. According to the Copyright Act, the owner has the exclusive right to display, distribute, reproduce, adapt or perform the protected work. This is a virtual legal monopoly, with only narrow exceptions.

When does protection begin?

In the United States, copyright protection begins as soon as a work of authorship is "fixed in a tangible medium of expression." That is, the work is protected as soon as it is on paper, audiotape, videotape, film or in some other reproducible form. No other formalities are required.

Under the current Copyright Act, there are benefits to federal registration and to placing a copyright notice on the work. But neither of these steps is a prerequisite to basic protection. Copyright protection begins automatically, unlike patents, which must be granted by the government.

Beginning authors often are under the mistaken impression that they must obtain some official approval or must at least mail a copy of their works to themselves before they can safely claim copyright. This is simply not true. Formalities such as mailing a manuscript to oneself and then leaving it in the sealed and postmarked envelope may later serve as evidence of the creation date, if that should become an issue. But this technique doesn't actually initiate the copyright protection.

Who owns the copyright?

The general rule is that copyright ownership vests initially with the person who actually created the work, the author. And if coauthors produce a work they become co-owners of the copyright, absent an agreement to the contrary.

However, authors must be aware of the all-important "work-made-for-hire" rule. If a writer is hired as an *employee* to produce material for an employer then the employer automatically owns all of the rights unless the parties expressly agree otherwise, in writing.

As a general rule, book authors and freelance magazine writers are considered independent contractors, not employees. But costly misunderstandings over copyright ownership sometimes arise when authors are hired to create work for others. This misunderstanding may exist, for example, when an author is commissioned by a publisher to write several specified chapters for a book, over a period of several months. Has the author now become an employee? If so, then all rights to the chapters automatically belong to the publisher. But if the author remains an independent contractor, then the author is presumed to retain copyright ownership in the work; the commissioning publisher is presumed to have merely a nonexclusive license to use the work for the one project discussed.

It is important for authors to have a clear, written agreement in cases where the professional relationship could conceivably be deemed one of employment. The agreement should cover copyright ownership as well as the deadlines, manuscript specifications, payment amount, and so on. For important projects, a lawyer's assistance may be advisable.

Absent a written agreement, the courts sometimes must be called upon to determine whether a writer was an employee or an independent contractor. The basic consideration in such cases is the degree of control exercised by the commissioning organization. The greater the control exercised, the more likely an author will be declared an employee.

How long does protection last?

For works created on or after January 1, 1978, the general term of protection is the lifetime of the author (or last surviving author, if there were co-authors) plus 70 years. In the case of works made for hire, copyright protection lasts until 95 years from the year of first publication, or 120 years from the year of creation, whichever expires first.

After these terms of protection expire, then the work of authorship falls into the "public domain." It then may be reproduced by anyone without fear of copyright infringement.

How is the copyright sold?

Copyright is considered a divisible form of property. This means that a copyright can be transferred to others, either in its entirety or in small pieces. When the entire copyright interest is transferred, this is called an "assignment" of the copyright. For example, book publishers often seek to obtain an assignment of the copyright as part of the deal with the author. If an author chooses to sell only a piece of the copyright, with the author retaining the bulk of the rights, this is called a "license." For example, the author of an article might license "first U.S. publication rights" to a magazine while retaining the rights to all other uses of the article.

344

Copyright licenses may be described and limited in virtually any way the contracting parties desire. They all fall into one of two categories, however: exclusive or nonexclusive. A license is exclusive if by its very terms it could not be granted to multiple parties. A license for first U.S. publication rights, for example, would be an exclusive license. For an assignment or an exclusive license to be valid, it must be made in writing. Nonexclusive licenses, on the other hand, are not required to be in writing.

In any event, whenever permission is given to others to use copyrighted material, it is important that the author know precisely what sort of copyright interest is being conveyed. Documentation is always advisable. Written copyright permissions or transfer agreements should reflect the nature of the project and should not carelessly fritter away an author's marketable interests. In recent years, for example, authors have learned that a distinct, marketable interest may exist in "electronic rights" to their works.

Copyright agreements themselves can take many forms, ranging from an informal, one-paragraph letter to a multi-page contract for subsidiary rights in a novel.

Is a copyright notice necessary?

Works published on or after March 1, 1989, are no longer required to include a copyright notice on published copies. Copyright protection now remains in effect even if a work is published without a notice. However, it is still highly advisable upon publication to attach a proper notice (e.g., "© 2007 by John Smith") because this precludes an infringer from claiming the defense of "innocent infringement" and it may help to ward off unauthorized copying. There is no requirement that copyright registration be obtained before a notice is used on the published material. The copyright notice should be placed in a conspicuous place, where someone would normally look for it.

Should registration be obtained?

Registration, like notice, is not required for copyright protection. However, works must first be registered with the federal Copyright Office before an owner can sue anyone for infringement. Other procedural and evidential advantages also exist for those who promptly register. For example, if registration is made within three months after publication of the work, the owner then maintains the right to collect attorney's fees and specified statutory damage amounts from infringers without having to prove actual monetary harm. Also, should there be a dispute over ownership to a copyright, the registration serves as court evidence (though not necessarily conclusive evidence) of valid ownership.

Registration is obtained by preparing the proper application form and then mailing it, along with a registration fee and a copy of the work (two copies if published) to the Register of Copyrights, Library of Congress, Washington, D.C. 20559. For books and most other kinds of textual materials the proper application form is Form TX. Often book publishers will handle the copyright registration on the author's behalf.

What if someone infringes?

When copyrighted material is used without authorization, the owner's first step usually is to send a letter informing the infringer of the owner's rights and demanding that the unauthorized use cease. In some cases there may also be a demand for compensation, followed by some negotiation, and ultimately a settlement agreement. Most copyright infringement problems are resolved through informal avenues such as these.

Occasionally, in cases of egregious and highly detrimental infringement, the first step may be to file a lawsuit for an injunction and damages. In any event, whenever unauthorized uses are discovered authors should immediately seek to enforce their proprietary rights. Failure to do so will lead to an erosion of those rights. If a work already has been published, typically the publisher will have a stake in protecting the copyright and will fund the necessary legal steps.

What may be borrowed from others?

Authors must be concerned not only with protecting their own copyrights but also with avoiding infringement of others'. In most cases, copyright infringement claims are based on some altered use of the protected material, such as extensive "borrowing" from a magazine article. It is permissible to extract *factual* content from others' literary works. (Remember, facts are not protected by copyright.) However, if the manner of expression is also reproduced, such that portions of the latter work are substantially similar to the former, then this may constitute infringement. Ultimately, it is for a jury to decide whether the latter work is "substantially similar."

In some cases even verbatim copying from others' works is permitted, however, under the doctrine of "fair use." As stated in section 107 of the Copyright Act: "The fair use of a copyrighted work...for purposes such as criticism, comment, news reporting, teaching, scholarship, or research, is not an infringement of copyright." This doctrine is not conducive to precise boundary lines, and courts weigh four factors to help determine whether an unauthorized use qualifies as "fair." Those factors are: the purpose of the use, the nature of the copyrighted work, the portion of the work used, and the effect of this use upon the market for the copyrighted work.

The fair use doctrine is a narrow exception to the owner's control over copyright. Typical examples include the quotation of excerpts in a book review or the quotation of short passages in a newspaper column in order to illustrate the columnist's point. But any copying that encroaches upon a portion of the copyright owner's potential market is highly unlikely to be considered a "fair use." Authors who wish to obtain a more thorough understanding of the fair use doctrine and its application by the courts should read the U.S. Supreme Court's decision in *Harper & Row v. Nation Enterprises*, 471 U.S. 539, a thoughtful 1985 case that is available in public law libraries and most college libraries.

What special precautions should coauthors take?

When two or more authors collaborate on a work, it raises additional questions about copyright ownership. The issues are much the same as with joint ownership of any other kind of property. For example, if three friends each chipped in to buy a car together, who would have the right to sell or lease it? Who would have the right to alter it? And if one of the friends died, would his share then pass to his heirs?

Similar questions arise with joint ownership of copyrights. Although these issues rarely seem to be pondered in advance, they should be. Ideally, coauthors should enter into a formal collaboration agreement that specifies, among other things, how the copyright will be owned among them and how copyright assignment or licensing decisions will be made.

Sources of further information

Many helpful publications explaining the basic copyright laws and the registration process can be obtained free from the Public Information Office of the Copyright Office, Library of Congress, Washington, D.C. 20559. The Public Information Office will also provide copies of the registration forms themselves. However, the Copyright Office will *not* offer legal advice, comment on the apparent validity of a copyright claim, or discuss questions relating to copyright infringement. On such matters authors should consult a copyright lawyer or the numerous copyright reference materials available in a good public library.

John D. Zelezny *is an attorney and the author of* Communications Law: Liberties, Restraints, and the Modern Media.

Writers' Resources

Questions to Ask Literary Agents

Suggested questions to ask agents
when offered representation

The following is a list—prepared by the Association of Authors' Representatives, Inc.—of suggested topics for authors to discuss with literary agents with whom they are entering into a professional relationship.

1. Is your agency a sole proprietorship? A partnership? A corporation?

2. Are you a member of the Association of Authors' Representatives?

3. How long have you been in business as an agent?

4. How many people does your agency employ?

5. Of the total number of employees, how many are agents, as opposed to clerical workers?

6. Do you have specialists at your agency who handle movie and television rights? Foreign rights? Do you have sub-agents or corresponding agents overseas and in Hollywood?

7. Do you represent other authors in my area of interest?

8. Who in your agency will actually be handling my work? Will the other staff members be familiar with my work and the status of my business at your agency? Will you oversee or at least keep me apprised of the work that your agency is doing on my behalf?

9. Do you issue an agent-author contract? May I review a specimen copy? And may I review the language of the agency clause that appears in contracts you negotiate for your clients?

10. What is your approach to providing editorial input and career guidance for your clients or for me specifically?

11. How do you keep your clients informed of your activities on their behalf? Do you regularly send them copies of publishers' rejection letters? Do you provide them with submission lists and rejection letters on request? Do you regularly, or upon request, send out updated activity reports?

12. Do you consult with your clients on any and all offers?

13. Some agencies sign subsidiary contracts on behalf of their clients to expedite processing. Do you?

14. What are your commissions for: 1) basic sales to U.S. publishers; 2) sales of movie and television rights; 3) audio and multimedia rights; 4) British and foreign translation rights?

15. What are your procedures and time-frames for processing and disbursing client funds? Do you keep different bank accounts separating author funds from agency revenue?

16. What are your policies about charging clients for expenses incurred by your agency? Will you list such expenses for me? Do you advance money for such expenses? Do you consult with your clients before advancing certain expenditures? Is there a ceiling on such expenses above which you feel you must consult with your clients?

17. How do you handle legal, accounting, public relations or similar professional services that fall outside the normal range of a literary agency's function?

18. Do you issue 1099 tax forms at the end of each year? Do you also furnish clients upon request with a detailed account of their financial activity, such as gross income, commissions and other deductions, and net income, for the past year?

19. In the event of your death or disability, or the death or disability of the principal person running the agency, what provisions exist for continuing operation of my account, for the processing of money due to me, and for the handling of my books and editorial needs?

20. If we should part company, what is your policy about handling any unsold subsidiary rights to my work that were reserved to me under the original publishing contracts?

21. What are your expectations of me as your client?

22. Do you have a list of Do's and Don'ts for your clients that will enable me to help you do your job better?

Reprinted by permission of Association of Authors Representatives, Inc.
aar-online.org

Submission Tracking Sheet

Photocopy this page and use for each work submitted

Title: _____

Notes:

①

Publisher: _____ Editor: _____ Phone: _____

Address: _____ Date submitted: _____ Multiple Submission? No Yes

Date to follow up: _____ Date followed up: _____ Follow-up note: _____ Date accepted: _____

Date rejected: _____ Pub date: _____ Payment due date: _____ Payment amount: _____ Clips received: _____

②

Publisher: _____ Editor: _____ Phone: _____

Address: _____ Date submitted: _____ Multiple Submission? No Yes

Date to follow up: _____ Date followed up: _____ Follow-up note: _____ Date accepted: _____

Date rejected: _____ Pub date: _____ Payment due date: _____ Payment amount: _____ Clips received: _____

③

Publisher: _____ Editor: _____ Phone: _____

Address: _____ Date submitted: _____ Multiple Submission? No Yes

Date to follow up: _____ Date followed up: _____ Follow-up note: _____ Date accepted: _____

Date rejected: _____ Pub date: _____ Payment due date: _____ Payment amount: _____ Clips received: _____

④

Publisher: _____ Editor: _____ Phone: _____

Address: _____ Date submitted: _____ Multiple Submission? No Yes

Date to follow up: _____ Date followed up: _____ Follow-up note: _____ Date accepted: _____

Date rejected: _____ Pub date: _____ Payment due date: _____ Payment amount: _____ Clips received: _____

⑤

Publisher: _____ Editor: _____ Phone: _____

Address: _____ Date submitted: _____ Multiple Submission? No Yes

Date to follow up: _____ Date followed up: _____ Follow-up note: _____ Date accepted: _____

Date rejected: _____ Pub date: _____ Payment due date: _____ Payment amount: _____ Clips received: _____

Standard Manuscript Format

There is no single correct physical format for a manuscript, but following common format conventions, as shown here, is a good way to say to an editor: "I am a professional." Always use letterhead-sized, white paper. Always be sure the print is dark and legible. Paper clip sheets together or use a manuscript box; never staple.

Author's Name
Street Address
City, State Zip
Phone Number
Social Security Number

Rights Available
Copyright © Year
Approx.: XXXX words

List the rights you're offering to sell.

Some say a copyright notice is the mark of a novice. Most editors won't care either way.

Round word count off to nearest 50 or 100.

Social security number is necessary for government reporting of payments.

TITLE OF ARTICLE, BOOK OR STORY

by Author's Name

Come down about one-third and type the title in all caps. Double space and type "by" and the author's name.

Lorem ipsum dolor sit amet, consectetuer adipiscing elit, sed diam nonummy nibh euismod tincidunt ut laoreet dolore magna aliquam erat volutpat. Ut wisi enim ad minim veniam, quis nostrud exerci tation ullamcorper suscipit lobortis nisl ut aliquip ex ea commodo consequat.

Duis autem vel eum iriure dolor in hendrerit in vulputate velit esse molestie consequat, vel illum dolore eu feugiat nulla facilisis at vero eros et accumsan et iusto odio dignissim qui blandit praesent luptatum zzril delenit augue duis dolore te feugait nulla facilisi.

Lorem ipsum dolor sit amet, consectetuer adipiscing elit, sed diam nonummy nibh euismod tincidunt ut laoreet

Leave four blank lines, then start the text.

Indent paragraphs.

Double space text. Do not right-justify it.

Left, right and bottom margins should be 1"-1½" wide.

Lastname/Title/4

Place a slug line: last name/a key word from the title/page number, one-quarter of an inch down, right justified, on all but first page.

Leave 1½" blank at top of sheet.

dolore magna aliquam erat volutpat. Ut wisi enim ad minim veniam, quis nostrud exerci tation ullamcorper suscipit lobortis nisl ut aliquip ex ea commodo consequat. Duis autem vel eum iriure dolor in hendrerit in vulputate velit esse

molestie consequat, vel illum dolore eu feugiat nulla facilisis at.

END

Drop 4 lines below end of text and type "MORE," except on the last page type "-30-" or "END."

Proofreader's Marks

Commonly understood symbols and marks are used to communicate changes to be made to manuscripts and other typeset material.

Mark	Meaning	Example	
ꟷTeꞇ	Let it stay	The ~~brown~~ wolf ran home.	ꟷTeꞇ
ℓ	Delete	The brown wolf ran homes.	ℓ
∧	Insert	The brown∧wolf ran home.	timber
⊼	Insert comma	The little∧brown wolf ran home.	
⊙	Insert period	The brown wolf ran home∧	⊙
;/	Insert semicolon	The wolf ran home∧the bear didn't.	;/
:/	Insert colon	You can't go back home∧However...	:/
∀	Insert apostrophe	It was the grey wolfs home.	
#	Insert space	The brownwolf ran home.∧	#
∀ ∀	Insert quotations marks	The wolf said,∀Yes!∀	
¶	Start new paragraph	The brown wolf ran home. ⌐The bear always walked in front...	¶
⌣	Close up space	The bro⌣wn wolf ran home.	
sp	Spell out	The wolf from the (USA) came in second.	sp
⌐	Indent left	The brown wolf ran home. ⌐	
⌐	Indent right	⌐The brown wolf ran home.	
tr	Transpose	The brown wolf ran⌢home.	tr
≡ or Cap	Set in capital letters	(t)he brown wolf ran home.	Cap
/ or lc	Set in lower case	The brown wolf RAN home.	lc
bf	Set in **boldface** type	(Wolves.) A large dog-like...	bf
ital	Set in *italic* type	The big wolf ran home.	ital
rom	Set in roman type	The brown wolf ran (home.)	rom

Royalties and Advances—
Some Benchmark Figures

Advances

Many smaller publishers and university presses offer no advances or only small advances. Larger houses offer advances based on a number of factors including sales projections and the author's history. The figures below are from a survey of author advances and should only be used as a guide: Advances may be negotiated.

Range: Low-High

Trade books

Fiction Hardcover	$5,000-$100,000
Fiction Paperback	$1,500-$56,000
Nonfiction Hardcover	$5,000-$150,000
Nonfiction Paperback	$1,000-$100,000

Mass-market paperbacks

Mystery	$5,000-$50,000
Romance	$1,000-$40,000
Science Fiction	$3,500-$40,000
Western	$1,500-$35,000
Young Adult	$1,000-$14,000
Other Original Paperback	$1,500-$35,000

Children's books	$0-$53,000

Textbooks

Elementary, Junior High & High School	$0-$5,000
College	$0-$50,000
Graduate	$0-$10,000

Professional books	$0-$20,000

Royalties

Royalties are figured on the number of copies sold by the publisher, less any copies returned to the publisher. Royalty rates listed here are shown as a percentage of the cover price—also known as the retail price or list price—of the book.

Often a contract will call for royalties to be paid as a percentage of the net amount a publisher receives for its sales of a book instead of as a percentage of the cover price. In the book trade, a publisher sells to the various wholesale and retail accounts at a discounted price to allow these accounts to resell the book at a profit.

A publisher might give a wholesaler a 50% discount off the cover price. In this case, on a $10 book, a 10% royalty paid on the net amount received by a publisher [$10 - ($10 x .50) = $5.00] would earn an author $.50 per book. This works out to be 5% of the cover price. Be sure you understand how your publisher will figure royalties.

It is customary for the author to share in any amounts received by the publisher for the sale of subsidiary rights, such as sales to book clubs or catalogs. These amounts are usually figured as a flat percent of the net amount received for these rights.

Prevalent range

Trade books

Fiction

Hardcover
First 5,000 books	5-10%
Next 5,000 books	10-12%
Thereafter	12-15%

Paperback
First 10,000 books	5-10%
Thereafter	8-15%

Nonfiction

Hardcover
First 5,000 books	5-10%
Next 5,000 books	10-15%
Thereafter	10-15%

Prevalent range

Nonfiction

Paperback
First 10,000 books   5-10%
Thereafter   8-15%

Mass-market books

Mystery
First 150,000 books   6-15%
Thereafter   8-15%

Romance
First 150,000 books   4-10%
Thereafter   7-15%

Science Fiction
First 150,000 books   7-10%
Thereafter   8-15%

Western
First 150,000 books   2-10%
Thereafter   4-15%

Young Adult
First 150,000 books   1-10%
Thereafter   1-12%

Other original paperback
First 150,000 books   5-15%
Thereafter   7-15%

Source: National Writers Union.
For a more complete listing of royalties and advances, see
National Writers Union Guide to Freelance Rates &
Standard Practice.

Average Book Print Runs

Print runs—the number of copies of a book printed—differ greatly from book to book and from publisher to publisher. Print runs are based on the publisher's best guess as to the number of copies that will sell in a relatively short period, usually not more than twelve months.

Conventional wisdom dictates that a publisher, especially a smaller publisher, who wishes to remain in business, be conservative with initial print runs, opting to reprint a book if sales warrant it.

Larger print runs may indicate greater support in terms of promotion and marketing for the title from the publisher.

	Range: Low – High
Trade books	
Fiction Hardcover	500 – 72,000
Fiction Paperback	750 – 500,000
Nonfiction Hardcover	800 – 100,000
Nonfiction Paperback	500 – 300,000
Mass-market books	
Mystery	5,000 – 150,000
Romance	10,000 – 500,000
Science Fiction	5,000 – 150,000
Western	5,000 – 100,000
Young Adult	10,000 – 150,000
Other Original Paperback	3,000 – 250,000

Source: National Writers Union
For a more complete listing of book print runs, see National Writers Union Guide to Freelance Rates & Standard Practice.

Sample Magazine Writer's Guidelines

Magazines and other periodicals often prepare tip sheets—called writer's guidelines—for writers who wish to submit freelance articles or stories. Although these guidelines vary in degree of completeness, most include the basics necessary for a writer to best formulate his or her submissions.

It is prudent to have read a periodical's guidelines prior to submitting your work. Check The American Directory of Writer's Guidelines, *available in bookstores and libraries, or look in the front of the publication for the editorial address and send an SASE with a short note to the managing editor requesting the guidelines be sent to you.*

Reproduced here are the guidelines for Transitions Abroad *to give you an idea of what a comprehensive set of guidelines includes.*

TRANSITIONS ABROAD

Transitions Abroad is a planning guide for cultural immersion travel. Founded by Clay Hubbs in 1977 to provide practical information on educational travel abroad, *Transitions Abroad* remains the leading magazine and web site for independent travelers who want to extend their time abroad through work, study, or low-cost travel. Its title suggests the changes that result from immersion in another culture. Our writers provide the details and "nuts and bolts" that readers need to make their own plans.

What We Are Looking For
The magazine's four major departments—Work, Study, Travel, and Living—all focus on immediately usable practical information gained from first-hand experience for readers who travel for something more than the sights. The editors are unable to check sources, so current and accurate information is essential. Sidebars include details that are not in the body of the article: contact names and addresses, web sites and email addresses, telephone numbers, costs. Well-researched supporting material and annotated web links in sidebars greatly increases the likelihood of publication.

Transitions Abroad is primarily a place for travelers to share information. Your contribution can either take the form of a full-length article or a brief summary on a topic related to work, study, travel or living abroad. Be as concise as possible and do not hesitate to offer your critical evaluations.

Note: The editors will sometimes shorten material submitted for other departments for inclusion in Information Exchange, which leads off each issue. Submissions that otherwise fit our guidelines but are too lengthy to include in the magazine (or to shorten for Information Exchange) may be published on our web site. Please tell us if you do not wish your material to be considered for Web publication. If you prefer to have your article published on the Web exclusively (which reaches over 3.5 million unique visitors a year), please email webeditor@transitionsabroad.com with an electronic submission, as the Web site has no space limitations or time constraints.

What We Do Not Want
Sightseeing or "destination" pieces that focus on what to see rather than on the people and culture; Personal travelogues or lengthy descriptions of personal experiences (unless readers can use the practical details in your account to make their own travel plans); Articles that represent travel as a form of consumption and objectify the people of other countries; Information that is readily available in guidebooks or from government tourist offices.

Departments for *Transitions Abroad* Magazine

Maximum length: 1,500 words. Average length: 800 to 1,000 words. Length restrictions do not apply for web-only submissions. For the magazine we must edit tightly because of space limitations. At least four feature-length articles are used in each issue: one each on Work, Study, Immersion Travel, and Living. Content must be information-based and not merely a travelogue or personal narrative description.

Immersion Travel Writers' Guidelines

This lead-off section of the magazine focuses on interaction with local people and cultures and the avoidance of superficial tourist routines. Articles may involve such things as a finding a home stay or a rural bed and breakfast, a 1- or 2-week language study course, or pursuing a special interest or activity like cooking, music, dancing, visual arts, writing, photography, hiking or biking.

To qualify for inclusion in the Immersion Travel section submissions should describe (and provide supporting information for) travel that involves active participation in the life of the host community: Cross-Cultural Travel is travel that includes interaction with the people of the host community. It goes beyond conventional tourism to the deeper experience that makes travel exciting, enriching, and educational...travel that includes immersion in another culture by living, working, studying (or playing!) alongside your hosts.

Community-Based Travel is travel that profits the host community. If an organized tour (see Ecotours and Cross-Cultural Travel below), the organizer and guides should, whenever possible, be from the host community.

These principles of immersion travel underlie the following subsections featured in the magazine, which are listed here alphabetically:

Activist Responsible Traveler

Many of us immersion travelers have stories about how direct exposure to human suffering or environmental destruction led us to contribute in some way to its alleviation. In what ways have you given back to the people in the countries where you have traveled?

Best Bargains

Current information on best-value-for-money travel opportunities. Be specific about dates, contacts, etc. in the text (no sidebars). Several used each issue. See the Budget Travel section of our site for examples.

Cross-Cultural and Alternative Tours

While our focus is on independent travel, we recognize that there are occasions when locally-organized tours are the least intrusive and most efficient ways to see the local sights.

Disability Travel

Travelers with disabilities have found plenty of opportunities for immersion travel, volunteering, interning, and studying abroad. In cooperation with the National Clearing House on Disability and Exchange (NCDE), *Transitions Abroad* encourages submissions on projects, programs, how-to information, and planning advice for travelers with disabilities. See the Disability Travel section of our site for examples.

Eco-Travel

Department editors Ron Mader and Deborah McLaren welcome information on how local communities abroad organize and profit from ecotourism, plus details on responsible ecotour organizers. See the Responsible Travel section of our site for examples.

Family Travel

Vacation overseas with the kids? Short-term and long-term family travel can be inexpensive and enriching. Submissions can focus on local family tour operators, homestays, vacation rentals, camping, and independently planned itineraries with an emphasis on cultural and community-based travel. See the Family Travel section of our site for examples.

Independent Travel Itineraries

Detailed itineraries that take independent and solo travelers off the tourist trail—whether to the less-visited areas of Europe or to remote regions of the rest of the world See the Independent and Solo Travel section of our site for examples.

Lifelong Learning

500 words maximum (longer pieces will be considered for the Education Abroad section which includes the experiences of teens, college students, post-grads, and seniors). Usually first-hand reports on a travel-study program or an independently organized learning experience such as a language-learning vacation. This could include cultural immersion experiences that travelers would find difficult to organize on their own. See the Educational Travel, Cultural Travel and Special Interest Tours, and Language Study sections of our site for varied examples.

Senior Travel

Among the most noticeable features of global travel today are both the age and the sheer numbers of older men and women taking active, adventurous vacations with a strong learning and service focus. Whether short-term vacations or retirement sojourns, editor Alison Gardner is looking for 50- to 80-year-olds to write about ecological, educational, cultural, and volunteer travel. Topics may include home stays and hospitality exchanges, international tours with substance, educational programs, and service-learning. See the Senior Travel section of our site for examples.

Solo Woman Traveler

More and more women are traveling solo or with other women. Submissions should emphasize the advantages of independent solo travel and precautions regarding health and safety. See the Women Travel section of our site for examples.

(Note: Due to space limitations in the magazine an abbreviated version may sometimes run in print and an extended version on the web site. This is true of all submissions.)

Working Traveler Writers' Guidelines

The working abroad section of the magazine deals with the varied ways for travelers to support themselves while living for an extended period abroad. For many, the work is not an end-in-itself, but provides the possibility for a more deeply rewarding experience though immersion in a foreign culture. For others, international work is a great way to build a global resume. Articles in this section should provide the practical information necessary to prepare for and to find work abroad of both a long- and short-term nature. Writers are encouraged to include an evocation of the specific culture within the context of an information-based article. As always, inclusion of annotated links and resources greatly increases the likelihood of publication.

International Careers

Submissions should focus on securing long-term jobs abroad and discussing ways to prepare for a successful overseas career. Emphasize practical information and insights based upon experience in an international career (which may include international work in the U.S.). See the International Careers section of our site for examples.

Teaching English Abroad

As the world rushes to acquire English, the new lingua franca of international commerce, diplomacy, and higher education, the bulk of job opportunities abroad are for English teachers. Your "credential" is simply being a native speaker of the English language. In this section we seek information on how to prepare to become an English teacher, choosing an ESL program, how to research and find a good job, and what to expect in the way of demands and rewards. See the Teaching English Abroad section of our site for examples.

Short-Term Work

Your experience in finding and maintaining a short-term job abroad (from crewing a yacht to working as a journalist) is of great interest to our readers, especially as a way to extend your stay. You should include resources and practical information for how readers can find a similar work experience. Articles can focus on topics such as the pros and cons of particular jobs around the world, tips on how to make the most of your job, and opportunities for creating your own work as a freelancer or entrepreneur. See the Short-Term Work section of our site for examples.

Volunteering

A very popular, fascinating and rewarding way to extend a trip abroad is to exchange work for free room and board (and often a small stipend). In other cases volunteer programs may be quite comprehensive—including language learning, internships, excursions, etc.—and the stipend is correspondingly higher. These are excellent ways to extend a vacation while participating in a useful and rewarding service. First-hand reports on how to do this are welcome. See the Volunteer Abroad section of our site for examples.

Internships Abroad

The best time to seek work abroad and to prepare for an international career is while you are a student or soon after graduation (though some internships also exist for those seeking a career change). You may be considering an overseas work experience for many reasons: an adventure, a chance to gain in-depth knowledge of another culture and of yourself, an inexpensive way to improve foreign language proficiency, or as preparation for an international career. First-hand reports on how to do this are welcome. See the Internships Abroad section of our site for examples.

Teaching K-12 and University

Travelers with K-12 certification have a wide range of options for teaching abroad. Articles in this section include work in private international schools, Department of Defense schools, teacher exchange programs and volunteer organizations. First-hand evaluations of experiences are welcome. See the Teaching Abroad section of our site for examples.

Education Abroad Writer's Guidelines

Transitions Abroad's Education Abroad section, which runs in every issue, deals specifically with international education for enrolled students. For this section the editors seek reliable and useful information and advice on educational opportunities abroad in articles of 1,000-2,000 words. To see a collection of articles by international educators recently published in *Transitions Abroad* go to the Study Abroad section of our site.

Note: Busy international educators are encouraged to email conference presentations, rough drafts, outlines, or ideas to Clay Hubbs (Clay@TransitionsAbroad.com), who will help you turn promising ideas or material into a polished piece for publication. *Transitions Abroad* maintains that anyone working in the field for more than five years has something valuable to say to his or her colleagues about what works in advising students. Send completed articles as an attached MS Word file to: Editor@TransitionsAbroad.com.

In every issue of *Transitions Abroad*'s Education Abroad section, you'll find:

Student to Student
Student Participant Reports
Study Abroad Adviser
Program News and Notes
Issue-Specific Columns (See "Columns" below)

Student to Student features articles in which currently enrolled or recently graduated students share information and experience with other students contemplating an educational experience abroad, whether formal study abroad, volunteering, or work abroad. Students write 1,000- to 1,500-word articles that emphasize essential practical information like: how they selected a program or arranged their own independent study or job or internship. Recent topics include: Study in Russia, Study in Australia: A Practical Guide, Winning a Grant to Work Overseas, Anti-Americanism Abroad, Study Abroad with a Disability, Sports and Study Abroad. Many more examples can be found in our archived section dedicated to Student to Student reports. All student-written articles are eligible for consideration in the annual *Transitions Abroad* Student Writers Contest.

Student Participant Reports. Students returning from a program abroad evaluate the program based on their own first-hand experience. Informational sidebars provide details on the program (contact info, costs, etc.) and a selection of similar programs—with contact info—so that other students can plan a similar experience. Many more examples can be found in our archived section dedicated to Student Participant Reports.

Both Student to Student and Student Participant Reports should focus on practical, usable information based on personal experience. Think about what you were looking for when you were planning to go abroad: What did you need to know? Where did you find it? What were the most challenging planning questions you faced (short-term versus long-term study, Independent study versus a program, an internship program versus creating your own internship, etc.)? Once you were abroad, what did you wish you had known before you left?

Since you returned, how have you been able to fit what you did and learned abroad into your life—academic and otherwise? Note: These are only suggestions to help you focus; don't attempt to answer them all.

Think of yourself as an adviser or counselor and your reader as someone like yourself before you went abroad. Be specific and to the point: Narrative descriptions of your own experiences and responses to them (diaries) are not generally helpful to someone preparing for their own trip unless your descriptions make clear how the reader can plan and carry out a similar program. If you write about a specific program (a "Participant Report"), be critical but remember that the appropriateness of the program depends upon the individual. What was right (or perhaps wrong) for you might be wrong (or right) for another student. If possible, provide examples of similar programs or opportunities for your reader to choose from. Study Abroad Adviser. Started in 1980 by the late Lily von Klemperer, a legend in international education, to provide practical information for advisers to use in their day-to-day work to make their efforts more effective, efficient, and rewarding. Recent topics have included:

The Benefits of Study Abroad, Debunking Reasons Against Studying Abroad, Top Ten Reasons for African-Americans to Study Abroad, etc. One article is selected for publication per issue. 1500-2000 words. Many more examples can be found in our Study Abroad Advisor archives.

Student Program News and Notes. Introduced by Lily von Klemperer in 1981 and now edited by Clay Hubbs, this section of short notices of new programs, changes in existing programs, and new resources for education abroad runs in every issue. Program directors are encouraged to send program updates and announcements to Editor@transitionsabroad.com with a copy to Clay@transitionsabroad.com.

Columns

Students and especially education abroad professionals are encouraged to submit articles of 1,500 to 2,000 words on the following topics to appear in selected issues of *Transitions Abroad*:

Jan/Feb — International Career Advisor

Focuses exclusively on student preparation for an international career. Recent topics: Build on an International Employment Profile, Living and Working Abroad.

Mar/Apr — High School Exchanges

Practical information on all educational opportunities abroad for high school students. May be written by administrators or by students (or both).Recent topics: Summer Abroad: Opportunities Abound for High School Students, An Australian Exchange, Amazon Teen Exchange in Ecuador.

May/June — Developing Countries Focus

Why and how to study in developing countries. Recent topics: Study Abroad in the Developing World, Why Study in Asia?, Why Study in Africa?

July/Aug — Service-Learning Advisor

Practical information and evaluations on service-learning opportunities for students. What are the opportunities? How can students find them? Is credit available for service learning? How can students tie service learning into their on-campus academic curriculums? What is the value of experiential education?

Sept/Oct — Work Abroad Advisor

Started by William Nolting in 1993. While every issue of *Transitions Abroad* features The Working Traveler section, Work Abroad Advisor is dedicated to information and experiences specifically for students or recent graduates. Work, including volunteering, is the only affordable education abroad choice for a great number of students. What are the opportunities? How can students find and use them? Recent topics: English Teaching Jobs Abroad, International Internships, Volunteering Abroad.

Nov/Dec — Point:Counterpoint

Introduced in 1990 by Bill Hoffa, a leading spokesman on international education and an author and editor of the most important reference guides for international educators, to call attention to trends and issues in international education, this column explores timeless topics and controversies in the field with no immediate "solutions" but which must be continuously addressed by all international educators. Recent topics: Coming Home from Study Abroad: Relationships, Roots and Unpacking, Defending Study Abroad, Virtual Advising, Traveling to Learn, International Education is not Commodity.

Living Abroad Writers' Guidelines

1,000 words maximum. The best way to learn about a country and its culture is to live there (or short of that to travel like a local). For longer stays nothing beats exchanging your home for a comparable home abroad or renting or buying a vacation home. Often you may extend your stay by working in the host country as well.

Making the move to live abroad is for many the ultimate transition -- often the fulfillment of a lifelongdream, in other cases the result of chance and circumstance. We are seeking inspiring articles which also provide in-depth practical descriptions of your experience moving and living abroad, including discussions of immigration, personal and family life abroad, housing, work, social interactions with the natives, food, culture, and potential prejudices encountered.

Apart from practical considerations what were the most important physical, psychological, and social adjustments necessary to integrate into the local communities? Feel free to include anecdotes about locals who may have aided in your adjustment to the physical conditions and social mores of the host community, as well as the role of other expatriates in providing information and support.

A listing or reference to the most important web sites, publications, and other resources which have aided you in the cultural adjustment process or enhanced your current life abroad is encouraged to help others who may find themselves in similar situations or even similar locations. Such sidebars should include supporting details and resources that are not in the body of the article.

As always, we do not seek diaries or personal blogs, but your own perspective in which the host country remains the primary focus, such that the color and taste of the people and land remain in the foreground. See the Living Abroad section of our site for examples.

Abroad At Home Writers' Guidelines

1,000 words maximum. The opening of borders between people and cultures through art and other forms of expression (music, film, literature, art, craft work, cuisine, etc.) is a bridge to other countries and cultures. Submissions should provide insights on the creative arts of another culture that may be embraced in our day-to-day life while not physically abroad. Resource sidebars may include web sites related to the subject and contact information for relevant groups, clubs, and organizations.

See Latin American Movies for an excellent example of an article which demonstrates the notion that artistic works from abroad continue to be transformative and educational even while experienced at home.

Information Exchange

Contributors are invited to use this opening section of the magazine to share letters to the editor, factual and current practical information, and tips on work, study, living, or ""'life-seeing"'" travel abroad. Be as brief as possible (250 words maximum). Payment for Information Exchange is a free one-year subscription or subscription-extension.

Submission Procedures for *Transitions Abroad* Magazine

Articles

Maximum length: 1,500 words. Average length: 800 to 1,000 words. We edit tightly for length. Manuscripts should be sent electronically and addressed to editor@transitionsabroad.com. Include your contact information. Please attach only Microsoft Word documents: if you use another format, please cut and paste your article into the text portion of your email message. We prefer that you do not send photos electronically until your article has been accepted for publication. If you do not submit your article via email (not recommended), you must provide an electronic version of your manuscript on disk (Macintosh platform) via regular mail. The author's name, address, phone and fax number, and email address should appear on at least the first page of the manuscript.

Photos

We strongly recommend that you let us know whether photos are available with your article. However, if you are submitting an article electronically, please do not submit photos electronically until your article has been accepted for publication. High resolution (300 dpi) digital or scanned photographs sent as JPEGS or TIFS via email are preferred. It is fine to send prints or digital photos on disc via postal mail at any time. Slides are accepted but not preferred. It is also fine to send electronic standalone photos at anytime. An SASE must be included to ensure the return of photographs. See Photographic Guidelines for all information on sending photos for the Magazine.

Other Submissions Considerations

Regular mail should be accompanied by an SASE. If sending by mail please include your email address! All material is submitted on speculation. We purchase one-time rights only; rights revert to writers upon publication. However, we reserve the right to reprint published articles in part or whole on our web site. We will consider reprinted material from publications outside our primary circulation area.

Since ours is not the usual travel publication, writers may want to browse the back issues on our website or review a recent issue of *Transitions Abroad* for style and content (See order form).

Contact Information	Electronic Submissions
Mailing Address	editor@transitionsabroad.com
Transitions Abroad	UPS or Fed-X
PO Box 745	617 Niles Rd.
Bennington, VT 05201	Bennington, VT 05201

Include a short biographical note at the end of each submission, including your email address. We include these on all published articles so that readers can contact you directly with their feedback.

Include your name, address, telephone numbers (day and evening), and email address on at least the first page of your manuscript.

Electronic submissions are preferred, however, if you are sending the manuscript in postal mail, include an envelope of adequate size and with the correct postage for return. We do not return material unaccompanied by SASEs.

Initial response time to manuscripts is about four to six weeks. We often request permission to hold a submission longer pending final decision. We record and file each submission and take great care with material "on hold" awaiting the appropriate issue. Unless you need your manuscript or photographs returned immediately, please do not telephone. We cannot provide status reports by phone.

Payment by *Transitions Abroad* Magazine

Payment is on publication, $2 per column inch (50-55 words), sometimes more for repeatcontributors. Minimum payment $25. For the most part our contributors are not professional travel writers but people with information and ideas to share; we are much more interested in usable first-hand information than in polished prose. We are always looking for experienced writers to become regular contributors or contributing editors. Fees for regular contributors are by agreement. Two copies of the issue in which your story appears will be included with payment.

Sample Book Publisher's Writer's Guidelines

Many book publishers have writer's guidelines available. You are more likely to meet with success if you obtain and follow a publisher's guidelines when submitting a book proposal. You may write a publisher requesting their guidelines—remember to send an SASE—or check The American Directory of Writer's Guidelines: More than 1700 Magazine Editors and Book Publishers Explain What They Are Looking for from Freelancers.

Prima Publishing's guidelines, shown below, are typical for a nonfiction book publisher.

Prima Publishing

A Division of Random House
3000 Lava Ridge Court
Roseville, CA 95661
(916) 787-7000

Guidelines for Submissions

PRIMA PUBLISHING, founded in 1984, publishes hardcovers and trade paperbacks in nonfiction categories including popular culture, current affairs and international events, travel, business, careers, legal topics, sports, cooking, health, lifestyle, self-help, and music. Prima also produces a line of computer books geared toward business, professional, and recreational users, and a line of video/computer game clue books.

Prima is among the fastest-growing independent publishers and maintains a solid backlist.

Please include the following information when sending a proposal to Prima Publishing:

Brief explanation of the book. What is the manuscript about and why would someone buy it? Like the short text written on the back cover of a book, the explanation should describe the contents of the book while also enticing the reader to know more about it. The overview is also an opportunity for the author to display his or her unique writing style.

Detailed table of contents and chapter outlines. Breaking the manuscript down into individual chapters, write a paragraph discussing the information in each chapter.

Sample chapter. The editor will need to see your best chapter in order to evaluate your writing.

Anticipated market for the book. Who is intended audience? Be as specific as possible. Quantify and target the audience as much as possible. Publishers are looking for profitable books and, especially if it is a new area for Prima, we need to know the size of the market and the likelihood of reaching it. Will it appeal to professionals in your area? If so, how will we reach them? Will it have appeal outside the usual trade bookstore channels? Are there books currently on the best-seller lists that reach the same type of market?

Competition for the book. Are there other books currently on the market that address the same or similar topics? How and why is your book different? Does your proposed book fill a niche presently open? Recognize the competition but tell us how your book will surpass that competition because of the added material or new slant it offers.

Author's Qualifications. What makes you the right person to write this book? Tell us about your career experience and educational credentials as well as your experience. Also of interest is your publishing history and why you came to write this book. Do you have periodical, journal, or book writing experience?

Additional guidelines. When submitting a proposal to Prima, or to any publisher, it is standard practice to include a self-addressed stamped envelope (SASE) in which your proposal or manuscript can be returned to you. Please allow six to eight weeks for a response to your proposal.

The Insider's Guide to Book Editors, Publishers, and Literary Agents by Jeff Herman provides detailed instructions on how to produce an effective book proposal. Other reference books are available through the public library or at your local bookstores.

Prima appreciates your thinking of our publishing program in connection with your work and wishes you luck with this and all of your publishing endeavors!!

Magazines and Newsletters of Interest to Writers

One surefire way to fine-tune your skills, keep up on the markets, and even resupply your enthusiasm for writing is by reading the many great periodicals available to writers. Here's just a sampling. Naturally subscription prices may change.

American Journalism Review For journalists and communications professionals, (301) 405-8803 University of Maryland, 1117 Journalism Building College Park, MD 20742-7111.

Byline General interest writer's magazine, (405) 348-5591, bylinemag.com, P.O. Box 5240, Edmond, OK 73083-5240.

Canadian Author Quarterly newsletter for writers in Canada, (705) 653-0323, fax (705) 653-0593, P.O. Box 419, 27 Doxsee Ave. N., Campbellford, ON K0L 1L0 Canada.

Children's Book Insider Useful market information for children's writers, also how-to articles, (970) 836-0394, 901 Columbia Road, Fort Collins, CO 80525, e-mail: mail@write4kids.com. write4kids.com

Communication Briefings Monthly newsletter compiling tips on management, writing and promotion, (703) 518-2318, 2807 N. Parham Rd. Richmond, VA 23294.

Editor & Publisher Covers the newspaper and syndicate publishing industry. Also publishes a detailed syndicate directory every summer, (800) 336-4380, 770 Broadway New York, NY 10003.

The Editorial Eye, Focusing on Publications Standards and Practices Monthly, newsletter on editorial subjects, including writing, editing, graphics, production, (703) 683-0683, fax (703) 683-4915, EEI, 66 Canal Center Plaza, ste. 200, Alexandria, VA 22314.

The Exchange, a Newsletter for Writers Who are Christian Quarterly newsletter. TheWordGuild.com.

Fiction Writer's Guideline, The Newsletter of Fiction Writer's Connection Monthly newsletter. FictionWriters.com.

Folio Covers the magazine industry, (203) 854-6730, 33 South Main St. Norwalk, CT 06854.

Freelance Success: The Marketing and Management Newsletter for Experienced Journalists and Nonfiction Writers Weekly newsletter. (877) 731-5411, e-mail: editor@freelancesuccess.com. 32391 Dunford St. Farmington Hills, MI 48334

Freelance Writer's Report Monthly newsletter with information for writers, (603) 922-8338, (603) 922-8339 fax, P.O. Box A, North Stratford NH 03590. writer-editors.com

The Gila Queen's Guide to Markets Newsletter of complete genre market news, plus articles, (973) 579-1537, P.O. Box 97, Newton, NJ 07860. gilaqueen.us.

Horn Book Magazine Covers children's literature, also the *Horn Book Guide*, reviews of children's books published in previous six months. (617) 628-0225 Roland Street suite 200 Boston MA 02129. hbooks.com

Locus, Science fiction newspaper, with reviews, articles, market news, etc., (510) 339-9196, P.O. Box 13305, Oakland, CA 94661. locusmag.com

Maine in Print Maine Writers and Publishers Alliance, monthly newsletter for writers, editors, teachers, librarians, etc., (207) 228-8263, 318 Glickman Family Library University of Southern Maine PO Box 9301, 314 Forest Avenue, Portland, ME 04104. mainewriters.org

Poets & Writers Bimonthly magazine for fiction writers and poets, with information on publication, grants, contests, etc., (212) 226-3586, 72 Spring St., Room 301, New York, NY 10012. pw.org

Publishers Weekly Weekly book publishing trade magazine, with reviews, book and publishing news, etc., (800) 278-2991, 360 Park Avenue South, New York, NY 10010. publishersweekly.com

Rising Star Newsletter on science fiction and fantasy markets, (603) 623-9796, 47 Byledge Rd., Manchester, NH 03104.

Roundup Magazine Bimonthly magazine with the latest trends in publishing, book reviews, marketing news, how-to articles, magazine of Western Writers of America, available without membership, (615) 791-1444, contact James Crutchfield, 1012 Fair St., Franklin, TN 37064. westernwriters.org

Scenario, The Magazine of Screenwriting Art, Quarterly, each issue features four complete screenplays with author interviews and essays, (212) 463-0600, 104 Fifth Ave. 19th floor New York, NY 10011

Science Fiction Chronicle Monthly with book reviews, market reports, information for writers, editors, publishers, etc., (718) 643-9011, 1380 East 17th St. Ste. 210, Brooklyn, NY 11230. dna.publications.com

Small Press Review/Small Magazine Review Monthly for and about the small press and small magazines, (530) 877-6110, P.O. Box 100, Paradise, CA 95967. dustbooks.com

Speculations Bimonthly magazine with related website, has markets and writing tips for SF, fantasy and other speculative fiction, e-mail: k.brewster@compuserve.com, 1111 W. El Camino Real, ste. #109-400, Sunnyvale, CA 94087.

The Writer monthly general interest writer's magazine, (617) 423-3157, 120 Boylston St., Boston, MA 02116. writermag.com

Writer's Digest Monthly general interest writer's magazine, (513) 531-2222, 1507 Dana Ave., Cincinnati, OH 45207.

Writer's Journal Bimonthly general interest writer's magazine. WritersJournal.com.

Selected Books
for Writers

Every writer must have a good dictionary and thesaurus, but other books on the craft of writing and taking care of the business side of writing are almost as important. There are scores of good books available. Here are a few selected titles worth seeking. Often the title explains the contents, but as writers ourselves, we couldn't keep from making a few notations.

1001 Ways to Market Your Books: For Authors and Publishers by John Kremer. Much of the promotion for a book is left to the author. This is *the* book for savvy authors who want to make their books best-sellers.

101 Best Scenes Ever Written: a Romp through Literature for Writers and Readers by Barnaby Conrad.

The ABC's of Writing for Children by Elizabeth Koehler-Pentacoff. Advice and anecdotes from 112 published children's authors.

The American Directory of Writer's Guidelines: More than 1700 Magazine Editors and Book Publishers Explain What They Are Looking for from Freelancers edited and compiled by Stephen Blake Mettee, Michele Doland, and Doris Hall. Most periodical and many book publishers have writer's guidelines which spell out exactly what that publisher is seeking. Included is key information about topics, voice, word counts, credentials required, who the average reader is and other criteria. With *ADWG* over 1,700 of these guidelines are available in one place. Use this resource to browse for ideas, fine-tune a submission, or locate a publisher for the piece—still languishing in your desk drawer—that you wrote ages ago.

The Associated Press Stylebook and Briefing on Media Law by Norm Goldstien. Newly updated and expanded. Want to know when to capitalize religious titles? Or what portion of the world actually constitutes the Far East? This is your book. Easy to use and surprisingly versatile.

Bird by Bird: Some Instructions on Writing and Life by Anne Lamott. This would be a good read, even if you had never thought of writing anything.

Characters and Viewpoint by Orson Scott Card. Expert advice on two tough topics.

The Chicago Manual of Style. A big book that is often the final word on usage, punctuation and form for authors, editors, copy editors and proofreaders. Also available on CD-ROM.

Comedy Writing Step-by-Step by Gene Perret. Foreword by Carol Burnett. 'Nuff said.

Damn! That's Funny by Gene Perret. The longtime head writer for Bob Hope shows how to write and sell comedy.

Damn! Why Didn't I Write That? By Marc McCutcheon. Bestselling author shows how to fill lucrative niches, year after year.

The Elements of Style by William Strunk, Jr. and E. B. White. This thin volume provides concise instruction in the essence of good writing. If a writer can have only one book on the craft of writing in his or her library, this is the one. Read it and reread it.

Emotional Structure: Creating the Story Beneath the Plot by Peter Dunne. It's about screen writing, but novel writers can benefit, too.

The Fast Track Course on How to Write a Nonfiction Book Proposal by Stephen Blake Mettee. Short and to-the-point.

Feminine Wiles: Creative Techniques for Writing Women's Feature Stories that Sell by Donna Elizabeth Boetig.

The Fiction Writer's Silent Partner by Martin Roth. If this doesn't help with brainstorming, nothing will. Out of print, but available from used book sources.

How to Get Happily Published: A Complete and Candid Guide by Judith Appelbaum. A classic. The name says it all.

How to Get a Literary Agent by Michael Larsen. Good, practical advice—interspersed with humor—from an experienced agent.

How to Write a Book Proposal by Michael Larsen. This step-by-step guide will not only result in a professional book proposal but will also act as a drill to help you fine-tune the book itself.

How to Write a Children's Book and Get It Published by Barbara Seuling. The definitive guide to all types of children's books, full of advice.

How to Write a Damn Good Novel and *How to Write a Damn Good Novel II: Advanced Techniques for Dramatic Storytelling* by James N. Frey. Damn good instruction from a damn good novelist.

How to Write and Sell Historical Fiction by Persia Woolley.

If You Can Talk, You Can Write by Joel Saltzman. An entertaining and informative read. Out of print, but available at used book sources.

The International Directory of Little Magazines & Small Presses edited by Len Fulton. This annual lists over 6,000 paying and nonpaying markets for your writing. It is the number-one resource for collecting the clips and credits often needed to get your work published by one of the bigger periodical or book publishers.

Kirsch's Handbook of Publishing Law by Jonathan Kirsch. Covers the full spectrum of legal issues facing an author or publisher. Out of print, but available from used book sources.

Let's Get Creative: Writing Fiction that Sells, by William F. Nolan. Nolan uses a brisk and humorous style to teach how to craft novels and short stories that sell.

LifeWriting: Drawing from Personal Experience to Create Features You Can Publish by Fred D. White, Ph.D.. This encompasses a broad range of personal experience writing.

Literary Market Place (LMP) and *International Literary Market Place*. *LMP* is a rather expensive two-volume set listing publishers, agents and others in the industry. Most writers use their library's copy.

On Writing: A Memoir of the Craft by Stephen King. This is not only the rags-to-riches story every writer dreams about, but it's also a manual of practical and inspiring advice, written in that fast-paced, can't-put-it-down Stephen King style.

Pitching Hollywood: How to Sell Your TV and Movie Ideas by Jonathan Koch and Robert Kosberg with Tanya Meurer Norman. Two successful movie and TV producers provide tips.

Quit Your Day Job! How to Sleep Late, Do What You Enjoy, and Make a Ton of Money as a Writer by Jim Denney. He lays out a sound, strategic plan for building a career as a full-time writer.

The Romance Writer's Handbook: How to Write Romantic Fiction and Get It Published by Rebecca Vinyard. This book has short, readable chapters with practical info on everything romance, including how steamy to make your love scenes.

The Self-Publishing Manual by Dan Poynter. This is the book most often recommended to new publishers—with cause.

Working Solo: The Real Guide to Freedom & Financial Success with Your Own Business by Terri Lonier. Written with not only writers in mind, but solid advice for anyone planning to quit his or her day job.

Writers' and Artists' Hideouts: Great Getaways for Seducing the Muse by Andrea Brown.

The Writer's Journey: Mythic Structure for Storytellers & Screenwriters by Christopher Vogler. Joseph Campbell did a great deal of landmark thinking and writing on myths, some of which comprise the oldest of human stories. He discovered these early stories share common elements—across time and cultures—that, when viewed beyond the literal, help to explain the essence of mankind's experience. In this book, Christopher Vogler concludes there is something fundamentally, perhaps even primordially, compelling about a story that is successful in capturing these elements. He takes Campbell's concepts, and, one by one, applies them to story writing, using examples to point out that today's best and most beloved novels and movies have achieved mythic dimensions by the incorporation of some or all of these common elements. A must-read for any serious fiction writer.

Writer's Market edited by Robert Lee Brewer. This book is a great place to begin checking out the markets for your writing. Published annually. There are other market books for specific genre, too.

Zen in the Art of Writing: Expanded by Ray Bradbury. Twelve essays written by a master. As much fun to read as it is informative.

Associations for Writers

Professional associations can be helpful, especially for writers, who often work alone. Groups provide not only networking, but also valuable information about markets, promotions, legal issues and more. Many of the national organizations have local chapters. To find smaller, local groups not listed here, check with your local library, bookstore, or community college writing program. When writing to any group, please include a self-addressed, stamped envelope, as many are nonprofit organizations run by volunteers.

Academy of American Poets
584 E. Broadway, Suite 1208
New York, NY 10012
(212) 274-0343
(212) 274-9427 fax
poets.org
The academy offers members readings and residencies, contests and fellowships, a newsletter, and book projects.

American Book Producers Association
160 Fifth Ave., Suite 625
New York, NY 10010-7000
(212) 645-2368
abpaonline.org
ABPA was founded in 1980 as the trade organization for independent book producers in the United States and Canada. Book producers provide all services necessary for publication except for sales and order fulfillment. They work with authors, agents, editors, designers, and all the other people involved in producing a finished book.

American Crime Writers League
12 St. Ann Drive
Santa Barbara, CA 93109
acwl.org

American Medical Writers Association
40 West Guide Dr.

Rockville, MD 20850
(301) 294-5303
(301) 294-9006 fax
amea.org

AMWA holds an annual conference, as well as regional meetings throughout the year and local chapter meetings. It was founded in 1940 for communicators in the biomedical and health sciences fields. Membership is open to anyone interested in health or medical communication, including freelance writers, publishers, doctors, pharmacists, veterinarians, and people at clinics, nonprofit associations or hospitals.

American Society of Journalists & Authors, Inc.
1501 Broadway, Suite 302
New York, NY 10036
(212) 997-0947
(212) 937-2315 fax
asja.org

ASJA is an association for published writers of nonfiction. Members receive a monthly newsletter with lots of market information, and can receive help with contracts or collection of payments. There is an annual conference and monthly dinner meetings, which nonmembers may attend.

Arizona Authors Association
P. O. Box 87857
Phoenix, AZ 85080
(623) 847-9343
azauthors.com

A networking group for writers, publishers, editors, typists, agents and others interested in books throughout Arizona. The group offers critique groups, workshops and a newsletter featuring information on contests, other writers' groups, bookstore news and more.

Asian American Writer's Workshop
16 West 32nd Street Ste. 10A
New York, NY 10001
(212) 494-0061
e-mail: desk@aaww.com
aaww.com

This New York-based nonprofit group is dedicated to the creation, publication and distribution of Asian American literature. It is a national network of writers, publishers, agents, illustrators, performing artists and others. Members receive a literary magazine three times a year, plus a literary journal, *Asian Pacific American Journal*, twice a year. AAWW holds seasonal workshops in New York, as well as in other parts of the country.

Association of Authors' Representatives
P. O. Box 237201, Ansonia Station
New York, NY 10003
(212) 353-3709
  Literary agents who are members of AAR subscribe to a code of ethics. AAR provides a list of questions to authors to help them in choosing an agent.

Association of Desk-Top Publishers
3401-A800 Adams Ave.
San Diego, CA 92116
(619) 563-9714

Association of Writers and Writing Programs
Tallwood House, Mail Stop 1E3
George Mason University
Fairfax, VA 22030
(703) 993-4301
(703) 993-4302 fax
awpwriter.org
  A membership in AWP includes six issues of *AWP Chronicle*, seven issues of *AWP Job List*, and discounts on the annual conference and other programs. Members can subscribe to a job placement service.

The Authors Guild
116 West 23rd Street Ste. 500
New York, NY 10011
(212) 563-5904
(212) 564-5363 fax
authorsguild.org
  Membership in the guild provides a variety of services, including a quarterly newsletter, a legal staff to review members' publishing agreements, health insurance and a guide to publishing contracts. Annual dues include membership in The Authors League of America.

The Authors League of America, Inc.
330 W. 42nd St.
New York, NY 10036
(212) 564-8350
  A sister organization to The Authors Guild (see above).

California Writers Club
1090 Cambridge St.
Novato, CA 94947
(415) 883-6206
calwriters.org

This group has a dozen area chapters in California. There are local meetings and a local newsletter each month, as well as a statewide monthly newsletter. There are three levels of membership: active (published writers), associate (trying to get published), and social (just interested). Dues include membership in one local chapter. The club holds a respected three-day conference (which includes a writing contest) at Asilomar on the California coast during odd-numbered years only. Attendance at the conference is not limited to members.

Canadian Authors Association
Box 419
Campbellford, ON K0L 1L0 Canada
(705) 653-0323
Canauthors.org.

This association has 16 regional branches. There are two levels of membership: Members for published authors, associate for not-yet-published. CAA publishes a variety of publications for members, including a directory and a writing guide. It offers writing awards and an annual conference.

Canadian Society of Children's Authors, Illustrators and Performers
104-40 Orchard View Blvd. Lower level entrance
Toronto, ON M4R 1B9 Canada
(416) 515-1559
canscaip.org

CANSCAIP focuses on Canadian markets for children's writing with a newsletter, workshops and a conference.

Cassell Network of Writers
P. O. Box A
North Stratford, NH 03590
(603) 922-8338
(603) 922-8339 fax
e-mail: info@writers-editors.com
writers-editors.com

Members get the *Freelance Writers Report*, access to a toll-free hotline for advice, a listing in the Writer Data Bank Referral Service, and a legal hotline for advice from an attorney about copyright.

Cat Writers' Association
256 Timbertop Rd
New Ipswich, NH 03071
www.catwriters.org
 CWA offers networking for people who write about cats, with a newsletter, writing contest, annual conference, membership directory and a mentoring program.

Copywriters Council of America, Freelance
CCA Building, 7 Putter Lane
Dept. JK02 P. O. Box 102
Middle Island, NY 11953-0102
(631) 924-8555
(631) 924-3890 fax
e-mail: CCA4DMCOPY@aol.com
 CCA is a professional organization of 25,000 freelance copywriters, journalists, editors, consultants and other creative talents specializing in communications, marketing and more. Members of CCA get referral business in their fields.

Crime Writers of Canada
3007 Kingston Road, Box 113
Scarborough, ON M1M 1P1 Canada
crimewriterscanada.com

Dramatists Guild
1501 Broadway, Suite 701
New York, NY 10036
(212) 398-9366
dramaguild.com
 A professional association of playwrights, composers and lyricists, the Dramatists Guild maintains contracts for all levels of production, from Broadway to small regional theaters, plus other important agreements such as collaboration contracts. The guild provides a toll-free number for members to get advice on theater-related business and marketing. It has a quarterly literary journal, regular newsletter, and directory of agents, contests, workshops, etc. Membership is available in several levels, from active (having produced a Broadway or other first-class production) to associate (any interested writer/composer) to student.

Editorial Freelancers Association
71 West 23rd St., ste. 1910

New York, NY 10010
(212) 929-5400
the-efa.org

EFA membership consists of self-employed editors, writers, proof-readers, researchers, desktop publishers and people in similar professions. Members receive a newsletter, directory, eligibility for insurance, and a job phone, which lists freelance and full-time jobs.

Educational Press Association of America
Rowan College of NJ
201 Mullica Hill Rd.
Glassboro, NJ 08028
(856) 256-4610
(856) 256-4926 fax
e-mail: edpress@aol.com

EdPress offers members a newsletter, membership directory, annual conference, awards, workshops, publication exchange and more.

Education Writers Association
2122 P Street, NW Suite 201
Washington DC 20005
(202) 452-9830
(202) 452-9837 fax
e-mail: ewa@ewa.org
ewa.org

Members include newspaper education reporters, public information officers of school districts and colleges, and other education writers. Dues include a guide to covering education and a number of other publications. EWA provides seminars, contests and fellowships to members.

Fiction Writer's Connection
P. O. Box 4065
Deerfield Beach, FL 33442
(954) 426-4705
e-mail: bcamenson@aol.com

Members receive free critiquing of the first 10 pages of their novel, free writing consultation, a newsletter with information about markets, contests, agents, etc.

Florida Freelance Writers Association
P. O. Box A
North Stratford, NH 03590

(603) 922-8338

ffwamembers.com

Just like its sister organization, Cassell Network of Writers (see above), FFWA members get the *Freelance Writers Report*, access to a toll-free hotline for advice, a listing in the Writer Data Bank Referral Service, and a legal hotline for advice from an attorney about copyright. FFWA members also receive a directory of Florida markets, a directory of members, and a special Florida insert in the monthly newsletter.

Freelance Editorial Association
P. O. Box 380835

Cambridge, MA 02238

(617) 643-8626

This is a volunteer organization that provides networking for freelance writers, editors, desk top publishers and others. Members receive a newsletter, a copy of *Code of Fair Practice*, and a listing in the group's Yellow Pages.

Friends of Mystery
P. O. Box 8251

Portland OR 97207

(503) 241-0759

friendsofmystery.org

Horror Writers Association
P. O. Box 50577

Palo Alto, CA 94303

e-mail: hwa@horror.org

horror.org/hwa/

HWA provides networking, an agent database, a newsletter, and even opportunities for publication in members-only anthologies. Members can be active (specific publishing credits) or affiliate (anyone interested in horror writing).

Independent Writers of Chicago
1800 Nations Drive, ste. 117

Gurnee, IL 60031

(847) 855-6670

IWOC is for writers in the Midwest. It offers a job referral system, membership directory, access to insurance, a monthly newsletter, legal referral service, a credit union and more.

International Association of Business Communicators
1 Hallidie Plaze, ste. 600

San Francisco, CA 94102
(415) 544-4700
(800) 776-4222
(415) 544-4747 fax
iabc.com

IABC members receive a newsletter and access to an electronic database of communication and public relations issues. IABC sponsors an annual conference and PeopleFinders, a system for networking with communicators in a specific industry or job function.

International Association of Crime Writers Inc., North American Branch

P. O. Box 8674
New York, NY 10116-8674
(212) 243-8966
e-mail: info@crimewritersna.org
crimewritersna.org

IACW is an organization of professional writers whose primary goal is to promote communication among writers and to promote crime writing. It has branches in many countries, including England, Germany, Mexico, Cuba, and Bulgaria. The organization at large sponors regional and international conferences, and the North American Branch publishes a quarterly newsletter, hosts several receptions, and sponsors a writing contest. Membership is open to published writers only.

International Women's Writing Guild

Gracie Station, Box 810
New York, NY 10028-0082
(212) 737-7536
(212) 737-9469 fax
Web site: iwwg.com

IWWG is a worldwide nonprofit organization open to all women, published or not. Benefits and services include a bimonthly newsletter, free announcement of members' newly-published works, access to health insurance, a directory of members, a listing of literary agents, and local chapters.

League of Vermont Writers

P. O. Box 172
Underhill, VT 05490
leaguevtwriters.org

The league is a volunteer organization for writers in 11 northeastern states, with meetings in various parts of Vermont. Members receive a newsletter with information on upcoming events, member news, book reviews, markets and more.

Maine Writers and Publishers Alliance
318 Glickman Family Library
University of Southern Maine
P. O. Box 9301, 314 Forest Avenue
Portland, ME 04104
(207) 228-8263

MWPA supports Maine writers and publishers with a monthly newsletter, workshops throughout the state on screenwriting, grammar, poetry, etc. and more. It is also a book wholesaler for Maine writers. Members have access to health insurance and can participate in readings. Call for dues.

Mid-America Romance Authors
P. O. Box 8625
Prairie Village, KS 66208
(816) 468-7695

MARA is a chapter of Romance Writers of America. It has monthly meetings, a monthly newsletter, a critiquing service, critiquing groups, and an annual writer's conference or retreat.

Mystery Writers of America
17 E. 47th St, 6th floor
New York, NY 10017
(212) 888-8171
(212) 888-8107 fax
mysterywriters.org

MWA is a nonprofit professional organization for published writers of mysteries. It promotes the interests and welfare of mystery writers and monitors tax and other legislation affecting writers. Chapters hold monthly meetings, and MWA holds an annual banquet at which it awards "Edgars," named after Edgar Allan Poe.

National Association of Science Writers
P. O. Box 890
Hedgesville, WV 25427
(304) 754-5077
(304) 754-5076 fax
nasw.org

NASW is open to science writers, editors and broadcasters. Public information officers dealing with science topics may join as associate members. Benefits include a newsletter, listings of job news, online services, workshops, and an annual meeting. Health and disability insurance are also available.

National League of American Pen Women, Inc.
The Pen Arts Building
1300 17th St. NW
Washington, DC 20036
(202) 785-1997
americanpenwomen.org
    The league promotes development of the creative talents of professional women in the arts. Membership through local chapters is by invitation.

National Society of Newspaper Columnists
1345 Fillmore Street Suite 507
San Francisco, CA 94115
(415) 563-5403
columnist.com
    Hosts an annual conference and publishes a very helpful networking newsletter.

National Writers Association
10940 S. Parker Road #508
Parker, CO 80134
(303) 841-0246
(303) 841-2607 fax
e-mail: info@nationalwriters.com
    This nonprofit association offers many services to writers, including research reports, advice on copyright and contracts, a bimonthly magazine, a newsletter, agent referral, and contests.

National Writers Union
National Office
113 University Place, 6th floor
New York, NY 10003
(212) 254-0279
(212) 254-0673 fax
e-mail: nwu@nwu.org
nwu.org/nwu/
    NWU is a labor union committed to improving the working conditions of freelance writers. Members have access to health insurance and job banks. They receive a quarterly magazine and can request copies of numerous resource

materials, including guides to book contracts, small claims court, copyright and fair use.

New Dramatists
424 W. 44th St.
New York, NY 10036
(212) 757-6960
(212) 265-4738 fax
newdramatists.org

New Dramatists is a service organization for playwrights, providing members with the time, space and tools to develop their craft. There are no dues or fees, but members are expected to participate in activities. To join, potential members must submit two full-length play manuscripts and an application form. Services include readings and workshops, workspace, overnight accommodations, even grants and fellowships.

North Carolina Writer's Network
P. O. Box 954
Carrboro, NC 27510
(919) 967-9540
(919) 929-0535 fax
ncwriters.org

This group has seasonal workshops, a bimonthly newsletter, numerous literary contests and many resources available to its members, including an annual guide to markets, grants, etc.

Outdoor Writers Association of America
121 Hickory St. ste. 1
Missoula, MT 59801
(406) 728-7434
(406) 728-7445 fax
owaa.org

OWAA is a nonprofit, international organization representing professional communicators who report and reflect on America's interest in the outdoors. Members receive a monthly newsletter and can attend meetings and conferences. Applicants must meet strict requirements for membership, and must work full-time in an approved field of outdoor writing or editing.

PEN American Center
568 Broadway
New York, NY 10012
(212) 334-1660

(212) 334-2181 fax

pen.org

PEN American Center is the largest of the 124 centers worldwide, with a membership of almost 3,000 literary playwrights, essayists, editors and novelists (whence the acronym). PEN has a multitude of programs to promote literature and to offer assistance to writers. Members are elected by the membership committee, but Friends of PEN is open to anyone.

Periodical Writers Association of Canada

215 Spadina Ave. Suite 123

Toronto, ON M5T 2C7 Canada

(416) 504-1645

PWAC.ca

Offers networking, professional development, mentoring, a newsletter and other services to professional freelance writers.

Playwrights Guild of Canada

54 Wolseley St., 2nd floor

Toronto, ON M5T 1A5 Canada

(416) 703-0201

(800) 561-3318 (Canada only)

(416) 703-0059 fax

e-mail: info@playwrightsguild.ca

Members must have produced at least one play and must be Canadian citizens or legal immigrants. They receive a bimonthly newsletter and can attend an annual general meeting.

Poetry Society of America

15 Grammercy Park

New York, NY 10003

(212) 254-9628

(212) 673-2352 fax

poetrysociety.org

This nonprofit cultural organization was founded in 1910 to promote wider recognition of poetry through readings, lectures, symposia, workshops and contests. Dues include a newsletter, a program calendar, and privileges to the group's 8,000 volume library.

Poets & Writers Inc.

72 Spring St. Suite 301

New York, NY 10012

(212) 226-3586

(212) 226-3963
e-mail: PWSubs@aol.com
pw.org

A nonprofit organization offering a central source of practical information for the literary community. The information center compiles *A Directory of American Poets and Fiction Writers* and provides answers to questions about writing. It is not a membership organization; it has no dues, and anyone may use the services.

Private Eye Writers of America
407 W. Third Street
Moorestown, NJ 08057

Public Relations Society of America
33 Maiden Lane 11th Floor
New York, NY 10038
(212) 995-2230
(212) 995-0757 fax
prsa.org

PRSA is the world's largest organization for public relations professionals. Members receive a number of publications and information, as well as chances to network with peers. Local chapters hold regular meetings, and the group holds an annual conference.

Criminal Justice Journalists
720 Seventh St. N.W. 3rd Floor
Washington, DC 20001
(202) 448-1717
reporters.net
e-mail: membership@reporters.net

The Reporters Network is a nonprofit organization promoting the Internet as a research and communications tool for working journalists.

Romance Writers of America
1600 Stuebner Airlines Rd., ste, 140
Spring, TX 77379
(832) 717-5200
rwanational.org

A worldwide network of romance writers, RWA holds an annual conference, gives awards, produces a newsletter, and offers a chance for published and unpublished writers to hone their craft. There is a fee for postage for outside the United States.

Science Fiction and Fantasy Writers of America
P. O. Box 877
Chestertown, MD 21620
e-mail: execdir@sfwa.org
sfwa.org

Membership in SFWA is for published writers. Active membership is open to authors who have published one book or three short stories in the science fiction or fantasy field. Associate membership is for beginning writers who have had just one publication. Members receive two newsletters and a membership directory.

Seattle Writers Association
P. O. Box 33265
Seattle, WA 98133
(206) 860-5207
Web site: http://members.tripod.com/seattlewriters-assoc/

SWA holds monthly meetings, September through May, and sends out a monthly bulletin. It sponsors a dozen critique groups and holds a winter workshop. But by far its most unusual program is the annual evening performance, which is something of a recital for writers. People submit poems, essays, novel excepts, etc. for judging, and the chosen pieces are read by the authors in a form of literary theater.

Sisters in Crime
P. O. Box 442124
Lawrence, KS 66044
(785) 842-1325
e-mail: sinc@sistersincrime.org
sistersincrime.org

Members are mystery writers, readers, editors, agents, booksellers, and librarians, who receive a quarterly newsletter, a membership directory and a catalog of members' books in print. Other publications are available for purchase, including ones on book promotion and author book signing.

Society of American Business Editors & Writers
Missouri, School of Journalism
134 Neff Annex
Columbia, MO 65211
(573) 882-7862
sabew.org

The purpose of SABEW is to promote superior coverage of business and economic news. Members must be business or economic reporters, writers or editors for newspapers, magazines, newsletters or other media, or teachers of journalism or business. Membership includes a newsletter, an annual conference, a jobs hotline, a membership directory and contests.

Society of American Travel Writers

1500 Sunday Drive Suite 102
Raleigh, NC 27607
(919) 861-5586, fax (919) 787-4916
satw.org

The society is for professional travel writers, editors, etc. and for public relations professionals in the travel industry.

Society of Children's Book Writers & Illustrators

8271 Beverly Blvd.
Los Angeles, CA 90048
(323) 782-1010

Full membership is open to published authors or illustrators, and associate membership is open to those not yet published. SCBWI has an annual conference and regional meetings. Members receive a newsletter and various other publications and are eligible for grants. The group offers a chance for members to critique each other's work.

Society of Professional Journalists

Eugene S. Pulliam National Journalism Center
3909 N. Meridian St.
Indianapolis, IN 46208
(317) 917-8000
spj.org

SPJ offers members career services and support, continuing professional education and journalism advocacy. The Society hosts national and regional conferences and dinner meetings. Members receive the *Quill Magazine*. Professional membership is open to people working more than half time as journalists or journalism educators. Other memberships are open to retired journalists, students (high school, college and post-graduate) or people who are not eligible for full membership.

The Society of Southwestern Authors

P. O. Box 30355
Tucson, AZ 85751
e-mail: wporter202@aol.com

SSA encourages and assists published and not-yet-published writers.

Members must be published or work closely with writing in an accepted position. Associate membership is open to unpublished writers. Members receive a newsletter and membership roster, and can attend monthly meetings and an annual conference.

Society for Technical Communication
901 N. Stuart St., Suite 904
Arlington, VA 22203
(703) 522-4114
(703) 522-2075 fax
e-mail: stc@stc.com
Web site: http://stc.org/
Dedicated to advancing technical communication, STC has regional and chapter events, seminars and workshops for members, as well as an annual conference. Members receive a newsletter and are eligible for competitions, grants and scholarships.

Songwriters Guild of America
1500 Harbor Blvd.
Weehawken, NJ 07086
(201) 867-7603
songwritersguild.com
(Branches in New York, Nashville, and Hollywood)
The guild collects royalties, reviews contracts, conducts workshops, provides advice from professionals, audits music publishers and more. Members receive a newsletter.

Western Writers of America
1665 East Julho Street
Sandy, UT 84093
westernwriters.org
Members must be published in fiction or nonfiction books or articles about the historical or contemporary West. WWA offers a membership directory, annual conference, contests and networking.

Williamette Writers
9045 SW Barbur Blvd., ste. 5A
Portland, OR 97219
(503) 452-1592
williamettewriters.com
WW is a nonprofit organization led by volunteers. Members receive a newsletter and have access to critique groups, a resource center and a screen-

play library. They can be listed on a writers' referral service. WW holds regular meetings, seminars, workshops and conferences. Members also get discounts at local retailers.

Association for Women in Communications
Severn Commerce Center
3337 Duke Street
Alexandria, VA 22314
(703) 370-7436
(703) 370-7437
Women in Communications offers a variety of services for people in all fields of the profession, including media, education, sales, marketing and fund development. Services include two newsletters, a membership and resource directory, career assistance, business and personal discounts, even business and personal insurance plans.

Writers Alliance
Box 2014
Setauket, NY 11733
(516) 751-7080
Writers Alliance is a support group for writers. It sponsors readings and publishes a quarterly newsletter for writers who use or want to learn about computers.

Writers Connection
P. O. Box 24770
San Jose, CA 95154
(408) 445-3600
Writers Connection offers forums to meet editors, information on where to sell, conferences, networking opportunities and other resources.

Writers Guild of Alberta
11759 Groat Rd.
Edmonton, AB T5M 3K6 Canada
(800) 665-5354
e-mail: mail@writersguild.ab.ca
writersguild.ab.ca

Writers Guild of America (East)
555 W. 57th St. Suite 1230
New York, NY 10019
(212) 767-7800

(212) 582-1909 fax

Web site: http://wgaeast.org

WGAE is a labor union representing professional writers in motion pictures, television and radio. Members must be published or employed in the field. The guild provides a registration service for literary material, which is one of the most popular services offered. WGAW also offers a variety of publications, including a newsletter, a listing of agents and a booklet on formatting screenplays.

Writers Guild of America west

7000 West Third Street

Los Angeles, CA 90048

(323) 951-4000

wga.org

WGA west is for writers west of the Mississippi River. Members must meet certain employment standards or have specific writing credentials to join. WGA west also provides manuscript registration, which is open to members and nonmembers.

Writers Information Network

P. O. Box 11337

Bainbridge Island, WA 98110

(206) 842-9103

(206) 842-0536 fax

christianwritersinfo.net

An association for Christian writers, providing a chance for professional development and networking. Members receive up to date information on religious book and magazine publishers. Critiquing, consulting and marketing are available for a fee.

Writers of Kern

P. O. Box 6694

Bakersfield, CA 93386

(805) 871-5834

A branch of California Writers Club, Writers of Kern also has affiliate members who are not members of CWC. Membership includes a newsletter, monthly meetings, networking, many active critique groups and an annual conference. WOK is starting "Junior Writers of Kern" to serve students at high school and younger.

Writers' League of Texas

1501 W. 5th St., Suite E-2

Austin, TX 78703
(512) 499-8914
(512) 499-0441 fax
writersleague.org

The Austin Writers' League offers monthly meetings, annual workshops, seminars and conferences, informal classes, study groups, a job bank, a Writers in Schools project and much more.

The Writers' Union of Canada
90 Richmond St. East, Suite 200
Toronto, ON M5C1P1 Canada
(416) 703-8982
(416) 504-9090
e-mail: Info@writersunion.ca
writersunion.ca

The Writers' Union of Canada is an organization for authors of books. It provides information on contracts, electronic publishing rights, tax law, literary rights and more. There is a manuscript evaluation service, and an annual contest for developing writers.

Web Sites
of Interest to Writers

More and more writers are taking to cyberspace, as evidenced by a Google search that turned up 340,000,000 documents about writing. Many websites have links to other writers' organizations, bookstores, research topics or additional sites considered of interest. Listed below are a few sites just to get you started. Remember the web is an everchanging, fluid entity and web addresses seem to change or become obsolete daily.

Academy of American Poets
poets.org

Agent Query is an online database of agents. They have search engines that will show you agents by genre, and there are articles about what to watch out for when choosing an agent.
agentquery.com

Amazon is an online bookstore, where readers can browse through almost every book in print and place orders. Amazon has information about authors and books, as well as reviews of many of the books it sells.
amazon.com

The **American Booksellers Association** site offers book news, events including live author chats, a searchable database of bookstores, and a reading room with reviews and articles from the *American Bookseller* magazine.
ambook.org

Bookwire has reviews, best-seller lists (including *Publishers Weekly* and *Boston Book Review*), links to author websites, lists of author appearances and much more.
bookwire.com

Canadian Authors Association
canauthors.org

Cat Writers Association
catwriters.org

The Children's Writing Resource Center offers information to writers of juvenile topics.
write4kids.com

Editor & Publisher magazine's site has links to major online newspapers, research information and classified ads (including job listings).
editorandpublisher.com

Hatrack River, one of the worlds created by science fiction writer Orson Scott Card, this site has a writers' group and young writers' group. (Besides SF, Card writes about writing.)
hatrack.com

Horror Writers Association
horror.org/hwa/

International Association of Business Communicators
iabc.com

International Women's Writing Guild
iwwg.org

My Virtual Reference Desk. This website serves as a home base to locate other WWW sites with information about everything from A to Z. Be sure to check out its "Virtual Facts on File" page.
refdesk.com/facts.html

National Writers Union
nwu.org

New Dramatists
newdramatists.org

One Look Dictionaries will search 936 online dictionaries for definitions. You can get translations of words, too.
onelook.com

The Online Writery offers support and networking including help with brainstorming, revising, researching and editing.
missouri.edu/~writery/

Poets & Writers is both a print magazine and an online e-zine. It is a non-profit organization providing resources for writers and information about writing opportunities.
pw.org

Preditors & Editors is an online database of editors, publishers and other information interest to writers. The site is especially known for its listings of untrustworthy agents and publishers.
anotherealm.com/prededitors

Public Relations Society of America
prsa.org

Public Safety Writers Association
policewriter.com

Purdue University Online Writing Lab. Need help with grammar, style or other similar writing problems? Then this is the site for you. And you'll find *The Elements of Style*, the classic E. B. White and William Strunk, Jr. book, online.
owl.english.purdue.edu/

The Reporters Network
reporters.net

Science Fiction and Fantasy Writers of America
sfwa.org

Shaw Guides provides a listing of writers' conferences.
shawguides.com

Sisters in Crime is an organization of mystery writers (men are welcome, too). From the internet chapter, you can find local chapters for networking in person.
sinc-ic.org

Society for Technical Communication
stc.org/

Troma Films offers scriptwriting contests on its home page.
troma.com

University of Chicago Division of Humanities. You can access *Roget's Thesaurus* on this award-winning site. From the site, you can also access *Webster's Unabridged Dictionary*.

humanities.uchicago.edu/forms_unrest/ROGET.html

Western Writers of America
westernwriters.org

The Writer's Edge. News and information on the Christian writing industry and a list of comprehensive resources.

writersedgeservice.com

Writers Guild of America West
wga.org

Writers Net offers a directory of literary agents and published writers, as well as free forums.

writers.net

The Writer's Resources site offers comprehensive information and links to sites to help writers with copyright, grammar and style, inspirational quotes, finding agents and publishers, getting freelance gigs and much more.

poewar.com

Writers Services has information and forums for writers.

writersservices.com

Writing.com Online Community. Includes writer's classified, newsletter, writer's forums, market information, special sections for beginners, young writers and children's writers and links of interest to writers.

writing.com

Writing World contains more than 600 online articles about a wide variety of topics, including rights and contracts and submitting manuscripts. There are articles of interest to both the beginning writer and the experienced one.

writing-world.com

Software for Writers

There are many computer programs on the market, including a handful of good word processors, to interest writers. Included are some programs specifically targeted for the writer, and this is a sampling of those.

Software versions and prices change often. These are just a sample of some of the more popular programs. You can find a wide variety of writer's software at http://www.amazon.com and at http://www.writerssupercenter.com. All programs are available in PC versions; a few have Mac versions.

Submission Software:

Ink Link: Manuscript Management Software
Ink Link Software
(866) 907-8737
inklinksoftware.com
Ink Link helps track manuscripts, writing income and expenses, organize markets and more.

Fiction Writing:

StoryCraft Fiction Development software
StoryCraft
(866) 907-8737
writerspage.com
StoryCraft bills itself as the only major software using Joseph Campbell's mythological hero's journey story arc system.

Writer's DreamKit
Write Bros.
(818) 843-6557
write-bros.com
Writer's DreamKit helps with developing characters, plotting, structure... all the basic elements of story telling.

StoryBuilder, The Fiction Writer's PC Tool

Seven Valleys Software
(866) 335-8929
svsoft.com
StoryBuilder helps you get over writer's block, helps you develop characters and plot, has genre-specific information, and more.

WritePro for Windows
FictionMaster
The Sol Stein Creative Writing Program
(800) 755-1124
writepro.com
WritePro has eight lessons for novelists and short story writers, walking you through creating characters, inventing suspenseful plots, making villains intriguing and much more. FictionMaster is an advanced program.

StoryBase
Ashelywilde, Inc.
(800) 833-PLOT
ashleywilde.com
StoryBase offers a clipboard of narrative writing prompts that can help jump-start writers of any genre. If you own the previous program, Plots Unlimited, the company has an upgrade discount. The book *Plots Unlimited* is still available.

Script Writing:

Movie Magic Screenwriter
Dramatica Pro
Story View
(800) 84STORY
screenplay.com
Software for script writers that can stand alone or be used together.

Scriptware
(800) 788-7090
http://scriptware.com
Scriptware is a full-fledged word processor with automatic screenplay formatting at a keystroke. Included are formats for TV and film, with a feature that allows you to import screenplays you've already written. Competitive upgrades are available for owners of some competitors' products.

At-Home
Writing Courses

Some courses offer college degrees; others simply offer instruction. Write or call for free information. Some offer work-at-your-own-pace instruction; others offer extensions on the time limits of the course for additional cost.

Writing Classes.com
(877) WRITERS
writingclasses.com
This site is one of the most comprehensive listings of online writing courses, and even includes a sample online course. Classes are available in all genres.

American Christian Writers
(800) 21-WRITE
watkins.gospelcom.net/americanchristianwriters/index.htm
Offers correspondence course, conferences, critique, software, publish on demand, books, etc.

Christian Writers Guild
(719) 495-5177
christianwritersguild.com
There are various levels of courses for adults and children.

Institute of Children's Literature
(800) 243-9645
institutechildrenslit.com
The original long-distance writing course, targeted toward children's writers.

Long Ridge Writers Group
(800) 624-1476
longridgewritersgroup.com
This program has been teaching writers by long distance for some thirty years. Programs include fiction, nonfiction, and children's.

Union Institute and University

(800) 336-6794

tui.edu

This program started out at Vermont College, the first college to specialize in brief-residency programs. Focus on short stories, poetry, essays, drama and fiction, under the guidance of a faculty mentor. Off-campus, accredited B.S. program, now with additional academic centers in California, Ohio, and Florida.

University of Massachusetts

(413) 545-0222

umassulearn.net

Online non-credit writers workshops for poetry, fiction and memoir includes editing, revising, critiquing, and coaching.

University of Tennessee

Distance Education and Independent Study

(800) 670-8657

anywhere.tennessee.edu

Home study courses offering instruction in writing fiction, nonfiction, poetry and more.

Winghill Writing School

(800) 267-1829

winghill.com

A distance education provider specializing in writing courses, including classes in fiction, children's, romance, and memoirs.

Writers College

(813) 236-7509

writerscollege.com

There are one-week seminars and classes lasting from four to six weeks on a variety of topics. Prices are very reasonable.

Writer's Digest School

wdwowadmin@fwpubs.com

writersonlineworkshops.com

Due to the high demand for online study, WD School has switched over to Internet courses only. The school still offers several courses, all for home study, at your own pace (to be completed in no more than two years): Elements of Effective Writing, Novel Writing Workshop, Nonfiction Book Writing Workshop, Writing and Selling Short Stories, and Writing and Selling Nonfiction Articles. There are advanced courses (in the advanced novel course, participants complete a novel).

Writers on the Net
writers@writers.com
writers.com
The first private writing school on the internet.

The Writer's Studio
(212) 255-7075
writerstudio.com
A variety of online courses

Write What You Know
(512) 445-7498
writewhatyouknow.com
This is the website of a writing coach and online instructor. Click on "services" for a list.

The Author's Bundle of Rights

According to United States copyright law, the writer's work is considered copyrighted from the moment it is written. This automatically gives the author ownership of a bundle of rights to his or her work. (Copyright laws differ from country to country so be sure to review and understand your country's copyright laws. In most instances, many of the terms and concepts listed here will still be applicable.)

This bundle of rights may be divided and sold in any number of pieces and with any limitations the author can conceive of and get a publisher to agree to. The writer assigns the right to use the work to publishers, according to the contract between the writer and the publisher.

Many experts suggest that writers list on the manuscript just what rights are being offered. For example, type "First North American Serial Rights" on the upper right hand corner of a short story or article, just above the word count. Always check your contract (or letter of acceptance from the editor) to see what rights the publication expects to receive.

This is just a brief summary of some of the components of the bundle rights. For specific questions, it is always best to consult an attorney who specializes in communications, copyright or publication law. For a more detailed look at copyright law, see the chapter titled "Copyright, What Every Author Should Know," beginning on page 342.

All rights— Just what it sounds like. When a writer sells "all rights" to a work to a publisher, this means the writer no longer has any say in future publication of the piece. If you want to use it again, say to include a short story in an anthology, you would have to get permission from the publisher to whom you sold the rights. It's always a good idea to avoid selling "all rights," unless the amount offered is very good or the writer decides that the sale— for prestige or another reason—is worth abdicating all rights to the piece.

Electronic rights— This is a term used to define a bundle of rights related to computer technology. It may include the right to reproduce the material on CD-ROMs, in online databases, in multimedia or interactive media, or with publishing-on-demand systems. Just like all other rights, an author may wish to assign certain electronic rights and retain others.

First North American rights— A specific form of first serial rights. This is an agreement to let a periodical use the material for the first time in any periodical within North America. This is the most common type of first rights used in the United States and Canada.

First serial rights— The right to be the first periodical to publish the material. May be limited geographically.

Foreign language rights— The right to reproduce the material in one or more foreign language. This also may involve geographic limitations.

Foreign rights— These include the right to publish the material outside of the originating country. These may be broken down by country or by some other geographical division such as European rights and may involve foreign language rights.

One-time rights— This is generally used when a writer sells an article to many non-competing newspapers or small magazines. This means the periodical buys non-exclusive rights to use the piece once.

Second serial rights— Also called reprint rights. This gives a periodical the chance to print a piece that has already appeared somewhere else. Like one-time rights, these are non-exclusive.

Simultaneous rights— The right to publish the material at the same time; purchased by two or more periodicals. This may be the case with publications with non-competing markets.

Subsidiary rights— This is a term that refers any secondary rights including, but not limited to,

> Audio rights
> Book club rights
> Character rights
> Condensation rights
> Dramatic rights
>> TV rights
>> Film rights
> Mass-market paperback rights
> Merchandising rights
> Trade paperback rights
> Translation rights

A wise author or agent retains as many subsidiary rights as possible or at least makes an agreement for the author to share in any revenue generated by the sale or use of such rights.

Glossary

Advance — The amount a publisher pays an author before a book is published. The advance is deducted from the royalties earned. Often an advance is paid in two or three parts: at the time the contract is signed, upon delivery of an acceptable manuscript, and, if in three parts, upon publication of the book.

All rights — See The Author's Bundle of Rights, page 412.

Article — Nonfiction prose written for a magazine or newspaper.

Assignment — When an editor asks an author to produce an article for an agreed-upon fee. See also On spec/On speculation.

Auction — Conducted—usually by an agent—when more than one publisher is interested in buying a book manuscript. Often conducted over a number of hours or days.

Back matter — The material at the end of a book, usually consisting of one or more of the following: appendixes, notes, glossary, bibliography, index. See also: Front matter.

Backlist — A publisher's list of books still in print. See also: Front list; Midlist.

Book packager — A company that puts together a book, working with writers, editors, graphic artists, and printers but does not sell the book to the public, instead selling the package to a publisher.

Book proposal — Specific written information on a proposed book. Includes an outline, sample chapter or two, markets and other such information. (See also: How To Write a Nonfiction Book Proposal: Sell Your Book Before You Write It, page 141.)

Byline — Author's name as it appears on a published article or story.

Chapbook — A thin book or booklet, usually of poetry or literary fiction.

Chapter book — Short, simple book used to graduate young readers from picture books.

Clips — Samples of an author's published work, usually photocopies of newspaper or magazine stories or articles.

Concept — A short statement that summarizes a screenplay, often just one or two sentences.

Contributor' copies — Copies of a magazine or other periodical containing the author's work, often sent as partial or complete payment for the work.

Copyediting — Editing a manuscript for grammar, punctuation, sentence structure, etc., not content.

Copyright — Legal protection of an author's work. Under U.S. law, copyright is automatically secured when the piece is written. Copyright registration is not required for protection. (See also: Copyright: What every author should know, page 350)

Conventional publisher — Contracts with an author for the right to publish his or her book, then edits, designs, prints and markets the book at the publisher's expense. Pays the author royalties based on the book's sales. See also: Self-publishing; Subsidy publishing; Vanity publishing.

Co-publishing — See Subsidy publishing.

Cover letter — Short letter introducing a manuscript or proposal. Not always necessary. See also: Query/Query letter.

Derivative work — A work produced by altering another work. May be a screenplay, translation or condensed version.

Electronic submission — Submitting a story, article or book on disk or over a modem. Many publishers now require this and a hardcopy.

El-Hi — Elementary school to high school market.

E-mail — Electronic mail sent via an online computer service or the Internet.

Fair use — Copyright law allows a small portion of copyrighted material to be quoted without infringing on the copyright owner's rights. The exact amount that qualifies is debatable. See also Plagiarism.

Feature — A human interest article, usually longer than a news story, focused on a trend, issue or person. Often written in a colorful manner.

Filler — A short piece used to fill space in a magazine or newspaper.

First serial rights — See The Author's Bundle of Rights, page 412.

Formula — Used to describe a fiction story—novel, short story, or movie—that uses predictable plots and characters.

Frontlist — Books published in the current season. See also: Backlist; Midlist.

Front matter — Also called "preliminaries," this is the material at the front of a book, usually consisting of one or more of the following: title page, copyright page, dedication, epigraph, table of contents, list of illustrations, list of tables, foreword, preface, acknowledgments, introduction. See also: Back matter.

Galleys — The first typeset proofs of a manuscript, used for proofreading and error correcting. A number of respected publications require galley copies of a book be sent to them three to four months prior to the publication date in order to be eligible for review in that publication.

Genre — General classification of writing, such as nonfiction, poetry, or novels, but primarily used to refer to categories within those: mysteries, science fiction, romances, business, children's, etc.

Ghostwriter — Author whose work is credited to someone else, by agreement. Autobiographies by famous people are often written this way, although it is now common for the ghostwriter to be acknowledged thus: By (famous person, in large print) with (ghostwriter, in smaller print).

Hard copy — Computer printout of material.

Hardware — The mechanical and electronic parts of a computer (or other machine). See also Software.

Home page — The first page of a World Wide Web document.

Honorarium — A small token, sometimes money, sometimes copies of the publication, given to the author.

Hypertext — Words used as a link to other text or illustrations in an electronic document. Usually accessed by a click of the computer mouse.

International reply coupon (IRC) — Purchased at a post office, and used in place of stamps for the return of a manuscript or editor's reply when submitting out of the country.

Internet — Started in 1969 as a U.S. Defense Department project, this worldwide computer network is now used for entertainment, research, shopping, etc. Accessed by modem through an online service or Internet server for a fee. See also: World Wide Web.

ISBN — International Standard Book Number, the number on books used for ordering, sales and catalogue information, usually used with a bar code that includes pricing.

ISSN — International Standard Serial Number, the number on a periodical used for identification and ordering, usually used with a bar code that includes pricing.

Kill fee — Fee paid for an article that was assigned but not published. Often a percentage of agreed-upon fee, usually either a standard at the magazine or agreed upon in advance.

Lead time — The time between the purchase of a manuscript and its publication, also the time between the planning of a magazine issue or book and its publication date. The reason magazines usually want Christmas articles and stories submitted in summer.

Libel — A published accusation that exposes someone to contempt or ridicule, loss of income or damage to reputation. Defenses include truth, consent, and fair comment. The publisher and the author can both be held liable.

List royalty — Royalty payment based on a book's list (also called retail or cover) price. Figured as a percentage. See also: Net royalty: Royalties.

Little magazines — Publications, often focused on literary, special interest, or political topics, that enjoy only limited circulation.

Mainstream — Fiction not fitting into a genre, often written with greater concern for characterization than genre fiction.

Mass-market book — Books appealing to a wider market; these are the smaller-sized paperbacks sold in drugstores and supermarkets as well as bookstores. See also Trade book.

Masthead — A listing of the names and titles of the staff of a publication.

Midlist — Non-genre fiction or nonfiction books that may make up the greater part of a publisher's list. Titles not expected to be blockbusters. See also: Backlist; Front list.

Model release — A form signed by the subject—or guardian of the subject—of a photograph granting permission to use the photo for the purpose stated on the form.

Modem — A computer device used to connect by telephone to other computers, online services or the Internet.

Ms, mss — Abbreviation for manuscript, manuscripts.

Multiple submissions — Sending a manuscript to more than one publication at a time. Generally encouraged by greeting card and filler-type publishers, and discouraged by book and magazine publishers, but gaining favor. Same as simultaneous submission.

Net royalty — Royalty figured as a percentage of the amount a publisher receives for a book after various wholesale discounts have been granted. See also: List royalty.

Novelette/Novella — Medium-length work of fiction. Might run anywhere from 10,000 to 50,000 words.

Novelization — A novel derived from the script of a movie. Generally not well respected by "real" novelists.

On spec/On speculation — When an editor agrees to consider an article without committing to publishing it. Usually used by editors when they are unsure of a writer's ability or have not worked with the writer before.

One-time rights — See The Author's Bundle of Rights, page 412.

Online service — Computer company, such as CompuServe, America Online, Prodigy, that offers access by modem to various entertainment, research, educational and other services. Usually also offer Internet access.

Op-ed — Short for opinion/editorial or opposite editorial (page) depending on who you ask. Describes a newspaper opinion piece printed in the editorial section of a newspaper, usually about 600-1,000 words.

Outline — A skeleton version of a book's story, often written first to aid in writing of the book, but also written later to give an agent or publisher an idea of the story. Usually under 15 double-spaced pages, often in the form taught in school with chapter headings and a descriptive sentence or two. See also: Synopsis; Treatment.

Over-the-transom — Term for material sent by a writer unsolicited to a publisher; comes from the times when authors would toss manuscripts through an open window above a publisher's door in hopes of attracting an editor's attention.

Payment on acceptance — The writer is paid when the publication accepts the article or story.

Payment on publication — The writer is not paid until the work is published, which can mean waiting for months.

Pen name — See Pseudonym.

Plagiarism — Stealing another writer's work and claiming it as your own.

Proofreading — Careful reading of a manuscript to catch and correct errors and omissions.

Proposal — See Book proposal.

Pseudonym — A name used on a work instead of the author's real name.

Public domain — Denotes material not protected by copyright laws. It may have never been copyrighted or the copyright has expired.

Query/Query letter — A one-page letter to an editor or agent to propose an article, story, or book. Should be an example of the author's best writing.

Remainders — Copies of a book sold at a greatly reduced price. Often the author receives no royalty, depending on the terms of the contract.

Reporting time — The time it takes an editor or agent to contact the writer regarding a query, proposal or manuscript.

Royalties — Payment from a publisher to a book author based on the book's sales. For hardcover books it generally ranges from 4-15 percent of the retail cover price; on paperbacks it is 4-8 percent.

SASE — Self-addressed, stamped envelope, required with all manuscripts for return or (if you don't need the manuscript back) the editor's reply.

Scene — In fiction writing, an individual unit of dramatic action, with or without dialogue, that, with other scenes, combines to make up the plot.

Self-publishing — When the writer arranges for all the production and marketing for his or her book. It takes more money and energy up front and brings a degree of financial risk, but usually offers greater control and the author/publisher gets to keep all the profits. Now seen as a legitimate alternative to traditional publishing. See also: Conventional publishing; Subsidy publishing; Vanity publishing.

Serial — Newspaper, newsletter or magazine published periodically, usually on a set schedule.

Sidebar — A companion piece to a newspaper or magazine article, usually shorter, which gives extra details or complementary information.

Simultaneous submission — See Multiple submission.

Slant — The emphasis or direction given to a story or article. Often done to fit the periodical's editorial mission.

Slush pile — The often large stack of unsolicited manuscripts in an agent or editor's office. Usually the last task in an editor's list of priorities.

Speculation — See: On spec/On speculation

Subsidiary rights — See The Author's Bundle of Rights, page 412.

Subsidy publisher — A publisher who charges the author to typeset and print the book but markets the book at the publisher's expense, usually along with the publisher's own titles. The publisher and the author share in any profits to the degree and by the method agreed upon in advance. This is often done with associations like historical societies. Comes dangerously close to vanity publishing and one should check out a subsidy publisher thoroughly before signing a contract. See also: Conventional publishing; Self-publishing; Vanity publishing.

Synopsis — A short summary of a novel or nonfiction book, perhaps one to two pages in length. See also: Outline; Treatment.

Tearsheet — The pages removed from a magazine or newspaper showing an author's work. So called because the author tears the pages out of the publication to save for a clip file. See also: Clips.

Trade book— Hardcover or larger size paperback book. Generally denotes a book that is published to sell in bookstores and to libraries. See also: Mass-market book.

Treatment — Short outline of a television or movie script. Generally 10-15 pages for a half-hour TV show, 15-25 for an hour, 25-40 for 90 minutes, 40-60 for a movie. See also: Outline; Synopsis.

Unsolicited manuscript — Any manuscript that an editor did not specifically ask to see. See also: Slush pile.

Vanity publisher — A vanity publisher charges an author to print and bind his or her book. Often this can be done for much less by going directly to a book manufacturer. (Book manufacturers are listed in *Literary Market Place* available at your library.) Vanity publishers often run adds in magazines and newspapers that say something like "Publisher in need of Manuscripts." Vanity publishers rarely offer editing assistance and a vanity publisher's imprint on a book is the kiss of death with most potential reviewers. Often a vanity press masquerades as a subsidy publisher offering a very limited amount of promotion and marketing. See also: Conventional publishing; Self-publishing; Subsidy publishing.

Word count — The number of words in a manuscript. Use a word processor's count feature, or count the number of words in a couple of lines to figure the average per line, then the average number of lines per page. Multiply number of words per line by lines per page by number of pages to get final count. Generally a double-spaced, typed document with one inch margins will have about 250 words per page.

Some standard word counts:

Nonfiction article	250 - 2,500 words
Nonfiction book	20,000 to 100,000 words
Novel	60,000 - 300,000 words
Novelette/Novella	10,000 to 50,000 words
Short story	1,000 to 10,000 words
Children's book	150 to 1,500 words
YA novel	15,000 to 50,000 words

World Wide Web (WWW) — A part of the Internet that uses hypertext to access information, often using formatted text, illustrations, motion, and sounds (depending on the user's computer's capabilities). See also: Internet; Hypertext.

Work for hire — Usually used to refer to the work of someone who is an employee of a company, but freelance writers can enter into this agreement in which the editor or other buyer purchases all rights to the writing. See also: The Author's Bundle of Rights page 412.

Writer's guidelines — Formal statement of what a periodical or book publisher requires. Writers should send a note to the managing editor requesting the guidelines. Always include an SASE. *The American Directory of Writer's Guidelines: What Editors Want, What Editors Buy,* available at bookstores and libraries, is a compilation of over 450 publisher's guidelines. (See also: Sample Magazine Writer's Guidelines, page 357, and Sample Book Publisher's Guidelines, page 363)

YA — abbreviation for young adult: books, stories or articles written for teenagers.

Index

About the Editor

Stephen Blake Mettee, founder and publisher, Quill Driver Books/Word Dancer Press, Inc. is the author of *The Fast-Track Course on How to Write a Nonfiction Book Proposal* and the editor of *The American Directory of Writer's Guidelines*.

Quill Driver Books publishes nonfiction books. QDB's authors include recognizable names such as Irving Stone, Dr. Ruth Westheimer, and America's most popular medical columnist, Peter H. Gott, M.D., as well as first-time authors.

QDB is recognized by industry periodical *Book Marketing Update* as one of the "Top 101 Independent Book Publishers" in the United States and by *Writer's Digest* as one the 100 most new-writer friendly book publishers in the United States.

Mettee is always in the market for exceptional nonfiction books. Contact him at the address below.

Quill Driver Books/Word Dancer Press, Inc.
1254 Commerce Way
Sanger, CA 93657

Please visit
QuillDriverBooks.com
and sign up for our free e-mail newsletter
on writing and getting published.